RESOURCE ECONOMICS

RESOURCE ECONOMICS

An Economic Approach to Natural Resource and Environmental Policy

Alan Randall

University of Kentucky

Grid Publishing, Inc., Columbus, Ohio

©COPYRIGHT 1981, GRID PUBLISHING, INC.
4666 Indianola Avenue
Columbus, OH 43214

Printed in the United States

1 2 3 4 ▦ 4 3 2 1

Library of Congress Cataloging in Publication Data

Randall, Alan, 1944-
    Resource economics.

    (The Grid series in agricultural economics)
    Includes index.
    1. Natural resources.   2. Environmental
policy.   3. Economics.   I. Title.
HC55.R36   333   79-22988
ISBN 0-88244-211-2

Contents

V. TECHNIQUES FOR EMPIRICAL ANALYSES

PREFACE

This is a book about natural resource and environmental policy and, in particular, the role of economic analysis in informing, analyzing, evaluating, and assisting in the development of that policy. Resource economics, to use the imprecise but mercifully brief term by which this subdiscipline is known, is seen as an applied, policy-oriented field of enquiry. It is seen as so thoroughly policy-oriented that it would not exist as an identifiable subdiscipline of economics if (a) all resource-related decisions were made by the decentralized, profit-seeking entrepreneurs of competitive micro-economic theory, and (b) the outcomes of such decisions were regularly and predictably efficient and just. If there were no need for resource and environmental policy, there would be no need for applied resource economics.

Although economics is the focal point and the unifying theme of this book, economics is not treated in isolation. A considerable respect is accorded the natural sciences, and legal, political and administrative concerns are substantially integrated with economic analysis whenever the opportunity arises. Throughout the book, real-world examples are used to illustrate important concepts; Section VI is entirely devoted to the use of resource economics principles in analyzing applied problems.

The organization of this book reveals the author's philosophy with respect to teaching resource economics. Following a chapter that provides a perspective on the resource and environmental problems of the modern world and a chapter that defines resources and identifies some important resource policy issues, the next eight chapters provide an intensive introduction to economics and, especially, the economic theory necessary to permit effective economic analysis of resource problems. These principles are illustrated with relevant examples, but the principles themselves are emphasized. Then, and only then, do we return to the applied sphere of institutional realities, techniques of quantitative analysis, and the integrated analysis of applied policy problems.

This book is directed toward upper-division undergraduate and beginning graduate courses in natural-resource and environmental economics. Such courses often attract a diverse group of students, whose common dimension is an interest in public policy with respect to natural and environmental resources. Some students bring a strong background in economics or agricultural economics into the course, hoping to gain an understanding of natural resource and environmental issues while, at the same time, acquiring new insights into the use of economics to solve policy problems. Others have a vital interest in natural resource and environmental issues, and an educational background that emphasizes the physical, engineering, natural, or social sciences. These students perceive a need to understand the economic aspects of natural resource and environmental issues, but have often had only little formal exposure to economics. Chapters 3 through 5 are intended to provide the necessary remedial work for these students.

It is likely that this book introduces more material than can be adequately covered in a one-semester course. This provides the teacher with the flexibility to tailor his particular curriculum to the needs of his students. Teachers whose students are neophytes and/or non-majors in economics may prefer to pass lightly over some of the more demanding materials in Chapters 6, 8, 9, 10, and 16, while supplementing the textbook with readings from some of the excellent survey-course-level textbooks on environmental economics and books of readings on environmental issues that are now available. Teachers of beginning graduate courses serving mostly majors in economics and agricultural economics may choose to leave Chapters 3, 4, and 5 for the students' bedtime reading, while supplementing the textbook with readings from the scholarly-journal and reference-book literature.

ACKNOWLEDGMENTS

Any individual's knowledge and approach to his subject is distilled from a wide variety of sources; mine is no exception. I have learned from my teachers, the elder statesmen of my profession, many of my contemporary colleagues who (like me) labor with a considerable degree of anonymity in the vineyards of natural resource and environmental economics, the famous and not-so-famous in other subdisciplines of economics and in other disciplines, and my students. With these kinds of sources, it is perhaps amazing that I have learned so little, for I surely have had the opportunities.

Preparation of a textbook is a labor-intensive task, in which I enjoyed considerable help. John Sjo convinced me to undertake the task, and provided constant encouragement, along with occasional and remarkably restrained prodding. Warren E. Johnston and John

Sjo read the entire manuscript; Angelos Pagoulatos and John R. Stoll read various sections. Their comments were thoughtful and helpful.

The Department of Agricultural Economics at the University of Kentucky provided moral and material support. Joanna Drzewien-iecki-Abugattas undertook to type the first draft of a lengthy manuscript from dictated tapes. Her painstaking work is most appreciated, and I was sorry to see her leave this fair city. Terry Combs, Mary Edwards and Wanda Hamilton ably completed the task. The final draft was typed, with blinding speed and amazing accuracy, by Terry Combs. Bill Nelson ably served as a research assistant.

In this, as in all my professional undertakings, I enjoyed the support of my wife, Beverley, and our children.

Alan Randall
Lexington, Kentucky

RESOURCE ECONOMICS

I. NATURAL RESOURCE AND ENVIRONMENTAL POLICY: THE CHALLENGE TO ECONOMISTS

Economic Growth, Resource Scarcity, and Environmental Degradation

Things were not always this way. For most of his relatively brief history, *Homo sapiens* was preoccupied with the endless struggle merely to survive: to find food and shelter for his family, and to protect himself as best he could from disease, pestilence and the depredations of wild animals and hostile interlopers. Man was, even then, set somewhat apart from the rest of the ecosystem by his superior intellect, his abilities of communication, his inquisitiveness, his aesthetic sensibility, and his spirituality which led him to pose and seek answers to great metaphysical questions of the meaning of life. But, not very far apart. Although man was winning the struggle for survival, it was not by a comfortable margin. His existence must have seemed precarious.

Slowly, man began to bend the ecosystem to his needs and to develop a social structure — a communication and organization system — which permitted him to direct his collective energies. He banded together in groups for defense, domesticated animals, and cultivated crops. He learned to use hides, wood, stone, bronze, and iron. He developed civilizations, cultures, art and literature, myth and religion. He also played his part in the creation of deserts, and the destruction of ecosystems. And, he refined techniques for torture, destruction, warfare, and the domination and enslavement of his fellow man.

Great civilizations grew, flourished, and, when they outgrew their resource bases and organizational structures, decayed.

What we now call progress came slowly and painfully. The limits seemed always close at hand. The historian, looking back across centuries and millenia, could discern key developments in social organization, which permitted increases in the scale and changes in the nature of the extended family, the tribe, the feudal domain, the state, the nation, and the empire. He could identify pivotal technical inventions — the wheel, the stirrup, the cannon — and the incremental developments in weaponry, land transportation and navigation that permitted man to more effectively exploit his environment (which, always, included more primitive human populations). Nevertheless, although life was surely eventful, most individuals could expect to see little technological change and little change in the real incomes of their communities (unless through redistribution by plunder or conquest) in their lifetimes.

For most of man's history, then, change came slowly. Increasing affluence was seldom hoped for, let alone expected as a right. Social, cultural and political institutions were geared to ensuring stability, rather than facilitating change.

THE FOUR HUNDRED YEAR BOOM

Sometime about five or six hundred years ago, the rates of technical, economic, social, political, and cultural change began to increase rapidly, first in Western Europe, and later around the world. These changes established the conditions that permitted the unprecedented economic progress of the last four hundred years.

The first manifestation of this abrupt change was the development of transoceanic navigation, which facilitated trade — an important generator of economic opportunity. Even more importantly, large sailing vessels, equipped with the vastly more potent weaponry made possible by the development of military uses for gunpowder, hugely expanded the resource base of Western Europe. There followed an age of intercontinental exploration and plunder, and piracy to redistribute the spoils. Initially, gold and precious objects were simply taken from Asia and the Americas, to enrich the homeland. Later, it was spices, oils, and minerals. Then a broad range of food, fiber, mineral, and human resources were exploited, to supply European economies with raw materials and enslaved labor. Colonies were established, to serve as bases for plunder, to operate mines, and, especially in the warmer climates, to produce food and fiber under the plantation system.

Back home, rapidly increasing wealth and ease of travel, which permitted cross-fertilization of ideas, encouraged technical developments at an exponentially increasing rate. First the Agrarian Revolution and then the Industrial Revolution radically changed both the techniques and the social organization of production. The domestic resource base was expanded, as uses were found for things, like petroleum, that were previously undiscovered or were known but considered useless. Developments in science and medicine permitted population growth at unprecedented rates. The non-European world increased, rather than decreased, in importance to Europe. It continued to provide food, fiber, minerals, and slaves. In addition, the colonies provided markets for the industrial surplus of Europe and homes for its surplus population. Areas sparsely settled and with particularly primitive indigenous populations — North America, Australia, southern Africa and parts of South America — became the frontier, to be tamed and developed by European populations. The resource base of the New World was huge, especially in North America. Drawing upon its European technology and cultural heritage, a steady flow of immigrants from Europe, and a massive resource base ripe for exploitation, the United States became, in less than three centuries, the dominant economic power in the world.

The European populations, in Europe and the New World, entered an age of increasing affluence. Some other populations, notably the Japanese, joined them. Technological progress continued apace, with developments unimaginable only a few centuries ago in electronics, computer science, air transportation, nuclear engineering, genetics, and medicine. Food, clothing, shelter, and protection from predators demanded an ever-decreasing proportion of real income, and discretionary consumption beyond the necessities of life now provided the incentive for the common man to work and to invest in increasing his own technical skills. Production and marketing were organized on a global scale. A combination of increasing discretionary income and the incentives provided by the international economic system freed individuals from the bonds of family, community, and place, and encouraged individualism and mobility. For many, location and interpersonal relationships became transitory, while income continued to grow. The range of choice seemed to be expanding exponentially.

The social-organization mechanisms, the legal system, and the institutional structure that developed during the Four Hundred Year Boom no longer promoted stability. Instead, they promoted industrial progress, resource exploitation, and the transfer of resources to those best able to utilize them. As one small example, in the face of the new possibilities of air transportation, the centuries-old common-law concept of land ownership was summarily changed. No longer did land ownership apply to the air space above land to the extent that a landowner could deny passage of an airplane through that air. When old concepts of ownership could potentially impede development of air transportation, it was the legal construct rather than air transportation that had to go. More generally, laws of nuisance and legal standing were interpreted to encourage industry and new resource uses even when these imposed costs — pollution, and noise, for example — on others.

The point of this thumbnail sketch of history is that the Four Hundred Year Boom is not typical of man's history. It was a most unusual time. Yet, it shaped the aspirations and expectations of twentieth-century man in the developed countries. It shaped his lifestyle and his intellectual orientation. It shaped the institutions under which production and human interaction are organized. And, it is the period that provides the experience upon which the technologists, economists, lawyers, and political scientists base their projections for the future.

What is the assurance that the trends of the Four Hundred Year Boom can be continued indefinitely? Rather than attempt a definitive answer, it might be appropriate to consider three important characteristics of the boom. First, it was based, to a significant degree, on plunder, colonialism and the exploitation of the resource base of non-European lands by technically advanced European peoples. It was not self-supporting, in geographical space, but depended on the exploitation of the world's resources for the primary and immediate benefit of a fraction of the world's population. Second, it was based, to a significant degree, on the exploitation of nonrenewable and exhaustible resources. Conservation of resources was not important, and recycling of resources was costly, compared to the costs of using newly extracted resources, and fundamentally limited by the laws of physics. The use of exhaustible resources represents withdrawals from the store of such resources. Thus, the boom was not self-supporting over time, but depended on the exploitation of resources that when used now are unavailable for future generations. Third, it depended, to a significant degree, on the progressive and irreversible modification of ecosystems. Land was converted to uses that were thought productive regardless of the changes wrought in its plant and animal communities. Agricultural and industrial wastes were released without concern for, and often without knowledge of, their ecological impacts. Thus, the boom was not ecologically self-supporting. These considerations do not prove that the Four Hundred Year Boom cannot be continued indefinitely. However, these three conditions cannot themselves be continued indefinitely on the planet Earth. Continued progress and prosperity, as man has come to define them, depend on some very substantial changes in the bases of economic activity.

SOME BENEFITS AND COSTS
OF ECONOMIC GROWTH

For its beneficiaries, the increasingly affluent citizens of the developed countries, the Four Hundred Year Boom has brought prosperity, freedom from anxiety about food and shelter, an extended life expectancy and a modicum of relief from pain, education to develop skills and the capacity for self-fulfillment, and leisure time. The common man owns products of industry and technology and can to some extent indulge a desire for status through consumption. He is typically educated beyond the mere needs of his employment, and has the time to indulge his creative instincts in hobbies, literature and popular culture through print, film, and broadcast media. While largely protected from constant crises of survival, he can indulge his need for excitement by contriving adventure through travel, sports, and all kinds of challenging and risky activities undertaken not from necessity but for fun. The common man is freed from drudgery to a degree enjoyed by only the very rich of past societies. He seems surrounded by choices, and if, indeed, he has little real power, he has always the hope and the expectation that his command over material goods will increase as time goes on.

This condition has not been achieved without cost. The ecosystem of vast expanses of the globe has been irreversibly changed, and its balance and diversity have diminished. This is not all bad: the civilization of man (which, on balance, civilized man has seen as a good thing) is incompatible with the ecosystem in which prehistoric man survived. Yet something of value, we instinctively feel, has been lost. In addition, there is evidence indicating that the gene pool has diminished and that, in many ways, the capacity of the environment to absorb wastes, handle extremes of weather (for example, the runoff from unusually heavy rains), and provide natural competition for pests has been reduced.

Pollution of land, air, and water has increased alarmingly. While it has been correctly observed that the concentration of some kinds of pollution in large cities has been reduced by the replacement of coal furnaces in the home with oil, gas, and electric heat and by vastly improved sanitation practices, new forms of pollution are becoming important and pollution has spread across the landscape. While emissions from the internal-combustion engine have become notorious, the rapid increase in the production of nearly indestructible synthetic chemicals and nuclear wastes poses perhaps a greater threat.

Modern methods of agricultural production have accelerated the loss of topsoil due to erosion of broad expanses of the finest cropland, and have made pollution from animal wastes, fertilizers, and pesticide residues almost ubiquitous.

Congestion in commercial centers and places of mass entertainment, in residential agglomerations, on the highways, and even in the outdoor recreation sites intended to provide opportunities to "get away from it all," has become a source of increasing frustration.

Although anxieties about food, shelter, and predators have largely disappeared, it seems they have been replaced by other anxieties about overweight, loss of youth, perceived underachievement as income earners and consumers, and alienation as mobility has severed, for many, the attachments to place, community and family. Some have expressed the view that the expansion of choice brought about by affluence is largely illusory. E. J. Mishan has written (and I paraphrase): while the carpet of choice is unrolled before us by the foot, it is rolled up behind us by the yard.[1] Alvin Toffler has argued that the sheer pace of change has disoriented the individual, who continually suffers from "future shock."[2] As an aside, perhaps we should note that the most fundamental assumption in economics, that human satisfaction is positively related to real incomes (the ability to purchase material goods and services), does not seem to have been borne out by human experience. At best, economists can claim that while that assumption is hard to validate, it is equally hard to refute.

Beyond these anxieties and neuroses, there is another set of concerns that are perplexing to the thoughtful. These include the rapid increases in the population of many already overpopulated countries in the early stages of economic modernization, the fears of resource exhaustion that were brought to a head by the oil embargo of 1973 and the subsequent massive increase in oil prices, and the concern for the effects of nearly indestructible wastes on the environment.

While all is not rosy in the affluent nations, the countries that are home for a vast majority of the world's population have obtained few of the benefits of the Four Hundred Year Boom. There is grinding poverty, malnutrition, poor sanitation, and short life expectancy. Some of these countries had always been poorly endowed with resources. Others have seen much of their resource base plundered, exploited by foreign corporations paying only a pittance to domestic menial labor, or exchanged for imported manufactured products in an international monetary system that favored the industrial nations. The Four Hundred Year Boom not only diminished the store of exhaustible resources in the lands that enjoyed its benefits, but also irreversibly limited the economic prospects of many countries that did not.

It is not impossible that current demands for international redistribution expressed through diplomatic channels and in various forums may escalate into more serious threats to world harmony. In addition, circumstances may arise, with respect to other important exhaustible resources, in which the redistribution imposed by OPEC-like cartels could be realized.

AN UNCERTAIN FUTURE

We live in a time when future prospects are uncertain. Not many years ago, the economist William J. Baumol wrote that it made little sense for present generations to consciously forego current consumption to invest in projects designed to benefit future generations, since history suggested that future generations would surely be richer than present generations, anyway.[3] It is not known whether Professor Baumol still holds this view, but it is clear that many other thoughtful individuals, laymen and specialists alike, are not as hopeful about the future as they once were.

It is clear that the bases which supported the Four Hundred Year Boom cannot continue to exist forever. Resource exhaustion and overloading of the environmental mechanisms for assimilation of wastes are serious threats to the survival of civilization on Earth. Increasing resource scarcity and the loss of environmental amenities threaten to reduce the quality of life.

In spite of all man's advances in technology and the policy sciences, extrapolation of past trends remains the customary method of predicting future trends. Yet, history is anything but linear. Instead, it reveals patterns of growth, stagnation, and decay, and abrupt changes in direction. Turning points are positively identified only in retrospect.

During the Four Hundred Year Boom, there have been periods of uncertainty and pessimism, economic stagnation and depression, and concern about overpopulation and resource exhaustion. The present time may be (and the technological optimists tell us it is) just another of these temporary pauses in man's progress toward an age of plenty for all. There are several possibilities for solution of the world's resource and environmental problems, but it is well-nigh impossible to evaluate them all in advance. New deposits of exhaustible resources may be found, and more efficient techniques of extraction may bring lower-grade deposits into production. Production processes and consumption habits may be modified to permit substitution of more plentiful resources for those that are approaching exhaustion. Ways may be found for economically utilizing things that now seem useless; those things would thus become resources. Energy from the sun and the earth's magnetic forces represents flow resources rather than exhaustible stocks. Technological developments to harness these resources not only would allow substitution of these energy sources for energy stocks, but also could provide the energy to permit vastly more efficient recycling of exhaustible mineral resources.

Increasing scarcity and higher prices of resources may encourage conservation and making do with less of some kinds of resources. People may find it relatively easy to change wasteful habits when waste becomes much more costly. Similarly, increasing awareness and immediacy of the real costs of environmental degradation may encourage much greater effort in preserving the quality of the environment.

Finally, those whose thought processes are most deeply rooted in the Four Hundred Year Boom look to high technology and interplanetary travel for the solution. They dream of orbiting solar generators beaming electricity back to earth, and mining and even colonizing the moon and the other planets. And, who knows, these may eventually occur.

A fairly well-balanced viewpoint may be something like the following. While there is no need to be totally despondent about the future of mankind, neither is there reason to place our faith with those who believe technology will solve all problems. All too often, it seems, technology helps solve a recognized problem but at the cost of introducing totally new problems, such as nuclear waste disposal, whose solutions are not evident. Solutions will not come easily, and will involve some combination of technology, resource substitution, conservation and population control. Hard decisions will need to be made, as every feasible course of action will have its costs as well as its benefits. Some courses of action will preclude others. There will be agonizing trade-offs among goals, since pursuit of some goals will involve sacrifice of others.

In a society that values democratic government and individual decision making, the role of the technologist, the physicist, the chemist, and the engineer will be important but limited. Sound solutions will also require the services of management experts, social scientists, and policy analysts. Among these, the role of the natural resource and environmental economist will continue to increase in importance.

QUESTIONS FOR DISCUSSION

1. In what ways do the last 400 years represent an unusual period in the history of humanity? Is it reasonable to expect the trends of rapid technological innovation and increasing material wealth, established in the developed countries during that period, to continue?
2. In what ways do you expect ethics, customs, and institutions developed during the agrarian, industrial, and technological revolutions to change in the future? (Your answer will surely be influenced by the way you answered question 1.)
3. Lynn White in "The Historical Roots of the Ecological Crisis" puts much of the blame for environmental degradation on the "Judeo-Christian ethic." Do you agree? Try to develop a counter-argument.
4. Did you read "The Limits to Growth" (by Meadows, et al.) and "The Age of Substitutability" (by Goeller and Weinberg)? Can these two pieces be addressed to the same world? Can you agree with either, or both, of them?

FURTHER READINGS

Beckerman, Wilfred. 1975. *Two Cheers for the Affluent Society: A Spirited Defense of Economic Growth.* New York: St. Martin's Press.

Goeller, H. E., and Alvin M. Weinberg. 1976. "The Age of Substitutability: What Do We Do When the Mercury Runs Out?," *Science,* 191: 683-689.

Heilbroner, Robert L. 1974. *An Inquiry into the Human Prospect.* New York: Norton.

Meadows, Dennis L., et al. 1972. *The Limits to Growth: A Report of the Club of Rome's Project on the Predicament of Mankind.* New York: Universe Books.

Mesarovic, M. D., and E. C. Pestel, 1974. *Mankind at the Turning Point: The Second Report to the Club of Rome.* New York: Dutton.

Mishan, Ezra J. 1967. *The Costs of Economic Growth.* New York: Frederick A. Praeger, Inc.

White, Lynn Jr. 1967. "The Historical Roots of Our Ecological Crisis," *Science,* 155(No. 3767): 1203-1207.

ENDNOTES

1. Mishan, Ezra J. 1967. *The Costs of Economic Growth.* New York: Frederick A. Praeger, Inc., p. 85.
2. Toffler, Alvin. 1970. *Future Shock.* New York: Random House.
3. Baumol, William J. 1968. "On The Social Rate of Discount," *The American Economic Review,* 58 (No. 4): 788-802.

Natural Resource and Environmental Policy

Let us consider some of the issues in natural resource and environmental policy that confront the world in the last years of the twentieth century. While mindful of the problems facing traditional societies and countries in the early stages of modernization, we devote most of our attention to the concerns of the countries that participated most fully in the Four Hundred Year Boom.

THE ISSUES

The issues we face are of the most fundamental kind. What do we want, what do we have to work with, and how can we best use what we have to get what we want? What are our goals and how can we most effectively mobilize our resources to achieve those goals?

How fast should we spend the world's bank account — that is, exhaust the world's stock of resources? At what rate should the irreversible alteration of the environment proceed? Under what terms should present generations trade material goods and services for environmental amenities, and vice versa? What restraints should present generations voluntarily accept, for the benefit of the future? All questions, big or small, broad and pervasive or narrow and localized, in natural resource and environmental policy fall within the rubric of one or more of the above general issues.

THE CONCEPT OF RESOURCES

A *resource* is something that is useful and valuable in the condition in which we find it. In its raw or unmodified state, it may be an input into the process of producing something of value, or it may enter consumption processes directly and thus be valued as an amenity. At this point, it may be easier to define what is not a resource. First, things that are unknown or for which no uses have been found are not resources, since they have no value. Similarly, things that, while useful, are available in such huge amounts relative to demands that they have no value, are not resources. "Resource" is a dynamic concept, and the possibility always exists that changes in information, technology and relative scarcity may make a valuable resource out of that which previously had no value. Second, things that are produced under human guidance in processes that combine resources, capital, technology, and/or labor, are not themselves called resources, although resources are always among the inputs used to produce them.

Resources are multi-attribute and thus have *quantity, quality, time,* and *space* dimensions. Air is a useful example. It is available in most places in such vast quantities relative to demand that it may seem more like a free good than a resource. Yet, in many places, the quality of air is impaired to some degree and thus air of better quality has a positive value (i.e., individuals and/or society are willing to spend money to obtain air of higher quality). In certain small, enclosed places — for example, manned space capsules — air (or its oxygen component) is very scarce and is highly valued. In the open environment, air quality may change as time passes. In the space capsule, the flow of oxygen is strictly limited by the amount initially available and the rate at which stocks can be replenished; exhaustion of the oxygen supply as time passes is quite feasible.

Some resources, the best examples being mineral deposits, exist in given stocks in a given place. These are called *stock resources,* or *exhaustible resources* since withdrawals from the stock lead eventually to its exhaustion. Their quantity is measurable, usually in terms of mass or volume. Their quality is often measurable in terms of chemical composition (e.g., mineral content of ores, or ash content of coal) but many also have more nearly intangible aspects, such as aesthetic properties. The distinction between the concepts of quantity and quality is simply that quantity is usually unidimensional (i.e., mass or volume) while quality is multi-attribute and may refer to any dimension or composite of dimensions (e.g., chemical composition, physical structure, and aesthetic attributes) that affects the value of the resource in use. Resource quality will be perceived differently, for different uses; and the less tangible (e.g., aesthetic) aspects of quality will be perceived differently by different users. The space dimension is the physical location of the deposit. The time dimension is important because extraction will reduce the quantity that remains and, in the absence of extraction, the natural process of entropic degradation will result in quantity and quality changes.

Other resources, a good example being the radiation from the sun, are called *flow resources*. The sun's radiation reaches the earth's atmosphere in constant quantities per unit of time. (This statement is adequate in terms of any time frame relevant for future planning; however, the sun's radiation will diminish over periods measured in billions of years.) The rate at which the sun's radiation reaches the earth's atmosphere and its quality at that point are beyond the control of man. A flow resource must be utilized when it is available. What is not effectively used now, or captured and stored for later use, is lost. Once the sun's radiation enters the earth's atmosphere, man's influence makes itself felt. The quality of the resource may be diminished by atmospheric pollution. The value man generates from the use of the sun's radiation depends on how he uses it. The storage of solar energy as biomass has always been possible, and can be manipulated by man. In the late twentieth century, man has become interested in other means of storage of solar energy in forms more immediately available for heating and cooling (solar power cells) and forms that are more readily transmissible (e.g., electric energy). Storage converts a flow resource into a *fund resource,* in that deposits and withdrawals can be made, and the rate of deposits and withdrawals can be manipulated by man, subject always to the rule that withdrawals (by man, and through natural entropic degradation) in any time period cannot exceed the initial fund plus deposits.

The quantity dimension of a flow resource is measured in mass, volume, or energy units, per unit of time. The quality dimension is, again, multi-attribute and is related to use: quality attributes will render uses feasible or infeasible (given the conditions of scarcity and technology at the time), and the intended use will make particular quality attributes more or less important. The time and space dimensions at which the flow is received constrain the uses that are possible. Storage may, at some cost, relax the time constraints, while transmission, again at some cost, may relax the space constraint.

This categorization of resources as exhaustible or flow resources, and the subcategorization of some flow resources as fund resources (water in a reservoir is another good example) is highly imperfect. There are overlaps, and some kinds of resources do not fit any category very well. Fossil fuels are usually classified as exhaustible, and for good reason. Yet, they represent stores of solar energy. Why, then, are they not called fund resources? The answer is that deposits occur over geological time, whereas the rate of withdrawal is limited only by capital, technology, and human restraint. It is the human concept of time that makes fossil fuels exhaustible, for all relevant policy purposes.

Biological resources (e.g., crops, forests, animal populations) represent a complex category of resources. They make use of the flow of solar energy, the flow (or fund) of hydrological resources, and the fund of soil nutrients. Fragile equilibria may be established independently of man, and man may manipulate the complex system to establish and maintain different equilibria. Given the flow of solar energy, the biological capacity for reproduction, and human restraint, biological resources are *renewable*. Not automatically self-renewing, but renewable given human restraint and sound husbandry.

Man derives value from the complex system of solar, atmospheric, geological, hydrological, and biological resources by using them as inputs in production processes, by consuming them directly, and by deriving satisfaction from the amenities they provide. These uses may involve *extraction* of exhaustible resources, *harvest* of renewable biological resources, *interception* of flow resources, and *withdrawal* from funds; these are the *consumptive* uses. Some uses are *nonconsumptive:* e.g., the use of plants to replenish oxygen, and the use of resources to provide aesthetic amenities. Even the nonconsumptive uses are not always totally benign. The aesthetic enjoyment of the outdoors, for example, often involves human invasions that diminish, selectively, the populations of animal and plant species.

The challenge to man is to effectively manage the resources of the planet, so as to maximize the satisfaction derived from these resources. The challenge has a time dimension that is absolutely critical. If mankind were willing to accept extinction or the demise of civilization within a few generations, resource extraction could proceed without restraint, and harvest of renewable resources could exceed equilibrium rates and thus bring about the demise of these resources. Wastes could be released into the geosphere, hydrosphere and atmosphere at rates that exceed the capacity of these resources to assimilate them, causing irreversible environmental damage. Such a strategy would increase mankind's consumption of material goods in the short run, but would soon bring on a horrible end to civilization. On the other hand, a human population that seeks the continuation of civilization into the indefinite future and the continuation of man's progress would take a very different approach to resource management. Resource extraction would be viewed as a temporary expedient while techniques of utilizing flow resources are perfected. The rates of harvest of renewable resources and release of wastes into the environment would be restrained to the levels consistent with long-run maintenance of the biological system. The present population would be very reluctant to create toxic wastes that are almost indestructible.

SOME SPECIFIC CHALLENGES

Man faces many specific challenges in the management of specific resources. Some examples may be helpful.

Consider the *land* resource. Land is useful as substrate — that is, it provides support for plants and animals, watercourses, buildings, transportation arteries, etc. It is useful as soil, a major component of life-supporting systems. And it is useful as a store of value: it stores stocks of minerals, fossil fuels, etc. Within these broad categories, and among them, the uses made of land influence other potential uses. Surface and open-cut mining drastically disturb the land surface and affect its suitability for agriculture, forestry, wildlife support, and residential and industrial use, as well as its aesthetic value. Urban uses of land (buildings, transportation arteries, parklands, etc.) reduce the amount of land available for agriculture and open space. For obvious reasons, it is much less costly to convert land from agricultural to urban uses than vice versa. So, mainte-nance of land in agricultural and open-space uses is a decision that can be readily reversed, whereas conversion of such land to urban uses is a decision which can be reserved only at great expense. Intensive cropping now may exacerbate soil erosion, and thus limit future agricultural production. Some kinds of land uses create nuisances that adversely affect other uses. Who wants to live next to a hog feedlot, a jetport, a sawmill, or a pornographic movie house?

Consider the *water* resource. It is useful for drinking and bathing, in residential uses; for heating, cooling, and cleansing, and as a solvent, in industrial processes; for commercial navigation, and recreational swimming, fishing, and boating; for waste disposal; and for ecosystem support, in agricultural and nonagricultural uses. There are potential conflicts within and among these uses. Intensive use in waste disposal reduces the value of water in ecosystem support and thus reduces its value in recreational uses; in addition, it increases the costs of treatment of water to make it fit for many residential, commercial, and industrial uses. Use of water for industrial cooling raises its temperature and may thus affect its usefulness in ecosystem support. In places like the American Southwest, the scarcity of water makes for vigorous competition among the various possible uses. The possibility of storing water in reservoirs introduces additional sources of conflict. Recreational and aesthetic uses of free-flowing streams are displaced while slack-water recreation opportunities are generated. Flood-control and flow-augmentation (to dilute pollutants during low-flow seasons) uses of reservoirs conflict with slack-water recreation uses.

The *air* resource is useful for life support, for visibility to facilitate movement and for aesthetic enjoyment, for transportation, for industrial processes, and for waste disposal. Again, there are conflicts within and among these uses. Intensive use for waste disposal restricts visibility and reduces the value of air for life support.

We have scarcely begun to consider the complexity of the interactions among resource uses. Uses that directly impact one of the land, water, or air resources often influence the value that can be derived from the other resources. Urban, industrial, and transporta-tion uses of land affect air quality. Impoundment of water in reservoirs inundates some land, while it may render other land more productive through irrigation, flood control, energy production, and navigation. Drainage of wetlands interferes with hydrological systems and may change flood patterns, groundwater systems and ecological systems. Land disturbance for surface mining, building, road construction, or agriculture may influence water quality. The paving of land to increase its value for transportation also increases water runoff. Fertilizers and pesticides to increase the agricultural productivity of land may reduce the quality of water and modify ecological systems.

Resources are typically used in combination. Air transportation requires air, obviously, but also land for takeoff, landing, and passenger movement to and from the plane. Industrial processes typically use land as space and support, and use minerals, water, and air in production and waste disposal. Studies have shown that land, water, and air (as sky), given that each has desirable aesthetic qualities, provide the greatest aesthetic satisfaction in combination. Agricultural production requires air, land, and water, and will be adversely affected by diminution of the quantity or quality of any of these.

In addition, although not the subject of this book, it is well to recognize *human resources*. Human labor, knowledge, and technical capacity are employed to derive benefits from natural-resource utilization. Modern societies invest heavily in the development of these human capacities, using human resources as complements to, and substitutes for, natural resources. Further, given the dominance of human beings in the earth's ecosystem, the organizing, planning and decision-making capacity of humans as individuals and societies is crucial to man's success in deriving satisfaction and ensuring the continuity of civilization.

All of these specific complementary and conflicting potential resource uses challenge man to use his organizational powers and to control his greed and selfishness in order to wisely allocate resources for the present and for the future. Man must maximize the net benefits (the amount by which the total value of the beneficial impacts exceeds the total value of the adverse consequences) from resource use, always seeking the proper balance between present benefits and future costs.

SOME COMMON ATTRIBUTES OF RESOURCE ALLOCATION PROBLEMS

Most resource use, management and conservation decision problems are perceived, and must be solved, in a very complex context. Consider some of the attributes of that context.

1. The resources of immediate concern are components of highly complex systems. The earth's resource system is a vast, complex, dynamic, interactive system. Attempts to modify individual components of that system will result in changes

elsewhere in the system. Yet, man's understanding of this system is very, very limited. So, the consequences of manipulating components of the system are not easy to predict. Often these consequences manifest themselves in unexpected ways, and are observed some considerable time after the initial stimulus. Cause and effect are difficult to link. The effects of new actions are difficult to predict: this is a major source of concern in a time of rapid technological progress. The language we use to describe these effects — "spillovers," "side effects," "unintended consequences" — is an indication of our ignorance and naivete, and of our remarkably poor understanding of the systems concept in general and the resources system in particular.

2. Most alternative courses of action have consequences that we perceive, from our limited base of knowledge, as both beneficial and adverse. What is seen as beneficial to one individual may quite likely be seen as adverse by another.

3. Any decision will influence many people, whose well-being will be affected differently and whose power to participate in decision making will vary widely. Thus, there are few resource-related decisions that are truly private, in the sense that all their impacts are confined to the individuals who voluntarily agreed upon the decisions.

4. In any society, resource-related decisions, whether initiated by private individuals and groups or by public decision-making bodies, are made within a complex institutional structure that assigns legal rights and liabilities and thus establishes the structure of incentives. That institutional structure is itself dynamic, and while it typically has conservative mechanisms to promote its continuity, it also has adaptive mechanisms to help it adjust to emerging realities of scarcity and power. In the kinds of modern economies that allow significant economic freedom for the individual, resource-related decisions at the public level often involve changes in institutions, with a view to changing the incentives facing individuals and thus the decisions individuals make.

Resource allocation policy problems are typically highly complex, since they concern complex physical and biological systems and must be solved within a complex social and institutional environment. Legitimate goals come into conflict, and individuals will balance their legitimate interests differently. The physical and biological systems present trade-offs: if we decide to pursue goal A purposefully, we will incur losses with respect to goal B; to maintain a satisfactory condition with respect to goal B, we must forego some of our potential success in the direction of goal A. What should we do? If we had full knowledge of the consequences of every possible action, the decision would not be easy. It would depend on our relative valuations: how much of A is worth how much of B? How much energy to encourage economic growth and permit material comfort is worth how much expense and how much risk of failure in nuclear waste disposal? In the very likely event that different people have different relative valuations, how will these be weighted to arrive at a decision for society? Given that we do not have full knowledge of the consequences of each action, not only relative valuations but also empirical estimates of the consequences, beneficial and adverse, will be different for different people.

APPROACHES TO SOLUTIONS

Who in his right mind would want to enter into a field of study where the problems are so complex, with so few simple solutions? A good question. The only response can be that if we ignore these problems, they will not go away. On the other hand, if we focus the best thinking and the soundest science on these problems, there is hope that better information can be made available. The alternative actions and their consequences can be more accurately identified, and an enlightened populace can make better decisions.

This process has a role for each of many, many fields of human inquiry: the physical, chemical and biological sciences to provide a factual understanding of the resources system; the engineering sciences to define the existing technical possibilities and develop new ones; the social sciences — psychology, anthropology, sociology, political science — and law to provide an understanding of the human social system and the complex rules it establishes to guide decision making; the analytical sciences — mathematics, systems analysis — and economics (which spans the social sciences and the analytical sciences) to provide the framework that permits understanding of the interrelationships of these systems and facilitates decision making; and the humanities — philosophy, ethics, history, and literature — to help define human aspirations and develop the social consensus about what is good and evil.

This book focuses on economics as an organizing framework and an analytical system of thought. Nevertheless, the focus on economics must not permit us to become forgetful of the role of the other subdivisions of human inquiry. True progress will come only from a combination of disciplinary, multidisciplinary, and interdisciplinary efforts ranging across the broad frontiers of knowledge.

QUESTIONS FOR DISCUSSION

1. It has been said that "resources are not, they become." What does this mean?

2. "Solar energy research is an effort to find ways to convert a flow resource into a fund resource, so that it may more effectively substitute for exhaustible resources." How would you explain this statement to an angel over the telephone?
3. "Few resource-related decisions are truly private." Explain.

FURTHER READINGS

Detwyler, Thomas R. 1971. *Man's Impact on Environment*. New York: McGraw-Hill.

Ehrlich, Paul R., John P. Holden, and Richard W. Holm. 1971. *Man and the Ecosphere*. San Francisco: W. H. Freeman and Co.

Murdock, William, and Joseph Connell. 1970. "All About Ecology," *The Center Magazine*, 3, Jan.: 56-63.

National Academy of Sciences. 1969. *Resources and Man*. San Francisco: W. H. Freeman and Co. for NAS-National Research Council. (Especially Chapter 2).

3

A Thumbnail Sketch of a Modern Economy

Economics is the study of economic systems, and therefore its concerns, the variables upon which it focuses, and its methodological approach are fashioned, to a substantial extent, by the characteristics of economic systems. For this reason, it makes good sense to undertake a quick overview of a typical modern economy prior to commencing our formal inquiries into the subject of economics.

WHAT IS AN ECONOMY?

There are many possible answers to this question, but one of the most serviceable is that an economy is a complex organizational system: a system for organizing the production of goods and services and their distribution among people. As such, it is inextricably linked with the natural system (the atmosphere, geosphere, hydrosphere, and biosphere) and the social system (the system of rules, customs, traditions, organizations, and communications networks that guides, constrains, and channels the interactions among people). Clear boundaries defining what is, and what is not, a part of the economic system do not exist. In fact, if that question is asked of many things, one by one, the answer that emerges is that virtually everything either is a part of the economic system or is linked to the economic system in important ways.

An economy includes *production* sectors that extract or capture natural resources and combine them with capital (which is, in a sense, the savings from previous production) and labor, in processes that utilize knowledge and technology (the fruits of investment in man's own productive facilities), to produce goods and services.

Immediately, it can be seen that production processes are subject to the availability of natural resources, capital, and labor, and to the technical characteristics of the production process. Further, they are subject to the inexorable laws of physics, the first of which is that energy-matter is neither created nor destroyed. So, production is a process not of creation but of conversion. Useful production converts matter and energy into more valuable forms of matter and energy — that is, into forms that are more serviceable in satisfying human demands. Efficient production maximizes the increment in value that results from the production process. Useful and efficient production typically generates some wastes (i.e., matter and energy of zero or negative value) along with its valuable outputs.

Consumption sectors are also included. People, acting individually and sometimes collectively, combine the outputs of the production sector (and, sometimes, natural resources directly) with their time, in processes that may utilize learned behaviors (consumption technologies), to obtain sustenance and satisfactions. Consumption processes are subject to the productivity of the society of which the individual is a member, the ability of the individual to command goods and services in competition with his fellows, and the laws of physics. Goods consumed do not disappear, but are converted to other forms of energy-matter, some of which are wastes (i.e., of zero or negative value).

As indicated in the preceding two paragraphs, production and consumption are activities of physical transformation, rather than creation and destruction. The concept of *materials balance,* which is based on the laws of physics, is helpful in developing a view of economic activity that recognizes the limits to production and consumption and the inevitability that residuals (discommodities that need to be disposed of, and waste energy, such as heat, that must be dissipated) will be created. An economy must, sooner or later, face up to the limits imposed by the laws of physics.

So, an economy includes production and consumption sectors, the former of which services the latter. However, the distinguishing feature of an economy is its coordination and organization function. Production, in a modern economy, requires the coordination of individuals in technologically complex production units, and the functional coordination of input procurement, scheduling of interdependent production processes, sales, and investment for future production. More importantly, the derivation of sustenance and satisfactions through consumption must be coordinated with the production process. Those goods and services that are needed or desired should be produced, and those forms of energy-matter that reduce rather than increase satisfaction must be avoided or rendered as harmless as possible. Inputs must be allocated to their highest valued uses, and goods and services must be distributed to those who value them most highly. People who control raw materials, capital goods, labor, and technical abilities must be encouraged to devote them to production, and the total output of the production process must be distributed among competing consumers. Transportation, storage, and financial services must be supplied, unless production and consumption are to occur at exactly the same time and place. Any modern economy devotes a major proportion of its resources to these coordination functions.

Information on the relative values of all inputs, goods, and services must be generated and made widely available. A common measure of value must be established, and used as currency, to facilitate trade and permit the storage of purchasing power. To provide incentives for production and to ration goods and services among competing consumers, these value measures must be translated into income for producers and expenses facing consumers.

To make rationing devices work effectively and to provide incentives, a detailed system of rights must be established and enforced. These rights must define the conditions under which individuals have access to inputs, goods, services, and the environment, and the proper relationships among people. Who, and under what conditions, may do what to whom?

Given an adequate system of rights, the value of goods produced or services provided becomes the revenue of the producer and the value of the inputs used becomes his cost. The residual is his income, which permits him to purchase goods and services for his consumption and to save for investment in future production. Here we have the rudiments of a simplified economic coordination system. The need of the individual for sustenance and his desire for additional consumption make income valuable to him and thus provide the incentives for production. If he can organize his production so as to be more effective in producing things others value highly, then he can increase his consumption and save and invest for an even more prosperous future. Thus, the relative values consumers place on different goods and services are reflected in production incentives. On the other hand, inputs, goods, and services that are scarce by virtue of limited resource availability or costly production processes will be made available only at great expense. This, in itself, will limit the quantities demanded and ration the supply among those who have high incomes, or who are willing to make great sacrifices, or both.

An economy, then, coordinates production and consumption, saving and investment, given resource scarcity, limited technology, the needs and desires of its citizens, and the system of rights.

HOW IS COORDINATION ACHIEVED?

To this point, everything that has been said is equally pertinent to an enterprise economy, a centrally planned economy, and a mixed economy in which central planning provides some goods and services and influences the incentives under which enterprise sectors provide others. These different forms of economic organization differ in the ways the coordination function is performed. Since the coordination function always involves incentives and rewards, economies that differ in their coordination mechanisms most likely achieve different results in terms of what is produced, how much of it is produced, and who gets to consume it.

First, consider *a pure enterprise economy*. In such an economy, rights must be exclusive, enforceable and transferable. Ownership of anything must guarantee the right to use it and to exclude others from using it. Ownership rights must be enforced, since a right that is unenforced is ineffective. There must be no restraints on the transfer of ownership rights. Individuals must be free to transfer ownership rights to others, and, given this freedom, they will choose to do so whenever they are offered something of greater value in return. Who determines value? The parties to the exchange, or trade, determine value. Since trade is voluntary, it will take place only when both parties are satisfied that it is beneficial to themselves — i.e., that each is convinced that he will receive something of greater value (to himself) than he gives up. Exclusive rights facilitate trade by assuring individuals that they can use what they own, that they cannot use what they do not own, and that they can obtain desired things they do not own only by giving up less desired things that they own.

Since individuals are not arbitrarily restricted in their choice of trading partners, each is free to seek the most favorable terms of trade (i.e., relative prices). Competition among buyers and sellers tends to result in convergence of individual offers and asking prices and the establishment of relative prices that remain stable until there is some change in market conditions (i.e., in demand, or relative scarcity). Introduce a currency, money, as a medium of exchange and a store of value, and these relative prices become the money prices with which we are all familiar.

Given a complete system of ownership rights, price serves the coordination function for the enterprise economy. Prices provide the incentives for production, since income is determined by the price and the quantity of goods and services sold. Prices ration goods and services among consumers since, for each consumer, the sum of his expenditures (price multiplied by quantity) on all items of goods and services cannot exceed his budget. Since prices for all goods and services are determined by supply-and-demand conditions, price movements provide an information system, signaling changes in scarcity and demand and providing incentives for producers and consumers to make adjustments to the new conditions.

Prices thus provide a feedback and self-correction mechanism in the market economy. A rise in the price of some commodity, reflecting increased relative scarcity, tends to encourage increased production and decreased consumption of that commodity, while simultaneously encouraging increased production and consumption of its substitutes, thus tending to correct the scarcity situation. Even for exhaustible resources, whose stocks are strictly limited, the price mechanism tends to correct scarcity problems, by encouraging exploration and resource discovery, discouraging consumption, and encouraging conservation, recycling and the production of substitutes.

Given that interest rates are prices of capital, the price system tends to stabilize the economy over time. Increases in interest rates, reflecting a shortage of capital, encourage saving while discouraging borrowing and delaying consumption, and thus generate more capital.

The price mechanism is the device that permits Adam Smith's famous invisible hand to perform its wondrous function, so that myriad decentralized decisions of individuals pursuing their own self-interest work, in aggregate, for the common good. Modern economists have proven, as we shall see in later chapters, that under certain quite demanding conditions not necessarily bearing much similarity to the real world, the price system generates completely efficient organization of the enterprise economy.

Not that the price mechanism is entirely without costs and disadvantages. It *is* costly to operate. It works best with exclusive property rights and widespread availability of information, but the establishment and enforcement of exclusive property rights and the provision of information are costly undertakings. The price mechanism works best when each buyer and seller operates on such a small scale that the decisions of any one acting alone cannot influence price. Yet, modern production processes often require such large-scale operations that individual firms have obvious opportunities to influence prices. Opportunities may exist for buyers or sellers to collude to influence price. Since the independent decisions that generate prices are made by individuals whose life spans are very brief compared with geological time or even the history of civilization, there is no assurance that prices provide adequate guides for decisions with long-lived consequences.

The price mechanism can be a cruel disciplinarian. Where production processes are subject to the vagaries of ephemeral weather patterns, as is the case with some agricultural products, violent price fluctuations may have a devastating impact on income of producers. Changes in technology may sharply reduce the value of plant and equipment rendered obsolete and the incomes of individuals whose skills are no longer so valuable.

There is a circularity between prices and incomes that is disconcerting to some who worry about whether the enterprise system is fair or just in the way it distributes incomes. Prices help determine incomes, but prices themselves are in part determined by incomes. Effective demand is desire backed up by spending money. Thus, in a price system, the things desired by the rich count for more. If income were more evenly distributed, it is predictable that relative prices would change.

Income is the reward for labor, skill, education, and training, and also for use of capital and resources owned. For the very rich, the greater portion of income comes from the latter sources. While capital and resources must be rewarded, to attract them to productive uses, the high incomes of their owners do not always seem fair and just to those who do not own much of value.

For these and other reasons, some societies have been reluctant to allow price, with a system of exclusive property rights, to function as the coordinating mechanism for their economies. Instead, *centrally planned economic systems* are operated.

Centralized planning agencies, dedicated (one hopes) to serving the best interests of the citizenry, are called upon to carry out the economic coordination function. Resources and the capital stock may be owned by the collective (i.e., the state) rather than the individual. In this way, income inequality attributable to capital and resource ownership is avoided. In addition, to the extent that the state takes a longer-term view of things than does the individual, resource uses that sacrifice longer-term benefits for the sake of more immediate gains may be avoided. Since there will be few, if any, very rich persons under such a system, resources will not be directed toward producing playthings for the rich, but toward satisfying the needs of the citizenry. Economic growth may be stimulated by encouraging saving and investment rather than immediate consumption. These are the laudable aims of some centrally planned socialist economies.

How are these broad social purposes to be translated into incentives encouraging individuals to offer their labor and invest in the development of their skills, and industrial managers to produce the things that are desired? The central planners typically establish a complex system of directives, production quotas, and rewards and penalties, backed up with continual exhortation that each individual do his best for the common good. These incentives will have varying degrees of effectiveness. However, the individual will respond most willingly when the course of action desired by the planners is also the one that increases his own welfare. Thus, rewards must be related to skill, effort, and willingness to make desired adjustments, and so a degree of income inequality inevitably appears. How do the planners know which directives to issue and what production quotas to establish? They must have a massive amount of information on relative scarcities, relative values, and the relative efficiency of alternative production processes. This information must be gathered and analyzed, in order to determine desired goals; then, incentives must be established for achievement of these goals. Notice that these are the functions that are performed by price in an enterprise economy. The coordination function in a planned economy is performed by a central agency using "shadow prices" (i.e., prices that are imputed, not observed) to replace market-generated prices.

A *mixed economy* makes substantial use of the price system to direct the activities of its enterprise sectors. However, the state retains the right to influence the patterns of production and consumption. The state may produce and distribute, outside the price system, certain goods which it believes are essential for national security or of overwhelming social value. It may attempt to influence the behavior of its consumers and its enterprise production sectors by "fine tuning" relative prices, directly or indirectly. It may do this in many ways: by taxation, subsidization, tariffs, import and export quotas, and public-sector purchasing, all of which influence prices directly; and by regulation and modification of the system of property rights, which influence prices indirectly.

The mixed economy is, then, an attempt to take advantage of the inherent efficiency of the price system as a coordination mechanism, without entrusting all aspects of economic performance to the price system. Price retains major roles in creating incentives and distributing rewards, while public policy seeks to provide some minimal level of consumption for the least effective income earners, to cushion the shock for those whose skills and resources are suddenly reduced in value by changes in market conditions, and to correct perceived resource misallocations that occur when the price mechanism fails to provide the "right" incentives. It is important to understand that the public-sector role in the mixed economy involves substantial planning: collection and analysis of information, establishment of goals, and creation of incentives for achievement of these goals. Thus, public-sector mismanagement and imperfect planning are quite possible. In a modern mixed economy, there is always room for sincere and vigorous debate as to whether the public sector is in general making things better or worse and whether particular public-sector programs should be introduced, modified, or abandoned; and economists are, and should be, among the leaders in that debate.

HOW IS THE PERFORMANCE OF AN ECONOMY MEASURED?

The ultimate goal of an economic system must be to provide satisfaction for the members of the society it serves. However, we are not especially adept at measuring individual satisfaction, let alone aggregating satisfaction across individuals. So, we make do with a variety of rather incomplete indicators of economic performance.

Are the production sectors operating at full capacity? One may examine such indicators as the percentage utilization of industrial plant capacity, and the unemployment rate (i.e., the percentage of all those offering themselves for employment who are unemployed). The unemployment rate is an indicator of underutilized human resources. However, it is also a measure of economic welfare, since unemployment almost always means reduced income for those affected and increased public-sector expenditures on support for their dependents. In a society that has made a virtue of work, unemployment may have debilitating social and psychological effects on those affected.

Is the price level, in aggregate, relatively stable? One may examine the rate of inflation, which indicates the annual rate of increase in the general price level. Inflation rates are measured by changes in the consumer price index or, for some purposes, the wholesale price index.

If one is interested in the performance of particular sectors, one may consult a host of indicators: sales, employment, investment in new plant and equipment, price indices, etc. However, if one is interested in the total performance of an economy, the indicator most commonly consulted is gross national product (GNP). Countries with large GNP are thought to be economically powerful. Those with large GNP per capita are considered successful and prosperous. Those whose GNP is growing rapidly are considered to be making good economic progress. Times of rapid growth in GNP are considered expansionary phases, when prosperity is on the rise and hopes are high. In democracies, governments like to be running for reelection in such times. Times of stagnation in GNP are called recessions and are likely to be times, also, of relatively high unemployment and underutilized industrial capacity.

How good is GNP as an indicator of economic well-being and, ultimately, of personal satisfaction in the aggregate? GNP is the total value of goods and services sold in a country, usually in one year. The standard of value is the price of goods and services established in the market. Thus, GNP has several problems as an indicator. First, a rise in the general price level, due to an inflationary increase in the money supply, will increase nominal GNP without any increase in economic well-being. This illusion of prosperity may be avoided by calculating real (i.e., deflated) GNP in terms of the level of prices prevailing in some base year. Other problems with GNP are not so easily circumvented.

GNP records expenditures without distinguishing between costs and benefits. The value of new cars sold (a benefit, presumably) is added to the incomes of those who earn their livings disposing of junk autos. However, the latter is a cost item and would, in a calculation based on efficiency concepts, be subtracted from, rather than added to, the former. While GNP is increased by resource extraction and, in the short run, by overexploitation of renewable resources, there is, in the calculation, no compensating entry of the value of resources lost. GNP is, in a real sense, a measure of the rate of throughput. It is simply not addressed to efficiency in production and consumption and net changes in well-being.

Based, as it is, on market values, GNP cannot consider changes in the production and enjoyment of goods and services that do not pass through markets. The value of services produced by housewives, home gardeners and do-it-yourself handymen does not influence GNP. You could, if you chose, conspire with your neighbor to increase GNP by taking in each other's washing. In a similar vein, many textbooks have made mention of the man who reduced GNP by marrying his housekeeper.

More important are the natural resources and environmental amenities whose values, for various reasons discussed in later chapters, are not reflected in markets. Pollution, which surely makes us worse-off in many ways, does not reduce GNP. On the other hand, the human health problems it causes will result in higher expenditures on medical services, and the corrosion it causes will result in more rapid replacement of durables. Thus, pollution actually increases GNP. If expenditures are made to reduce polluting emissions or cleanse polluted environments, these will increase GNP. While industrial output is rising, generating benefits, it also results in loss of amenities (tranquil environments, a sense of wonderment at the harmony of nature, pleasant and peaceful scenery), and an increase in noise, congestion, pollution, and psychic stress. These costs, which surely reduce the net benefits from increased industrial output, do not reduce recorded GNP.

If it is true, as some have argued, that environmental damage and amenity loss grow exponentially as industrial output increases, then it is quite possible that GNP is not only an inaccurate indicator of human and social well-being but also a truly perverse indicator. A stage may be reached in which GNP is rising while people are actually becoming less well-off, all things considered.

Since "economic growth" is taken to be synonymous with growth in GNP, this discussion provides a warning against single-minded pursuit of economic growth. Such a policy is not really the pursuit of happiness. Rather, it is, to a significant extent, a policy of substituting priced or "material" goods and services for unpriced goods, services, and amenities. Since both the priced and the unpriced categories provide satisfaction, continued replacement of the unpriced with the priced will eventually lead to reductions in total satisfaction.

For those concerned about the long-term prospects for human civilization, the single-minded pursuit of economic growth will be unattractive, since it would diminish the prospects of future generations by speeding the conversion of stocks of resources to flows of priced goods and services.

THE PROBLEM WITH PRICE

The above discussion of the weaknesses of GNP as an indicator of economic progress strongly suggests that there is a whole class of goods and services for which price fails to fulfill the coordinating function in the enterprise economy or the modern mixed economy. How could that be?

Remember that the price system is based on a complete system of exclusive and transferable rights. For some important categories of goods, services, and amenities, exclusive and transferable rights have not been established. In some cases, tradition and/or social consensus militates against the establishment of such rights: "there are some things that just should not be *owned*; the public should have access to some of nature's treasures." In other cases, it is not feasible to establish and defend exclusive rights. Ambient air, ocean fisheries, and, in some uses, water have physical characteristics that make ownership by individuals prohibitively expensive to enforce. Without exclusive rights, there can be no voluntary exchange and no meaningful price. The individual cannot reap personal rewards for the maintenance, conservation, and improvement of such goods and services. Nor does he suffer direct personal costs as a result of his use, misuse, abuse, and overuse of them. Price fails to provide incentives and thus fails in its coordination function. The individual is denied the opportunity to balance his production and consumption across the range of priced and unpriced goods in the manner he might desire.

But all is not lost. Individuals through collective action may define and enforce ingenious kinds of rights, which establish the proper incentives. Rules, customs, and traditions may be established that provide reasonably effective and enforceable rights short of ownership. A planning sector may establish shadow prices that do a reasonably good job of providing the proper incentives.

In an economy that provides a major role for its enterprise sectors and thus assigns important duties to its price system, the task of the natural resource and environmental economist is to identify and analyze the weaknesses of the price system and possible solutions to the problems that arise from those weaknesses.

QUESTIONS FOR DISCUSSION

1. If an economy is a complex organizational system for coordinating production, consumption, and distribution of goods, services, and amenities, what role is played by *rights* in any economy?
2. At an economics seminar, an elderly professor rose and said, "Speaker X understands that prices allocate resources, and Speaker Y understands that prices determine incomes; I seem to be the only person here who understands that prices do both." What relevance does that comment have to the political controversy surrounding deregulation of oil prices and a "windfall profits tax" on oil companies?
3. Is there any reason to expect centrally planned economies to create less environmental degradation than enterprise economies?
4. What are the reasons why GNP is not an accurate measure of social well-being?

FURTHER READINGS

Barkley, Paul W., and David W. Seckler. 1972. *Economic Growth and Environmental Decay: The Solution Becomes the Problem.* New York: Harcourt Brace Jovanovich. (Chapters 4 and 5.)

Boulding, K. E. 1966. "The Economics of the Coming Spaceship Earth," in *Environmental Quality in a Growing Economy,* ed. Henry Jarrett. Baltimore: The Johns Hopkins Press.

Friedman, Milton. 1962. *Capitalism and Freedom.* Chicago: The University of Chicago Press.

Galbraith, J. K. 1958. *The Affluent Society.* New York: Houghton Mifflin.

Galbraith, J. K. 1967. *The New Industrial State.* New York: Houghton Mifflin.

Heilbroner, Robert L. 1970. *Between Capitalism and Socialism.* New York: Vintage Books, Random House.

Heilbroner, Robert L. 1972. *The Worldly Philosophers.* New York: Simon and Shuster. 4th edition.

Kneese, A. V., R. U. Ayres, and R. C. d'Arge. 1970. *Economics and the Environment: A Materials Balance Approach.* Washington: Resources for the Future, Inc.

Nordhaus, William, and James Tobin. 1972. "Is Growth Obsolete?" in National Bureau of Economic Research, *Economic Growth. Economic Research: Retrospect and Prospect.* Fifth Anniversary Colloquium V. New York: Columbia University Press.

4

The Role of Economics

Economics is the study of economic systems, and has been defined as the study of choice in an environment of scarcity. Without scarcity, the choices actually made are inconsequential. However, given scarcity, every possible choice has its costs: action A will preclude action B, and the costs of action A are equal to the benefits that would have resulted from B, if B had been chosen. In this kind of environment, every choice has consequences and the individual who chooses well will achieve the highest possible satisfaction that his means permit. Societies that choose well increase the range of possible choices for their citizens, over the long haul.

Since economic systems are so complex and their ramifications have so many kinds of influences, economists have tended to specialize, and identifiable subdivisions in the subject matter have arisen. *Macroeconomics* is the study of movements in aggregate economic variables — total production and income, the price level, the interest rate, employment, saving and investment, etc. — and the choices governments may make in directing and stabilizing the performance of those variables. *Microeconomics*, sometimes called *price theory*, studies the decisions of the consumer, the supplier of inputs, and the producing firm as they each attempt to optimize their choices given the opportunities confronting them. Using a logic developed from the study of individual decisions, microeconomists analyze supply-and-demand conditions and the movements of prices for particular commodities and inputs. This permits them to predict the impacts of changes in any *one* of the following — prices, input costs, the technology of production, consumer preferences — on the behavior of the *others*. *General equilibrium theory* is the study of the interactions in the whole vast system, and the performance of the coordination mechanism as it seeks equilibrium in times of stability and makes adjustments in times of change. *Welfare economics,* which in its most complete form encompasses microeconomics and general equilibrium theory, examines the performance of economic systems in terms of efficiency and income distribution.

The use of economic concepts along with *statistical methods* (called *econometrics* when the economic and statistical analyses are fully integrated) and *operations research techniques* permits sophisticated quantitative analysis of economic questions. Not only is it possible to predict in what way a change in some economic variable A will affect B; one can also predict the size of the impact.

There are many applied specialties in economics, in which the basic conceptual frameworks described above are applied to the analyses of particular kinds of economic problems. Some of the better-known include agricultural production economics, marketing and industrial organization, international trade and development, economic policy, labor economics, public finance, regional economics, and natural resource and environmental economics.

Natural resource and environmental economics applies economic theory and methods of quantitative analysis to public-policy problems in the provision, allocation, distribution, and conservation of natural resources and environmental amenities. As such, it is a (major) subfield of the broader field of *social microeconomics,* in which microeconomics and welfare economics are applied to the solution of problems of public-policy concern. The focus is on social costs and benefits of proposed actions and public-policy solutions to problems that have impacts across individuals, firms, industrial sectors, economic classes, and, often, regional and national boundaries. In social microeconomics, the analysis of individual producer and consumer decisions is seldom the ultimate goal. Rather, it is an intermediate step in the analysis of public-policy issues.

The approach is always *analytical:* the most logically sound methods of analysis and the best available data are brought to bear on the issues at hand. The analysis is pursued until the logical conclusion is reached, even if that conclusion turns out to be uncongenial to the personal inclinations of the analyst. Where possible, refutable hypotheses are posed, and tested rigorously (i.e., with sound data, in a logically consistent analytical framework). Always, the economist's reasoning, his analytical framework (often called a "model"), his data and his conclusions are exposed forthrightly to the examination and criticism of others. In these ways, *scientific objectivity* is actively sought.[1] Polemics, pamphleteering, and outright advocacy are left to others, or to the economist in his nonprofessional role as a citizen and a human being.

The objectives of social microeconomics include those that come under the definition of *positive economics;* i.e., to learn how the economic system works and how it interacts with the social and ecological systems, and to examine and eventually predict the impacts of changes in particular variables on the behavior of other parts of the system. However, its objectives go beyond positive economics, narrowly defined. In policy analyses, means must be related to ends (goals) in a rational and systematic way. Means must be marshaled efficiently to achieve ends. Ends must frequently be modified and renegotiated, when it is found that the available means are simply insufficient to achieve all ends simultaneously. Finally, since society's ends are not simply given, but arise from the complicated process of negotiation among individuals and groups, and since ends are seldom final goals (e.g., human dignity) but rather immediate goals (e.g., opportunities for employment), ends themselves must be critically examined to determine their implications and their philosophical underpinnings, and the findings of such analysis must be given public exposure. In these ways, social microeconomics, without abandoning its analytical approach, breaches those areas that some have called *normative economics*.

THE ECONOMIC WAY OF THINKING

The economics discipline is alive and vital. It has developed, with a good deal of sophistication and in substantial detail, an approach to its subject matter that is accepted by many of its practitioners. This mainstream approach, or methodology, serves both as an organizing framework for much of the research and scholarship undertaken by economists and as a focus for the continuing methodological debate and intellectual ferment within the economics profession.

The mainstream economists fall into several loose groupings. The middle ground is occupied by those who find the mainstream economic methodology useful, and even quite powerful, but who realize that it has some perplexing limitations, especially when applied to policy analyses. The reader who is not already familiar with these limitations will be acutely aware of them, after studying Section II. To one side of the middle, there is a group of free-market zealots, who see the economic system in very simple terms, and who cannot understand why others fail to see what, to them, is obvious. They divide their time between proselytizing for free-market solutions among non-economists and attempting to keep the other groups of mainstream economists on the straight-and-narrow. To the other side of the middle, there is an ill-defined group of those who are quite uneasy about the limitations of mainstream economics in policy analysis, and suspicious that the zealots confuse methodology and ideology, but are unable to develop a coherent alternative to the mainstream methodology. The best of these "in-house critics" are competent in the use of the mainstream methodology, and their work is, if anything, improved by their awareness of its limitations; the worst of them offer a criticism that is less coherent than that which they are criticizing.

Outside of the mainstream, there are Marxists, various kinds of more or less romantic socialists, and even a few anarchists.

Economics is not a monolith. The questions with which economics grapples are both important and interesting, and economics has attracted its share of intelligent and articulate individuals. I sincerely hope that, sooner or later, some of my readers will be attracted to an in-depth study of, and perhaps active participation in, the philosophical and methodological debates that enliven economics. In the interim, however, a brief exposure to a simplified exposition of mainstream economic methodology must suffice.

The fundamental tool of mainstream economic methodology is *abstraction*. The economy is a complex system that interacts with other complex systems. The process of abstraction is an attempt to make the intractable tractable, by identifying and concentrating on crucial variables to the exclusion of less important variables. This process is absolutely essential. The man who says "everything depends upon everything else" is in a sense correct, but he has neither advanced understanding nor provided useful information.

The economist constructs an abstract *model,* a much simplified version of reality that strips away layer upon layer of detail while leaving the essential components of the system under study basically intact. Alternatively, the model may not replicate any actual components of the system: *so long as it works like the essential components of the system work, it will suffice.* Given that the model "works," simplicity is a positive virtue. If two models achieve similar results, the simpler is preferred. Perhaps it is wise to expand upon the phrase "achieve similar results." One test is prediction. The economist often evaluates models on the basis of how many different things they predict and under how wide a range of conditions, and how reliable are the predictions.

In economist's models, or abstractions, *assumptions* play a crucial role. Since not all empirical magnitudes and interrelationships are known, and since reality insofar as it is known is complex, it is often necessary to make assumptions about the imperfectly known, or to simplify those things that are known. The use of assumptions is an essential strategy in the economist's search for simplicity.

Without exception, mainstream economic models start with the assumption that decisions are made by *rational individuals.* "Rational" does not mean that they think like you or me, or that if placed in the same circumstances they would decide as you or I would decide. For that matter, "rational" is not a synonym for "sensible," as the latter term is popularly used. Rationality, in this context, means merely that the decision process is coherent and logically consistent. It is assumed that individuals are capable of ranking alternatives. For any pair of alternatives, the individual will prefer A to B (or vice versa), will consider A at least as desirable as B (or vice versa), or will be indifferent between A and B. Preferences are transitive — that is, if A is preferred to B and B is preferred to C, A must be preferred to C. Finally, the individual's preferences, given the constraints which he faces, will determine his choice.

In this framework, *preferences* are treated as data of the most fundamental kind. Value, in the economic sense, is ultimately derived from individual preferences, not from the opinions of political, cultural, and/or spiritual leaders about what is good and what is bad (although it is recognized that these opinions may influence individual preferences).

The other body of data which is taken as fundamental is *resource availability,* which is limited by resource stocks and flows and, it is becoming increasingly recognized, by the laws of physics that govern the conversion of energy-matter from one form to another and the entropic degradation of energy-matter.

Technology — i.e., the store of knowledge about ways to get things done — places strict limits (in a static time sense) on the capacity of man to use available resources to produce things he values. However, technology is treated in economics as not so fundamental as preferences and resource availability, since man can and does influence technology, as time passes, by investing in its development and implementation.

At any given time, a society's technology and resource availability determine *society's opportunity set,* which is a set of all possible choices, bounded by the constraints upon the society. The cultural, religious, and political institutions of a society serve the purpose of further constricting that society's opportunity set, by defining some possible choices as unacceptable.

In a competitive process, the society's opportunity set is partitioned into *individual opportunity sets.* The individual's opportunity set is an array of the alternatives facing that individual, with *prices* or *opportunity costs* attached to each, and bounded by the constraints that impinge upon the individual. Given his individual opportunity set, the rational individual makes choices on the basis of his preferences. In a dynamic context, individual choices in one time period may influence the individual's opportunity set in later time periods and, in aggregate, individual choices will influence the society's opportunity set in later periods.

Now that the basic elements of a typical mainstream economic model have been identified, the model must be constructed. Model construction is an exercise in pure logic. The basic elements are organized into a logical system, which is activated by a set of *motivational assumptions.* If preferences and constraints together determine choice, the economist who can precisely define the constraints can make considerable progress in predicting choice by making some simple and manageable assumptions about preferences. The individual is assumed to prefer more to less, for all of those things he positively values. However, the incremental satisfaction he obtains from each additional unit of a homogeneous good is diminishing. These motivational assumptions are basic to all mainstream economic models. For particular purposes, the economist may make some more specific assumptions: the consumer may or may not be concerned about uncertainty with respect to his future income; the producer may single-mindedly maximize profit in the present time period, or he may seek not only current profits but also leisure and the security that comes from long-term survival of his firm.

Given a set of motivational assumptions, the economist's model becomes a precise and functional system, wherein changes in the magnitude of some variables lead inevitably to changes in other variables.

How is such a model used? First, it is used to predict. In theoretical exercises, the actions of one hypothetical individual may be predicted, whereas in empirical work, it is more common to predict the behavior of aggregates (e.g., the actual and potential producers and consumers of a particular commodity and its substitutes). What is predicted? Most commonly, the changes in behavior (i.e., decisions made) that result from changes in the pattern of relative scarcity. Changes in income, in the relative prices of goods bought and sold, and in production technology all change the pattern of relative scarcity confronting the individual. For a whole society, changes in population, individual tastes and preferences in aggregate, technology, and the resource base change the pattern of relative (and absolute) scarcity.

How would one expect the individual to react to an increase or decrease in his income? . . . to a change in the price of a commodity he values? . . . to an invention that increases his productive capacity? . . . to change in the rate of taxation? . . . to a subsidy that benefits a competitor? . . . to the introduction of a new product on the market? . . . to a law prohibiting trade in a commodity he does not produce but is accustomed to using? What would be the aggregate effect, in a given country, of a rise in the price of a commodity it exports? . . . a rise in the price of an increasingly scarce exhaustible resource it imports? . . . a technological improvement? . . . the imposition of a new tax, or an increase in the rate of an existing tax? . . . an attempt to prohibit markets in a commodity desired by many? . . . an income supplement for those who earn low incomes in the market? . . . a program to provide certain commodities to low-income individuals at less than the market price?

From prediction, it is a short step to policy analysis. In fact, the simplest form of policy analysis is prediction — prediction of the impacts of proposed policy changes upon relevant variables such as incomes, quantities supplied and demanded, and prices.

The social microeconomist is typically a policy analyst; in the case of most interest to us, a natural resources policy analyst. Thus, he is primarily interested in examining the impacts of changes in institutions upon opportunity sets and economic outcomes. Examples of such institutions include laws, regulations, guidelines, and other policy pronouncements; taxes, administered prices, and other attempts to modify and direct the pattern of trade; and public investments. Positive analyses are essential, in order to permit prediction of the effects of changes in these kinds of institutions. In performing these kinds of analyses, the economist typically uses one or another variant of the mainstream economic model discussed above. However, as he seeks to inform the process of institutional choice (that is, the policy-making process), the social microeconomist finds himself increasingly confronted with normative questions: which of the various policy alternatives is most desirable?

These kinds of questions introduce a special kind of difficulty. While it is always possible to make reasonable judgments about what is good for an individual (and the economist typically uses the criterion that whatever gives the individual the most of what that individual wants is good), it is very difficult to say what is good for a society when, as is typically the case, individuals are not unanimous as to their preferences. In addition, the socioeconomic system is fundamentally competitive. That is, increments in the satisfaction enjoyed by one individual or group must often come at the expense of other individuals or groups. In such an environment, the identification of the preferred policy alternative must always involve the adjudication of conflicting claims for satisfaction among individuals. There must be a way to weigh the claims of individuals against the claims of other individuals. This problem is known as the *aggregation problem* in normative social microeconomics.

Three quite different types of approaches to the aggregation problem have substantial currency among various groups of mainstream economists. The *social welfare function approach* assumes that it is possible for a society to develop a social consensus as to the proper distribution of satisfaction among its members. The *Pareto-safety approach* backs off that kind of judgment; instead, it simply takes as self-evident that any innovation that makes at least one person better-off without making others worse-off must be desirable, and refuses to make judgments about the desirability of innovations that do not meet that criterion. The *benefit cost approach* simply adds up the gains and losses that accrue to individuals to determine the total or aggregate net benefit; it makes no distinction as to the validity of conflicting claims among individuals. However, in so doing, the benefit cost approach necessarily makes a judgment that a dollar gain to a wealthy man is sufficient to cancel out a dollar loss to a very poor man. In both the Pareto-safety and the benefit cost approaches, social judgments are budget-based; that is, in making social judgments, the preferences of individuals are weighed according to their budgets. Each of these three quite different approaches to the aggregation problem is discussed in detail in Chapter 6.

As this discussion has suggested, the differences of opinion among mainstream economists on the subject of methodology become more pronounced as the subject moves from positive analysis into normative analysis. Virtually no one disagrees that economic models are useful in prediction and that efforts to improve their performance in prediction represent a sound investment of economists' time and skills. There is some, but not much, disagreement that economic research is useful or at least potentially useful in policy analysis. Some, however, argue that the economist should stop at the prediction of effects of policy alternatives, while others argue that he should take an active role in the selection of preferred policies. Among those who take the latter position, there is considerable disagreement about the appropriate criteria by which to select preferred policies.

RESOURCE ECONOMICS

Resource economics is a branch of social microeconomics. Thus, it takes the social microeconomic approach to positive and normative economic analyses. The concern is with the economic effects of policy decisions at the aggregate level; individual decisions are primarily of interest as generators of data.

The major concerns of resource economics are resource allocation in the present and in the future, and the distributional outcomes of resource-allocation decisions. How should a society allocate its resources now and in the future, and in what manner should the fruits of those resource-allocation decisions be distributed among the members of a society? To raise these questions assumes that there is something at stake. One does not question systems that are generally acknowledged as perfect. Thus, resource economics, by its very existence as a serious field of inquiry, raises questions about the effectiveness of existing market and institutional structures in allocating resources, in adjudicating among the claims of individuals in the present generation, and adjudicating among the claims of present and future generations.

As its name implies, resource economics focuses on policy questions with respect to natural resources: land, in its many dimensions (as soil; as an organizer of spatial relationships; as substrate for buildings, roads, etc.; and as store of mineral wealth); water; air; and the ecological system. Resource economics seeks to analyze problems in the allocation of these resources, to identify the causes of those problems, and to identify and examine alternative programs, policies, and projects being proposed as solutions. It focuses on the benefits and costs of alternative programs, policies, and projects, and the incidence of those benefits and costs: geographic incidence, incidence among economic sectors, incidence across socioeconomic classes, and intertemporal incidence. Resource economics approaches the analysis of these issues from the peculiar perspective that we have described as the economic way of thinking. It focuses on prices and costs, on opportunity sets, and on the way in which alternative policies impact prices, costs, and opportunity sets. Even more fundamentally, it focuses on individual preferences and, at the most basic level of analysis, takes individual preferences as fundamental indicators of value. What people want is taken to be the most serviceable indicator of what is good.

QUESTIONS FOR DISCUSSION

1. Distinguish between positive and normative economics.
2. "Identification of the preferred policy alternative must always involve the adjudication of conflicting claims for satisfaction among individuals." Explain.
3. "Resource economics, by its very existence as a serious field of inquiry, raises questions about the effectiveness of existing market and institutional structures in allocating resources, in adjudicating among the claims of individuals in the present generation, and adjudicating among the claims of present and future generations." Does this mean that the resource economist is necessarily a radical? Radical in what respect(s)?

FURTHER READINGS

Friedman, Milton. 1953. "The Methodology of Positive Economics," in *Essays in Positive Economics.* Chicago: The University of Chicago Press.
North, Douglass C., and Roger Leroy Miller. 1973. *The Economics of Public Issues,* 2nd ed. New York: Harper and Row.
Samuelson, Paul A. 1976. *Economics. An Introductory Analysis.* New York: McGraw-Hill. 10th edition.

ENDNOTE

1. See Karl Popper. 1957. "Philosophy of Science: A Personal Report," in *British Philosophy in Mid-Century,* ed. C. H. Mace. London: George Allen and Unwin.

II. ALLOCATION, DISTRIBUTION, AND ECONOMIC WELL-BEING: SOME ECONOMIC THEORY FOR NOW

In this and the following sections, we take time out from our study of the economics of natural resource problems, in order to develop the tools of economic analysis that can make that study more effective. This section deals with the theory of social microeconomics in a static, or timeless, context. We examine the individual consumer, the individual firm, and the development and functioning of markets. Then we consider the efficiency of those markets and their effectiveness in promoting the well-being of society. The interrelation between markets, institutions, and the structure of legal rights is examined, and the influence of institutions and rights on efficiency and social well-being is considered. Since resource economics is, more than anything else, a study of the problems that arise from imperfections in the markets for natural resources, we develop the theory of market imperfections and inefficiency.

Chapter 5 presents a simple exposition of the theory of the consumer, the firm, and market equilibrium. For many students this will be a revision of materials initially encountered in a Principles of Economics course. However, the presentation is sufficiently simple that, with patience and persistence, the student who is new to microeconomic theory will be able to grasp this material. Chapter 6 discusses economic efficiency and social well-being, subjects that are often first encountered in a graduate course in welfare economics. Nevertheless, the basic concepts of welfare economics are essential for the study of social microeconomics. So, in Chapter 6, these concepts are developed using a simplified verbal and diagrammatic logic that builds directly on the material in Chapter 5. Students who understand Chapter 5 will have no unusual difficulty understanding the concepts presented in Chapter 6. In Chapter 7, we introduce the concept of property rights, thus taking advantage of some significant conceptual developments in the theory of welfare economics that have occurred in the past two decades. The interrelations between property rights, economic efficiency, and social well-being lie at the very heart of an adequate theory upon which to base analyses of resource economics problems.

Chapters 5, 6, and 7 provide rather impressive testimony to the usefulness of markets. But Chapter 8 examines the problems that arise from the imperfections in markets. While market imperfection alone is never a sufficient condition for governmental economic activity, and while economists are in continuous debate as to whether the appropriate response to market imperfection is governmental enterprise, regulation, or some relatively simple refinement in the rules under which markets operate, there is general agreement that market imperfections represent serious economic problems. If markets functioned pervasively and perfectly, there would be little reason to expect resource economics, along with many other branches of applied economics, to exist.

5

The Consumer, the Firm, and the Market

Markets, when they work well, are wondrous devices of quite awesome simplicity. Their ostensible purpose is quite limited: to facilitate trade, the process by which people exchange goods and services with one another. In serving this purpose, however, markets generate and transmit the signals (i.e., prices) that direct the production, distribution, and consumption of a considerable array of goods and services. By rewarding the producer who switches to a less costly production process or to the production of a new kind of output that is preferred by consumers, and by rewarding the consumer who changes the mix of things he consumes in response to changes in their relative prices, market prices direct the activities of independent and selfish individuals in directions that are mutually beneficial to all.

What can the student of natural resource and environmental economics learn from the study of markets? There are many markets which work well, effectively allocating resources and distributing the product, while making continuous, if not entirely painless, adjustments to changes in the pattern of relative scarcity. My freshman biology teacher frequently stressed that the remarkable thing about the human body is not that it occasionally fails, resulting in weakness, pain, illness, or injury, but that it works so well for so much of the time. The study of economics has led me to feel much the same way about markets.

The resource economist needs not only to respect markets, but also to understand how they work. Such understanding is basic to an informed and educated respect. It also provides the fundamental perspective and basic tools for an understanding of the market imperfections that exist. Resource economics is, in large part, the study of market imperfections. In order to recognize market imperfections, diagnose their causes, and suggest solutions, it is necessary first to acquire a deep understanding of perfect markets.

Markets have a logic and a momentum of their own. Economists frequently insist "there is no free lunch." Actually, one does not need economics to tell one that; physics will serve that purpose. However, economics drives the lesson home, again and again. It is understandable that, in times of persistently low product prices, farmers may feel strongly that prices should be supported above market levels, and many citizens may sympathize with them. Economics does not say that such a strategy is impossible, but it does point out the impediments to a successful program of price supports and the costs, in terms of valuable products sacrificed, of such a program. If a society persists in attempting to achieve a price-support goal, economics can offer considerable insight into the least costly way of getting the job done.

It is equally understandable that in times of rising retail prices, citizens may feel strongly that price ceilings should be enforced. Attempts may be made to control prices in general, or specific prices such as those of gasoline or rental apartments. Economics can point out the impediments to successful programs, the resource and opportunity costs of implementing such programs, and, with reasonable precision, the least costly method of implementing them.

Casual and informed observers, alike, see increasingly acrimonious competition for water in arid lands (especially in places like the American Southwest, where there are substantial rural and urban populations). They see environmental degradation and pollution. And, they see some curious inconsistencies in the way some natural amenities, such as access to outdoor recreation sites, are provided to, and rationed among, the public.

At first glance, these problems may not seem to have much to do with economics. After all, to the extent that these problems are resolved at all, they are resolved in the political arena. Yet, economics has much to offer. It can explain why these problems are persistent, what forces work to exacerbate them, and how the incentives established in the political arena may be perverse and counterproductive. Economics, by identifying causes of these problems, points the way to their solution. If there are several possible solutions, as there usually are, economics can often identify good reasons to predict that particular solutions are likely to be more effective, and/or less costly in terms of productive opportunities foregone, than others.

Toward the end of this chapter, these problems and policy issues are again raised. At that place, the economic logic of markets is applied to problem definition, and to the identification of causes and impediments to solutions. Possible solutions, while not carefully analyzed, are suggested.

However, it is necessary to crawl before one can walk. Therefore, we must first erect the structure of market logic, before we can effectively use it. Let us begin by constructing a simple market and examining its workings.

THE CONSUMER

Our concept of "the consumer" is just a simple little abstraction, by which we focus on the individual human being in his role as a user of goods, services, and amenities. In his consumer role, which is just one of many roles he plays, man uses his budget, which typically consists of time and money, to assemble a mix of goods, services, and amenities that will provide him with satisfactions. Given sufficient budget, he will first satisfy biological needs, and then various less pressing wants and desires, the fulfillment of which nevertheless provides him considerable satisfaction. At this point it should be noted that the economic concept of consumption is sufficiently broad to include goods, services, and amenities. Thus, everything the individual "consumes" is not literally consumed in the physical sense of the word. Some goods (i.e., food) are eaten, and thus transformed into energy and waste products; but the economic act of consumption applies equally well to personal services that provide convenience, entertainment spectacles that are enjoyed, and quiet mountain lakes that impart a sense of tranquility to the beholder. In economics, the idea of consumption does not necessarily imply rivalry in the sense that what I consume is unavailable for you. There is a class of goods, called indivisible goods, that are consumed in a nonrival manner. Their enjoyment by one does not diminish their capacity to provide enjoyment by others. (Nonrival goods are of importance in resource economics, and will be discussed in Chapter 8; in the intervening sections, we will deal with goods for which there is rivalry in consumption.)

Now we return to the concept of satisfaction. Economists use the term *utility* to describe the satisfactions that an individual enjoys from consuming goods, services, and amenities. Utility is a relative concept. Although it is meaningless to try to compare several alternative prospects in terms of the numerical value of the utility they would provide, it is both possible and meaningful to compare alternatives on the basis of the relative utility they promise. Each individual is able to rank the alternatives as more or less desired and, most likely, is able to select one particular alternative as most preferred — that is, offering the prospect of the most utility. There is no good reason to expect that, if several individuals were each independently making such a ranking, each of them would select the same alternative as the most preferred.

The *ordinal* nature of utility (i.e., the concept that utility is amenable to rank orderings but not to absolute numerical quantification) is a fundamental concept in economic analysis, which has some very important ramifications. The most significant of these is the impossibility of choosing among alternatives for society, each of which may enrich some while impoverishing others, without recourse to ethical propositions. More on that in Chapter 6.

The concept that goods, services, and amenities provide utility is expressed in the *utility function:*

$$U = f(Z_1, Z_2, \ldots\ldots Z_n),$$

where $Z_1, \ldots\ldots Z_n$ represent the various goods and services and amenities that yield satisfaction to the individual.

The utility function describes mathematically the relationship between the individual's total satisfaction and the goods, services, and amenities he enjoys. It will most likely be different for each individual. The utility function is an expression of the individual's preferences among the total array of goods, services, and amenities that are available.

In order for the utility function to be useful as a tool of analysis, it is necessary to assume that: (1) the individual has full information about the array of alternatives from which he can choose, (2) his mind has the capacity to consider all the alternatives and to develop a consistent preference ranking among them, and (3) this preference ranking will be stable at least during the period of the analysis. It is also necessary to assume that the individual's preferences among alternatives are consistent with the relative amounts of satisfaction each alternative, if chosen, would provide him.

These are rather strong assumptions. There are limits on the capacity of the human mind to apprehend and process information. And, information gathering can be an expensive process. Further, the relationship between preferences and utility is not so clear and certain as it seems at first glance. Preferences are not satisfactions but, rather, expectations of future satisfactions. Yet, all of us can remember purchases, or other consumption decisions we have made, that have disappointed us. Actually, it is likely that preferences correspond quite closely with satisfactions for those items with which we are very familiar and about which we make decisions quite frequently; but for unfamiliar items about which we must make decisions only infrequently, preferences can be nothing more than a "best guess" about the satisfaction the item will provide.

Overall, the assumptions behind the utility function are fairly reasonable, and they are justified because they greatly facilitate economic analysis, which would be very difficult without them. Nevertheless, it behooves the economist to be constantly alert for circumstances in which these assumptions may be especially unrealistic.

The Indifference Map

For ease of analysis, assume that the consumer can choose among only two kinds of goods, Z_1 and Z_2. Then, his utility function is simply:

$$U = f(Z_1, Z_2).$$

If the utility function is continuous and each of the two goods Z_1 and Z_2 is continuously divisible, it is possible to derive an *indifference map* between Z_1 and Z_2 for the consumer. An indifference map is simply a set of *indifference curves*. An indifference curve is a locus of all of the combinations of two kinds of goods that yield the same level of total utility or satisfaction to the consumer. In Figure 5.1, we see a portion of the consumer's indifference map between the goods Z_1 and Z_2. Three indifference curves, I', I'', and I''' are shown. All the combinations of the goods Z_1 and Z_2 that lie on the indifference curve I' yield exactly the same amount of utility. Thus, 10 units of Z_1 and 45 units of Z_2, taken together, yield as much total satisfaction as 25 units of Z_1 and 15 units of Z_2. The consumer would be (barely) willing to move from point *a* to point *b* (if the move was costless), since either point yields the same utility; and in so doing he would be willing to give up 30 units of Z_2 in order to obtain 15 additional units of Z_1. Thus in the range from *a* to *b,* his average rate of substitution between Z_1 and Z_2 is -2. At any point on an indifference curve the slope of the indifference curve is equal to the consumer's *rate of commodity substitution (at the margin)* between the two goods.

Although the consumer obtains exactly the same amount of total utility from all the possible combinations on the indifference curve I', and thus is indifferent between all those combinations, he obtains a greater amount of total utility from any point on the indifference curve I''. For example, at the point *c,* he had 20 units of Z_1 and 45 units of Z_2; while at the point *d,* he has 25 units of Z_1 and 28 units of Z_2. He is, of course, indifferent between the points *c* and *d* since he obtains the same total amount of utility at either point. However, he clearly prefers any point on the indifference curve I'' to any point on the indifference curve I'.

Indifference maps have several properties that greatly facilitate economic analysis and, at the same time, make perfectly good sense. If both Z_1 and Z_2 are *commodities* (i.e., the consumer considers both goods desirable and, all other things being equal, would prefer to have more of both goods), each indifference curve will include a segment that slopes downward to the right. If the consumer obtains *diminishing marginal utility* (i.e., as he consumes more and more units of each good in a given time period, the additional — or marginal — utility he obtains from each additional unit of the good diminishes), the indifference curves will be convex to the origin. Consider a ray drawn from the origin, for example, through the point *d.* As the consumer moves out along that ray, he moves to successively higher and higher indifference curves, and each higher indifference curve represents a higher level of total utility. Since there are an infinite number of possible levels of total utility, there are an infinite number of indifference curves in any indifference map; in Figure 5.1 three of the infinite number of indifference curves that exist are selected for display.

Indifference curves may never cross, since crossed indifference curves would be a logical impossibility. Because every point on a

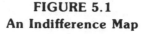

FIGURE 5.1
An Indifference Map

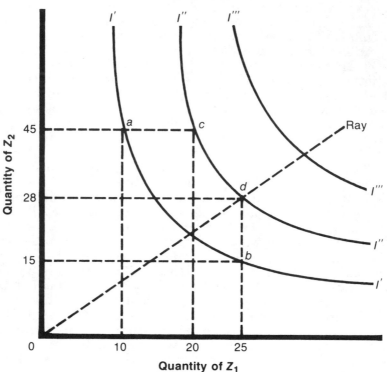

particular indifference curve represents the same level of utility and because indifference curves farther from the origin represent higher levels of utility than indifference curves closer to the origin, there cannot be an indifference curve, say I', that at some points represents higher total utility than another indifference curve I'', at other points represents lower total utility than I'', and at the point of crossover represents exactly the same utility as I''. Such a construct would be logically impossible.

The Budget Line

The consumer seeks always to maximize his utility, within his *opportunity set*. The opportunity set is simply an array of all the possible alternatives from which he can choose, with their prices attached, and bounded by the constraints that the individual faces. In a simple analysis, like the one we are now conducting, it is customary to focus on a single constraint, the consumer's budget constraint, which is defined as the total amount of money he has available to spend.

FIGURE 5.2
Budget Lines

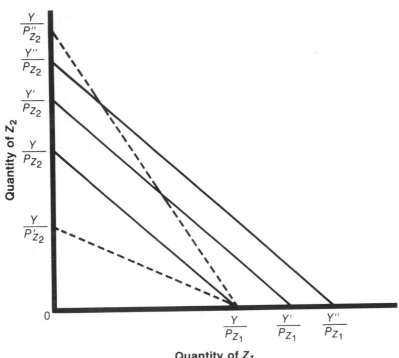

Quantity of Z_1

Consider a consumer with a total budget of Y. If the price per unit of the commodity Z_1 is P_{Z_1} and the price per unit of Z_2 is P_{Z_2}, and, as before, Z_1 and Z_2 are the only goods from which he can choose, it is possible to construct a *budget line* (Figure 5.2). The budget line is the locus of all combinations of the goods that can be purchased if the entire budget is spent. If, for example, the entire budget Y is spent on Z_1, the amount of Z_1 that can be purchased is exactly equal to Y/P_{Z_1}.

If instead, the entire budget is spent on Z_2, the total quantity of Z_2 that would be purchased is Y/P_{Z_2}. If the prices per unit of Z_1 and Z_2 are unaffected by the quantities of Z_1 and Z_2 purchased, the budget line may be drawn as a straight line joining the points Y/P_{Z_1} on the Z_1 axis and Y/P_{Z_2} on the Z_2 axis. The slope of this budget line is $-(P_{Z_1}/P_{Z_2})$.

If the individual's income changes but prices do not change, the budget constraint shifts to a new position parallel to the original budget constraint. The budget constraints for the incomes Y' and Y'', which are progressively higher than the income Y, lie progressively to the right of the budget line Y, and are parallel to it.

If income remains constant, as does the price of one of the goods, Z_1, while the price of Z_2 changes, the slope of the budget line will change. If the price of Z_2 were to increase to P'_{Z_2}, the point Y/P'_{Z_2} would lie closer to the origin. Thus, the new budget line for the income Y and prices P_{Z_1} and P'_{Z_2} is less steeply sloped than the original budget line. If, on the other hand, the price of Z_2 decreases to P''_{Z_2}, the point Y/P''_{Z_2} lies further from the origin. The new budget line for the income Y and the prices P_{Z_1} and P''_{Z_2} is more steeply sloped than the original budget line.

The budget line is a very serviceable analytical construct, and can be used with confidence in cases where the following assumptions are reasonable: (1) the consumer has full information about Y, P_{Z_1} and P_{Z_2}, and (2) P_{Z_1} and P_{Z_2} are unaffected by the quantities of Z_1 and Z_2 purchased. The first of these assumptions causes no great concern. However, the second assumption has great economic significance. It is valid when the purchases of any one consumer are so small relative to the total volume of sales in the market that no consumer, no matter how he chooses to allocate his budget, has any influence on prices. If, in addition, we make an analogous assumption about producing firms (that is, each firm is so small relative to the total market that no firm is able to directly influence the price at which its product is sold), these two assumptions, taken together, are the classical assumptions of perfect competition. For many kinds of goods and services, these assumptions are accurate, or at least a reasonable representation of reality. However, in a complex modern economy, there are some industries that are not perfectly competitive.

Return to the budget constraint for the income Y and the prices P_{Z_1} and P_{Z_2}. That budget line and the two axes of the diagram form a triangle. No point outside that triangle is feasible. Points inside the triangle are perfectly feasible but would represent incomplete utilization of the budget. Combinations of purchases that lie on the budget line totally exhaust the budget. So, the triangle formed by the budget line and the axes completely defines the consumer's opportunity set; combinations outside that triangle are infeasible, combinations inside the triangle are feasible but leave some of the budget unused, and combinations on the budget line totally exhaust the budget.

Notice that Figures 5.1 and 5.2 are expressed in exactly the same axes: the quantities of Z_1 and Z_2. Notice, also, that Figure 5.1 expresses the consumer's preferences, while Figure 5.2 defines his opportunity set. If we were to superimpose the budget line for Y, P_{Z_1} and P_{Z_2} (from Figure 5.2) upon Figure 5.1, we would construct a diagram capable of showing how the consumer can choose from his limited opportunity set in order to achieve the maximum possible satisfaction. Figure 5.3 is such a diagram. Note that indifference curve I^* is tangent to the budget line at the point a. The indifference curve I'' is infeasible, since it lies always outside the opportunity set. There is a segment of the indifference curve I' that is feasible. However, the indifference curve I^*, being further from the origin, represents a higher level of total satisfaction than indifference curve

FIGURE 5.3
The Utility-Maximizing Consumption Bundle

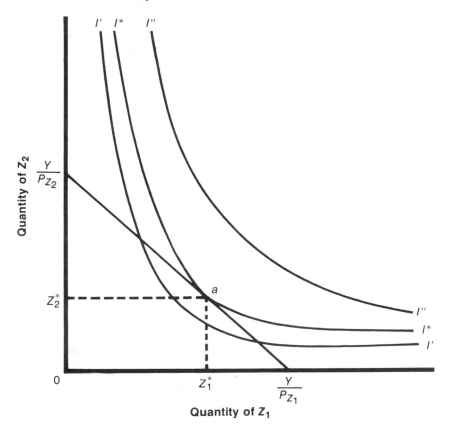

I'. Thus, the single feasible point, a, on I^* represents the greatest total satisfaction that the consumer can obtain, given his limited opportunity set. The point a represents a *consumption bundle* of Z_1^* and Z_2^*. This particular consumption bundle is therefore the *utility maximizing consumption bundle* for this particular consumer, given his preferences, his limited budget, and the commodity prices he faces.

Remember that, at any point on an indifference curve, the slope at that point (i.e., the slope of a straight line tangent to the indifference curve at that exact point) is the rate of commodity substitution (RCS) between the two commodities Z_1 and Z_2. On the indifference curve I^*, there is only one point, point a, at which the rate of commodity substitution between Z_1 and Z_2 is exactly equal to the ratio of the prices of Z_1 and Z_2; i.e.:

$$\text{RCS}_{z_1 z_2} = \frac{P_{z_1}}{P_{z_2}}.$$

This is a *necessary condition* for utility maximization. This condition is always met at points like point *a*, where an indifference curve is just tangent to a budget line. The *sufficient condition* for utility maximization is that the indifference curves must be nonconcave; they must be convex, or, as a special case, they may be straight lines.

To validate this contention, try the following exercise. Take a sheet of working paper and draw a diagram similar to Figure 5.3, except that the indifference curves are concave to the origin. Demonstrate for yourself that, in that case, the point of tangency between the indifference curve and the budget line determines the consumption bundle that generates the least possible satisfaction for the consumer while exhausting his budget. If indifference curves were typically concave, analysis of the type shown in Figure 5.3 would identify utility minimizing, rather than utility maximizing, consumption bundles. But, as we have seen, there are very good reasons to believe indifference curves are typically convex.

INDIVIDUAL DEMAND

With the analytical apparatus developed in Figure 5.3, it is quite easy to derive the individual's demand curve for either of the commodities Z_1 or Z_2. Let us hold income Y constant, along with the price of Z_2, while allowing the price of Z_1 to vary. In that way we can derive a demand curve for Z_1, under the assumption that income and prices of other goods do not change. As we have already seen, the budget line may be modified, to express a change in the price of one good while income and the price of the other good do not change, by varying its slope. In Figure 5.4, an array of budget lines, radiating from the point Y/P_{z_2}, is shown. Each of these budget lines is relevant for a different price of Z_1. The budget line 1 is relevant to the price P'_{z_1}, the highest price for Z_1; the budget line 2 is relevant to the price P''_{z_1}, an intermediate price for Z_1; and the budget line 3 is relevant to the price P'''_{z_1}, the lowest price for Z_1. Now, superimpose the consumer's indifference map upon this array of budget lines. At the point *a*, the indifference curve I' is tangent to the budget line 1; at the price P'_{z_1}, the consumer will purchase Z'_1 units of the good Z_1. At the point *b*, the indifference curve I'' is tangent to the budget line 2; at the price P''_{z_1}, the consumer will purchase Z''_1 units. At the point *c*, the indifference curve I''' is tangent to the budget line 3; at the lowest price P'''_{z_1}, the consumer will purchase Z'''_1 units.

Now we move to Figure 5.5, which depicts a price-quantity relationship. The horizontal axis is expressed in quantity of Z_1

FIGURE 5.4
The Effect of Changes in the Price of Z_1

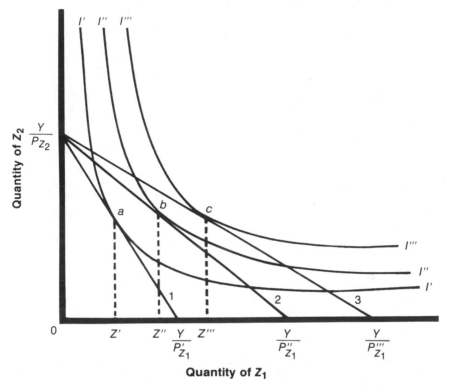

Quantity of Z_1

purchased, while the vertical axis is expressed in terms of the price of Z_1. Since, for each of the points a, b, and c (Figure 5.4), we know the price of Z_1 and the quantity of Z_1 taken, it is easy to draw a demand schedule for Z_1. At point a, the price is P'_{Z_1} and Z'_1 units are purchased; thus the point a', corresponding to point a, can be located in Figure 5.5. Points b', corresponding to P''_{Z_1} and Z''_1, and c', corresponding to P'''_{Z_1} and Z'''_1, can be similarly located in Figure 5.5. The demand curve is constructed by simply joining the points a', b', and c'. It slopes downward to the right, and as it does so, it becomes flatter.

Changes in Income

Take a sheet of working paper and draw a diagram similar to Figure 5.4. Draw a set of budget lines for the budget Y', which is some amount larger than Y. For each set of prices (i.e., P_{Z_2} and P'_{Z_1}, P_{Z_2} and P''_{Z_1}, and P_{Z_2} and P'''_{Z_1}), the new budget line will be parallel to, and to the right of, the budget line for the total budget Y. Now, superimpose an indifference map over the new budget lines and find a new set of tangency points d, e, and f. Now, on your working paper, draw a

FIGURE 5.5
The Demand Curve for Z_1, Given That Income and the Price of Other Goods Remain Constant

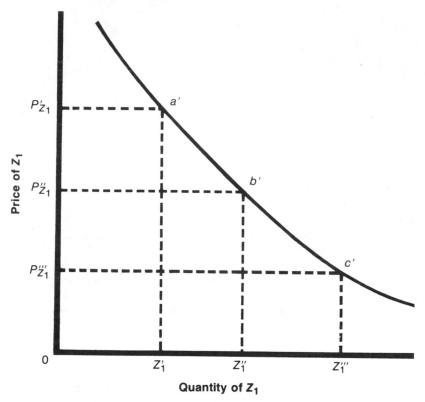

diagram similar to Figure 5.5. Locate the points d', e', and f', and join them to form a new demand curve for the good Z_1, at the new income Y'. Observe that, with the increased income, the demand curve shifts to the right. As it happens, this is a quite general finding: if income increases, the whole demand curve will shift rightward, whereas if income decreases, the whole demand curve will shift leftward. This is true for normal and superior goods, but not for inferior goods.

Changes in the Prices of Other Goods

Remember that the demand curve shown in Figure 5.5 is the demand curve for the good Z_1, given that the price of Z_2 and the budget remain constant. If the price of Z_2 were to change, it is quite possible that the demand curve for Z_1 would shift. If Z_1 and Z_2 were close *substitutes* (for example, beef and pork), an increase in the price of Z_2 would lead the consumer to divert his budget to the purchase of the substitute, Z_1. The result would be a shift in the demand curve for Z_1 to the right. A decrease in the price of Z_2 would, similarly, attract additional purchases, and the demand curve for Z_1, which is now relatively more expensive than Z_2, would shift to the left. If Z_1 and Z_2 were *complements* (for example, bread and butter, which make each other more attractive to the consumer), an increase in price of Z_2 would make both Z_1 and Z_2 less attractive to the consumer and would shift the demand curve for Z_1 to the left. A decrease in the price of Z_2 would make both Z_1 and Z_2 more attractive to the consumer and would shift the demand curve for Z_1 to the right.

DEMAND FOR THE OUTPUT OF AN INDUSTRY

In the case of ordinary private goods, the demand curve for the output of an industry can be derived by horizontal summation of the demand curves for all the individuals who use that industry's product. In Figure 5.6, the individual demand curves of three different consumers for the good Z_1 are shown. If there were only three buyers for Z_1, the demand curve for the output of the industry that produces Z_1 can be derived from the information contained in these three individual demand curves. At the high price P'_{Z_1}, the quantities of Z_1 demanded by the individuals are Z'_{11}, Z'_{12}, and Z'_{13}; the total quantity of Z_1 demanded at price P'_{Z_1} is Z'_{1T}, which is equal to $Z'_{11} + Z'_{12} + Z'_{13}$. At the lower price P'''_{Z_1}, the total quantity of Z_1 demanded is $Z'''_{1T} = Z'''_{11} + Z'''_{12} + Z'''_{13}$. This procedure can be repeated for all other prices, including the intermediate price, P''_{Z_1}.

We have derived the demand curve, D_T, for the industry that produces the commodity Z_1, by the process of horizontally summing the individual demands at each price in order to obtain total demand at that price, and then drawing a curve through the total demands at the various prices. Notice that the industry demand curve slopes downward and to the right, and has a more gentle slope than the individual demand curves.

Elasticity of Demand

Elasticity of demand is a concept that deals with the responsiveness of quantity demanded to changes in other relevant variables. The *price elasticity of demand* of Z_1 is the proportional change in the quantity of Z_1 demanded as a result of a change in the price of Z_1. That is:

$$\frac{\Delta Z_1}{\Delta P_{Z_1}} \cdot \frac{P_{Z_1}}{Z_1} .$$

Price elasticity of demand is almost always negative. The demand for Z_1 is called *price elastic* if the price elasticity of demand is greater (in absolute value) than -1. If the price elasticity lies between 0 and -1, the demand for Z_1 is called price inelastic. The demand for things

FIGURE 5.6
The Industry Demand Curve for Z_1

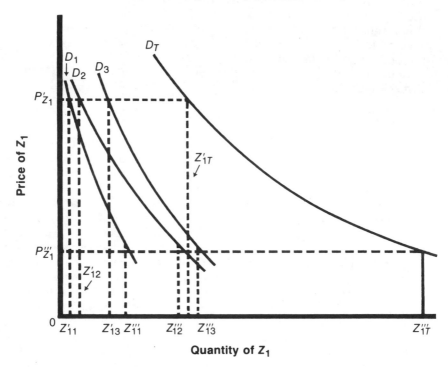

that are sometimes called "necessities of life" is usually price inelastic, while the demand for discretionary items is often price elastic. For example, the demand for the broad category, all foods, in a single country is price inelastic. However, the demand for particular food items, especially items in the luxury category, is often price elastic.

Estimates of price elasticity of demand provide very useful information for policy analysts. Suppose it were thought important to encourage conservation of oil. If the demand for oil were price elastic, increases in the price of oil to consumers would be an effective way to reduce the quantity demanded. However, if the demand for oil were price inelastic, price increases would be a much less effective way of encouraging conservation.

Cross-price elasticity of demand measures the responsiveness of the quantity of one commodity, say Z_1, demanded to changes in the prices of another commodity, say Z_2. That is:

$$\frac{\Delta Z_1}{\Delta P_{Z_2}} \cdot \frac{P_{Z_2}}{Z_1} \ .$$

Cross-price elasticity of demand may be positive, zero or negative. If Z_1 and Z_2 were good substitutes for each other, the cross-price elasticity of Z_1 with respect to Z_2 would be positive. If Z_1 and Z_2 were complements, the cross-price elasticity of Z_1 with respect to Z_2 would be negative; the quantity of Z_1 consumed would decrease in response to an increase in the price of Z_2.

Another very important demand elasticity concept is *income elasticity of demand*. It deals with the response of the quantity of a commodity demanded to a change in the consumer's income. That is, for Z_1:

$$\frac{\Delta Z_1}{\Delta Y} \cdot \frac{Y}{Z_1} \cdot$$

For *superior goods,* income elasticity of demand is greater than 1. For *normal goods,* income elasticity of demand is positive, but less than 1. For *inferior goods,* the income elasticity of demand is negative. As income rises, the quantity of a superior good demanded rises at a more rapid rate, while the quantity of a normal good demanded rises at a less rapid rate. For inferior goods, quantity demanded falls as income rises.

Estimates of income elasticity of demand are very useful in predicting changes in quantities of goods demanded. In times of rising prosperity, the growth industries are those that produce goods for which the income elasticity of demand is high. In relatively wealthy countries, where the basic nutritional needs of most citizens are satisfied, the income elasticity of demand for most foods at the farm level is relatively low, whereas the income elasticity of demand for processing and packaging services that increase the convenience of food items is higher. This accounts, in large part, for the growing farm-retail price spread for food items in the wealthy countries.

While there are few reliable estimates, there is much discussion of the income elasticity of demand for environmental quality amenities such as clean air and clean water. If the income elasticity of demand for such amenities is substantially greater than 1, as some have guessed that it is, one would predict that prosperous societies would spend a greater proportion of their total incomes on attaining environmental quality, while impoverished countries would spend a lower proportion of their total incomes for these kinds of amenities. Within a single country, a relatively high income elasticity of demand for environmental quality would suggest that these kinds of amenities are typically of greater concern to upper-income citizens than to lower-income citizens.

Some thoughtful observers believe that this kind of discussion is much too simplistic to be meaningful. It is likely that those things loosely grouped together as "environmental quality amenities" actually consist of a number of very different goods and services. The income elasticities of demand for such basic environmental quality services as sanitation, and air and water quality conducive to good health and normal life spans, are probably quite low. These things are quite likely viewed by most as "necessities of life." On the other hand, the income elasticity of demand for high levels of atmospheric visibility in remote wilderness areas may well be quite high.

THE FIRM

The economic analysis of the producing unit (i.e., the firm) is in a number of important respects quite similar to that for the consumer. On the other hand, there are some significant differences.

The *production function* for some good, Z, is a mathematical relationship between the quantities of the various inputs used in the production of Z and the total amount of Z produced. The production function can be expressed:

$$Z = f(X_1, X_2, ..., X_n),$$

where $X_1,...,X_n$, are the inputs used in the production of Z.
In classical economics, these inputs were often characterized as land, capital, and labor. The production processes for most goods are much more carefully defined than that. The exact nature of the inputs is much more specific: for example, fertilizer with a specific chemical composition.

The production function is a physical, rather than an economic, relationship and expresses the production technology of the firm. If a new technology were introduced, the production function would change. In fact, the history of technological progress in modern societies is a history of the repeated introduction of new technical processes that change the production functions for commodities produced.

How does the firm decide which combination of inputs it should use to produce its output? Consider a production process in which the output of Z is determined by the utilization of two variable inputs, X_1 and X_2. Its production function can be expressed as:

$$Z = f(X_1, X_2).$$

Working with only two inputs is an analytical convenience that permits us the simplicity of two-dimensional diagrams; the kind of results we can derive in two dimensions can be derived for n kinds of inputs using vector calculus.

Given that X_1 and X_2 are both variable inputs, they may be used in various combinations to produce a given output of Z. An *isoquant* is the locus of all of the possible combinations of two inputs X_1 and X_2 that can be combined to produce a specific quantity of the output Z.

Isoquants are in many ways similar to indifference curves, and the analysis of the producing firm that will follow is quite similar to the analysis of the individual consumer. The major difference encountered in the analysis of production is that the quantity of output is cardinally measurable. Output is measurable in terms of specific quantities, and it is clear that twenty bushels of corn is exactly twice as much as ten bushels, and one million acre feet of stored water is exactly twice as much as five hundred thousand acre feet. On the other hand, utility is measurable only ordinally. We can say that indifference curves farther from the origin represent greater total utility than indifference curves nearer the origin, but we cannot say exactly how much greater.

The *isoquant map* for the production of Z using X_1 and X_2 is shown in Figure 5.7. Assuming that Z is perfectly divisible, there is an infinite number of isoquants for Z. In Figure 5.7, three representative isoquants are shown. If, as would be expected, the firm experiences diminishing marginal productivity for both X_1 and X_2, its isoquants will necessarily be negatively sloped and convex to the origin in the region of potentially efficient production. At any point

FIGURE 5.7
An Isoquant Map

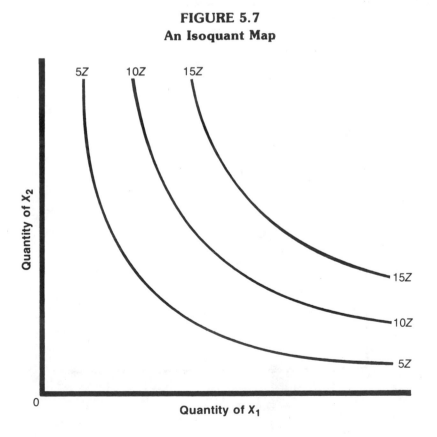

on an isoquant, the absolute value of the slope of the tangent to the isoquant is equal to the *rate of technical substitution* of X_1 for X_2 in the production of Z.

As with indifference curves, isoquants farther from the origin represent greater quantities of total output than isoquants nearer the origin; and isoquants may never intersect.

THE EFFICIENT COMBINATION OF INPUTS

If the producing firm is in a perfectly competitive industry, its purchases of the inputs X_1 and X_2 will not be sufficiently large to influence the price of X_1 and X_2. Under these circumstances, an *isocost line,* a construct analogous to the budget line in the theory of consumer demand, may be constructed. The slope of the isocost line is simply the negative of the price ratio of the two inputs, that is, $-(P_{X_1}/P_{X_2})$. The exact position of the isocost line depends on the price ratio of the inputs, and also on the total amount the firm is willing to spend on inputs. Assume, for the moment, that the firm faces a strict constraint on operating capital. It can spend only the amount C on inputs for production, but no more. Using information on that capital constraint and the price ratios, a precise isocost line may be specified, as in Figure 5.8.

FIGURE 5.8

An Isocost Line

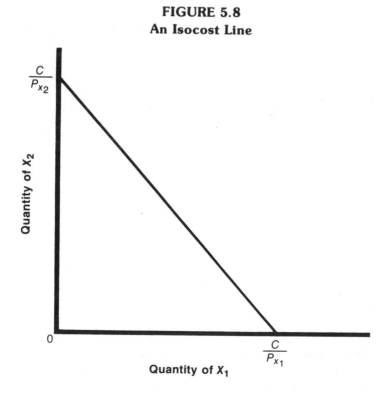

Quantity of X_1

The producer's problem is to find the *output-maximizing combination of inputs, given a cost constraint*. Given the cost constraint, C, this problem is solved by finding the isoquant that is tangent to some point on the isocost line (Figure 5.9). The tangency point specifies the exact combination of inputs X_1 and X_2 that will maximize output given the cost constraint. The maximum output is Z^*, and the output-maximizing input combination is X_{1Z^*} and X_{2Z^*}. Observe that, at this output-maximizing combination of inputs, the rate of technical substitution (RTS) of X_1 and X_2 is equal to the price ratio of the two inputs; that is:

$$\text{RTS}_{X_1,X_2} = \frac{P_{X_1}}{P_{X_2}}.$$

It may be that the firm manager does not face a rigid constraint on operating capital. He may, instead, conceptualize his problem as finding the *least-cost combination of inputs to produce a given output* of Z. Let us say he wants to produce five units of Z. Then he will identify the isoquant, $5Z$, and seek the combination of inputs that will minimize the cost of producing that level of output. He will do this by identifying the isocost line C^*, which is just tangent to the isoquant $5Z$. The point of tangency will identify the least-cost combination of inputs (X_{1C^*} and X_{2C^*}, in Figure 5.9). If he wants to know exactly how much it will cost to purchase the least-cost combination of inputs to produce $5Z$, he may use the formula:

$$C^* = P_{X_1} \cdot X_{1C^*} + P_{X_2} \cdot X_{2C^*}.$$

At the cost-minimizing combination of inputs to produce a given output:

$$\text{RTS}_{X_1,X_2} = \frac{P_{X_1}}{P_{X_2}}.$$

This condition, that the rate of technical substitution of inputs is equal to the ratio of input prices, is common to the solutions for the cost-constrained output-maximizing problem and the "least cost to produce a given output" problem. It is the *necessary condition* for efficiency in the production of a single output. If we had considered the production of two outputs, Z_1 and Z_2, this necessary condition would be stated thus: RTS_{X_1,X_2} in the production of Z_1 is equal to RTS_{X_1,X_2} in the production of Z_2, and both are equal to the ratio of prices of X_1 and X_2. The *sufficient condition* for efficiency in input utilization is that the isoquants be nonconcave. They should be convex to the origin or, as a special case, linear. If the isoquants were concave, satisfaction of the necessary condition would have the embarrassing result of minimizing the output for a given cost

FIGURE 5.9

The Output-Maximizing Combination of Inputs, Given a Cost Constraint; and the Least-Cost Combination of Inputs to Produce a Given Output

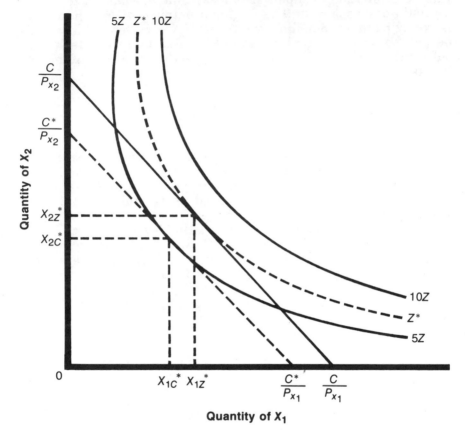

constraint or maximizing the cost of producing a given amount of output.

Consider what happens when the cost constraint is progressively relaxed while the prices of the inputs X_1 and X_2 remain unchanged. We can draw three isocost lines, 1, 2, and 3, all parallel, so that the isocost line 1 represents the locus of all combinations of the two inputs that can be purchased with the amount of operating capital C', and the isocost lines 2 and 3 are defined similarly for the operating capital budgets C'' and C''', respectively. As the operating capital budget becomes progressively larger, the isocost line moves further from the origin.

Now, for each isocost line, find the combination of the two inputs that maximizes output. Use the necessary condition, that the rate of technical substitution of X_1 for X_2 should be equal to the ratio of the

FIGURE 5.10
The Expansion Path

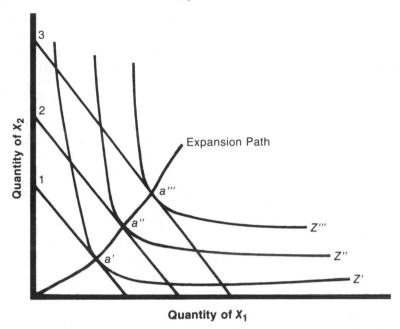

Quantity of X_1

prices for X_1 and X_2, and remember that the (absolute value of) slope of an isocost line is equal to the price ratio. For each operating capital budget, the output-maximizing combination of inputs may be identified: a' for the operating capital constraint C', a'' for C'' and a''' for C''' (Figure 5.10). A line joining the origin, the points a', a'' and a''', and all other points of tangency between isocost lines and isoquants is called an *expansion path*. The expansion path is the locus of all the output-maximizing combinations of inputs, as the constraint on operating capital is progressively relaxed. It shows how the efficient combination of inputs changes as output, and total expenditure on operating costs, increase. A particular expansion path is unique for input prices and technology; a change in the price of either input or in the technological information expressed in the production function would be sufficient to generate a new expansion path.

PROFIT-MAXIMIZING LEVEL OF OUTPUT

At this point, we have succeeded in determining the least-cost combination of inputs to produce a given output, or the output-maximizing combination of inputs given a strict constraint on operating capital. Now we need to determine the preferred level of output for the firm. To this point, we have implicitly assumed that the firm operator seeks to obtain the maximum possible output for a given expenditure on operating costs, or to find the least expensive way of producing a given level of output. Now we need a more general assumption about the motivations of the firm operator.

A simple but very serviceable assumption about the motivation of firm operators is that they seek to maximize profit. Since profit for the firm owner is identical to the income with which the same individual can act effectively as a consumer, this is probably not a bad assumption. In relatively simple economic analyses, the assumption of profit-maximizing motivation is almost always used. In more complex analyses, where information is incomplete and uncertainties abound, where firm performance in one period of time will influence long-run survival and growth of the firm into the future, and where firm operators may be concerned not just with immediate profit but also with security, long-run survival and the enjoyment of leisure time, more complex assumptions about the motivations of firm operators are used. Nevertheless, all other things being equal, firm operators typically prefer more profit to less. So the motivational assumption of profit maximization is highly serviceable in many kinds of economic analyses.

Profit is defined, for the purposes of simple analyses, as the difference between total returns (TR) and total costs (TC); i.e.:

$$\pi = TR - TC$$

where π denotes profit.

We assume that the producing firm is in a perfectly competitive industry. The quantity of output it produces is so small, relative to the total output of the industry in which it operates, that the output decisions of the firm have no influence on the prices it pays and receives.

The Total-Cost Curve

A total cost curve is simply a schedule relating total production expenses to the quantity of output. For example:

$$TC = h(Z)$$

is the general formula for the total cost curve for producing the commodity Z. It states, simply, that the total cost of producing Z is some mathematical function of the quantity of Z produced. The total cost curve is derived from the production function:

$$Z = f(X_1, X_2, ..., X_n)$$

and information about the unit prices of the inputs. The total cost of producing some specific amount of Z is:

$$TC = P_{X_1} \cdot X_1 + P_{X_2} \cdot X_2 + ... + P_{X_n} \cdot X_n,$$

where $X_1, X_2, ..., X_n$ refer to the specific quantities of the inputs that, when used together, make up the least-cost combination of inputs to produce that quantity of Z.

The total cost curve is, then, a schedule relating the total costs of producing Z to the quantity of Z produced, provided that for any specific quantity of Z produced, the inputs are used in the least-cost combination.

Costs in the Short Run and the Long Run. Total costs change as the quantities of variable inputs change. If the quantities of some kinds of inputs are unchanged (i.e., *fixed*) no matter how much of Z is produced, the costs of these fixed inputs will play no part in determining *how much* of Z should be produced; they will be of interest only in determining whether Z ought to be produced at all. How could the quantity of an input be fixed? Under what conditions would a firm manager be totally unable to manipulate the amount of an input used in production? The answer is: it is all a matter of time. If a farmer has already cultivated his land and planted his crop, the costs of performing those tasks are no longer relevant to any decisions he may be called upon to make during that growing season. For the rest of that growing season, the costs of soil preparation and planting must be considered fixed. As the growing season progresses, the farmer will make many more decisions, one by one. He will decide how much to spend on controlling weeds and pests, at what time and in what manner to harvest the crop, and, after harvest, how much to invest in storage and marketing strategies that may increase the price he receives for his crop. After each of these various tasks is completed, the expenditures outlaid to perform that task must be considered fixed, for that cropping season. His decisions will be based only on the costs that face him in the future — that is, those costs that are still variable in that growing season.

If he encounters adverse climatic conditions or a sharp fall in prices for his product, it may become apparent to him that the total revenue he can expect from his crop is less than the total costs, fixed plus variable, of producing it. However, he will continue crop husbandry, harvesting, and marketing, as long as the total return from his crop seems likely to exceed the costs of current and future operations alone. At any point in the growing season, he will base his production decisions on total revenue and variable costs. Only if his expected total return is so low that he cannot recover harvesting and marketing expenses, will he simply abandon his crop just prior to harvest time.

But, what about next year's growing season? Before he begins to prepare his land for planting, he will make his best estimate of the total revenue from next year's crop. He will perform the very first task of the new cropping season if, and only if, the expected total revenue from the crop exceeds the total direct costs of its production. At the very start of the growing season, all the direct enterprise costs of producing that crop are variable. However, he still has some fixed costs: for example, the costs of owning the land and machinery he uses. Those costs are fixed, until such time as he seriously considers whether to quit farming completely. If he takes a very long view of his decision problem, even the costs of owning his land and his machinery are variable.

The definition of fixed and variable costs depends entirely on his *planning horizon,* the time period over which he makes decisions. In the *short run,* for example, during a crop-growing season, some cost items are usually fixed while others are variable. In the *long run* all costs are variable, since the individual could simply liquidate the resources he uses for farming and invest them in some entirely different activity. Returning for a moment to the analysis used to find the least-cost combination of inputs X_1 and X_2, that analysis would be valid for both the short run and the long run if the production function for Z was simply:

$$Z = f(X_1, X_2).$$

However, if the production function for Z was:

$$Z = f(X_1, X_2 | X_3, ..., X_n)$$

(that is, inputs X_1 and X_2 are variable while inputs X_3 through X_n are fixed), that analysis would be valid only for the short run. In that case, a long-run analysis would need to consider all inputs, X_1 through X_n, as variable.

A typical long-run total cost curve, labeled LRTC, is shown in Figure 5.11. Long-run total cost is zero, when output of Z is zero; it rises quite rapidly as small amounts of Z are produced; then rises less rapidly as larger amounts of Z are produced, taking advantage of more efficient plant sizes; and, finally, commences to rise rapidly again, as the output of Z becomes very large and the firm experiences difficulty in efficiently managing such a large-size operation.

A short-run total cost curve, labeled SRTC, for the same firm is also shown in Figure 5.11. When output is zero, short-run total costs exceed zero: the fixed costs still must be met. Thus, short-run total costs at zero output are equal to C_f, fixed costs, and total fixed costs (TFC) may be represented in Figure 5.11 by a horizontal straight line passing through the cost axis at the point C_f. The TFC line is relevant, of course, only in the short run. The SRTC curve approaches the LRTC curve gradually, as output of Z increases to a level that can effectively utilize the fixed inputs. SRTC just touches LRTC at the point E in Figure 5.11. As output continues to increase, SRTC again begins to diverge from LRTC, on the high side. In the short run, fixity of some resources makes it more costly to expand output than in the long run, when all inputs are variable. For example, one could increase output with a fixed plant size by working more hours per day, but overtime wage rates and increased maintenance expenses may make that strategy quite costly. In the

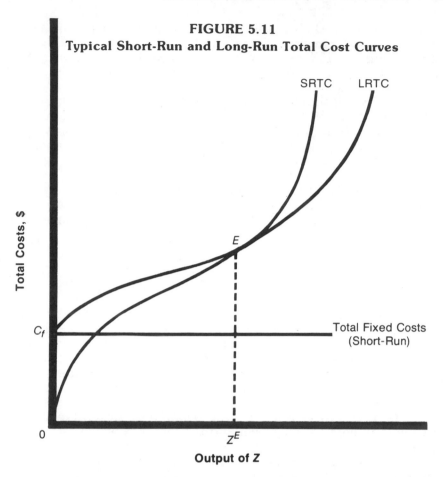

FIGURE 5.11
Typical Short-Run and Long-Run Total Cost Curves

long run, however, the same increase in output could be achieved in a less costly manner by judicious increases in plant size.

Average and Marginal Costs. For any level of output, *average cost* is simply total cost divided by total output. In the short run, it is possible to differentiate between average fixed costs, AFC, and average variable costs, AVC. Average fixed cost is simply TFC divided by the level of output. Since TFC does not change with output, AFC approaches TFC for very small outputs, but becomes very small for very large outputs. Total variable costs, TVC, for any level of output in the short run is simply the total costs of producing that output minus TFC. Average variable cost, AVC, for any level of output is, then, TVC divided by the quantity of output. For production processes with the kind of total cost curves depicted in Figure 5.11, AVC is a U-shaped curve. Average total costs, ATC, for any level of output is simply AFC + AVC for that level of output. The average total cost curve is also a U-shaped curve, but is tilted a little, relative to the AVC curve; it is considerably higher than AVC when output is low and AFC is large, but only a little higher than AVC when output is large and AFC is small.

In the long run, TFC and AFC are zero, since all costs are variable. Thus, AVC is equal to ATC, or simply average cost, AC, for each level of output.

Marginal cost is the change in total cost attributable to a one-unit change in output. Short-run marginal cost refers to the change in cost resulting from a one-unit change in output when only the variable inputs change. Long-run marginal cost, on the other hand, refers to the change in cost resulting from a one-unit change in output, when all inputs are variable.

Although the definition of marginal cost differs slightly between the short run and the long run, the calculation to determine marginal cost is similar. The marginal cost of, for example, an increase in output from Z' to Z'' is

$$MC'' = TC'' - TC'$$

or the increase in total cost caused by expanding production from Z' to Z''. For a production process with total cost curves shaped like those in Figure 5.11, the marginal cost at low levels of output is less than the average cost. At some greater level of output, marginal cost commences to rise, and to rise more rapidly than average cost. Eventually, some level of output is reached at which the marginal cost curve cuts the average cost curve; and for even higher levels of output, marginal cost exceeds average cost. These general relationships hold in both the short run and the long run, when total cost curves are shaped like those in Figure 5.11. However, long-run average and marginal cost curves are sloped more gently than their short-run counterparts, as shown in Figure 5.12. The short-run marginal and average cost curves denoted SRMC' and SRAC' are relevant when the fixed inputs are held at the level F'. Similarly, SRMC'' and SRAC'' are relevant when the level of fixed inputs is F''; and SRMC''' and SRAC''' are relevant when the level of fixed inputs is F'''. Notice that, for all four pairs of cost curves, SRMC' and SRAC', SRMC'' and SRAC'', SRMC''' and SRAC''', and LRMC and LRAC, the marginal cost curve intersects the average cost curve at the lowest point on the average cost curve.

Output and Supply. In the short run, the firm operator will determine the quantity of Z to produce, after considering the price of Z, and the marginal cost and average variable cost of producing Z. Assuming that the total output of the firm represents such a small contribution to total industry output that the decisions of the firm have no influence on the market price of Z, P_Z may be represented by a horizontal line, as in Figure 5.13.

In the short run, the firm will determine its output by the following rule: It will produce the quantity of output at which price is just equal

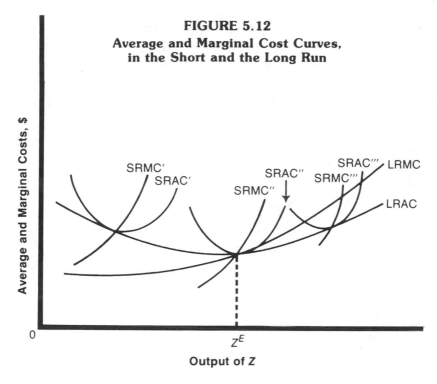

FIGURE 5.12
Average and Marginal Cost Curves,
in the Short and the Long Run

to marginal cost, so long as price is equal to or greater than average variable cost. At the price P'_Z, MC is just equal to AVC, and the firm will produce Z' units of output. At any price lower than P'_Z, no output at all will be produced. At the price P''_Z, the unit price of output is exactly equal to MC at the point where it intersects ATC, and the firm will produce Z''. At prices successively higher than P''_Z, the firm will produce increasing amounts of output, at each price applying the decision rule $P = \text{MC}$. Notice that the firm makes zero profit when $P = \text{ATC}$. Yet, the firm continues to produce in the short run at prices between P' and P''. At prices in this range, the firm's revenue is equal to or greater than its total variable costs, but less than its total costs.

   The *short-run supply curve of the individual firm* can be identified, using the information provided in Figure 5.13. The short-run supply curve has two segments: the straight vertical line OP'_Z, at which output is zero for all prices less than P'_Z; and that segment of the marginal cost curve that lies above and to the right of the point at which MC intersects AVC.

   We saw earlier how the demand for the output of an industry could be determined by the simple process of horizontal summation of the individual demand curves of consumers for that product. In the case of supply curves, things are seldom quite so simple. If the whole industry that produces the commodity Z is a relatively insignificant user of all inputs it uses, and therefore the total industry output of Z

FIGURE 5.13
Marginal Cost and the Short-Run
Supply Curve for the Single Firm

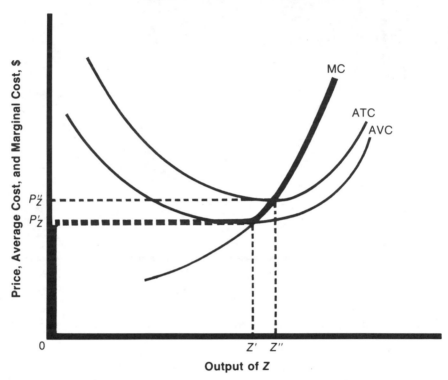

has no significant influence on the price of any of the inputs used in the Z industry, the process of horizontal summation of individual firm supply curves would be adequate for deriving the *industry short-run supply curve*. However, that is often an unreasonable assumption. Many industries, taken as a whole, purchase significant quantities of the inputs they use, so that the activity in those industries does have an influence on the price of inputs. In these cases, the effect of industry output on the price level of inputs introduces a complicating factor. As industry output expands, and input prices increase, each firm's marginal cost curve would be shifted to the left. It would require a quite complex analysis to determine the industry's short-run supply curve under these conditions. However, it is reasonable to presume that the industry's supply curve is somewhat more steeply sloped when input prices increase in response to an increase in output.

In the long run, each firm will cease production if price falls below long-run average cost (Figure 5.14). No firm would continue production in the long run, if to do so entailed continuous losses. At any price above the intersection of LRMC and LRAC, the firm will

FIGURE 5.14
Long-Run Equilibrium Price and Output

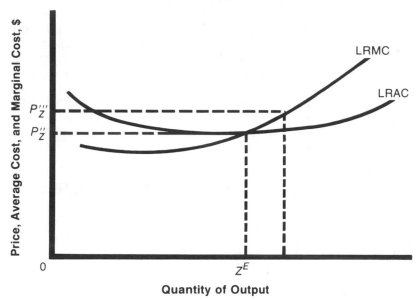

Quantity of Output

determine its level of output according to the rule $P_z = \text{LRMC}$. However, at prices such as P_z''', which is higher than the intersection of LRMC and LRAC, the firm is clearly enjoying a profit. In the long run, since all inputs are variable, such a situation is unlikely to persist. Resource mobility permits firms to move in and out of industries in response to changes in the profit picture. When the price of Z exceeds the minimum LRAC, the profitability of the Z industry is likely to attract new firms. The output of those entering firms will increase total supply. Assuming that the demand curve for Z slopes downward, as demand curves usually do, the activities of the new entrants would drive the price of the commodity Z downward toward P_z''. If the price of Z were to fall below P_z'', it would not remain there long, since firms would suffer losses and would exit. Thus, in the long run, and in the absence of changes in production functions or input prices, resource mobility will exert a strong tendency toward stabilizing the price of Z at P_z''.

At price P_z'', since $P_z'' = \text{LRAC}$, there are *no "pure profits,"* as economists define them. Firm operators make a living, and each of the firm's inputs is rewarded at the going rate. An accountant would be able to identify rewards to the firm owner and to the investments he has in the firm, and would probably call these "profit." However, since these various inputs are rewarded at only the normal rate of return (or, as economists say, recover only their opportunity costs), no "pure profits" are enjoyed by the firm owner.

In the short run, it is usually impossible to derive the *industry supply curve* by simple horizontal summation of individual-firm supply curves. In the long run, the relationship between industry and firm supply curves is even more complex. The activities of firms in aggregate may, as in the short run, influence the price of inputs. In addition, the possibility of new firms entering the industry, in response to changes in the price of its product, complicates the picture still further. Nevertheless, we know that industry supply curves typically have positive slopes, in the long run. Even if economists have difficulty providing a simple demonstration of how the long-run supply curve for an industry may be derived from the long-run marginal cost curves of the actual and potential firms in that industry, careful statistical analyses confirm, in most cases, the economists' prediction of a positively sloped long-run supply curve.

DEMAND, SUPPLY, AND MARKET EQUILIBRIUM

The analyses to this point have made use of a number of quite specific assumptions. Now, we pause to remind ourselves of these various assumptions.

1. *Motivational Assumptions.* We assume that the consumer seeks to maximize his utility, or satisfaction from the consumption of goods and the enjoyment of services and amenities. We assume the producer seeks to maximize his profit. Since the producer's profit provides his income, and income is believed to be positively related to utility, our assumptions concerning the motivations of consumers and producers are, to a significant degree, consistent one to the other. The consistency, however, is imperfect, since leisure is also believed to be positively related to utility, but the maximization of leisure is most likely incompatible with the maximization of profits.
2. *The Static Time Frame.* This assumption enables us to assume that the utility functions of consumers and the production functions that specify the technological relationships between inputs and outputs in production remain unchanged throughout the analysis. On the other hand, we assume that the time frame is sufficiently long to allow individual decision makers to absorb information and to make all the adjustments that are necessary as they go about their business of maximizing utility or profit. The author's favorite cynic has been known to refer to the static time frame as "the infinite instant: that period of time which is sufficiently short that nothing changes, but sufficiently long to permit all adjustments."
3. *Full Information.* We assume that consumers have, in advance, complete information about product performance and the satisfactions that various goods, services, and amenities will provide them. We assume that producers have complete information about the production functions for the production processes

from among which they choose. We assume that both producers and consumers have full information about all relevant prices.

4. *Convexity Assumptions.* We assume that as consumption of any commodity is increased while the consumption of other commodities is held constant, the marginal utility to the consumer is positive but diminishing. Similarly, we assume that as the use of any input in a production process increases while the other inputs are held constant, diminishing marginal productivity is encountered. These assumptions are sufficient to permit the economist the analytical convenience of assuming that indifference curves and isoquants are convex to the origin.

5. *Resource Mobility.* Resources are assumed, at least in the long run, to be mobile. That is, they can be transferred from one use to another in response to economic incentives such as price changes.

6. *Commodities and Inputs are Homogeneous.* We assume that each unit of each identifiable commodity and input is undifferentiated from other units of the same commodity or input. Thus, the consumer will have no preference as to which producer provides the commodities he purchases, and producers will have no preferences among alternative suppliers of the same input.

7. *Large Industries, Small Individuals.* We assume that the purchases of each consumer represent such a small proportion of the total output of any commodity that the decisions of an individual consumer have no influence on the price of that commodity. Similarly, we assume that each producer produces such a small proportion of the total output of a given industry that his actions have no influence on the price of the product or of the inputs used in its production.

These assumptions together permit us to develop a simplified analysis of demand, supply, and market equilibrium under perfect competition. Parenthetically, it should be noted that not all of these assumptions are necessary assumptions of the perfect competition model of market equilibrium; some are simply the necessary assumptions of the very simplest kind of perfect competition models. The assumptions of resource mobility and large markets consisting of large numbers of producers and consumers each trading quite small quantities of homogeneous products are the fundamental assumptions of perfect competition. It is possible within the perfect competition framework to relax many of the other simplifying assumptions listed above, and the scholarly literature in economics contains many examples of analyses that attempt to do that. The economist may work with more complex motivational assumptions, with a dynamic rather than a static time frame, with utility functions and production functions that do not always yield convex indifference curves and isoquants, and with the concept that information is expensive and thus can never be complete or perfect at less than prohibitive expense, all without violating the fundamental concept of perfect competition.

The *demand curve* for a commodity is a schedule relating the quantity of the commodities purchased to its price. Demand curves are expressed diagramatically in price-quantity space (that is, in the positive quadrant of a diagram with price on the vertical axis and quantity on the horizontal axis), and typically slope downward to the left. As price rises, smaller quantities of the commodity are demanded.

The *supply curve* is a schedule relating the quantity of a commodity produced to its price, and typically slopes upward to the right. As prices increase, making the commodity more attractive to producers, increased quantities are produced and find their way into the market. Since the supply curve and the demand curve are both expressed in price-quantity space, it seems useful to form a single diagram by superimposing the supply curve for a given commodity on the demand curve for the same commodity. In this way, a *market diagram* is formed.

The equilibrium price for the commodity Z in the market depicted in Figure 5.15 is P^e. At that price, Z^e units of Z are produced and

FIGURE 5.15

Demand, Supply, and Equilibrium Price

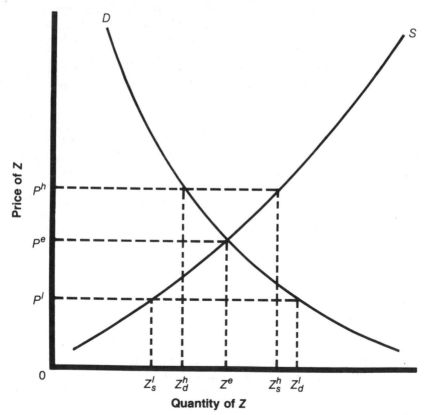

exactly that many units are purchased. As economists say, the market is cleared. At the higher price P^h, the quantity of Z demanded is Z_d^h, while quantity supplied is Z_s^h, which is substantially larger. At the price P^h, a *surplus* of $Z_s^h - Z_d^h$ exists. Notice that when the amount Z_s^h is supplied on the market, the demand price for that quantity is not P^h, or even P^e; it is lower than P^e. The excessive quantity of Z supplied as a result of the high price P^h provides a stimulus driving price downward. As price is driven downward, larger quantities are demanded. The market comes to equilibrium at the market clearing price P^e. If, on the other hand, price was P^l, lower than P^e, quantity demanded would be Z_d^l while quantity supplied would be Z_s^l. A *shortage* of $Z_d^l - Z_s^l$ would exist in the market for Z. That shortage would tend to drive price upward, while the rising price would tend to attract more of the commodity Z from suppliers. Eventually, the market would reach equilibrium at the price P^e.

The market thus has a built-in tendency to reach equilibrium. Price serves to ration goods among consumers. Higher prices discourage consumption, while lower prices encourage it. Price, since it is directly reflected in the incomes of producers, provides incentives for production. Higher prices encourage increased production, while lower prices discourage production. Working on both the demand and the supply sides of the market, price directs the allocation of resources.

The terms surplus and shortage refer to differences between quantity demanded and quantity supplied at *particular prices*. At the high price, a surplus existed; at the low price, a shortage existed. At the equilibrium price, quantity supplied equaled quantity demanded, and the market was cleared. The market is a device that, when working well, eliminates shortages and surpluses. That does not mean that a system of markets guarantees Utopia. The elimination of shortages does not mean that everybody has as much of every commodity as he or she would like. The elimination of surpluses does not mean that every producing firm receives the prices and revenues it would like. It simply means that markets have a strong in-built tendency to find the economic equilibrium by establishing the price at which quantity demanded equals quantity supplied, given the utility functions and production functions, the incomes, and the resource availability that exist.

Support Prices and Ceiling Prices. Suppose that, for reasons thought good, the government attempted to maintain the price of some commodity above equilibrium levels. Call the commodity wheat, and let P^h be the price which the government attempted to maintain. What would be the result of such a policy? Figure 5.15 provides the answer. The quantity of wheat produced would exceed the quantity demanded at the price P^h, and a surplus would be generated. This surplus, as we have seen, would, if left in the market, provide a powerful stimulus for a fall in wheat prices. But, the government is committed to maintain the price of wheat at P^h. Clearly, the surplus must be removed from the market. The government can do this, by purchasing it from the farmers and keeping it out of the hands of consumers. While fundamental conditions remain the same, the government must repeat this activity each year. What can it do with its wheat purchases? It can store ever-increasing quantities of wheat, it can deliberately destroy wheat, or it can give wheat (or sell it at very low prices) to consumers who could not afford to buy wheat at P^h or even P^e. Alternatively, the government can attempt to limit the quantity supplied to the same amount as the quantity demanded at price P^h. It could do this by guaranteeing the price P^h, and restricting production by acreage controls or marketing quotas. In fact, in the past 40 years, one or another variant of all of these policies has been tried.

It is not impossible to support prices above their equilibrium level, and from time to time both private enterprise speculators and governments have performed useful functions by supporting prices during brief periods when prices would otherwise be unusually low. However, to support the price of any commodity above its equilibrium level year after year is expensive and usually involves waste of resources or government controls of production, or both.

In other circumstances, governments have attempted to place price ceilings on certain commodities, so that the price may not exceed some level that is set below the equilibrium price. Return to Figure 5.15 and call the commodity rental housing. A government may simply pass a regulation that the price of rental housing (the monthly rent) must not exceed P^l. At the price P^l, the quantity of rental housing demanded exceeds the quantity supplied and there is a shortage of rental housing. There are some seeking rental housing who would be willing to pay a greater amount than the established price ceiling. The government would need to undertake an expensive effort to enforce the price-ceiling regulations, in order to stop those willing to obtain rental housing by paying above ceiling prices from doing so. A "black market" would arise, unless government enforcement efforts to prevent it were effective. As time passes, the shortage of rental housing would remain, as the price ceiling reduces the incentives for entrepreneurs to provide more rental housing. If rent ceilings were placed on some classes of housing but not on other classes, the housing market would be distorted as production of rent-controlled types of housing lagged while production of uncontrolled classifications of housing proceeded apace. Alternatively, the government could attempt to control the price of rental housing to renters at P^l, while paying some higher price to the owners of housing. In other words, it could provide rent subsidies that enable the owners of rental housing to receive more than the renters are paying. Again, governments in various places have tried all these strategies. The point is not that it is impossible to control prices at some level below the equilibrium, but that to do so for an extended period of time involves coercion or wasted resources, or both.

Shifts in Supply and Demand. Earlier in this chapter, when the demand curve was first derived, it was noted that any demand curve drawn on a two-dimensional diagram expresses the relationship between the price of a commodity and the quantity of that commodity demanded, assuming that income and the price of other commodities remain unchanged. Increases in income will most likely shift a demand curve rightward, while decreases in income will shift it to the left. Increases in the price of substitutes will most likely shift a demand curve to the right, while decreases in the price of substitutes will shift it to the left. Increases in the prices of complements will most likely shift a demand curve to the left, while decreases in the price of complements will shift it to the right.

The supply curve represented on a two-dimensional diagram is also a relationship between the price of a commodity and the quantity of that commodity (in this case, quantity supplied). It is also subject to shifts, if other important variables change. A decrease in the price of inputs will most likely shift a supply curve to the right, by lowering costs of producing the commodity supplied. Likewise, an increase in the price of inputs will most likely shift a supply curve to the left. Development and implementation of superior technology will change the production function, so that more of the commodity can be produced with the same variable inputs. So, improvements in technology shift the supply curve to the right. Let us examine what happens to equilibrium prices and equilibrium quantities when shifts occur in demand and/or supply curves.

Consider an initial market equilibrium at the intersection of demand curve D' and supply curve S', so that price is P' and quantity is Z'. Hold the supply curve constant at S' while shifting the demand curve to the left. When demand is represented by the curve D'' and supply remains at S', both price and quantity decrease, to P'' and Z'', respectively. If on the other hand, demand were to shift to the right, as represented by the demand curve D''', both price and quantity would increase to P''' and Z''', respectively (Figure 5.16).

Now, hold demand constant at D' while permitting the supply curve to shift (Figure 5.17). If supply were to shift leftward to S'', price would rise and quantity would fall, to P'' and Z'', respectively. If supply were to shift rightward, to S''', price would fall and quantity would rise, to P''' and Z''', respectively.

It is always conceivable that supply and demand may both shift. In Figure 5.18, the demand curve and the supply curve both shift to the right, in such a way that price and quantity both increase. However, in Figure 5.19, the demand curve and the supply curve both shift to the right, but in such a way that price decreases while quantity increases. If both curves shift in the same direction, the effect on equilibrium price is not predictable unless one has information on the slope of the supply curve, the slope of the demand curve, the extent of the shift of the supply curve and the extent of the shift of the demand curve.

The analyses just completed represent simple examples of a

FIGURE 5.16
Shifts in Demand

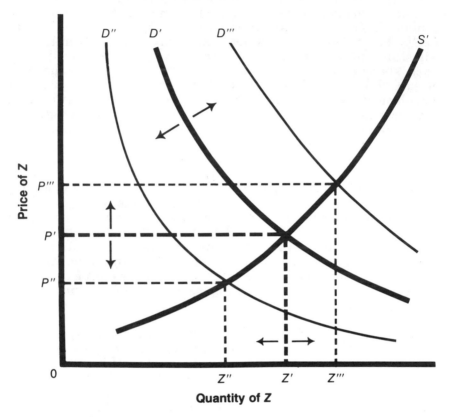

Quantity of Z

process called *comparative static analysis.* This kind of analysis compares the equilibria achieved under different kinds of conditions, and is very useful because it provides a simple and straightforward method of examining the outcomes to be expected if conditions were to change. It is called comparative static analysis because it compares static equilibria under two or more sets of conditions, on the assumption that for each set of conditions all adjustments have been completed. It does not address itself to examining the process of adjustment.

This kind of comparative static analysis finds application in the analysis of many different kinds of economic problems. The student should practice this kind of analysis, until it can be done easily. Think of examples of events that would result in a shift in one or both of the supply and demand curves, and analyze the effect on price and quantity. What is the effect on wages and employment opportunities for a category of skilled workers when a machine is invented that performs their task more effectively? What would be the effect of adverse climatic conditions during the growing season

FIGURE 5.17
Shifts in Supply

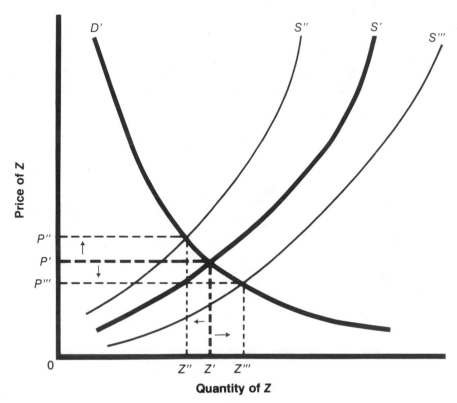

on the price of lettuce? If regulation of airline passenger fares tends to keep them above equilibrium levels, what would be the effect of deregulation on airline fares and the number of passengers?

EXAMPLES OF THE USE OF MARKET-EQUILIBRIUM ANALYSIS IN NATURAL RESOURCE ECONOMICS

Markets for many natural resources are imperfect. That, more than anything else, accounts for the existence of the subdiscipline of natural resource economics. Quite specialized forms of economic analysis are often necessary, if concepts developed for the analysis of perfect markets are to be made useful in the study of problems pertaining to natural resources. Nevertheless, there are many problems in natural resource economics which can be analyzed fruitfully, if not completely, with simple demand, supply, and market equilibrium models. Below, we present three such examples.

The Market for Irrigation Water. In many parts of the world and in many periods of history, from ancient Babylon to the Murray River basin of Australia and the American Southwest in modern

FIGURE 5.18
Shifts in Demand and Supply

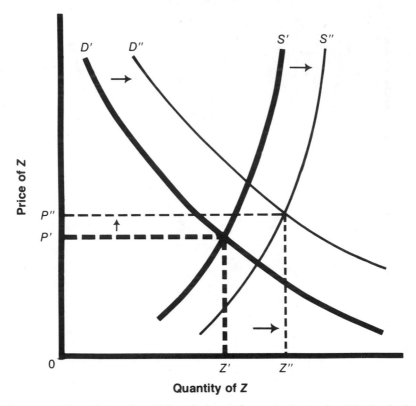

Quantity of Z

times, arid and semi-arid lands have been irrigated with the help of gigantic public-works projects that store water, divert it, and deliver it to the irrigated lands. For our purposes here, the American Southwest of modern times makes a very interesting example.

At any time, the supply of irrigation water in the American Southwest can be represented by a vertical line. Supply is completely inelastic — that is, unresponsive to changes in the price of irrigation water — at any given time. The position of the vertical supply curve for irrigation water depends on a complex set of hydrological facts (rainfall, snowfall, runoff, river-system capacity, evaporation and seepage, etc.), and on the development and operation of public-works projects that affect the capacity to store water and the uses that can be made of water once it is stored. Such a supply system is clearly unresponsive in the short run to changes in the demand price for water: thus, our assumption of an inelastic supply line.

When the irrigation system in the Southwest was in its early stages of development, it was feasible to shift the supply line to the right, time and time again, by building new water storage and

FIGURE 5.19
Shifts in Demand and Supply

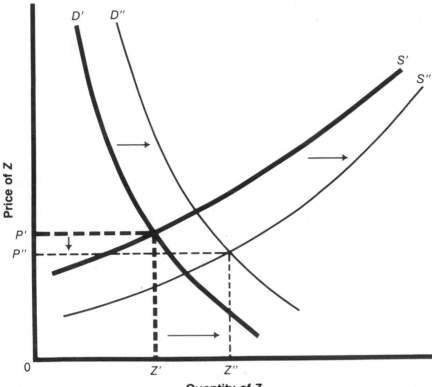

Quantity of Z

delivery systems. However, there are some who argue that, in the late twentieth century, it is no longer possible to systematically shift the supply curve to the right by building more public-works projects. The best damsites have already been used, and the stored water is "recycled" over and over again in agricultural uses to the extent that it was decided to build a desalination plant near the Mexican border to remove agriculture-caused salinity in the Colorado River water delivered to Mexico.[1] It is possible that building more dams in the Colorado River system would result in the delivery of less rather than more water, since additional dams would increase the rate of evaporation and seepage of water from the system. Since surface water appears to be completely utilized, and ground water is being utilized at a rate faster than it can be naturally replenished, an argument can be made that the supply curve for irrigation water in the Southwest is more likely to shift to the left than to the right in the future. For these various reasons, an inelastic and unshifting supply curve for irrigation water, even in the long run, is a serviceable analytic assumption.

The demand for water in the American Southwest can be divided into two broad categories: agricultural and urban. Since there are several major rapidly growing cities in the Southwest, since these cities rely for their water on the same river systems as does agriculture, and since residential and industrial uses of water are relatively high-valued, urban demands are competing more and more directly with agricultural demand for water, as time passes. Let D^u represent the demand for water in urban uses and D^a represent the demand for water in agricultural uses. The total demand for water, D^t, is simply the horizontal summation of D^u and D^a. If the price of water, set not by a market but by the government, is P, all demands at that price are met and there is a small surplus of water. Quantity of water demanded, W_d, is less than quantity supplied, W_s (Figure 5.20).

With the passage of time, however, urban demand for water shifts to the right. The new urban demand curve is $D^{u'}$, while the agricultural demand curve remains D^a and the new total demand curve for water is $D^{t'}$. At the government-determined price, P, there is now a serious shortage of water. Quantity demanded, W_d' exceeds quantity supplied, W_s (Figure 5.20). The price of P is no longer sufficient to ration the available water among the various users. Either the price must be permitted to rise, or some other rationing method must be found. When prices are set by government agencies, they can no longer respond to simple pressures of supply and demand; they respond also to political pressures. If the government is understandably reluctant to allow the price of water in agricultural uses to rise, some more elaborate method of rationing water among competing users must be found.

Suppose that the government reasons that urban users can afford to pay more for a given quantity of water than can agricultural users. Then, it may establish a dual price system, setting the price of urban water at P^u while maintaining the price of agricultural water at P^a. This effectively segregates the market for water. When urban users have siphoned off the quantity of water they demand, $W^{u'}$, at the price P^u, agricultural users may then satisfy their demands at the price P^a. Some surplus of water remains; W_d is now less than W_s (Figure 5.21). The dual price system for allocation of water has been effective in allocating the available water among competing users.

As still more time passes, the urban demand for water increases to $D^{u''}$. Suppose, again, that government agencies are understandably reluctant to raise the prices of water for either class of user. At P^u for urban users and P^a for agricultural users, not all demands can be satisfied and a severe shortage of water is observed; W_d'' is greater than W_s (Figure 5.21).

Under political pressure from agricultural users, the government may choose to restrict the quantity of water available to urban users to the amount W_s''. Thus the supply curve of water for urban users is arbitrarily placed at S^u. Then, $S^t - S^u$ becomes the supply of water available to agricultural users (i.e., S^a). Notice that neither market is cleared. At P^u and S^u, there is a shortage of water for urban uses; that

FIGURE 5.20
Demand and Supply of Water

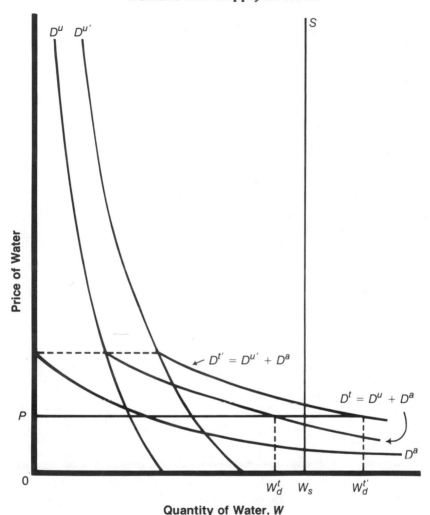

Quantity of Water, W

is, $W_s^{u''}$ is less than $W_d^{u''}$ (Figure 5.22). At P^a and S^a, there is a shortage of water for agricultural uses; that is, W_d^a (which is equal to $[W_s^{u''} + W_d^a] - W_s^{u''}$) is greater than $S^a = S^t - S^u$.

If it is a matter of government policy that neither P^u nor P^a be permitted to rise, non-price rationing devices must be found. The government may establish elaborate systems of water allotments. Each user may be permitted to divert some given quantity of water at the relevant price (P^u if an urban user, and P^a if an agricultural user). These allotments then become valuable, and a "black market" in water may arise. If the government is successful in preventing black markets, the value of the water allocations to urban

FIGURE 5.21
A Two-Price System for Water

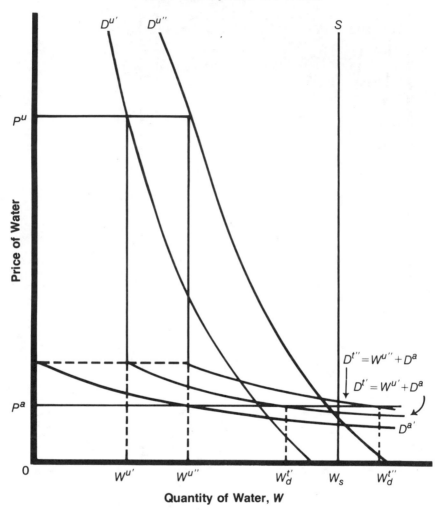

Quantity of Water, W

residential consumers, urban industrial users, and farmers will become capitalized into the value of real estate. The only way in which a farmer could increase his use of water would be to purchase additional land that carries a water allotment of its own. Urban users would face a similar situation.

This analysis is quite instructive. It indicates what happens when demand continues to shift to the right, while supply is both vertical and unshifting. It shows what happens when governments, for understandable political reasons, refuse to permit prices to rise to market-clearing levels. It shows what happens when government agencies attempt to segregate the market for a single commodity. And it provides a good starting point for anyone interested in

FIGURE 5.22
A Two-Price System for Water, with Rationing of Water in Urban Uses

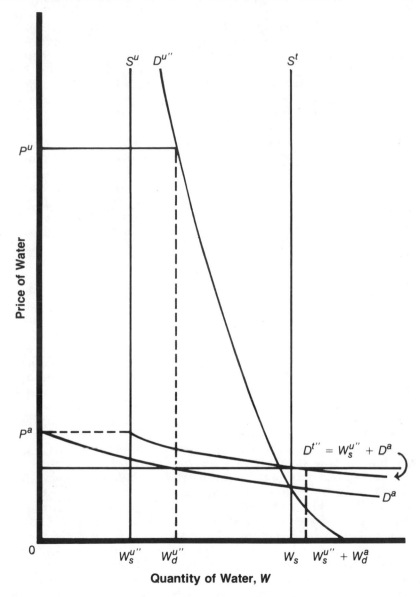

Quantity of Water, W

understanding the very complex politics of water in the American Southwest.

The Market for Pollution Control. Pollution control is expensive. The act of polluting provides no pleasure to the polluter, and the resulting pollution is offensive to the receptor. It is perfectly reasonable to assume that polluters pollute only insofar as doing so is cost-saving to them. Thus, pollution control, the act of reducing pollutant emissions, is expensive to the polluter. A polluting firm may reduce its emissions by reducing its total output of salable commodities, or by increasing its use of pollution-control inputs. A polluting consumer may decrease his pollutant emissions by reducing his participation in polluting activities, or by purchasing emission-control devices (for example, for his automobile). For the polluting firm, pollution control is cost-incrëasing and for the polluting consumer, pollution control is utility-decreasing. In both cases, therefore, the supply curve for pollution abatement (the act of reducing polluting emissions) is positively sloped.

There is a demand for pollution abatement. Consumers obtain greater satisfaction from a pollution-free environment. Producing firms find that a clean environment reduces their cost of operation. For example, if clean water is delivered to the firm, the firm will no longer have to meet the expense of water treatments prior to using water in its production process. Clean air would reduce the firm's cost of maintenance of its plant, since the corrosive effects of air pollutants would be eliminated. So, there is clearly a demand for pollution abatement, and it is most likely a typical downward-sloping demand curve.

Yet it is very difficult to observe operating markets for the control of many common types of pollutants. Market prices for pollution abatement go unobserved, and it does not seem likely that the equilibrium quantity of pollution abatement (Figure 5.23) is provided. Why? Figure 5.23 provides a rather significant hint. The demand curve for pollution abatement is presented as a broken line. Markets in pollution abatement are very poorly developed, especially on the demand side. For reasons that are discussed in detail in Chapters 8 and 21, it is difficult for the individual, acting as an individual, to purchase his preferred amount of pollution abatement and to be assured that he will receive exactly the amount purchased. Thus, the broken demand curve for pollution abatement represents a true demand, but an *ineffective* demand. The very poorly developed market in pollution abatement does not permit the demand curve to become effective.

Although supply and demand curves for pollution abatement clearly exist, and there are good reasons to believe that these supply and demand curves are similar to the supply and demand curves for many other commodities, the market for pollution abatement is ineffective. One does not observe the equilibrium price being generated, nor the equilibrium quantity of pollution abatement being provided. What can be done about this? There are many possible solutions, and many of these are discussed in Chapters 8 and 21. All of them involve government activity in one way or another. Government may seek to establish the kinds of property rights that would permit the broken demand curve of Figure 5.23 to become an effective demand curve. Alternatively, government may attempt to establish, by taxation, the equilibrium price for polluting

FIGURE 5.23
The Market for Pollution Abatement

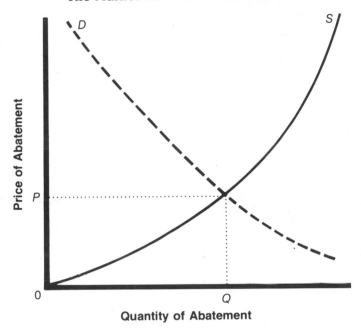

Quantity of Abatement

emissions, and charge that price to firms and individuals that choose to emit pollutants. Government may take a different approach, and seek to impose restrictions on polluting emissions at the individual level. This strategy is commonly referred to as the use of emissions standards.

Each of these separate strategies has its difficulties and its advantages. None of them seems to be perfect. The problems we have observed in the market for pollution abatement are quite typical of the problems resource economists observe in any market where property rights are ill-defined. And, ill-definition of property rights may result either from societal preferences as implemented by government, or from the physical nature of goods, like ambient air, that are indivisible and nonexclusive from the point of view of the individual.

The Market for Outdoor Recreation. For many years, and in many countries, governments have set aside areas of land that are especially attractive from a scenic or ecosystem point of view, and have made these available to tourists and recreators for their enjoyment. Since these lands are often viewed as part of the national heritage, it has often been a conscious governmental decision that markets in the enjoyment of this land should not be established. Ability to pay a market-established going price is not thought to be a suitable criterion for determining who should get to enjoy the amenities of such lands.

Consider a national park, of limited size, with a limited recreational carrying capacity. To simplify the example, assume that camping is an essential part of the recreation experience, that camping is permitted only in designated areas, and that the number of campsites is strictly limited. Thus the supply curve for campsites in this national park is strictly inelastic (that is, vertical) and unshifting. Assume that the government has established a campsite fee at the level P. Demand for campsites may be represented by a typical downward-sloping demand curve. When demand is D', all of the demand effective at the price P is satisfied, and some surplus, unused campsites remain; that is, C'_d is less than C_s (Figure 5.24). With increasing affluence and increasing ease of

FIGURE 5.24
Growing Demand in the Market for Outdoor-Recreation Amenities

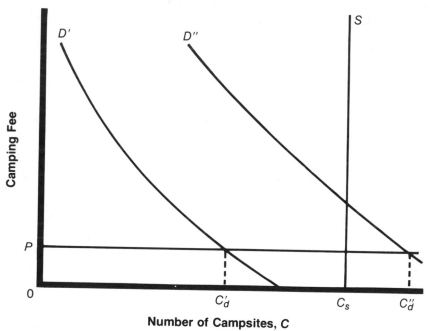

Number of Campsites, C

transportation, the demand for outdoor recreation in attractive sites has increased very rapidly in recent years. With the passage of time, demand shifts to the right and D'' becomes the demand curve for campsites. Now there is a severe shortage of campsites at the going price; that is, C''_d substantially exceeds C_s (Figure 5.24). If the government is reluctant to allow the camping fee to rise to the market-clearing price, some non-price rationing device must be found.

Typically, campsites are allocated on a first-come, first-served basis. People seeking campsites form queues and, if the queues are sufficiently long and are established sufficiently early in the day, prospective campers from distant places may choose to leave home very early in the morning or to arrive in the locality the previous night and sleep over in motels, in order to establish a favorable position in the queue. Thus, time and perhaps non-camping expenditures are substituted for camping fees as devices to ration a restricted number of campsites among a larger number of prospective campers. Those who are willing to invest more time than others will find their demand for a campsite satisfied. However, the agency that operates the national park is unable to collect this "time in queue" and spend it. The policy of maintaining price at low levels and using time as a supplementary rationing device limits the budget of government agencies charged with the provision and operation of outdoor recreation areas.

It is often the case that demand for outdoor recreation depends on the season. The supply of campsites is vertical and fixed year-round. However, the demand for campsites in the middle of winter, D^w, is located far to the left. In winter there is a very substantial surplus of campsites; that is, C_d^w is much less than C_s (Figure 5.25). In summer,

FIGURE 5.25

Seasonal Variation in the Market for
Outdoor-Recreational Amenities

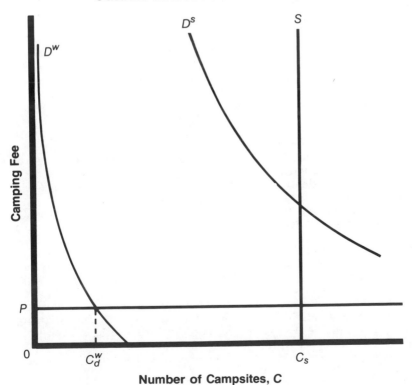

Number of Campsites, C

the demand for campsites, D^s, shifts far to the right. At the going price, there is a very severe shortage of campsites.

In winter, the going price serves as a rationing device, when rationing is unneeded. In summer, the going price is totally ineffective as a rationing device and must be supplemented with "time in queue."

It is quite possible that the agency that operates the national park could maximize both the number of users who get to enjoy the park and its revenues by setting camping fees at zero during the winter and permitting them to rise to the market-clearing level during the summer. In the long run, such a strategy may be effective in shifting the supply curve of high-quality outdoor recreation sites to the right, since it would permit the agency to acquire a sufficiently large budget to gradually purchase and develop additional high-quality recreation sites. However, it would be a highly controversial strategy, since there are many who believe that access to high-quality outdoor recreation sites should not be restricted to those who can afford to pay a market-determined use fee. Parenthetically, it should be noted that, in the United States, there is a certain irony to this proposition. Many of the finest outdoor recreation sites in the U.S. are quite distant from major population centers. Access to those sites is in fact effectively restricted to those who can afford to pay; not those who can afford to pay the entrance fee, but those who can afford the expense of travel to get there.

QUESTIONS FOR DISCUSSION

1. If a malnourished person were given an income supplement exactly equal to the cost of enough additional food to permit him to achieve a specified nutritional standard, would you expect him to actually achieve the nutritional standard? If, under these conditions, he did actually achieve the nutritional standard, what would that imply about the shape of his indifference curves?
2. What would you expect to be the sign and the approximate magnitude of each of the following elasticities:
   (a) the income elasticity of demand for white-water canoeing?
   (b) the price elasticity of demand for electricity?
   (c) the demand elasticity of natural gas with respect to the price of oil?
3. In what way would you expect the availability of mass-transportation services to affect the price elasticity of demand for gasoline in metropolitan areas?
4. "Increases in production costs are always passed on entirely to the consumer." Under what conditions would this statement be strictly true?
5. "The industry demand curve can be accurately derived by horizontal summation of individual demand curves. However, the industry supply curve cannot be accurately derived by horizontal summation of individual-firm supply curves." Is this true? Why?
6. "If the price rises, demand will decrease." True or false?

7. Is it reasonable to conclude that price controls, for many years, contributed to the shortage of natural gas in the U. S.? Explain.
8. Since relatively little air-pollution abatement is bought in unregulated markets, is it reasonable to conclude that there is little demand for it?
9. Since relatively few buggy whips are bought in unregulated markets, is it reasonable to conclude that there is little demand for them?

FURTHER READINGS

Barkley, Paul W., and David W. Seckler. 1972. *Economic Growth and Environmental Decay; The Solution Becomes the Problem.* New York: Harcourt Brace Jovanovich. (Chapter 6.)

Ferguson, Charles E., and Charles S. Maurice. 1974. *Economic Analysis.* Homewood, Illinois: R. D. Irwin.

Ferguson, Charles E. 1975. *Microeconomic Theory.* Homewood, Illinois: R. D. Irwin. 4th edition.

Kelso, Maurice M., William E. Martin, and Lawrence E. Mack. 1973. *Water Supplies and Economic Growth in an Arid Environment; an Arizona Case Study.* Tucson: University of Arizona Press.

Quirk, James P. 1976. *Intermediate Microeconomics.* Chicago: Science Research Associates.

ADVANCED READING

Henderson, James Mitchell, and Richard E. Quandt. 1971. *Microeconomic Theory: A Mathematical Approach.* New York: McGraw-Hill. 2nd edition.

ENDNOTE

1. The proposed desalination plant has again become controversial, due largely to some quite massive increases in its projected costs. See James M. Perry. 1979. "Plans to hold down Colorado River's Salt Content and avoid Irking Mexico are Hit by Rising Costs." *Wall Street Journal.* June 21: p. 46.

APPENDIX: A FURTHER METHODOLOGICAL NOTE ON MAINSTREAM ECONOMICS

In Chapter 4, the pivotal role of assumptions in the process of abstraction that permits the construction of economic models is discussed. In the present chapter, simplifying assumptions are used time and time again and are, indeed, very helpful in permitting the construction of simple, easily manipulable and yet serviceable models.

For various purposes, economists make assumptions about (1) human motivations, (2) the nature of the interrelationships among components of economic systems, and (3) the empirical magnitudes of important variables and parameters. In all three areas, assumptions may be used as substitutes for knowledge: to complete the system, it may be necessary to assume something about those things that are unknown. In the first two areas, assumptions may also be used to simplify the model: even when the economist has considerable knowledge about a complex relationship, he may choose to substitute a simple set of assumptions for the much more intricate reality that exists.

While economists are nearly unanimous about the virtues of simplicity, some economists (and many students in economics courses) are uneasy about the lack of realism of some of the assumptions commonly used in economic analysis. This uneasiness has spawned many of the more amusing tales that circulate among economists — on the whole, a not especially humorous group. I cannot resist retelling two of them. Following a shipwreck, an economist, an engineer, and a physicist found themselves on the shore of a deserted island. When they had recovered sufficiently from the trauma of it all, they took inventory and found that their food supply consisted of one can of beans. But no one had a can opener. After a period of silence, the physicist said, "Let's build a fire. The heat will increase the pressure within the can and eventually explode it." It was objected that the beans would be scattered all over, and contaminated with foreign matter. Then the engineer said, "We could drop a large boulder from a great height and the force would overcome the resistance of the can, breaking it open." Again, the proposed solution seemed imperfect: the beans thus released would probably be rendered inedible. After a long silence, the economist spoke up. "Let us *assume* we have a can opener," he said.

The second of these tall tales concerns an economist who, after imbibing too much at an economists' banquet, was found stumbling around beneath a street lamp, by a policeman. On inquiry, the economist said he was looking for his keys. "Where did you drop them?" "Back there, in that dark alley." "Then, why don't you look there?" The economist answered, "Because this is where the light is."

While experienced economists know there is a grain of truth behind the jocularity, the issues revolving around the realism or unrealism of assumptions are considerably more subtle.

A model is intended to preserve some of the essential elements of reality while eliminating the excruciating detail. Thus, realism, *per se,* is not necessarily a virtue in an economist's model. Rather, the primary virtues sought are simplicity and robustness. Robustness refers to the ability of the model to yield sound predictions about the behavior of the system under study (often called "the real world"), under a wide variety of circumstances.

It has been argued, most forcefully by Milton Friedman, that predictive power, not realism, is the primary test of a model. From the set of models that yield accurate predictions (i.e., those that pass the primary test), the best model may be selected on the bases of simplicity and versatility. Of several models of similar versatility, the simplest is the best. Thus realism (to the extent that realism and simplicity are opposed) is not a virtue, but a detriment.

It is impossible to deny the correctness of Friedman's position, thus stated. On the other hand, Friedman's philosophy, on careful examination, offers less than it would appear at first glance. His primary test is an *ex post* test: after the fact, we will know whether the model predicted accurately. We cannot know in advance that predictions will be accurate. Further, and this is crucial, we cannot deduce that, because a model predicted accurately in the past, it will predict accurately in the future.

A model that is a thoroughly unreal representation of an actual system may predict accurately, year after year. Then, when some variable that is a crucial part of the actual system but is ignored in the model changes its behavior, the model suddenly fails. A case in point is the model used by many utility companies to predict sales of electricity. It was so simple and unreal that it assumed quantity demanded was unrelated to price! From 1930 to 1972, this model predicted sales accurately. During that period, the price of electricity behaved with remarkable regularity, falling steadily (in real terms). However, in 1973, the real price of electricity started to increase, as a result of increasing costs of fuel feedstocks. Since that time, this disarmingly simple and formerly reliable electricity demand model has been wildly inaccurate in its predictions. More complex models, including a price variable, have predicted sales much more accurately.

Where does this leave the economist, in his search for simple yet accurate models? Models that have predicted poorly in the past can be discarded with a good deal of confidence. Models that have predicted well in the past may be used with considerable, but by no means total, confidence. It would be a wise precaution to examine the structure of such models carefully, to ensure that the assumptions on which they are based are a reasonable, if much simplified, representation of reality. By this I mean that a model, even if it has predicted well in the past, should be considered suspect if it is counterintuitive and at substantial variance with what is known about reality.

However, many of the policy-oriented analyses made by resource economists are forward-looking. Their conclusions cannot be tested against actual outcomes (the prediction test) until after the policy is implemented, by which time it may be too late to say "I'm sorry." The results of other analyses, such as those (discussed in Chapter 16) that attempt to estimate that which cannot be observed (e.g., the "prices" of non-market goods) may never be directly testable against reality.

In these cases, a major part of the important function of professional criticism, to keep the analyst on the straight and narrow, involves examination of the assumptions used. To what extent does the conclusion rely upon a particular assumption? Is that assumption consistent with what is known, or is it at least plausible, given what is known?

Professional self-examination and criticism must rely heavily on careful examination of the model used and the assumptions upon which it is based. In addition, of course, the analyst should use all the ingenuity at his command to devise opportunities for use of the prediction test. Together, these approaches to validation of policy-oriented models are imperfect. Yet, together they provide a better test than can be obtained using neither approach or either one alone.

FURTHER READINGS

Buchanan, James M. 1959. "Positive Economics, Welfare Economics, and Political Economy." *Journal of Law and Economics*. 1, Oct: 124-138.
Friedman, Milton. 1953. "The Methodology of Positive Economics," in *Essays in Positive Economics*. Chicago: The University of Chicago Press.
Nagel, Ernst. 1963. "Assumptions in Economic Theory." *American Economic Review*. 53: 211-219.
Samuelson, Paul A. 1963. "Problems of Methodology: Discussion." *American Economic Review*. 53: 231-236.

ADVANCED READING

Boland, Lawrence A. 1979. "A Critique of Friedman's Critics." *Journal of Economic Literature*. 17: 503-522.

6

Efficiency and Economic Well-Being

By now, we have learned some things about markets: the conditions for individual utility and profit maximization; the conditions for efficient adjustment of individual consumption and production to given, market-generated prices; and the process by which markets equilibrate supply and demand, and generate prices. As was demonstrated in Chapter 5, well-functioning markets perform very useful services; and analyses based on market logic are useful in diagnosing the problems caused by poorly functioning markets and the impediments encountered when political jurisdictions attempt to override market forces.

Natural resource and environmental economics is, for the most part, concerned with problems that arise when markets in natural resources and environmental amenities perform poorly, and with identifying and evaluating possible solutions to those problems. To perform these tasks, it is necessary to establish *criteria* by which to judge current performance of resource and environmental markets, and to evaluate alternative solutions. It is necessary to have a clear concept of what is good, in order to identify what is not so good and what might be an improvement.

This chapter is about criteria. Economic efficiency is one commonly proposed criterion. How is efficiency defined? How is it related to prices, resource availability, preferences, and production technology? What are the ethical implications of using efficiency as a criterion for policy evaluation? Maximum economic well-being for a whole society (or, in abbreviated form, maximum social well-being) is another criterion. How is it defined? What are its ethical implications? How is it related to economic efficiency? Is it a workable criterion, in practice? The same questions may be asked about other possible criteria: Pareto-safety, maximum value of social product, etc.

To my mind, one of the most admirable aspects of economics is the logical rigor with which it approaches the criterion problem. The result of this inquiry is enlightening, but perhaps disappointing: there is no easy solution and, perhaps, no perfect solution.

Every natural resource and environmental economist (in fact, everyone who works in any branch of economic policy studies) needs to know the rudiments of the analyses presented in this chapter. Less advanced students will find this chapter quite demanding, but the effort required to master its contents will be well spent. A solid, gut-level understanding of the issues raised here is the best antidote to the naiveté and misplaced zeal that can make the half-baked economist and the half-baked environmentalist ineffective in their sincere efforts to improve the condition of the world.

Maximum economic well-being (sometimes called maximum economic welfare) is the highest economic goal to which a society can aspire. It is a condition in which the society is as well-off as it can possibly be, given its resource base, its production technology, and the tastes and preferences of its members. If one thinks a little about the idea of economic well-being, it becomes clear that economic well-being must be a complex concept. It must involve economic efficiency, since it is difficult to imagine how a society could achieve maximum economic well-being while inefficient. Efficiency, itself, is not an especially simple concept; it involves efficiency in production, trade, and consumption. Yet, economic efficiency alone is insufficient to insure maximum social well-being. The concept of economic efficiency does not deal very effectively with the distribution of the rewards of economic activity: the question of who gets what. A meaningful concept of social well-being, on the other hand, must face up to the distributional issue.

Maximum social well-being, as we shall see, proves to be an elusive concept. It is, nevertheless, instructive to undertake the search for a workable set of economic criteria for the achievement of maximum social well-being. The search will identify some useful things that economics can say for sure about maximum social well-being, and it will also provide us with an understanding of why there are some things about social well-being that economics simply cannot say for sure. The search for economic conditions for maximum social well-being is instructive, and its results are both illuminating and frustrating.

ECONOMIC EFFICIENCY

In casual conversation, one encounters many meanings for the term efficiency. Some speak of efficiency as simply "doing the job well," without raising the question of whether it is worthwhile to undertake the job at all. Others speak in terms of "maximum production" or, a little more accurately, of "maximum production from some given level of inputs" or "cost minimization for a given level of output." Even these latter concepts of efficiency are very incomplete. In this book, the term efficiency always means global efficiency or *Pareto-efficiency*.[1] Pareto-efficiency (named for the economist and philosopher Vilfredo Pareto) is a concept of complete efficiency in which production, trade, and consumption are all organized efficiently within a total system context.

Let us undertake to build a model of a simple economy, literally from the ground up. In so doing, we will derive the necessary and sufficient conditions for Pareto-efficiency and maximum social well-being.

In Chapter 5, we found out how the manager of a producing firm can allocate inputs so as to produce the maximum output using a given operating capital budget, and how a consumer can allocate his fixed budget among various commodities so as to maximize his utility. In both cases, the analysis was quite similar. The analysis of production used isoquants and isocost lines, while the analysis of consumption used indifference curves and budget lines. Isocost lines and budget lines are simply straight lines whose position is determined by the size of the producer's operating capital constraint or the consumer's budget, and whose slope is determined by the ratio of prices facing the producer or the consumer. In our search for Pareto-efficiency and maximum social well-being, we cannot make use of isocost lines and budget lines. We seek, among other things, to derive the price ratios that are efficient. Therefore, we cannot start out the analysis by assuming anything about prices. We do, however, make rather substantial use of isoquants and indifference curves.

Let us construct a very simple model of a whole economy.[2] This economy consists of two individuals, whom we shall call 1 and 2; two commodities, which we shall call B and W (for bread and wine); and two inputs, which we shall call L and D (for labor and land — it is unclear why D should denote land, but land cannot be L since that letter has already been assigned to labor; there is a suspicion abroad that D really stands for dirt). It may seem strange to develop a model of an economy that consists only of two persons, two commodities, and two resources, but there is a very good reason for so doing. It permits us to make effective use of two-dimensional diagrams. Rest assured that all the results which we can derive with our two-dimensional diagrams can also be derived for a much larger economy, in n dimensions, using vector calculus.

The production functions are:

$$B = h_b(L_b, D_b)$$
$$W = h_w(L_w, D_w),$$

where L_b = the amount of labor devoted to the production of bread,

D_b = the amount of land devoted to the production of bread, and

L_w and D_w are defined similarly, for wine.

It is assumed that the production technology remains constant throughout the analysis, and that all units of each of B, W, L, and D are homogeneous in quality.

The utility functions are:

$U_1 = f_1(B_1, W_1)$, and

$U_2 = f_2(B_2, W_2)$,

where U_1 = the level of utility enjoyed by the consumer 1,
B_1 = the amount of bread consumed by 1,
W_1 = amount of wine consumed by 1, and
U_2, B_2, and W_2 are similarly defined for consumer 2.

The utility functions are assumed to remain unchanged during the course of the analysis; that is, the tastes and preferences of each individual do not change.

It is assumed that the marginal productivity of each input in the production of each output is positive but diminishing; and that the marginal utility of each consumer from the use of each commodity is positive but diminishing. Thus, all isoquants derived from the production functions and all indifference curves derived from the utility functions will be convex to the origin.

EFFICIENCY IN PRODUCTION

The production functions for bread and wine provide sufficient information to permit the derivation of the isoquant maps for bread and wine (Figure 6.1). Isoquant maps alone, however, provide insufficient information for determining the conditions of efficiency in production. In analyses of the single firm in isolation, the economist can always use price information to construct a budget line. However in the analysis of the efficient organization of the whole economy, price information must be derived, not assumed at the outset. How, then, can the production problem be solved? If we assume, quite reasonably, since this is an analysis of a whole economy, that resources are in fixed supply ($L_b + L_w = \bar{L}$ and $D_b + D_w = \bar{D}$), we can use this information to solve our problem. In Figure 6.1, we use the assumption of fixed resources to place bounds upon both isoquant maps. Even if all labor were used in the production of bread, there are limits to the amount of bread that can be produced. Quantities of bread that require more than the total supply of labor are simply infeasible, even if no wine at all is produced. Using this kind of logic, we can place bounds upon the isoquant maps. The broken lines in Figure 6.1 provide the boundary for the section of each isoquant map that is feasible, given strictly limited resource supplies.

Formation of the Edgeworth Box

The feasible section of each isoquant map in Figure 6.1 is a rectangle, and, since the dimensions of each of these rectangles were determined from the same information (that is, the total amount of labor and land available to the economy), each rectangle must be the same size as the other. This fact permits us to form the Edgeworth box.

Start with the bounded isoquant map for bread. Then, take the isoquant map for wine and turn it over, so that the origin for wine is now at the top right-hand corner, the amount of land used in the production of wine increases as one moves left along the land axis, and the amount of labor used in the production of wine increases as one moves down along the wine axis. The amount of wine produced increases as one moves down and to the left, from the wine origin. Figure 6.2 shows the result of this maneuver. Now, place the wine origin at the intersection of the broken lines on the bread isoquant map. This completes the formation of the Edgeworth box (Figure 6.3).

The Edgeworth box is a perfect rectangle. Its length is determined by total availability of land in the economy, and its height is determined by the total availability of labor. The production box we have just formed contains an infinite number of isoquants. As one moves away from the bread origin in the lower left-hand corner, one encounters isoquants representing increasing quantities of bread. As one moves away from the wine origin at the upper right-hand corner, one encounters isoquants representing increasing quantities of wine. Thus, as one moves northeast inside the box, production of bread increases while production of wine decreases; as one moves southwest, production of wine increases and production of bread decreases.

FIGURE 6.1
The Isoquant Maps, Bounded by
Fixed Resource Supplies

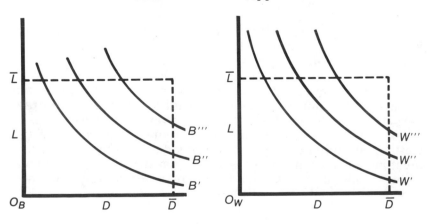

FIGURE 6.2
Formation of the Edgeworth Box: Step 1

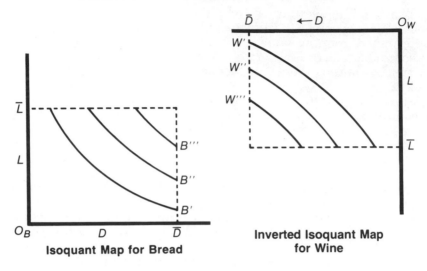

Isoquant Map for Bread   **Inverted Isoquant Map for Wine**

FIGURE 6.3
Formation of the Edgeworth Box: Step 2

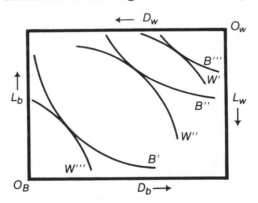

Let us pause a moment to examine the analytic properties of the Edgeworth box (Figure 6.4). First, its exterior dimensions are uniquely determined by resource availability. Second, any point inside a production box is uniquely defined in terms of resource allocation and output. Consider the point p, which point is simply chosen at random and has no special significance. By drawing perpendicular lines horizontally and vertically from p, resource allocation (that is, L_b, L_w, D_b and D_w) is uniquely defined. Since the box contains infinite numbers of both bread and wine isoquants, there must be one of each type of isoquant passing through the point p. Thus, the output of both bread and wine is also uniquely defined for any point in the Edgeworth box.

FIGURE 6.4

The Information Content of a
Production Edgeworth Box, and the
Derivation of the Production Efficiency Locus

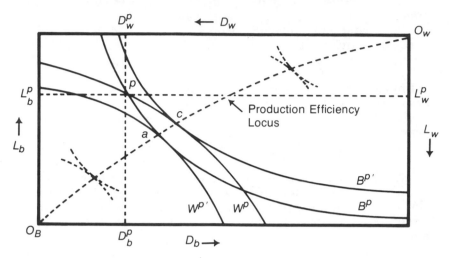

The Production Efficiency Locus

At the point p (in Figure 6.4), the bread isoquant, B^p, intersects the wine isoquant, W^p. Could there possibly exist one or more resource allocations more efficient than that at point p? Consider first the bread isoquant, B^p, at the point a. With the resource allocation represented by the point a, it is possible to produce as much bread as at the point p and a greater quantity of wine. The point a must therefore represent a more efficient resource allocation than the point p. Consider now the wine isoquant, W^p. At the point c, the bread isoquant $B^{p'}$ is just tangent to the wine isoquant W^p. At c, it is possible to produce as much wine as at point p, and more bread. The point c must represent a more efficient allocation of resources than the point p. Between the points a and c, there is a series of points of tangency between bread and wine isoquants. At each of these points of tangency, there is more of both bread and wine produced than at the point p. All these points must also represent more efficient resource allocations than the point p.

The segment, ac, must represent a locus of combinations of inputs, each of which is more efficient than the input combination at the point p. For any point inside the Edgeworth box, other than points at which there is a tangency between a bread isoquant and a wine isoquant, it is possible to find a similar line segment representing more efficient resource allocations. If the analysis we performed with respect to the point p were repeated for all other points inside the Edgeworth box, a curved line passing from the bread origin through points a and c to the wine origin would be found. This line is the locus of all of the points of tangency between bread and wine isoquants within the Edgeworth box. It is called the *production efficiency locus,* which is defined as the locus of all possible combinations of land and labor that are efficient in the production of bread and wine. For any point off the production efficiency locus, a line segment joining more efficient resource allocations can be found on the production efficiency locus.

In our search for the efficient organization of our model economy, we have made substantial progress. We have eliminated every point off the production efficiency locus. But we are still left with an infinite number of points on the production efficiency locus, and any one of those could be the resource allocation that is consistent with global efficiency. So, it is not possible to define a completely efficient economic organization by looking only at production.

The analysis to this point has taught us something important about production efficiency. It can be achieved only with resource allocations that lie on the production efficiency locus, and every point on the production efficiency locus has something in common. Since each is a point of tangency between a bread isoquant and a wine isoquant, the slope of the bread isoquant must be equal to the slope of the wine isoquant at that point. Thus, the rate of technical substitution (RTS) of the inputs must be equal in the production of each commodity, at every point on the production efficiency locus. That is,

$$(RTS_{D.L})_B = (RST_{D.L})_W.$$

EFFICIENCY IN CONSUMPTION

If there is no way to completely identify the conditions for economic efficiency by looking at production information alone, perhaps it would be helpful to use the information about tastes and preferences contained in the individual's utility functions. Construct a diagram whose axes are expressed in terms of the commodities, bread and wine. Since every point on the production efficiency locus is uniquely determined in terms of the quantities of bread and wine it represents, it ought to be possible to transfer the information contained in the production efficiency locus to the new diagram expressed in commodity space (i.e., whose axes are defined in terms of quantities of the different commodities). For each point on the production efficiency locus, simply determine how much bread and how much wine that point represents; and then identify a point in commodity space representing exactly the same amount of bread and wine. When this process is completed for all points on the production efficiency locus, a unique efficient *production possibilities curve,* corresponding to the production efficiency locus, is derived (Figure 6.5).

The utility functions for the consumers, 1 and 2, provide sufficient

FIGURE 6.5
The Efficient Production Possibilities Curve

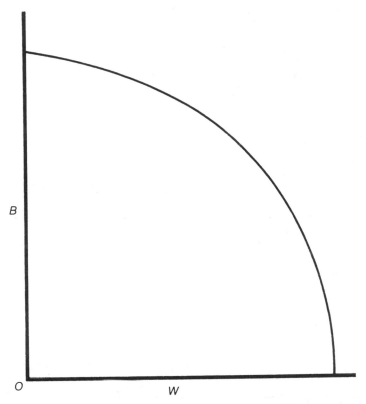

information to permit the derivation of the indifference maps for those consumers (Figure 6.6). Note that the efficient production possibilities curve and both indifference maps are expressed in the same commodity axes. Let the origin of Figure 6.7 represent the origin for the production possibilities curve diagram *and* the origin for consumer 1's indifference map. Now, arbitrarily select a point d on the production possibilities curve. Construct perpendicular lines to the bread and wine origins, from the point d. The point d now defines a product mix; at the point d on the efficient production possibilities curve, B^d units of bread and W^d units of wine are produced. Remember that there is nothing special about the point d. Selecting the point d merely permits us to ask the hypothetical question: if the model society chose to allocate its resources in such a way as to produce B^d units of bread and W^d units of wine, how would the consumers choose to distribute that bundle of commodities among themselves?

Notice that a rectangle, $O_1 B^d d W^d$, has been formed (Figure 6.7). The rectangle already contains individual 1's indifference map, with

108

FIGURE 6.6
The Indifference Maps

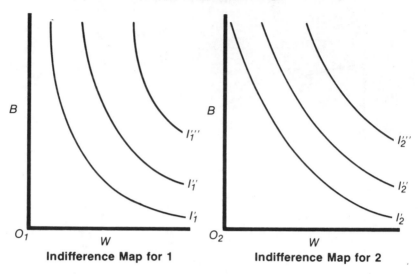

Indifference Map for 1   Indifference Map for 2

FIGURE 6.7
Derivation of the Consumption Efficiency Locus

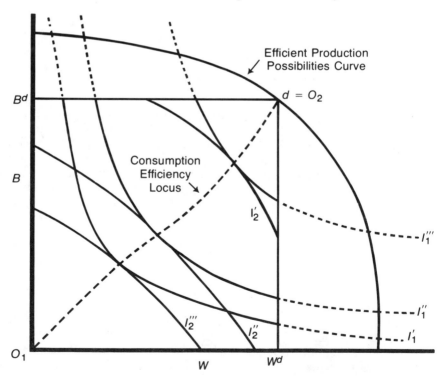

its origin at the point O_1. We can take individual 2's indifference map and turn it around, just as we did the isoquant map for wine, and place its origin at the upper right-hand corner of that rectangle (i.e., let $d = O_2$). By so doing, we have formed an Edgeworth box for consumption. The exterior dimensions of the consumption box are uniquely determined by the efficient production possibilities curve and the unique, but arbitrarily selected, point d on that curve. Thus, the dimensions of the consumption box represent quantities of the commodities bread and wine.

The consumption box is literally full of indifference curves: indifference curves for individual 1, whose utility increases as one moves from the lower-left origin, upward and to the right within the box; and indifference curves for individual 2, whose utility increases as one moves from the upper-right origin, downward and to the left within the box. Any point within the consumption box is uniquely specified with respect to commodity distribution (B_1, B_2, W_1, and W_2) and the ordinal levels of utility enjoyed by 1 and 2. Using the same logic as we used to find the production efficiency locus, the *consumption efficiency locus* may be identified. It is a curved line from the point O_1 to the point $d = O_2$, connecting all the points of tangency between indifference curves for individual 1 and indifference curves for individual 2. The consumption efficiency locus is defined as the locus of all distributions of commodities that are efficient in consumption. Points off the consumption efficiency locus represent commodity distributions that cannot possibly be consistent with global efficiency.

Notice that we have made further progress in our search for the efficient organization of our model economy. For the product mix represented by point d, which we know is efficient in production, all commodity distributions except those lying on the consumption efficiency locus have been eliminated as surely inefficient. But we are still left with an infinite number of points along the consumption efficiency locus, each of which is a candidate for selection as the efficient commodity distribution. Actually, as we shall see a little further on, the situation is really worse than that. The point d on the efficient production possibilities curve was selected quite arbitrarily, and any other point on that curve could have been selected with equal plausibility. For each other point on the production possibilities curve, a new consumption efficiency locus, unique to that point, exists. But more on that later.

For any arbitrarily selected product mix on the efficient production possibilities curve, the consumption efficiency locus represents a locus of potentially efficient commodity distributions. The consumption efficiency locus is a locus of points of tangency between indifference curves and, at any point on it, the slope of the tangent to the indifference curve for consumer 1 must equal that for consumer 2. Thus, the following condition must hold at any point on the consumption efficiency locus: the rate of commodity substitution

110

between bread and wine for consumer 1 must equal that for consumer 2. That is:

$$(RCS_{W.B})_1 = (RCS_{W.B})_2.$$

The Utility Possibilities Curve

Construct a diagram, such as Figure 6.8, in which the axes are expressed in terms of the levels of utility enjoyed by the individuals 1 and 2. Since utility is an ordinal rather than a cardinal concept (that is, differing alternatives can be ranked in terms of the relative amounts of utility they provide the individual, but it is not possible to say exactly how much utility each alternative provides), these utility axes must be expressed in ordinal rather than cardinal terms. Just as we took the production efficiency locus from its input space and mapped it into commodity space to derive the efficient production possibilities curve, we can take the consumption efficiency locus from its commodity space and map it into utility space to derive the *utility possibilities curve*.

FIGURE 6.8
The Utility Possibilities Curve, Given the Product Mix B^d, W^d

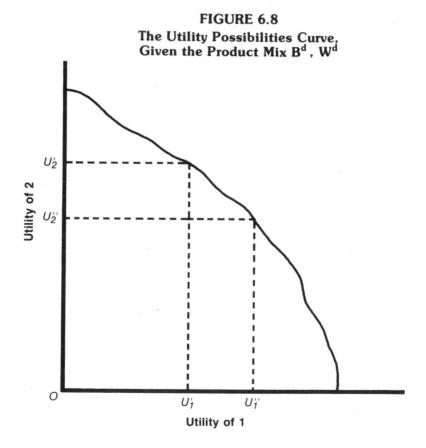

Visual examination of Figure 6.8 clarifies a point that the more alert observer will have already deduced from Figure 6.7. Starting from some point off the consumption efficiency locus, it is always possible for two individuals to make a mutually beneficial trade; that is, they can make a trade that increases the utility of both or, at least, increases the utility of one without reducing the utility of the other. However, for any given product mix, once the individuals have traded to a point on the consumption efficiency locus, any further utility gains for one must come at the direct expense of a utility reduction for the other. In Figure 6.8, any movement along the utility possibilities curve (which is simply the consumption efficiency locus mapped between utility axes) involves a utility gain for one of the individuals at the direct expense of a utility loss for the other.

THE GRAND UTILITY FRONTIER

Remember that the point d on the efficient production possibilities curve was selected, in quite arbitrary fashion, in order to permit us to answer the question "what if the product mix were B^d, W^d...?" Clearly, we have yet to find the most efficient product mix. We do this in an iterative fashion, repeating the analytical process for every other point on the efficient production possibilities curve — literally an infinite number of points. For each possible product mix represented by a point on the efficient production possibilities curve, a unique consumption efficiency locus can be found and can be mapped in utility space to derive a unique utility possibilities curve. When all possible points on the efficient production possibilities curve are considered, an infinite number of utility possibilities curves can be generated.

A representative sample of these utility possibilities curves is shown in Figure 6.9. Observe that the different utility possibilities curves intersect the U_1 and U_2 axes in different places; that many of the curves intersect each other; and that some curves lie wholly inside others. This last case occurs when one product mix dominates another.

Examine the outermost boundary of the feasible section of the utility possibilities diagram. Points that lie outside the outermost curve segment are infeasible, and points that lie inside the outermost curve segment are clearly inefficient. However, the boundary itself is not a smooth continuous curve, as is the efficient production possibilities curve. Rather, it is a series of segments of different utility possibilities curves. If one wants to move along the boundary, from the highest possible level of U_1 to the highest possible level of U_2, one does not move along a continuous curve, but instead one continually switches from one utility possibility curve to another, always moving along the outermost curve segments. The path one would follow is a line joining the outermost segments of the various utility possibilities curves. This line, which is not a true

FIGURE 6.9
Utility Possibilities Curves and the Grand Utility Frontier

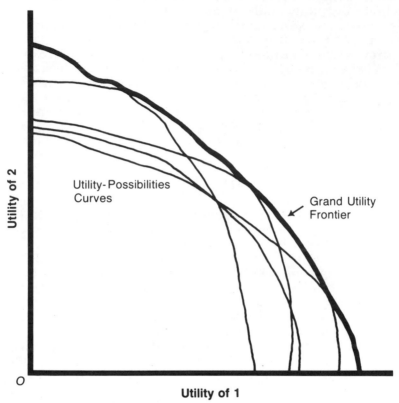

curve, but a frontier or envelope curve, is known as the *grand utility frontier*. By identifying the grand utility frontier, we have completed our search for Pareto-efficiency. We have eliminated all input combinations that do not lie on the production efficiency locus. We have eliminated all commodity distributions that do not lie on a consumption efficiency locus. Finally, we have eliminated all segments of consumption efficiency loci that do not lie on the grand utility frontier. Points inside the grand utility frontier are feasible but inefficient, and points outside the grand utility frontier are infeasible.

At any point on the grand utility frontier, the following proposition is true: it is impossible to reorganize the economy in such a way as to make one individual better-off without simultaneously making another individual worse-off. From any particular point on the grand utility frontier, movements in the feasible section of the northwest quadrant may make individual 2 better-off but at the expense of individual 1, who will be made worse-off (Figure 6.10). Movements in the feasible section of the southeast quadrant may

FIGURE 6.10

From Any Point on the Grand Utility Frontier, It is Impossible to Reorganize the Economy to Make One Individual Better-off Without Making Another Worse-off

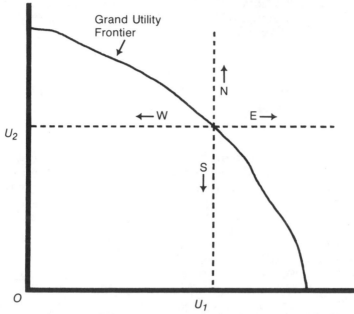

make individual 1 better-off, but at the expense of individual 2. Movements in the southwest quadrant are always feasible, but will make both individuals worse-off. Only movements in the northeast quadrant would make both individuals better-off (or, on the boundaries of the northeast quadrant, would make one individual better-off without making the other individual worse-off). However, no movements in the northeast quadrant are feasible, given the resource availability, production technology, and utility functions we assumed at the outset.

Pareto-efficiency is defined as a situation in which everyone is so well-off that it is impossible to make anybody better-off without simultaneously making at least one person worse-off. It is a situation in which all possibilities for voluntary trades, which would reallocate resources or redistribute commodities in more efficient ways, have been exhausted. There are no more opportunities for voluntary trade and there are no more opportunities to improve the efficiency of the economic system. In a sense, Pareto-efficiency is a situation so efficient that it is impossible to reallocate resources or redistribute commodities in order to make things more efficient. Once Pareto-efficiency has been attained, all gains to individuals must come at the expense of other individuals.

All points on the grand utility frontier are, obviously, Pareto-efficient. Once again, there is clearly an infinite number of such points. In our search for efficiency we have eliminated a multitude of input combinations that are clearly inefficient, a multitude of commodity distributions that are clearly inefficient, and a multitude of segments of utility possibilities curves that represented inefficient product mixes. We have made great progress. But we are still left with an infinite number of Pareto-efficient solutions arrayed along the grand utility frontier.

NECESSARY AND SUFFICIENT CONDITIONS FOR PARETO-EFFICIENCY

Select, completely arbitrarily, any point e on the grand utility frontier. The point e, then, has the virtue of being an efficient organization of our model economy, but has no special characteristics to distinguish it from other points on the grand utility frontier that also represent efficient organizations. So an examination of the economic characteristics of the point e will enable us to draw some general conclusions about the nature of Pareto-efficiency.

The point e is on the grand utility frontier, but also on one particular possibility curve (since the grand utility frontier is nothing more than an envelope of segments of utility possibilities curves). Take the utility possibility curve so identified (Figure 6.11), and return it to commodity space, from whence it originally came. The point e' in Figure 6.12 refers to the point on the consumption efficiency locus that corresponds to the point e on the utility possibilities curve.

Note that the consumption efficiency locus with which we are now working is not just any consumption efficiency locus, but the specific consumption efficiency locus derived from the specific utility possibilities curve that touches the grand utility frontier at the point e. Thus, the consumption efficiency locus runs from the point O_1 to the point e'' on the production possibilities curve. Construct a consumption box by drawing perpendicular lines from e'' to the bread and wine axes. Now, $e'' = O_2$. The point e'' defines the unique *product mix, B^e and W^e,* that is associated with the efficient point e. The point e' defines the unique *distribution of commodities* (B_1^c, B_2^c, W_1^c, and W_2^c associated with the efficient point e. The point e' is the point of tangency between a specific indifference curve for 1 and a specific indifference curve for 2. At the point e' the slopes of those two indifference curves are equal. At that point, the slopes of the two indifference curves determine the marginal trading ratios of the two commodities; i.e., the ratio of the prices of the commodities. Thus, at the point e':

$$(RCS_{W,B})_1 = (RCS_{W,B})_2 = \frac{P_W}{P_B} .$$

FIGURE 6.11

The Efficient Economic Organization Represented by Point e Is Arbitrarily Selected for Examination

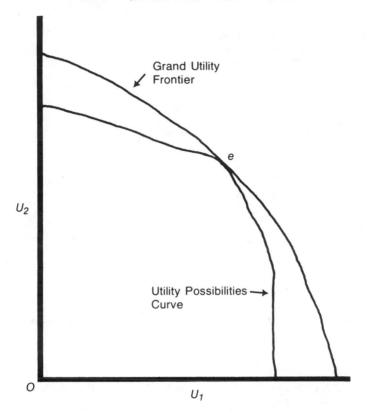

The rates of commodity substitution for both individuals are equal, and they are equal to the price ratio of both commodities.

It is also true that the slope of the tangent to the indifference curves for 1 and 2 at point e' is equal to the slope of the tangent to the production possibilities curve at e''. (In a two-dimensional, diagrammatic analysis, it is not possible to prove this contention. However, the student may rest assured that it is a quite simple matter to provide a proof using differential calculus.) The slope of a production possibilities curve at any point is equal to the rate of product transformation between the two commodities; i.e., the marginal rate at which one commodity must be sacrificed in order to increase output of the other commodity. Thus, the rate of product transformation must be equal to the price ratio of the two commodities. That is:

$$(\text{RPT}_{W,B}) \;=\; \frac{P_W}{P_B} \cdot$$

116

FIGURE 6.12

**Efficient Product Mix, Commodity Distribution and
Commodity Price Ratios**

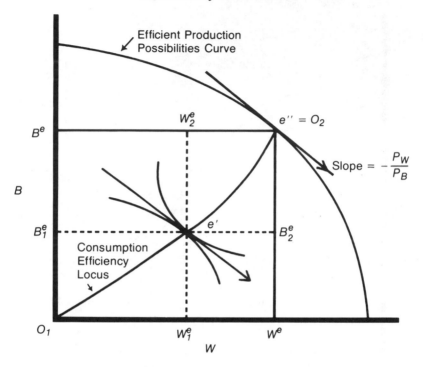

Since the tangents at point e' and point e'' are of equal slope, we have:

$$(\text{RCS}_{\text{W,B}})_1 \ = \ (\text{RCS}_{\text{W,B}})_2 \ = \ (\text{RPT}_{\text{W,B}}) \ \ = \ \frac{P_{\text{W}}}{P_{\text{B}}} \ .$$

The efficient production possibilities curve was derived, at the outset, from the production efficiency locus. Thus, it is possible to map the efficient production possibilities curve back into input space, restoring the production efficiency locus, and identifying the point e''' that corresponds to point e'' on the efficient production possibilities curve (Figure 6.13). The point e''' uniquely identifies the efficient *resource allocation* (L_b^e, L_w^e, D_b^e, and D_w^e) associated the point e on the grand utility frontier. A particular bread isoquant is tangent to some particular wine isoquant at the point e''', and the absolute value of the slope of that tangent must be equal to the price ratio of the inputs. That is:

$$(\text{RTS}_{\text{D,L}})_\text{B} = (\text{RTS}_{\text{D,L}})_\text{W} = \frac{P_\text{D}}{P_\text{L}}$$

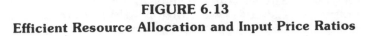

FIGURE 6.13
Efficient Resource Allocation and Input Price Ratios

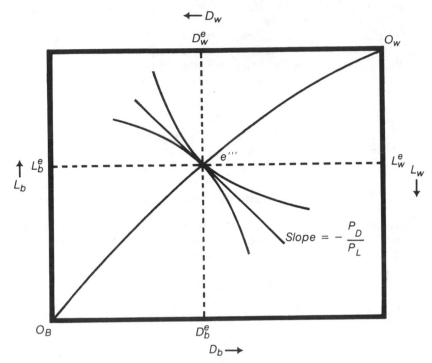

For the particular Pareto-efficient solution e, we have now uniquely defined the efficient resource allocation, product mix and commodity distribution. We have also identified the efficient price ratios. If we had chosen to solve the same problem using differential calculus, and if we assumed a specific supply of money in the economy, we could derive efficient prices for all commodities and all inputs, in money terms: P_L, P_D, P_B, and P_W.

Starting out with a set of production functions, a set of utility functions, and the information that resources are available in certain fixed quantities, *and arbitrarily selecting a unique point on the grand utility frontier,* we have derived unique answers to every meaningful question about the efficiency aspects of our model economy: How can resources be efficiently allocated to the production of commodities? What is the efficient mix of commodities to produce? What is the efficient distribution of commodities among consumers? What set of commodity prices is efficient? And, what set of input prices is efficient?

NECESSARY CONDITIONS FOR PARETO-EFFICIENCY

There are three necessary conditions for Pareto-efficiency:

efficient resource allocation, efficient product mix, and efficiency in consumption. A summary condition, which may be derived by combining the conditions for efficient product mix and efficiency in consumption, establishes the necessary linkage between production and consumption decisions.

Efficient Resource Allocation. The rate of technical substitution of any pair of inputs should be equal for all firms in the production of all commodities that use those inputs, and should be equal to the ratio of the prices of the inputs:

$$(RTS_{D,L})_B = (RTS_{D,L})_W = \frac{P_D}{P_L}, \quad \text{for all firms.}$$

Efficient Product Mix. The rate of product transformation of any two commodities should be equal for every producing firm, and should be equal to the ratio of commodity prices:

$$(RPT_{W,B}) \text{ firm } 1 = (RPT_{W,B}) \text{ firm } 2 = \dots = \frac{P_W}{P_B}.$$

Efficiency in Consumption. The rate of commodity substitution for any two commodities should be equal for each consumer, and equal to the ratio of commodity prices:

$$(RCS_{W,B})_1 = (RCS_{W,B})_2 = \dots = \frac{P_W}{P_B}.$$

The Summary Condition. By combining the second and third conditions, it is possible to derive the general condition that relates production and consumption. The rate of commodity substitution for any two goods should be equal for all consumers, and it should be equal to the rate of product transformation for the same two commodities for all firms, and both should be equal to the ratio of commodity prices:

$$(RCS_{W,B})_1 = \dots = (RPT_{W,B})_1 = \dots = \frac{P_W}{P_B}.$$

THE SUFFICIENT CONDITION FOR PARETO-EFFICIENCY

The sufficient condition for Pareto-efficiency is that all isoquants and indifference curves must be non-concave (i.e., convex or, as a special case, straight lines) in the relevant ranges. Convex isoquants necessarily imply that the efficient production possibilities curve will be concave to the origin in the relevant range.

The necessary and sufficient conditions together guarantee Pareto-efficiency. With the necessary conditions alone satisfied, it is possible that we should suffer the embarrassment of minimizing that which we wish to maximize. If the isoquants and indifference curves were concave to the origin, fulfillment of the necessary conditions would result in achievement, not of Pareto-efficiency, but of the "Dostoevsky minimum" — that situation in which everybody is so badly-off that it would be impossible to make anyone worse-off without accidentally making somebody better-off.

MAXIMUM SOCIAL WELL-BEING

All points on the grand utility frontier are Pareto-efficient. That means that it is possible, for any point on the grand utility frontier, to repeat the kind of analysis we have just performed for the point e. For any point on the grand utility frontier, there will be a unique and efficient resource allocation, product mix, commodity distribution, and set of price ratios. However, the empirical magnitudes of each of these will most likely be different for any two points on the grand utility frontier. Figure 6.14 shows a commodity space diagram similar to Figure 6.12. The points e' and e'' corresponding to the point e on the grand utility frontier are shown; also shown are the points f' and f'' corresponding to some different point, f, on the grand utility frontier. Note that the product mix is different at f'' than it is at e''. Commodity distribution is different at f' than it is at e'. Even the ratio of commodity prices, P_W/P_B, corresponding to the point f on the grand utility frontier is different from that corresponding to the point e. Since the points f'' and e'' on

FIGURE 6.14
Different Efficient Solutions Imply Different Product Mixes, Commodity Distributions, and Commodity Price Ratios

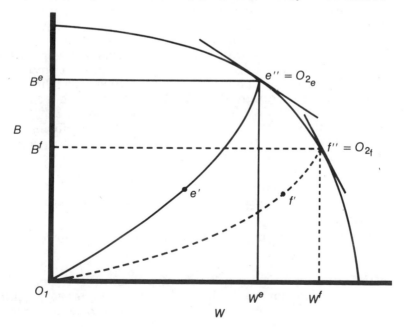

the efficient production possibilities curve map to the points f'' and e''' on the production efficiency locus, one can easily imagine that the ratios of input prices, P_L/P_D, would be different for the two different efficient solutions denoted by the points f and e. While the solutions denoted by the points f and e on the grand utility frontier are both Pareto-efficient, they imply different resource allocations, product mixes, commodity distributions and price ratios. Is there any way for a society to choose among efficient points on the grand utility frontier?

Consider the function $W = w(U_1, U_2)$, where $W =$ social well-being. This has been called the social welfare function (SWF), or the Samuelson-Bergson social welfare function (after two famous economists of the twentieth century).[3] W is expressed as a function of U_1 and U_2; that is, the levels of utility enjoyed by the individuals 1 and 2. The existence of such a function assumes that there is some way to develop a consensus across society as to how utility should be distributed among individuals, and that this function is capable of expressing such a consensus. The SWF is the societal analog of the individual utility function. Just as an indifference map can be derived from an individual utility function, *a social indifference map* can be derived from a social welfare function.

A social indifference curve is the locus of all possible combinations of utility levels for the individuals 1 and 2 that would result in the same level of social well-being. The social indifference map is expressed in utility axes. The social indifference map shown in Figure 6.15 indicates that the society whose preferences it represents has a relatively weak preference for equality of well-being among its members: its best-off member would have to become better-off at a rapid rate in order to compensate for a relatively small diminution of the well-being of its worst-off member.

Remember that the grand utility frontier was also expressed in utility space. It is possible, as in Figure 6.16, to superimpose the social indifference map upon the grand utility frontier. The point of tangency at which the highest feasible social indifference curve just touches the grand utility frontier is the *bliss point,* the point of maximum social well-being. The bliss point is Pareto-efficient, since it is on the grand utility frontier. Of all the Pareto-efficient points on the grand utility frontier, it is most preferred, since it permits the highest possible level of maximum social well-being.

Necessary Conditions for Maximum Social Well-being. The necessary conditions for maximum social well-being are:

1. Pareto-efficiency, and
2. Tangency between the grand utility frontier and the social indifference curve.

Sufficient Condition for Maximum Social Well-being. The sufficient condition for maximum social well-being is that a unique, true tangency exist between the grand utility frontier and a social

FIGURE 6.15
The Social Indifference Map

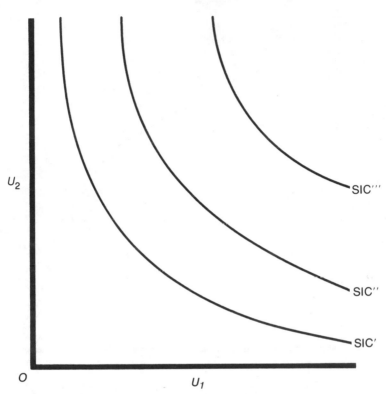

indifference curve. Parcto-efficiency implies that the grand utility frontier, although not necessarily smooth, will be generally concave to the origin. The social indifference curve is a smooth curve, but there is no essential reason why it must be convex to the origin. Convexity implies that the society cares rather strongly to avoid extreme deprivation of any of its members. However there may be societies that simply do not feel that way. Thus, it is possible for a social indifference curve to be a straight line or even concave. The sufficient condition will be satisfied if the social indifference curve and the grand utility frontier are of such shapes that there is a single true point of tangency between the two.

The social indifference curve and the social welfare function can exist only under some rather strong assumptions about the ability of society to achieve a consensus as to how economic well-being ought to be distributed among its members. Therefore, it is well to note that the sufficient condition for maximum social well-being requires that the social-welfare function exist.

FIGURE 6.16
The Maximization of Social Well-Being

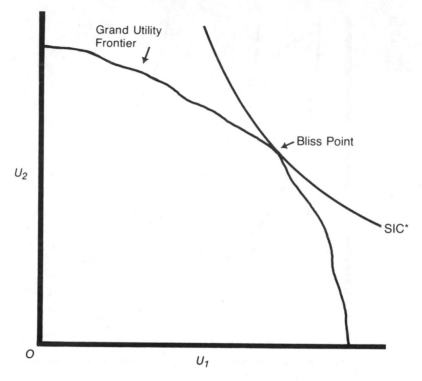

THE EXISTENCE OF THE
SOCIAL WELFARE FUNCTION

The social welfare function (SWF) is a mathematical relationship precisely expressing the societal preference as to how economic well-being (or, if you will, utility) should be distributed among the individual members of society. How could such a societal preference be established?

Some (many?) individuals may have developed personal philosophies about how the rewards of economic activity should be distributed. However, these personal philosophies are likely to vary widely from one individual to another. Further, even those individuals who have developed personal philosophies about distribution in general are likely to take a less detached approach to impending events that threaten to make themselves worse-off while making others better-off. For these reasons, we cannot expect the SWF to emerge from unanimous agreement among citizens.

Perhaps a dictator could specify the SWF for society. This solution would be unsatisfactory to all persons who adhere to even a minimal set of precepts about individual dignity. It is also unrealistic, since the single dictator would have no capacity to enforce his chosen social welfare function on everyone else. (Real-world "dictators" are not individuals making decisions unconstrained by the wishes of others; typically, they rule with the express support of one or more powerful factions and the tacit consent of the "silent majority." "Dictators" who lose these bases of support tend to enjoy brief regimes followed by long exiles or, for the less fortunate, violent deaths.)

Since we cannot expect the SWF to emerge from unanimous consent, and we would not accept (as either ethical or practicable) a SWF imposed by a dictator, we must search for ways in which the consensus implicit in the social welfare function concept could be established more or less democratically.

Although various kinds of political and governmental institutions are in varying degrees effective in adjudicating among the claims of competing individuals, coalitions, and philosophies, nothing that can be identified as a social welfare function seems to emerge from the process.

If a social scientist, armed with carefully designed questionnaires and a well-tested attitude measuring scale, were to bypass the political process and seek to estimate the SWF from surveys of citizens, it is unlikely that he would be successful. First, he would need to collect and analyze a truly horrendous quantity of data. But that is a relatively minor problem. His major problem would be that, in order to force the conflicting observations from individuals into the form of the SWF, he would need to invent a whole set of rules for making the various trade-offs. But that would solve the problem only by circumventing it; the analytical process assumes in advance the SWF that it sets out to find.

Kenneth Arrow, Nobel laureate in economics, has developed a very interesting, rigorous, mathematical proof of a proposition that some interpret as showing that the SWF cannot exist in a democratic society.[4] Arrow set out to find what he calls a *constitution,* a decision rule that always, when applied to any problem, yields a consistent answer. Any constitution acceptable to a democracy should, Arrow reasoned, meet several conditions: (1) it must be consistent with individual rationality; (2) individual rationality must be translated into collective rationality (for example, if any one of a set of possible alternatives were to rise in the ranking of one individual without falling in the ranking of any other individual, it should rise, or at least should not fall, in the social ranking); (3) neither individual nor collective preference orderings should be influenced by alternatives that are irrelevant (i.e., that are not elements of the opportunity set from which selections must be made); (4) the social preference ordering should not be imposed from outside the society; and (5) no individual should be a dictator (a dictator is defined as one whose preference ordering is always the social preference ordering, regardless of the preferences of everyone else).

Arrow was able to show, using a very simple analysis in which three individuals, 1, 2, and 3, ranked three alternatives, A, B, and C, that a democratic majority voting process is unable to yield a decision rule that never violates any of the five conditions. If the individuals have the following preference orderings (where the preferred alternative is stated first and the least preferred last):

individual 1:	A	B	C
individual 2:	B	C	A
individual 3:	C	A	B,

simple majority voting would yield the following result: A is preferred to B by a two-to-one majority; B is preferred to C by a similar majority; and C is preferred to A by a similar majority. This yields a social preference ordering of A B C A, which quite clearly violates the conditions of rationality. If A is preferred to B and B is preferred to C, how could C possibly be preferred to A?

Arrow's theorem, the "impossibility theorem," is controversial on two general sets of grounds.

First, some have questioned the idea of a constitution. Perhaps it is possible for a society to reach a workable consensus about the meaning of social well-being without that consensus meeting the strict criteria for a constitution. The economist Paul Samuelson (he of the Samuelson-Bergson SWF) insists that Arrow's constitution is a logical construct quite different from the SWF.[5]

Second, many have questioned the conditions that Arrow required. Is it necessary that a reasonable social decision rule meet every one of those conditions? While there has been almost thirty years of debate on that question, it must be noted that new and more sophisticated versions of Arrow's theorem have been developed, each dropping one of Arrow's conditions.

Many analysts have focused on the voting process itself, considering different kinds of voting processes in order to identify those that may avoid Arrow's paradox.[6] Some have demonstrated that, with a large number of alternatives to rank, and a large number of individuals voting, Arrow's paradox occurs very infrequently. Others have shown that when almost everyone conceives the alternatives in roughly the same way on some objective scale (for example, height in feet, or cost in dollars), even though individuals may have very different preferences among the alternatives, Arrow's paradox will not be observed. Other theoretical analyses have shown that various voting strategies commonly observed in the real world of political and committee decision processes (for example, vote trading, and voting strategies based on game-theoretic principles) may successfully avoid the Arrow paradox.

While the Arrow theorem and the multitude of more specialized impossibility theorems that have been more recently developed[7] are impressive exercises in logic, it is not clear that these kinds of theorems conclusively prove that a SWF cannot exist.

Nevertheless, while scholars may argue about the possibility of the existence of a SWF, there is literally no one who can make a serious and plausible claim to knowing precisely the SWF for any society. While the SWF is a useful device for developing the theoretical principle of maximum social well-being, the social microeconomist is simply unable to make use of the SWF in carrying out quantitative analyses of practical economic problems.

CRITERIA FOR ECONOMIC POLICY

In the absence, for all practical purposes, of a precisely specified social welfare function, what can the practicing resource economist say for sure about the social desirability of various alternative policies? He does, as we have seen, know some things about economic efficiency. But the grand utility frontier presents an infinite number of Pareto-efficient solutions, each with different distributional consequences. Efficiency alone provides no guidance as to how a society may rationally choose among these.

Since the present generation of economic analysts lacks the necessary social preference information to implement the maximum social well-being criterion, and the theoretical analyses along the line initiated by Kenneth Arrow cast serious doubt that social welfare function information will ever be available, it is appropriate to examine criteria for normative social microeconomics that do not depend on the SWF notion. As we examine potential criteria by which to measure economic performance, we shall be especially concerned with two indicators of economic performance: *efficiency,* as defined in earlier sections of this chapter, and *economic injury.* Economic injury is defined as a reduction in individual utility as a result, direct or indirect, of a public policy decision. Our definition of economic injury is thus quite similar to the popular notion of a "windfall loss."

For the purposes of the analyses that follow, the grand utility frontier is expressed in income axes, rather than utility axes. This procedure is helpful, since it permits a discussion more relevant to the real world in which income, not utility, is measured. There is some justification for replacing utility axes with income axes, since utility is believed to be positively correlated with income. However, as any good economist knows, it is not a strictly legitimate procedure: utility is ordinal and not subject to interpersonal evaluation, whereas income is cardinal and may be summed across individuals.

EFFICIENCY AS A CRITERION

Efficiency, alone, may be used as a criterion by which to judge alternative economic policies and public-sector activities. Some economists, impressed with the logical and empirical difficulties inherent in the social welfare function concept, insist that the economist is qualified by his professional training to speak of efficiency and to use efficiency as a criterion, but to go no further. This point of view regards the economist as professionally trained to identify policies that would eliminate waste, but as having no professional qualifications which would permit him to judge between alternative efficient solutions, each of which has different distributional consequences.

Consider Figure 6.17. Point *a,* lying inside the grand utility frontier, is clearly inefficient. Points *b, c,* and *d* are all on the grand utility frontier and thus all efficient. An economist using efficiency as the sole criterion would find that policies that would move the economy to points *b, c,* and *d* all represent improvements over point *a,* and are all equally desirable. Examine the northeast quadrant with its origin at point *a.* Remember that all possible situations in which at least one party is made better-off while no party is made worse-off, starting from point *a,* lie within that northeast quadrant.

FIGURE 6.17
Efficiency as the Criterion

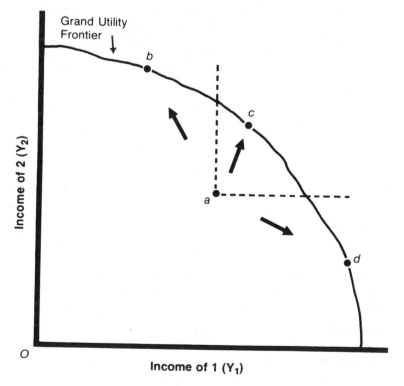

Thus, of our three efficient solutions, $b, c,$ and $d,$ only c is a solution in which neither party is injured. Starting at $a,$ a policy that resulted in the efficient solution b would result in economic injury to 1, while a policy resulting in d would result in economic injury to 2.

Economic efficiency, alone, is a criterion that eliminates inefficient (i.e., wasteful) solutions, but it provides no distinction between policies that result in economic injury for some and policies that result in economic injury for no one. Under this criterion, it is irrelevant whose ox is gored.

CONSTANT PROPORTIONAL SHARES

Consider a criterion that defines as an improvement any solution that results in greater income for one, so long as literally everybody's income increases proportionally. Under this criterion, everyone must benefit from a policy change, and each must benefit in strict proportion to his initial income. In Figure 6.18, there are three inefficient starting points $a, b,$ and $c,$ all of which lie within the grand utility frontier. Draw a series of rays, from the origin passing through each of the points $a, b,$ and $c,$ and continue the rays out to the grand utility frontier, thus defining the points $a', b',$ and c' that

FIGURE 6.18

Constant Proportional Shares

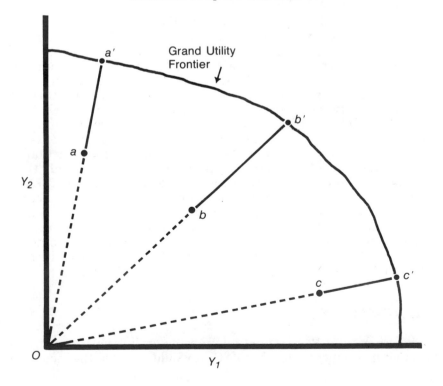

are Pareto-efficient. Starting at a, for example, any point on the line segment aa' represents an improvement, while a' represents the optimum policy.

Under the constant proportional shares criterion, a movement toward efficiency is necessary for a proposed policy to be considered an improvement, while an optimum policy is Pareto-efficient. However, from any starting point, only one point on the grand utility frontier is acceptable, while all other efficient solutions are eliminated. There can be *no real injury:* that is, no one can be made worse-off. In addition, there can be *no relative injury:* no one can be made worse-off relative to anybody else.

Notice, however, that at point a, 1 had a low income relative to 2, while at situation c, 2 had a low income relative to 1. At a', individual 1's income has not improved relative to that of individual 2; similarly, at c', individual 2's income has shown no relative improvement compared to 1's. The constant proportional shares criterion does not permit those who were badly-off at the outset to become relatively better-off as a result of new policies. Real or relative redistributions of income are prohibited. It may be argued that individuals who suffered a low income at, say, point a did so as a result of some past economic injury. That line of argument suggests that the constant proportional shares criterion permits no *new* relative economic injury, while embedding and reinforcing past patterns of relative economic injury.

It is not common to find serious proposals that the constant proportional shares criterion should be rigidly implemented throughout a whole economy. However, from time to time one does see arguments that it should be partially implemented. For example, labor unions sometimes argue for wage increases on the grounds that such increases are necessary to maintain a historical relationship between labor income and total income. Similarly, one occasionally encounters proposals that those on institutionally determined incomes — for example, social-security recipients — should have their incomes maintained at some constant fraction of GNP. At the time of this writing, there are serious proposals that total public-sector revenues be pegged at some proportion of GNP. University professors, throughout the past decade, have complained loudly, but ineffectually, that their incomes have fallen dramatically relative to GNP. All these arguments amount to proposals that the constant proportional shares criterion should be used, at least in certain circumstances, as a benchmark by which to judge the "fairness" of institutionally determined incomes.

PARETO-SAFETY

The criterion of Pareto-safety defines as an improvement (i.e., a Pareto-improvement) any change that would increase the income of

FIGURE 6.19
Pareto-Safety

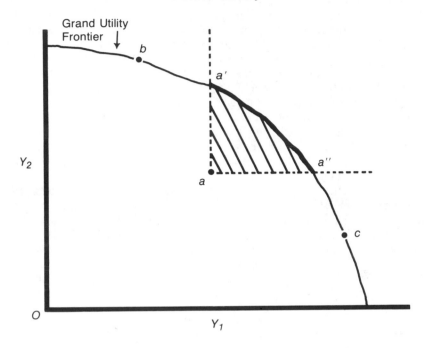

at least one person while reducing nobody's income. The northeast quadrant of Figure 6.19 defines the Pareto-safe region starting at point a. Any policy that would result in a movement to any point in the northeast quadrant would be considered an improvement; any policy that would result in a movement to any point on the segment $a'a''$ of the grand utility frontier, which lies within the northeast quadrant, would be considered an optimal policy. There is no acceptable basis for judgment among points that lie on that grand utility frontier segment.

A policy is judged to be an improvement if it results in a northeasterly move toward the grand utility frontier. Optimal policies require that efficiency be achieved. However, policies that result in moves from the inefficient point a to the efficient points b and c would not be considered improvements, much less optimal. No new real economic injury is permitted. However, relative economic injury is permissible: it is not essential that every individual in a society maintain his proportional share of income, only that no one actually lose real income. Pareto-safety permits relative redistribution of income as the total income of society grows, but no redistribution so great that any party actually receives less income. To this extent, the criterion of Pareto-safety at least partly embeds and reinforces past patterns of injury.

MAXIMUM SOCIAL WELL-BEING

There is surely no need at this point for a reminder of the difficulties inherent in the idea of a social welfare function. Nevertheless, it is interesting and instructive to evaluate maximum social well-being as a policy criterion, using the same indicators of economic performance that we have used to examine other criteria.

The social indifference map, superimposed upon the grand utility frontier (Figure 6.20), is presented using broken lines, to reinforce the logical doubts and empirical uncertainties that surround the notion of a social welfare function. From point *a*, any situation lying above the SIC passing through point *a* would be considered an improvement. The optimal situation would be at the point of tangency between the grand utility frontier and the highest feasible social indifference curve — i.e., the bliss point.

Notice that the SIC passing through point *a* intersects the grand utility frontier at two points. The segment of the grand utility frontier bounded by those two points of intersection defines the set of efficient solutions that would be regarded as improvements, starting from point *a*. No efficient solution lying outside that segment would be considered an improvement. Not only that, but moves from the efficient points *b* and *c* to the inefficient point *a* would be considered improvements. The criterion of maximum social well-being permits

FIGURE 6.20
Maximum Social Well-Being

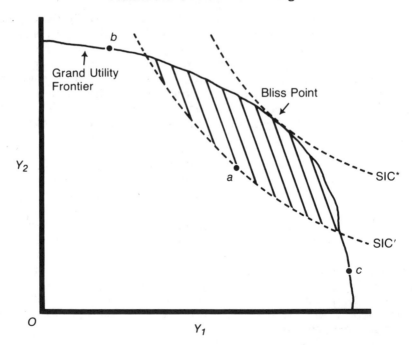

real economic injury, within limits. Those limits are defined by the shape of the social indifference curve, itself. In general, economic injury to individuals is permitted, so long as a social consensus exists that the outcome represents an improvement in social well-being.

While few would argue that the criterion of maximum social well-being is, or has ever been, rigidly applied, some of the policy discussion and some of the political decisions in a typical modern mixed economy are at least suggestive of an underlying social welfare function notion. One observes programs to assist the poor, the elderly, the unemployed, the disabled, and those children whose parents are unable or unwilling to adequately provide for them. Such programs, which accept a real redistribution of income from those who are economically successful to others who are less effective at providing for themselves in economic competition, seem to be based at least loosely on the social welfare function idea. In public-policy discussions, the term "the public interest" tends to surface rather frequently. The idea that there exists a "public interest," which cannot be expressed with complete adequacy by economically generated price signals, is also suggestive of the social welfare function notion.

MAXIMUM VALUE OF SOCIAL PRODUCT

One special form of the social indifference curve is a straight line, extending to both axes, of slope −1. Such a social indifference curve provides that each and every dollar of income be weighted equally, regardless of to whom it accrues. The value of society's output is to be calculated, without distributional weights, and that policy which results in the larger value of social product is preferred. Starting from point a, the set of possible improvements is defined by a line of slope −1 passing through point a; all points above that line are considered improvements, according to the criterion of maximum value of social product (Figure 6.21). The optimum solution, a', is determined by the tangency of the grand utility frontier with the highest feasible line of slope −1.

Under this criterion, an improvement need not necessarily represent a movement toward efficiency. From either b or c, a move to a — that is, away from efficiency — would be an improvement. However, the optimal solution must be efficient. Economic injury is permissible, so long as the sum of the dollars gained by the gainers exceeds the sum of the dollars lost by the losers. Thus, the criterion of maximum value of social product is totally neutral with regard to income redistribution. Income redistribution is never required for its own sake, and policies that happen to redistribute income are never prohibited so long as the total dollars gained by the beneficiaries exceed the total dollars lost by the losers.

In modern mixed economies, no one seriously suggests that the criterion of maximum value of social product should be applied,

132

FIGURE 6.21
Maximum Value of Social Product

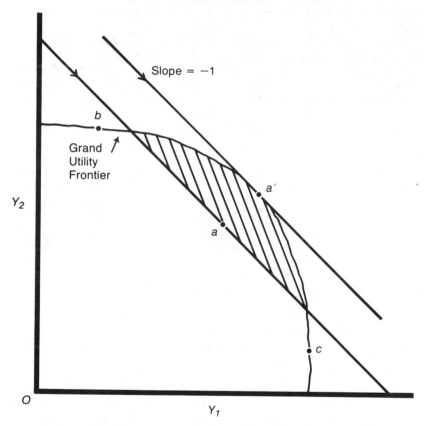

pervasively and without exception, to all policy decisions. However, this criterion is widely applied for certain classes of decisions. For example, the benefit cost criterion, that the benefits to whomsoever they accrue should exceed the costs, is synonymous with the criterion of maximum value of social product. The idea that the best economic policy is the one that maximizes the rate of economic growth, or growth in GNP, is related to the criterion of maximum value of social product in the following way: GNP, for reasons discussed in Chapter 3, is a highly unsatisfactory measure of a nation's economic productivity; however, if GNP were an adequate measure of the value of social product, the criterion of maximum value of social product would be a criterion of maximum GNP.

COMPOSITE CRITERIA

The normative criteria for economic policy discussed above are all single criteria. None seems entirely satisfactory. Objections to some are raised on ethical and philosophical grounds, while objections to others are based on pragmatic grounds; and, it seems, most of these criteria are vulnerable to objections on both kinds of grounds. There are, of course, other single criteria that could be, and have been, seriously proposed.

The reasonable objections to the various possible single criteria have led some thinkers to seriously propose the use of multiple or composite criteria. For example, some have proposed the use of the criterion of maximum value of social product, with the proviso that no policy that would make the poor worse-off is acceptable. That kind of criterion could be described as maximum value of social product, subject to Pareto-safety for the poor but not for the rich. It is quite possible to generate other composite criteria.

For example, consider the following criteria, to be implemented simultaneously: (1) policies that reduce the value of social product are unacceptable; (2) the income of the well-off individual, 2, should not be increased; (3) permissible redistribution will not proceed past the point of equality (i.e., individual 1 will not be permitted to become richer than individual 2); and (4) the optimal policy will be that policy which, while satisfying conditions 1-3, results in the maximum attainable value of social product. As Figure 6.22 demonstrates, it is possible, with a composite criterion such as this, to define a zone of policy improvements and an optimal policy. The optimal policy, which would move the economy to point a', is an efficient policy. Permissible economic injury is defined by the conditions that make up the composite criterion.

A NOTE ON COMPENSATION TESTS AND THE "POTENTIAL PARETO-IMPROVEMENT"

Some authors, feeling that the only reasonable objection to the Pareto-improvement criterion is that very few potential policy actions satisfy it, have proposed *compensation tests*.[8] For example, starting with policy situation A, *if* it is possible to introduce policy A' so that those who gain *could* afford to compensate the losers and have some gains remaining, the change from A to A' is a *potential Pareto-improvement*. The idea is that the possibility of compensation expands the set of policy actions that would result, potentially, in Pareto-improvements.

Just what kind of criterion is established, using this kind of compensation test? The answer depends entirely on whether or not the compensation is actually paid. If the compensation must be paid, the compensation test criterion reduces to the *actual Pareto-improvement*, albeit with compensation. If the compensation need not be paid, the compensation test criterion requires only that the sum of the gains (in dollar terms), to whomsoever they accrue, exceed the sum of the losses. In that case, the potential Pareto-improvement criterion is identical to the *maximum value of social product* criterion.

FIGURE 6.22
A Composite Criterion

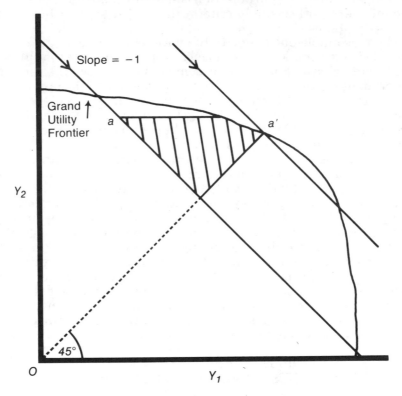

THE THEORY OF SECOND-BEST

Although the various kinds of normative economic policy criteria take markedly different approaches to determining the acceptability of economic injury, they all seem to have one thing in common. For all these various criteria, the optimum policy solution lies on the grand utility frontier; that is, Pareto-efficiency is one characteristic outcome of the optimal policy.

This observation has led some economists to propose that for purposes of evaluating economic policy alternatives the economist should concentrate his attention on the efficiency characteristics of these alternatives, and thereby avoid the logical and pragmatic difficulties that arise when the economist attempts to establish distributional criteria. In the real world, however, a problem arises when the economist attempts to identify policies that would yield efficiency improvements.

In a typical modern mixed economy, inefficiencies abound. Since inefficiency is defined as a situation in which the necessary and sufficient conditions for Pareto-efficiency are not fulfilled, anything that would cause violation of those conditions must cause inefficiency. Since the necessary conditions require that, at the margin, various rates of substitution and transformation be equal to relevant price ratios, inefficiency may arise from anything that distorts price ratios. Distortion in price ratios may result from monopolistic or noncompetitive market conditions, market failures (the externalities, indivisibilities in consumption, and nonexclusiveness problems that will be discussed in Chapter 8), and various well-meant governmental policies that restrict opportunities for trade or attempt to modify the outcomes of trade (for example, price controls, subsidies, import quotas, prohibition of trade in certain commodities, and most kinds of taxes).

In a modern mixed economy, it is both economically and politically infeasible to restructure the total economy, in one massive upheaval, to establish the conditions for economic efficiency simultaneously in all sectors. Of practical necessity, economic policy must be undertaken in piecemeal fashion. The impacts of particular laws, regulations, policies, or public investments are usually, for these practical reasons, studied one by one or in small groups called "policy packages." The assumption, beloved of economists, that "all other things remain equal," is put to exhaustive use in these kinds of analyses.

Given that inefficiencies abound throughout the whole economy, does it make sense to undertake economic analyses and pursue policies aimed at encouraging efficiency in a particular sector or with respect to a particular policy or public investment? Common sense would seem to suggest that it does: that one must start someplace, and it would surely be beneficial to establish the conditions for efficiency with respect to at least one previously inefficient circumstance within the economy. Unfortunately, the conclusion suggested by common sense does not hold water as a general proposition.

R. G. Lipsey and K. Lancaster, about twenty years ago, developed and proved the *general theory of second-best*.[9] This proposition may be stated in several ways, and it is useful to do so, since each of the various, slightly different statements of the theory suggests a slightly different perspective on its application.

1. If there is introduced into a general equilibrium system a constraint that prevents the attainment of one of the conditions for Pareto-efficiency, the other conditions for Pareto-efficiency, although still attainable, are in general no longer desirable.
2. Given that one of the conditions for Pareto-efficiency cannot be fulfilled, an optimal situation (in efficiency terms) can be achieved only by departing from all the other conditions for Pareto-efficiency.
3. There is no *a priori* way to judge between various situations in

which some of the conditions for Pareto-efficiency are fulfilled while others are not.
4. It is not necessarily true that a situation in which more, but not all, of the conditions for Pareto-efficiency are fulfilled will be superior to one in which fewer are fulfilled.

The general theory of second-best has been interpreted as proving that if Pareto-efficiency is unattainable, there are no simple and general sufficient conditions for an improvement in efficiency (given fixed resources, and unchanging technology and preferences). Thus, a policy of seeking piecemeal improvements in efficiency would seem to be totally unreliable.

The theory of second-best would seem to strongly suggest that, in practical situations where many sources of inefficiency exist and all cannot be simultaneously eliminated, the economist's reliance on the necessary conditions for Pareto-efficiency as a guide to piecemeal policy is without foundation. The economist who, somewhat shaken by the controversy surrounding the existence of a social welfare function, withdrew to the concept of Pareto-efficiency (on the grounds that "at least, economists can draw definitive conclusions about economic efficiency") now stands helpless, as the theory of second-best casts doubt upon the validity of economic analyses and economic policies that seek to bring efficiency in a piecemeal fashion to an imperfect economy. But all is not lost.

The Lipsey-Lancaster proof of the general theory of second-best relies upon a very simple mathematical analysis. O. A. Davis and A. Whinston have re-examined that proof.[10] They discovered that, if one makes an assumption about the relationships within the economy that is different from the assumption made by Lipsey and Lancaster, the theory of second-best no longer holds. Specifically, when the mathematical functions defining economic interaction are *separable,* an improvement toward efficiency may be achieved by applying the necessary conditions for Pareto-efficiency to one aspect of a generally inefficient economy. At first glance, the difference between the theory of Lipsey-Lancaster and that of Davis-Whinston appears to rest entirely upon differences in assumptions about mathematical functional forms. What could that have to do with economics?

It turns out that the difference with respect to assumptions about functional forms is economically significant. In general, the mathematical functions describing interactions between economic sectors will be separable when all the interactions among those economic sectors are defined by efficient price ratios. Thus, the necessary conditions for Pareto-efficiency may be introduced into one or more of the sectors whose interactions are defined by separable functions, without encountering the second-best problems raised by Lipsey and Lancaster.

In general, second-best problems will not be encountered when the sources of economic efficiency under analysis are of the following types: production indivisibilities, corner or boundary solutions, interdependent utility functions, and any situation where one or a small group of individuals or firms fails to maximize utility or profits, as the case may be, for individual reasons. Introducing efficient input use, or efficient commodity distribution, within a sector will always result in an improvement in overall economic efficiency. On the other hand, second-best problems do occur when price ratios are distorted by monopoly, uncorrected externality, and nonoptimal policies (for example, nonoptimal tariffs or taxes).

There is a substantial category of economic problems in which the theory of second-best is not relevant. However, the category of economic problems that do encounter the second-best situation is obviously also quite substantial. For this latter category of economic problems, exactly what constraints does the theory of second-best place upon the scrupulous economic policy analyst?

The theory of second-best is expressed in non-quantitative terms. It states simply that, when the relevant conditions exist, it is inappropriate to insist that the necessary conditions for Pareto-efficiency be implemented in a piecemeal fashion. In these situations, the scrupulous economic policy analyst cannot simply lean back in his armchair and advise the policy maker to set the price ratios facing an inefficient sector equal to the relevant rates of substitution and transformation. "Armchair analyses" are not permissible. However, in any case where the theory of second-best holds, it is always conceptually possible, and may often be practically feasible, to perform quantitative analyses in order to determine the necessary conditions for an improvement in efficiency. When these conditions are found, they will surely deviate from the necessary conditions for Pareto-efficiency. Nevertheless, they will be conditions for an improvement in the efficiency of the inefficient economy (or, in professional economic jargon, conditions for a second-best optimum). Armchair analysis is out, but, even in the second-best situation, careful quantitative analyses are capable of determining conditions for an improvement in efficiency.

WHAT CAN THE ECONOMIST DO?

In this chapter, necessary and sufficient conditions have been defined for Pareto-efficiency and for maximum social well-being. Nevertheless, this chapter must have provided a disillusioning experience for the neophyte economist who had hoped to use economic analyses to solve all the world's problems.

The social welfare function, which is essential to the derivation of the conditions for maximum social well-being, is unknown, and, even more damaging, impressive arguments have been made that a social welfare function satisfying a number of axioms of logic and reasonable conditions for democratic choice processes cannot exist. So, economists cannot define the conditions that would generate the best of all possible worlds, except in an entirely abstract formulation. This ought not be surprising, nor ought it be considered evidence of intellectual weakness on the part of economists. Several millennia of intense intellectual activity by theologians and philosophers have failed to definitively solve the same basic problem: how shall humankind determine what is good and what is evil? It is surely unfair to expect economics (which made its debut as a branch of moral philosophy) to definitively answer these questions in its brief, two-hundred-year, history.

In the absence of a social welfare function, economists have considered a number of other criteria by which policy proposals may be judged as good or bad. All these criteria identify efficiency as one necessary condition for an optimum. However, some do and some do not require a movement toward efficiency in order for a proposed policy to be considered an improvement. Each of the proposed policy criteria encounters serious ethical questions, not the least of which is the substitution of a cardinal income scale that permits additivity across individuals for the ordinal utility scale that does not permit interpersonal utility comparisons. Even if the income scale is accepted on ethical or, more likely, pragmatic grounds, each of these possible criteria places a different limit upon acceptable economic injury to individuals.

Those that accept economic injury, subject only to the restriction that, in aggregate, social well-being or the value of social product must be increased, are criticized by some because of the economic injury they permit. Other criteria — such as constant proportional shares, which permits no real or relative economic injury, and Pareto-safety, which permits no real economic injury — are criticized by others, with equal sincerity, on the grounds that, in any economy with a long and dynamic history, past patterns of economic injury would be suddenly embedded, reinforced, and carried forward into the future.

In this chapter, we have learned something about the economic and ethical implications of various criteria for economic policy, but we have not solved the criterion problem. The argument that the economist is not equipped by his professional discipline to solve this problem, and that therefore it should be left to "the decision-maker," is unhelpful, since it fails to face up to the question of the legitimacy of the decision-maker's power. Similarly, the argument that the solution of the criterion problem should be left to the political process is unhelpful, since there is no assurance that the political process itself is perfect. The author's personal viewpoint, which (it must be forthrightly stated) may not be shared by all or even most economists, is that the economist is no more qualified than others to specify criteria for economic policy; nor is he less qualified.

The theory of second-best is perhaps more worrisome to economists since, while many of them have never claimed to be able to solve the criterion problem, most felt that economic theory permitted them to say some very definitive things about economic efficiency and the road thereto. The theory of second-best, as modified by Davis and Whinston, defines the set of economic circumstances under which armchair analyses are not permissible. In such cases, it does not rule out the possibility of quantitative analyses to identify, piecemeal, conditions that would yield an improvement in economic efficiency. This kind of quantitative analysis is always conceptually possible, but it is often beyond the reach of the economic analyst, for any one of several reasons: the complexity of the economic system under study, the limiting nature of certain assumptions and techniques that facilitate economic analysis, and simple constraints upon the time and money that can be invested in economic analyses. The optimal investment in economic analysis prior to a policy decision is itself an economic question. Thus, piecemeal or "partial equilibrium" analyses are often used, for obvious pragmatic reasons, in situations where careful consideration of the theory of second-best would counsel a much more general analysis. In such circumstances, the theory of second-best provides a caveat to the economist, and those who make use of economic analyses. In the real world, this is often as much as is done with the theory of second-best. It is, frankly, honored more often with lip service than with complete and adequate analysis. And many well-trained and sincere economists (for example, E. J. Mishan[11]) argue that partial equilibrium analyses to identify opportunities for piecemeal improvements in efficiency do not often result in major errors, especially when, at the outset, the inefficiency is great.

As a practicing resource economist, the author is very much aware of the limitations to social microeconomic policy analyses that are introduced by questions concerning the existence of the social-welfare function and by the theory of second-best. However, he does not allow these concerns to immobilize him. He is convinced that economic analysis is capable of casting significant light on many economic policy questions, including many questions that involve the use, management, and conservation of natural and environmental resources.

Finally, it must be observed that there are some economists who counsel, more often orally than in writing, that welfare economics theory, social microeconomics, and resource economics are best avoided as subjects of inquiry because "there is so much uncertainty and so little that is known for sure." However, all branches of economics ultimately face the same unknowns. The economist who stops short of asking these difficult questions does not avoid the uncertainties, he only stops short of them.

QUESTIONS FOR DISCUSSION

1. "The economist can identify inefficiency, and point out the way to make

the situation efficient. Beyond that, his professional expertise is exhausted." Evaluate this statement critically.

2. "The pursuit of *maximum value of social product,* without reference to Pareto-safety, would leave citizens at the mercy of their government." Discuss.

3. "There is no *public interest,* but there is a *'public interest' interest."* Explain and evaluate this statement.

4. Does the *theory of second-best* leave the economist without a supportable basis for policy prescription, in a world where efficiency is pervasive?

5. An economist, famous for his pioneering efforts in using computer techniques to determine "optimum policies," once told a seminar audience, "Arrow has five axioms, and gets no solution; I have only one axiom: there *will* be a solution!" Identify the ethical positions underlying that economist's statement, and contrast them with those underlying the Arrow theorem.

6. Evaluate the following proposition: the formal proof that a perfectly competitive economy, in a static context, tends to achieve a Pareto-efficient equilibrium provides a sufficient basis for relying on market forces to solve a wide variety of real-world problems, many of which are outside the traditional scope of economics.

FURTHER READINGS

Arrow, Kenneth J. 1967. "Public and Private Values," in *Human Values and Economic Policy.* Sidney Hook (ed.). New York: New York University Press. Part I, A: 3-21.

Bator, R. M. 1957. "The Simple Analysis of Welfare Maximization," *American Economic Review.* 47(Mar): 52-59.

Baumol, William J. 1965. *Welfare Economics and the Theory of the State.* Cambridge: Harvard University Press. 2nd edition.

Buchanan, James M., and Gordon Tullock. 1962. *The Calculus of Consent.* Ann Arbor: University of Michigan Press.

Davis, O. A., and A. B. Whinston. 1965. "Welfare Economics and the Theory of Second Best," *Review of Economic Studies.* 32(Jan): 1-14.

Lipsey, R. G., and R. K. Lancaster. 1956-1957. "The General Theory of Second Best," *Review of Economic Studies.* 24(1): 11-33.

Mishan, E. J. 1962. "Second Thoughts on Second Best," *Oxford Economic Papers* (New Series). 14(Oct): 205-217.

Mueller, Dennis C. 1976. "Survey on Public Choice," *Journal of Economic Literature.* 14(June): 395-433.

Quirk, James P. 1976. *Intermediate Microeconomics.* Chicago: Science Research Associates.

Samuels, W. J. 1972. "Welfare Economics, Power and Property," in Wunderlich and Gibson (ed.), *Perspectives of Property.* University Park: The Pennsylvania State University. (Parts I, II, and III.)

ADVANCED READINGS

Arrow, Kenneth J. 1976. *Social Choice and Individual Values.* New York: Wiley. 2nd edition.

Henderson, James Mitchell, and Richard E. Quandt. 1971. *Microeconomic Theory: A Mathematical Approach.* New York: McGraw-Hill. 2nd edition. (Chapter 7.)

Quirk, James P., and Rubin Saposnik. 1968. *An Introduction to General Equilibrium Theory and Welfare Economics.* New York: McGraw-Hill.

ENDNOTES

1. The term Pareto-efficiency, as used in this book, is synonymous with Pareto-optimality as used by many other authors. Here "Pareto-efficiency" is preferred, since the concept to which both terms refer is an efficiency concept; it is a *social optimality* concept only under some highly restrictive assumptions discussed later in this chapter.
2. The following analysis is based upon that presented in Bator, R. M. 1957. "The Simple Analytics of Welfare Maximization," *American Economic Review.* 47(Mar): 22-59.
3. See Bergson, Abram. 1938. "A Reformulation of Certain Aspects of Welfare Economics." *Quarterly Journal of Economics.* 52: 311-334; and Samuelson, Paul A. 1948. *Foundations of Economic Analysis.* Cambridge: Harvard University Press.
4. See Arrow, Kenneth J. 1951. *Social Choice and Individual Values.* New York: John Wiley and Sons.
5. See Samuelson, Paul A. 1967. "Arrow's Mathematical Politics," in *Human Values and Economic Policy.* Sidney Hook (ed.). New York: New York University Press. (Part I, C.)
6. Black, D. 1948. "On the Rationale of Group Decision Making," *Journal of Political Economics.* 56(Feb): 23-34.
   Black, D. 1958. *The Theory of Committees and Elections.* Cambridge: Cambridge University Press.
   Buchanan, J. M., and G. Tullock. 1962. *The Calculus of Consent.* Ann Arbor: University of Michigan Press.
   Coleman, J. S. 1966. "The Possibility of a Social Welfare Function," *American Economic Review.* 56(Dec): 1105-1122.
   Coleman, J. S. 1970. "Political Money," *American Political Science Review.* 64(Dec): 1074-1087.
   Tullock, G. 1959. "Problems of Majority Voting," *Journal of Political Economics.* 67(Dec): 571-579.
   Tullock, G. 1967. "The General Irrelevance of the General Impossibility Theorem," *Quarterly Journal of Economics.* 81(May): 256-270.
   Tullock, G. 1970. "A Simple Algebraic Logrolling Model," *American Economic Review.* 60(June): 419-426.
   Tullock, G., and C. D. Campbell. 1970. "Computer Simulation of a Small Voting System," *Economic Journal.* 80(Mar): 97-104.
7. See, for example, Kelly, Jerry S. 1978. *Arrow Impossibility Theorems.* New York: Academic Press.
8. Hicks, J. R. 1939. "The Foundations of Welfare Economics," *Economic Journal.* 49: 696-712.
   Kaldor, Nicholas. 1939. "Welfare Propositions in Economics," *Economic Journal.* 49: 549-552.
   Scitovsky, T. 1941. "A Note on Welfare Propositions in Economics," *Review of Economic Studies.* 9(Nov): 77-88.
9. Lipsey, R. G., and R. K. Lancaster. 1956-1957. "The General Theory of Second Best," *Review of Economic Studies.* 24(1): 11-33.
10. Davis, O. A., and A. B. Whinston. 1965. "Welfare Economics and the Theory of Second Best," *Review of Economic Studies.* 32(Jan): 1-14.
11. Mishan, E. J. 1962. "Second Thoughts on Second Best," *Oxford Economic Papers* (New Series). 14(Oct): 205-217.

7

Property Rights, Efficiency, and the Distribution of Income

We have defined the necessary and sufficient conditions for Pareto-efficiency. The question that now faces us is: what kinds of economic organization are conducive to the achievement of efficiency?

Conceptually, it is possible for a directed economy in a totalitarian state to achieve Pareto-efficiency. To do so, the director of the economy would need to effectively set all of the price ratios equal to the relevant rates of substitution and transformation. That is, he would need to establish an efficient set of incentives for production, and an efficient set of price ratios (or some equally effective indicators of the terms of trade) to efficiently ration goods among consumers and to encourage efficient commodity substitution in the face of changes in relative scarcity. To establish these efficient signals, or "shadow prices," the economic director would need to gather and accurately process a massive amount of economic information. The enormity of the information-gathering and computation tasks has led most economists to suspect that the achievement of Pareto-efficiency in a directed economy, although conceptually possible, is most unlikely. In practice, these difficulties, along with a penchant for permitting political goals and considerations to interfere with economic planning, have led to obvious inefficiencies and economic dislocations in most planned economies.

On the other hand, it is not merely conceivable that a perfectly competitive, free-enterprise economy may achieve Pareto-efficiency. The competitive economy uses the price system to provide an inbuilt mechanism that tends to move the economy in the direction of efficiency. Using a highly abstract theoretical model in a static analysis, it has been shown that a competitive economy tends to reach equilibrium and that the competitive equilibrium is Pareto-efficient.[1] The remainder of this chapter will be devoted to an exploration of the institutional conditions under which a competitive economy may achieve Pareto-efficiency and to the implications of different institutional structures for both efficiency and the distribution of economic well-being.

A competitive economy relies upon prices as signals to direct independent producers and consumers to behave individually in such a way that the aggregate outcome of their independent endeavors is efficient. To achieve this result, the competitive economy relies upon free and unrestrained trade. The necessary conditions for Pareto-efficiency are, in fact, marginal conditions for efficient trade. Pareto-efficiency is achieved when all potential gains from trade in all sectors of a (perfect) economy are exhausted. The institutional conditions that encourage the achievement of efficiency in competitive economies are, thus, institutional conditions that facilitate trade.

PROPERTY RIGHTS

Imagine, for a moment, a society in which it was illegal to interfere with, or in any way impede the activities of, any person attempting to take any automobile for his own use. This would certainly be a radical change in the laws with which we are familiar. Not only would "automobile theft" be legal, but the term itself would have no meaning. How would such a law affect the production, use, and exchange of automobiles?

An individual in need of transportation would simply take the nearest convenient automobile, drive it to his destination, and abandon it there. When the time came to return, the individual would simply take the same automobile, or another, and drive it home or to wherever else he wanted to go. For a brief period after a law like this had been established, things would probably work fairly well. Since most people who go someplace eventually return, one would expect that automobiles, in general, would tend to be located where they are needed. A person in need of transportation would, therefore most likely find an abandoned automobile nearby.

As time passes, one would expect to see some major changes in the patterns of production, maintenance and use of automobiles. People would continue to purchase gasoline for automobiles, but they would soon learn to put only enough fuel for the planned trip in the gas tank. Automobiles with some fuel remaining in the tank would be the first to be taken by others in need of transportation. One could predict a sudden increase in the demand for portable gasoline containers, since anyone planning a trip away would be wise to carry with him sufficient gasoline to make it back (in a different automobile) at least as far as the first gas station.

Quite soon, one would begin to notice a deterioration in the quality of the society's automobile stock. No one would pay to have major maintenance or repairs performed upon an automobile he had recently picked up and expects to abandon soon. Given this decline in the quality of the automobile stock, prudent persons would carry tool kits along with their portable fuel containers, so that, if the need arose, they could perform minor repairs en route.

The automobile stock would age quite rapidly, since no one would have any incentive to purchase a new automobile. Automobile manufacturers would go out of business, suffering major capital losses, and causing a sudden increase in the supply of workers on the labor market. These outcomes could be avoided only if the government decided, on the grounds that an "automobile emergency" existed, to use tax revenues for the purpose of purchasing new automobiles that would be strategically placed around population centers. But, for the purposes of this little parable, assume that government chooses to forego that alternative. In addition to the effects on the market in new automobiles, one would also expect used-car dealers, automobile auctions, and manufacturers of all but the least expensive replacement parts to go out of business.

In a relatively brief period of time following the introduction of laws that abolished the concept of automobile theft, the automobile markets with which we are familiar would completely disappear, along with the industries that manufacture, exchange, and service automobiles. There seems no question that the society would be worse-off, since automobile transportation (which we must assume to be strongly desired, since it is purchased in large quantities when effective and unrestricted markets exist) would soon be effectively removed from individual opportunity sets.

This somewhat fanciful parable is helpful in understanding the crucial role of property rights in the economy. What are the characteristics of an adequate set of property rights?

OWNERSHIP

One rather simple legal change, the abolition of the concept of automobile theft, would be sufficient to eliminate markets in automobiles within a relatively brief time. This legal change is simple, yet quite radical. It would effectively abolish the concept of ownership.

Ownership is a legal device that assigns the right to use. In a market economy based on the concept of private property, payment results in ownership. Ownership carries with it the right to use, subject to various possible restrictions. The least restrictive kind of ownership is *exclusive ownership,* which carries with it the right to use and to determine who, if anyone, else may use and under what conditions. Exclusive ownership is the legal antonym of *res nullius,* which is a Latin term meaning literally "nobody's property." Our imaginary law that would abolish the concept of automobile theft would effectively reduce ownership rights in automobiles to the *res nullius* situation.

Ownership is an essential precondition for trade. Who in his right mind would pay for something without assurance that he could use it? Or, conversely, who in his right mind would pay to use something when he could not be stopped from using it free of charge?

SPECIFICATION OF RIGHTS

Individuals independently exercising their various ownership rights may often come into conflict. My hog feedlot may reduce the satisfaction you enjoy from your home in an expensive new subdivision. Your neighbor's failure to maintain his property in good condition may also reduce the satisfaction you derive from your property. A factory owner's use of his property may reduce the satisfactions of others (property owners and nonowners) by creating excessive noise, releasing pollutants into a flowing stream, and expelling pollutants through a smokestack into the atmosphere. This latter example expands the possibility of conflicts introduced by ownership, to include not only conflicts among owners but also conflicts between owners and nonowners.

To permit resolution of these conflicts, it is insufficient merely to declare that exclusive ownership exists. It is also necessary to specify the rights that accompany ownership. When different owners come into conflict, whose rights predominate? When owners and nonowners come into conflict, what rights are assigned to the property owner simply because he owns property and what rights are assigned to the nonowner simply because he is an individual human being? Clearly, restrictions must accompany ownership rights. If anyone could use anything he owns in any way he pleases, utter chaos would ensue.

In order that exclusive property rights may achieve their fullest effectiveness, thus permitting resolution of conflicts among owners and between owners and nonowners by trade, property rights must be completely specified. The rights that accompany ownership must be specified in detail, along with the restrictions that apply to owners and the corresponding rights of nonowners.

TRANSFERABILITY

If trade is to be effective in allocating resources and in resolving conflicts, rights must be transferable. An individual who desires to acquire a specific right must be permitted to make an offer to some other individual who already owns that right. An individual who is willing to relinquish a right he owns, in exchange for some consideration of greater value to him, must have the right to sell. In that way, rights can gravitate to their highest-valued uses. Restrictions on the transfer of rights (as opposed to restrictions on use, necessary for the complete specification of rights) are sources of inefficiency. Such restrictions erect barriers to the achievement of equality between price ratios and the relevant rates of substitution and transformation.

Since complete specification of rights entails the specification of a variety of different kinds of rights associated with a particular thing (i.e., a particular piece of property), complete transferability of rights requires that the different types of rights associated with ownership of a particular thing should be transferable independently of one another. For example, the cause of efficiency is served when the government-created right to market, say, tobacco may be transferred independently of the ownership rights pertaining to land. Further, efficiency is served when the rights pertaining to land ownership may be subdivided in many ways, and the subdivided rights transferred. This permits leasing, renting, sharecropping, easements, and rights of way, all of which work to make land utilization more efficient than it would be if ownership rights were undivided and, for example, someone seeking to run a transmission line across another's farm had only two options: purchasing the whole farm in fee-simple title or abandoning his plan.

To the uninitiated, the idea of trade in rights may sound a little strange. One tends to think of trade as the physical transfer of things — that is, property objects. Yet the fundamental characteristic of trade is the transfer of rights, rather than the physical transfer and removal of things. When one "buys" land, one does not pick up that piece of land and carry it home. Rather, one acquires certain specified rights to make use of that land. Even in the case of a small item purchased from a department store, the fundamental characteristic of trade is not physical removal but the transfer of the right to remove and use. Removal, alone, can be accomplished by shoplifting; but shoplifting is considered not a transfer of ownership rights, but a violation of them.

ENFORCEMENT

Incentives most certainly exist for violation of the rights pertaining to ownership and transfer of property. To steal is cheaper than to buy, if the thief is assured that he is unlikely to be apprehended and penalized. Pollution is an inexpensive method of waste disposal, if the polluter is assured that the rights of others (owners and nonowners) will not be enforced.

To be effective, a system of rights must be enforceable, and effectively enforced. An unenforced right is effectively no right at all. Returning, momentarily, to the automobile example, the unsatisfactory results in the automobile market are attributed to the abandonment of exclusive ownership rights in automobiles and their replacement with *res nullius*. However, exactly the same results would occur if, instead, exclusive ownership rights to automobiles remained on the books but enforcement broke down entirely.

Effective enforcement involves discovery of violations, apprehension of violators, and imposition of appropriate penalties. The complete specification of rights should include the specification of penalties for their violation. Then, perfect enforcement guarantees that those penalties will be imposed in the event of a violation. To be effective, the specified penalties should be sufficiently large that they exceed the benefits anyone could hope to obtain from violation. If enforcement is imperfect, as it must always be in the real world, the expected value of penalties (i.e., the amount of the penalty multiplied by the probability that it will actually be imposed) must exceed any possible gains a violator could hope to obtain.

THE DEFINITION OF PROPERTY RIGHTS

We are now in a position to define the concept of property rights. Property rights specify the proper relationships among people with respect to the use of things, and the penalties for violation of those proper relationships.

PROPERTY RIGHTS AND ECONOMIC EFFICIENCY

In an economy that is otherwise conducive to efficiency (i.e., that does not include monopolies, indivisibilities in consumption, or continually declining cost curves), *nonattenuated property rights* ensure Pareto-efficiency.[2] A set of nonattenuated property rights is:

1. Completely specified, so that it can serve as a perfect system of information about the rights that accompany ownership, the restrictions upon those rights, and the penalties for their violation.
2. Exclusive, so that all rewards and penalties resulting from an action accrue directly to the individual empowered to take action (i.e., the owner).
3. Transferable, so that rights may gravitate to their highest-value use.
4. Enforceable and completely enforced. An unenforced right is no right at all.

The alert reader will notice something a little strange about this definition of nonattenuated rights. Whereas the efficiency conditions for economic activity require that any production or consumption activity be pursued until its marginal benefits are equal to its marginal costs, the definition of nonattenuated rights suggests that the specification, transfer, and enforcement of rights should be carried to the point of perfection. However, specification, transfer, and enforcement are all costly activities, and the pursuit of perfection in these activities may result in prohibitive costs. These costs have been called *transactions costs* or, by some,[3] ICP (for information, contracting, and policing) costs.

These costs are not "money down a rathole," but are expended in exchange for valuable transactions services. In a modern economy, the transactions industry is quite massive. It includes sales personnel and their support staffs back at the office, agents of all kinds, attorneys, the police and judicial systems, and the large and growing private-sector enforcement system, which includes everyone from the mundane night watchman to the glamorous "private eye." If one thinks about it, one concludes that almost everyone who wears business dress to work and a good many others are employed in the transactions industry. It is clearly no minor industry, and transactions costs are clearly no trivial expense.

Accordingly, the definition of nonattenuated property rights provided above is clearly an ideal, and is strictly correct only if transactions services are costless. In a more realistic economic model, Pareto-efficiency is achieved if, in addition to all the other necessary and sufficient conditions, investment in specification, transfer, and enforcement of property rights proceeds to the point at which the marginal conditions for efficiency are satisfied.

PROPERTY RIGHTS AND THE NONUNIQUENESS OF PARETO-EFFICIENCY

Remember the grand utility frontier. It is the locus of all of the attainable solutions to the general economic problem that are Pareto-efficient. Each Pareto-efficient solution is associated with a different distribution of utility or, loosely, income. Conversely, the Pareto-efficient solution is unique only if the distribution of income is first specified. In the simple two-dimensional formulations used in Chapter 6, income was used as a surrogate for the multifaceted concept of economic well-being. One very significant facet of economic well-being is the rights the individual enjoys: rights associated with property objects, and other kinds of rights.

To say that, for efficiency, property rights must be nonattenuated does not, in and of itself, tell us everything we need to know about property rights. One can conceive of many different sets of rights with respect to a particular kind of property object, all of which are exclusive, transferable, and enforced, but each of which is specified differently from the others. The polluter may have unrestricted access to the environment for use in waste disposal; or, the receptor may have the right to insist that polluting emissions be restricted to zero. Alternatively, it is possible to consider intermediate specifications: for example, the polluter may release x tons of effluent annually, while the receptor is entitled to insist that no more than x tons be released.

It is perfectly possible that nonattenuated rights with either extreme specification, or any one of the multitude of possible intermediate specifications, could be established. Any one of these possible specifications of nonattenuated rights would lead to efficiency, but the efficient solution would be different for each different specification of rights. The idea that efficiency is nonunique, and that a unique efficient solution can be defined only by prior specification of the distribution of income (cf. Chapter 6), may now be extended. Efficiency is nonunique, and a unique Pareto-efficient solution may be identified only by prior specification of the distribution of income, wealth, and legal rights, which include property rights.

Conservative Reinforcement

Each different specification of nonattenuated property rights gives rise to a different Pareto-efficient solution. Each different Pareto-efficient solution involves different resource allocation, commodity distribution, and price ratios (Chapter 6). So, prices themselves are functions of property rights. More specifically, the prices that are efficient under one specific nonattenuated specification of property rights would be inefficient under a different specification of property rights.

The interrelationship between property rights and prices has an important implication for empirical economic analysis of the impacts of alternative specifications of rights. If the output generated under (nonattenuated) property-right specification A were valued according to its own efficient prices, it would be found to be an efficient bundle of output. Similarly, if the output generated under property-right specification B were evaluated according to its own efficient prices, it would be found to be efficient. However, if the output generated under property-right specification A were valued according to the prices that would be efficient under specification B, and vice versa, both bundles of output would be found to be inefficient.

The same general idea remains true when, as is usually the case, neither property-right specification A nor B is perfectly nonattenuated. To value the output generated under specification A using prices relevant to specification B, and vice versa, would introduce a downward bias into the resulting estimates of the value of social product.

Unfortunately, this problem arises, more often than not, in empirical research that attempts to predict the economic outcome of potential changes in the specification of property rights. The output under the existing specification of rights and the output under the proposed specification are both valued using existing, observed prices. Yet, those prices themselves were generated under the existing structure of property rights. This analytical practice necessarily introduces a bias into the analysis, and the bias is necessarily in favor of the existing specification of property rights. This bias has been called *conservative reinforcement,* because it tends to reinforce the existing situation.[4] The proposed specification of rights is clearly handicapped by any evaluation procedure that values the output generated under both the existing and the proposed structure of rights according to prices pertinent to the existing structure. Whenever customary techniques of empirical economic analysis are used to predict the economic impacts of institutional change, the danger exists that conservative reinforcement may be introduced into the evaluation process.

PROPERTY RIGHTS AND INSTITUTIONS

The discussion of property rights, to this point, has emphasized efficiency aspects. We have seen that any specification of property rights, so long as rights are nonattenuated, may lead to the attainment of an efficient solution. Yet, different specifications of rights will lead to efficient solutions that differ, perhaps quite radically, in the resultant distribution of economic well-being.

This kind of discussion is valid, and serves a useful purpose in the discussion of economic policy. On the one hand, it suggests that, if Pareto-efficiency alone is all that is desired, the role of government in economic affairs may be largely confined to the specification of a nonattenuated set of property rights. On the other hand, it suggests that a government, which seeks the attainment of economic efficiency and of certain specific goals with respect to the distribution of economic well-being, may seek to specify nonattenuated property rights, while manipulating the precise specification of those rights in order to achieve its distributional goals. Nevertheless, this kind of discussion, in and of itself, can be quite misleading. It fails to recognize the role of property rights within the total institutional structure, and the role of institutions, broadly conceived, in a dynamic society.

Institutions are the "going concerns" (to use a phrase made famous by the late John R. Commons[5]) which order the relationships among individuals within society. Institutions include laws, constitutions (which have been called "laws about making laws"), traditions, moral and ethical strictures, and "customary and accepted ways of doing things." The market, as idealized by economic theorists or as implemented in the practice of commerce, is itself an institution. Institutions, of one kind or another, direct, control, restrain, or, at least, influence almost every activity and almost every interpersonal relationship in a complex modern society. Time and time again, anthropologists have marveled at the complexity of the elaborate institutional structures that exist in technologically primitive societies. The alternative to a complex institutional structure in primitive and modern societies, it seems, is anarchy.

Institutions restrict individual freedom by limiting the harm an individual can impose on others. By the same token, institutions enhance the freedom of individuals by ensuring them of protection from the harm that others may do them. Institutions define the "rules of the game" and, by so doing, help to define the structure of incentives facing individuals.

Institutions also work to ensure their own continuity, through the conscious and unconscious shaping of the thought patterns and ethical systems of each new generation.

In the long run, social change is inevitable. Patterns of scarcity change, technological progress changes the opportunities confronting individual and societies, and demands change, as populations grow or decline and individual tastes and preferences are modified. In this broad process of change, institutions play a crucial but delicate role. They must accommodate change. However, they must restrict the rate of change and preclude changes thought to be thoroughly undesirable. Orderly social and economic interaction requires an environment of considerable stability. Life and comfort are precarious when all things are negotiable. Thus, the institutional structure must resist change, placing barriers in the way of all change so that only those proposals for change that have substantial support can be implemented. On the other hand, institutional structures that are entirely rigid are eventually doomed. When the pressures for change become massive, the alternative to peaceful change is bloody revolution.

The institutional structure is inextricably intertwined with the moral and ethical system of society. Institutions that are consistent with the moral and ethical values of the society in which they exist will be relatively easy to enforce: compliance will be substantially voluntary. On the other hand, institutions that are at variance with the value system of the society will experience little voluntary compliance, and may be enforced only with substantial effort. Even with regard to the relationship between institutions and value systems, we encounter the inevitable tension between adaptability and stability. Institutions shape, and are shaped by, moral and ethical value systems.

Property rights are just one facet of a total institutional framework. This places very significant restrictions on the manipulation of property rights for social and economic policy purposes. While any specification of nonattenuated property rights may lead to efficiency, many possible specifications will be at variance with the moral and ethical value system of society. These specifications are simply not realistic policy options. Further, all societies have chosen, for their own unfathomable reasons, to classify some things as simply inappropriate for exclusive ownership and unrestricted trade. Thus, the establishment of a completely nonattenuated set of property rights, essential for the achievement of Pareto-efficiency, is itself at variance with the moral and ethical value system of any society.

For this reason, the wise and pragmatic resource economist will recognize the limits to what can be attained through manipulation of property rights and the specification of nonattenuated property rights. There will be some problems for which workable, if not Pareto-efficient, solutions may best be achieved with some other kind of institutional structure. It is well to realize that nonattenuated property rights and *res nullius* are not the only two possible structures of rights. Instead, they represent the extremes on a continuum of possible structures. In many societies, and for many different problems, some variation of *res communis* (property held in common), often with quite elaborate rules relating individual contributions to individual rewards, provides a workable, if not Pareto-efficient, institutional framework that has the distinct advantage of compatibility with the social value system.[6]

QUESTIONS FOR DISCUSSION

1. "Everybody's property is nobody's property." Evaluate this statement critically.
2. "The air pollution problem could be solved by simply specifying exclusive rights to air." Do you agree?
3. Why are there oyster farms, but no salmon farms?
4. "To say that, for efficiency, property rights must be nonattenuated does not, in and of itself, tell us everything we need to know about property rights." Explain, and expand upon, this statement.
5. "Institutions must accommodate change, while restricting the rate of change." Does this seemingly contradictory statement make sense?

FURTHER READINGS

Cheung, S. 1970. "The Structure of a Contract and the Theory of a Nonexclusive Resource," *Journal of Law and Economics.* 13: 49-70.
Ciriacy-Wantrup, S. V., and Richard C. Bishop. 1975. " 'Common Property' as a Concept in Natural Resources Policy," *Natural Resources Journal.* 15: 713-729.
Furubotn, Eirik, and Svetozar Pejovich. 1972. "Property Rights and Economic Theory: A Survey of Recent Literature," *Journal of Economic Literature.* 10: 1137-1162.
Randall, A. 1975. "Property Rights and Social Micro-economics," *Natural Resources Journal.* 15: 729-738.
Randall, A. 1978. "Property Institutions and Economic Behavior," *Journal of Economic Issues.* 12: 1-21.

ENDNOTES

1. Arrow, Kenneth J. 1951. "An Extension of the Basic Theorems of Classical Welfare Economics," in *Proceedings of the Second Berkeley Symposium on Mathematical Statistics and Probability.* J. Neyman (ed.). Berkeley: University of California Press. 507-532.

2. See Cheung, S. 1970. "The Structure of a Contract and the Theory of a Non-Exclusive Resource," *Journal of Law and Economics.* 13: 49-70.
3. For example, Thomas D. Crocker. See his 1971 "Externalities, Property Rights, and Transactions Costs: an Empirical Study," *Journal of Law and Economics,* 14: 451-464.
4. See Samuels, W. J. 1972. "Welfare Economics, Power and Property," in *Perspectives of Property.* Wunderlich and Gibson (ed.). University Park: The Pennsylvania State University. (Parts I, II and III.)
5. Commons, John R. 1924. *Legal Foundations of Capitalism.* Madison: The University of Wisconsin Press.
6. See Ciriacy-Wantrup, S. V., and Richard C. Bishop. 1975. " 'Common Property' as a Concept in Natural Resources Policy," *Natural Resources Journal.* 15: 713-729.

8

Sources of Inefficiency

The economic arena is one of conflict. Given that resources are scarce, that production possibilities are limited by technology, and that individuals are both selfish and insatiable, how could it be anything else? In Chapters 5 through 7, there is developed a view of markets as incredibly effective devices for conflict resolution. If the structure of rights is hospitable to the fullest development of markets (i.e., is nonattenuated), markets establish prices that provide incentives for production, generate personal incomes, ration commodities among consumers, and provide a continuous flow of information about relative scarcity. In this way, markets allocate resources and distribute commodities, without the need for external direction, in a manner that ensures globally efficient outcomes from the independent decisions of self-motivated individuals. The market derives its effectiveness from nonattenuated property rights, and performs its functions through the instrumentality of efficient relative prices.

As is well known, not all individuals and societies see markets in such a favorable light. Many are frankly alarmed by the instabilities, myopia, and perceived waste and distributive injustice generated by uncontrolled markets.[1] Some would counsel the abandonment of the market mechanism and its replacement with other conflict-resolution institutions, which are typically promoted as "more humane."

This chapter is not addressed to those concerns. Instead, the fundamental efficacy of markets as devices to direct the allocation of resources is accepted. This chapter undertakes a much more limited inquiry: to explore the existence and nature of what has been called "market failure" or, more charitably, "market imperfection." It will be seen that there are circumstances in which the outcomes of free markets are inefficient. Not surprisingly, these circumstances typically involve the attenuation of property rights and/or fundamental inefficiencies in pricing.

155

In this chapter, we develop economic analyses that are especially pertinent to many natural resource and environmental economics problems. The formal analyses of externality, indivisibility in consumption, and nonexclusiveness are essential to an understanding of the air- and water-pollution problems. In the course of these analyses, the relationship between pollution and prices is elucidated, the potential for solutions through trade is evaluated, and the effectiveness of regulatory approaches, emissions taxes and marketable pollution rights is discussed in some detail.

The analyses of indivisibility in consumption and nonexclusiveness are also pertinent to many other problems in natural-resource allocation: for example, the management of fish and wildlife populations, the maintenance of the scenic beauty of outdoor environments and the diversity of natural environments, the management of public lands, the exploitation of oil and groundwater pools, and the provision of natural resource services and environmental amenities by public-sector agencies. In these contexts, the economic analyses of provision of services, pricing, and rationing among users help identify possible solutions to the inefficiencies and waste that arise.

The analyses of congestible public goods and "natural monopoly" are pertinent to the provision of outdoor recreation facilities, roads and bridges, and public utilities (e.g., water, telephone service, electricity, and natural gas).

The logic of economics is helpful in understanding why imperfections in the markets for these goods, services, and amenities occur, and in predicting the consequences of these imperfections. It is helpful also in suggesting possible solutions, and in predicting the responses of individuals and firms to those solutions, if implemented. In that way, alternatives can be evaluated, with a degree of reliability, prior to implementation. In some cases, there is no entirely satisfactory solution; but, even in these cases, economic logic can help us understand why no perfect solution exists, and can assist us in identifying the most effective of the various available imperfect solutions.

EXTERNALITY

A nonattenuated structure of rights, being exclusive, brings the rewards and penalties — or, if you prefer, the benefits and costs — of any action to bear upon the actor. However, in the real world we observe actions that are taken not because the benefits from the action exceed the total costs, but because the actor finds it possible to impose some or all of the costs upon others. In such a circumstance, the action will be taken whenever the total benefits to the actor exceed whatever proportion of the total costs he must bear. Pollution occurs, not necessarily because the total benefits of waste disposal into the environment exceed the total costs, but because the benefits of such waste disposal exceed the costs that are borne by the polluter. Pollution is just one member of a general class of phenomena called *externality,* a rather cumbersome term that denotes the inefficiencies that arise when some of the benefits or costs of an action are external to the decision maker's calculus; that is, some of the benefits accrue to, or some of the costs are imposed upon, individuals who play no part in the decision.

An externality[2] is said to exist whenever:

$$U_j = U_j(X_{1j}, X_{2j}, ..., X_{nj}, X_{mk}), j \neq k$$

where X_i $(i = 1, 2, ..., n, m)$ refer to activities, and j and k refer to individuals.

That is, an externality is said to exist whenever the welfare of some individual j is affected by those activities under his control, but also by some activity, X_{mk}, which is under the control of somebody else, k. Externality is obviously a very broad concept, referring to any situation in which the utility of one individual is influenced by an activity under the control of another. If one thinks about it a little, it becomes apparent that almost any activity involves externality. Clearly, if externality is to be an analytically useful concept, it must be defined more precisely.

A *relevant externality* exists whenever the *affected party, j,* has a desire to induce the *acting party, k,* to modify his behavior with respect to the activity X_{mk}. An externality becomes relevant whenever the affected party is not indifferent to it. Thus, the class of activities that may be called relevant externalities remains huge. For example, any activity which changes the pattern of relative scarcity and thus changes prices facing an individual could be called a relevant externality to that individual. But the ability of markets to adjust prices to reflect changing relative scarcity does not cause inefficiency; instead, it is useful precisely because it permits efficiency. A concept of externality that focuses upon inefficient externalities is necessary.

A *Pareto-relevant externality* exists when it is possible to modify the activity, X_{mk}, in such a way so as to make the affected party, j, better-off without making the acting party, k, worse-off. When a Pareto-relevant externality exists, there is the unrealized potential for a Pareto-improvement. Thus, Pareto-relevant externalities can exist only when the economy is not Pareto-efficient. Finally, we have a definition of externality that focuses on externalities that result in inefficiency. From now on, we shall, unless it is explicitly stated otherwise, use the term externality to mean Pareto-relevant externality.

THE ALLOCATIVE EFFECTS OF EXTERNALITY

It is useful to distinguish two types of Pareto-relevant externality.

An *external diseconomy* exists when the affected party, *j*, is made worse-off by activity X_{mk}, and has a desire to induce the acting party, *k*, to reduce the level of that activity. The external diseconomy is Pareto-relevant if it is possible to reduce the level of the activity X_{mk} in such a way as to make at least one party better-off and no party worse-off. Examples of external diseconomies include polluting emissions and effluents from industrial processes, non-point pollution from construction sites and farming operations, polluting emissions from consumption activities (e.g., automobile-exhaust emissions, and tobacco smoke), and any activity that imposes noise, ugliness, or other offensive impacts on affected parties.

An *external economy* is an externality in which the affected party, *j*, is made better-off by the activity X_{mk}, and therefore has a desire to induce the acting party, *k*, to increase his level of that activity. A Pareto-relevant external economy exists when it is possible to increase the level of the activity, X_{mk}, in such a way so as to make at least one party better-off while making no one worse-off. External economies may occur when, for example, one firm invents a new product or an improved production process, which is then available for other firms to use free of charge; when one firm provides specialized job training for its employees, who are then free to enter the employment of other firms who did not bear the expense of job training; when individuals who have themselves immunized against a contagious disease not only protect themselves but also protect others by reducing the probability of an epidemic; when individuals, by investing in their own education, also contribute to the creation of a more civilized society, which benefits everyone; and when an individual who invests in the beautification of his own property raises the value of neighboring property and provides pleasure for passers-by.

The economic analyses that follow concentrate, for the most part, upon external diseconomies. However, that should provide no problem for the reader who has a special interest in external economies. Everything that applies to external diseconomies applies also to external economies, but with the sign changed. One needs simply to refer to the definitions: an external diseconomy reduces the welfare of the affected party, who would prefer a reduction in the level of the external diseconomy; an external economy increases the welfare of the affected party, who would prefer an increase in its level.

Price Effects of Externality

Consider a simple Pareto-relevant external diseconomy in consumption. The utility of the individual *j* is affected by a vector of activities under his control, $X_{1j},...,X_{nj}$, but also by the activity X_{mk}, which is not under his control. Since it is an external diseconomy, the individual's marginal utility for increments in X_{mk} is negative.

The individual's budget constraint is:

$$Y_j - \sum_1^n p_i X_{ij}, \qquad i = 1,...,n$$
$$i \neq m$$

where Y_j = the income of j

P_i = price of i

Since j is unable to influence the level of the activity X_{mk}, that activity does not appear in his budget constraint; and the price, to him, of its effect upon him (i.e., $f[X_{mk}]$) is effectively zero.

If the individual j maximizes his utility subject to his budget constraint, the first-order conditions for a maximum are that the RCS between any two consumption activities is equal to the ratio of the prices of those activities. For any pair of activities in $X_{1j},...X_{nj}$, this condition causes no problem: the marginal utility from each of these consumption activities is positive, as is the price of each activity. However, a problem arises with respect to the RCS between any activity, X_{ij} and the external diseconomy, $f(X_{mk})$. Since the marginal utility from X_{ij} is positive while marginal utility from $f(X_{mk})$ is negative, and since the price, p_i is positive, the condition for efficiency in consumption,

$$RCS_{X_{ij},f(X_{mk})} = \frac{p_i}{p_{f(X_{mk})}},$$

can be satisfied only if the price of $f(X_{mk})$ facing the individual j is negative. However, that price is zero. Thus, the efficiency condition is violated.

Pareto-relevant externalities are simply manifestations of inefficient pricing. Efficiency can be achieved, where a Pareto-relevant externality exists, only if the correct price, negative for a diseconomy or positive for an economy, is placed on the externality.

If the price of the externality, $f(X_{mk})$, were not zero but, rather, an efficient negative price, that price would influence the behavior of both the affected party and the acting party. The affected party would have an incentive to tolerate the activity, X_{mk}, since his income (i.e., the budget that he has available for purchase of other goods and services) would rise as the level of the activity, X_{mk}, increases. The acting party would have an incentive to reduce the level of the activity, X_{mk}, since his income would fall as the level of the external diseconomy, $f(X_{mk})$, rises. Observe that these price incentives are simply the opposite of the incentives that positive prices introduce into the markets for typical commodities: positive prices induce the consumer to economize on his purchases, and the producer to supply the commodity. Thus, the efficient negative price for an external diseconomy results in the treatment of that diseconomy as if it were a simple discommodity (i.e., anything that provides negative utility for the consumer, who would be willing to pay positive amounts to get rid of it). Conversely, the efficient positive price for an external economy would result in its being treated just like any other commodity.

The Resource-Allocation Effects of Externality

Assume there is a Pareto-relevant externality associated with the activity, X_{mk}, such that $f(X_{mk})$ is priced at zero. Now, we examine the allocative effects of this externality, for a variety of pertinent situations: the cases of external diseconomies and economies, and the cases of externality in production and in consumption.

Consider the production of electricity using coal-burning steam electric generators, a process that results in the external diseconomy of air pollution. Each firm creates wastes in its production process, and uses the air resource for waste disposal; thus, the air resource is serving as an unpaid input into the production process for electricity. Under these conditions, the price of electricity is P_e, and the quantity of electricity is Q_e (Figure 8.1).

Now, assume that the correct negative price were placed on the air pollution, thus requiring the firm to pay the efficient price for the use of the air resource in waste disposal. This would increase the costs of producing electricity, and thus would shift the supply curve of electricity to the left. Given the new supply curve, S_e^*, the price of electricity would be P_e^* and the equilibrium quantity of electricity would be Q_e^*. This is a quite general conclusion, which can be stated as follows: when a Pareto-relevant external diseconomy in production exists, the price of the product associated with the external diseconomy will be too low, and its output will be too great.

This permits an interesting insight into the idea, which is in common circulation, that pollution controls tend to restrict production and raise prices. In general, that is true; however, the restricted production is the efficient amount and the higher price is the efficient price. Efficient pollution controls reduce production and raise prices only because, in their absence, prices are inefficiently low, output is inefficiently large, and an inefficiently large quantity of pollution is released.

The analysis of an external economy in production is logically similar. Consider a production process in which two outputs — for example, communications services and new technology — are produced, only the first-mentioned of which is priced. Under these conditions, the equilibrium output of communications services is Q_c and the equilibrium price is P_c. If the efficient positive price were placed upon the new technology jointly produced with communications services, the supply curve of communications services would be S_c^*, which lies to the right of S_c (Figure 8.2). The equilibrium price would be P_c^* and the equilibrium quantity would be Q_c^*. In general, if a Pareto-relevant external economy in production exists, the price of

FIGURE 8.1
Allocative Impact of External Diseconomy

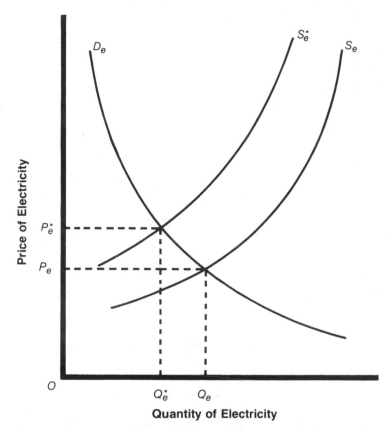

the commodity produced jointly with the external economy will be too high, and its output too small.

Externality in consumption has a similar allocative result. If polluting emissions from automobiles were unpriced, that Pareto-relevant external diseconomy in consumption would result in the cost to the consumer of automobile travel being too low and the quantity of automobile travel services used being too high, compared with efficient prices and quantities. Similarly, if individuals who improve the external appearance of their property, by so doing, create unpriced benefits for others, the cost of beautification to the property owner will be too high and the amount of such beautification will be too low, relative to the efficient levels.

EXTERNALITY AND PROPERTY RIGHTS

Pareto-relevant externality, being inefficient, is symptomatic of the attenuation of property rights. For example, where the air may

FIGURE 8.2
Allocative Impact of External Economy

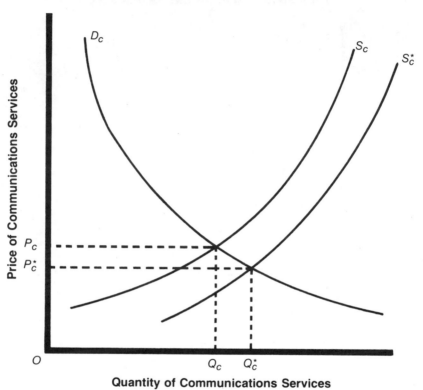

Quantity of Communications Services

be polluted at will, the situation is tantamount to *res nullius*. Individual, exclusive property rights to ambient air cannot be effectively specified or enforced. The air is nobody's property, and no individual bears a direct cost for using it for waste disposal, nor does any individual gain a direct benefit from restraining his air-polluting activities.

The Pareto-relevant external economy that occurred when communications services were produced jointly with new technology is also a result of incompletely specified and nonexclusive property rights. It may be remedied, to a considerable extent, by the legal device of patents, which provide the inventor with property rights in his discoveries.

INSTITUTIONAL SOLUTIONS TO EXTERNALITY PROBLEMS

We have seen that a Pareto-relevant external diseconomy is an inefficient situation that can be remedied if an efficient negative price is placed upon the externality. For a simple externality involving only two parties, the requirement of a negative price could be satisfied in either of two ways. The acting party could pay compensation to the affected party, the amount of compensation increasing as the level of the external diseconomy increases. Alternatively, the affected party could bribe the acting party to reduce the level of the external diseconomy. A positive price for *reductions* in the level of the external diseconomy is equivalent to a negative price for the external diseconomy itself.

Under what circumstances might one expect to find acting parties offering to pay compensation to affected parties? The right to create external diseconomies may be valuable to acting parties. If that right is not otherwise available to them, acting parties may offer to buy it. Thus, when affected parties are entitled to insist that uncompensated external diseconomies be reduced to zero, acting parties may have an incentive to offer compensation in exchange for permission to create some positive level of diseconomy.

Similarly, an affected party would bribe the acting party to reduce the level of external diseconomy, only if: (1) he has no right to force the acting party to desist; (2) at the margin, he is willing to pay for a reduction in the diseconomy; and (3) he is assured that, by paying the bribe, he is actually buying a guarantee of relief from the external diseconomy.

Given that the external diseconomy imposes disutility on the affected party, and that a reduction in the level of the external diseconomy would impose disutility on the acting party, a nonattenuated set of property rights is all that is needed to encourage trade between the involved parties, thus establishing an efficient negative price for the external diseconomy. But who will offer a payment to whom? The party disadvantaged by the specification of rights is the one who will offer payment.

The Coasian Market Solution

Consider a simple Pareto-relevant external diseconomy, involving two parties, one acting and one affected, in a legal environment of nonattenuated rights. Assume that transactions costs are zero, and that there are no income effects. Under these rather idealized circumstances, we now examine the market for abatement of the external diseconomy.

Figure 8.3 is a quite typical market equilibrium diagram, adapted for use in analyzing the market for abatement of external diseconomies. Since external diseconomies are discommodities, the abatement thereof is a commodity. But abatement is a kind of double negative: that is, the desirable act of reducing an undesirable effect. Thus, abatement cannot proceed beyond the initial level of the external diseconomy. Therefore, the market diagram is bounded on the right by a vertical line intersecting the horizontal axis at the point of complete abatement — i.e., the point where there is zero external diseconomy remaining. The horizontal axis may be read in two ways: from the left to the right, starting at zero abatement and

164

FIGURE 8.3

The Coasian Market Solution, Assuming Zero Transaction Costs and Zero Income Effects

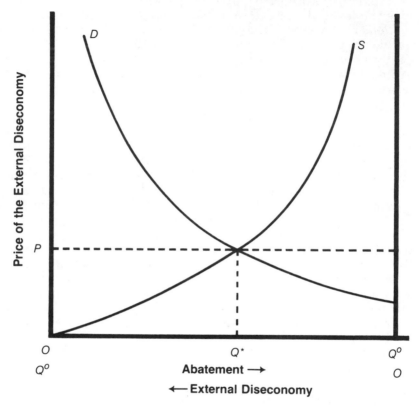

ending at a level of abatement equal to the initial level of external diseconomy, Q°; or from the right to the left, starting at zero external diseconomy and ending at the initial level of the external diseconomy, Q°.

The affected party has a demand for abatement. If he is a consumer, the demand curve reflects the money value of the marginal utility he would obtain from abatement; if a producer, the demand curve reflects the value of the marginal damages to his production process that would be avoided by abatement. It is reasonable to assume that the demand curve for abatement slopes downward and to the right. The acting party has a supply curve for abatement. If he is a producer, the supply curve reflects the incremental production expenses necessary to provide increasing levels of abatement; if a consumer, the supply curve reflects the incremental expense of providing abatement and/or the marginal disutility to the acting party of reducing the level of a pleasurable consumption activity in order to abate the external diseconomies it creates. Since the initial level of the external diseconomy, Q°, is exactly the equilibrium amount when the external diseconomy is unpriced, it is reasonable to expect the supply curve for abatement to pass through the origin and to slope upward to the right.

Consider, first, what would happen under a nonattenuated *full liability rule, L^f*. Such a rule specifies that, on appeal from affected parties, the authorities will enforce a requirement that external diseconomies be limited to zero. This kind of rule is completely specified, enforced, and transferable. Transferability is achieved through the requirement that the affected party's right to relief from external diseconomies will be enforced only on appeal by the affected party. The authorities would permit the creation of external diseconomies in the absence of such appeal. Herein lies the possibility of trade.

Imagine the following scenario. Upon perceiving the presence of an external diseconomy, the affected party notifies the acting party that he intends to appeal to the authorities for enforcement of the L^f rule. Since the L^f rule would surely be enforced upon appeal, resulting in complete abatement at substantial cost to the acting party, the acting party offers compensation in the hope of inducing the affected party to accept some positive level of external diseconomy. For any given level of external diseconomy, the acting party would be willing to offer compensation as great as his supply price for abatement, but no greater. The affected party would be willing to accept compensation as low as his demand price for abatement, but no lower. Given the usual perfect-market assumptions, an equilibrium would be reached, in which the amount of abatement provided is Q^*, the amount of external diseconomy remaining is $(Q^\circ - Q^*)$, and an amount of compensation equal to $P(Q^\circ - Q^*)$ is paid by the acting party to the affected party. Note that for amounts of abatement exceeding Q^*, the unit compensation received by the affected party exceeds his demand price for abatement. Thus, he is willing to enter into an agreement under which less than complete abatement is provided. Similarly, the acting party is willing to abate units of externality up to and including Q^* since, for those units, his cost of abatement is less than the compensation the acting party would demand. Under the L^f rule, Q^* is the efficient level of abatement. The marginal costs of providing more abatement exceed the marginal benefits, while the marginal costs of providing less abatement are exceeded by the marginal benefits.

Notice that the efficient abatement of an external diseconomy does not, in general, result in its complete elimination. Some external diseconomy remains. The efficient level of abatement eliminates all Pareto-relevant external diseconomy. The external diseconomy remaining is simply not Pareto-relevant. It would be impossible to further modify the externality in such a way as to make at least one party better-off without making another party worse-off.

Now, consider the nonattenuated *zero liability rule, L^z*. Such a rule states that affected parties have no right to relief from external diseconomies unless they choose to purchase such a right. If the right were purchased, it would be enforced on appeal to the authorities. In the absence of trade between the involved parties, the level of external diseconomy would be Q°, and zero abatement would be provided. The affected party, having no right of relief from the external diseconomy, must tolerate it, or bribe the acting party to reduce the level of external diseconomy. The affected party is able to offer bribes as high as his demand price for abatement, but no higher. The acting party is willing to accept bribes as low as his supply price for abatement, but no lower. Given the usual perfect-market assumptions, an agreement will be reached wherein the level of abatement provided is Q^*, the amount of externality remaining is $(Q^\circ - Q^*)$, and a total bribe equal to $P \cdot Q^*$ is paid to the acting party. This market outcome is efficient, and results in the elimination of all Pareto-relevant externality.

Given nonattenuated property rights, trade between the parties involved in an externality situation will eliminate Pareto-relevant externalities, and result in an efficient situation. Under the assumptions of this simple example, the allocation of resources is independent of the specification of nonattenuated rights. The L^f rule results in the same equilibrium level of abatement as the L^z rule. Only the distribution of income is influenced by the specification of rights. Under L^f, a payment is made by the acting party to the affected party; under L^z, payment is made by the affected party to the acting party. L^f and L^z are, of course, merely the endpoints on a continuum of possible specifications of property rights with respect to external diseconomies. It is quite possible to conceive of intermediate liability rules, which would permit acting parties to create some limited amount of external diseconomy, while enforcing that limit in the event that an affected party should appeal to the authorities on the grounds that the limit has been exceeded.

The above analysis demonstrates the Coase Theorem, which had its origins in the writings of R. H. Coase.[3] That theorem states that given nonattenuated property rights, trade among involved parties will eliminate Pareto-relevant externalities, resulting in an efficient solution. Further, the final allocation of resources will be invariant to the initial specification of property rights.

The Coasian analysis has made a number of important contributions to the understanding of externality and, more generally, of the functioning of markets. It suggests that market phenomena may be more pervasive than was generally recognized, and that market behavior is likely to occur whenever gains from trade exist, even in arenas customarily considered to be outside the market. It has elucidated the concept of property rights, and has led economists to analyze trade in rights, rather than in objects. Since the development of the Coase theorem, economists are much more careful than they once were about using terms such as "market failure" and recommending governmental regulation of market activity as the solution to perceived inefficiency.

On the other hand, there have been some economists who have misused the Coase theorem to falsely conclude that the establishment of a transferable liability law, *any* transferable liability law, is all that governments need do in situations of perceived inefficiency, and that the particular specification of the liability law chosen is unimportant.[4] This kind of logic led some to argue, in a caricature of the Coasian analysis, that there is no need for explicit policies to handle the problem of, say, air pollution because, in the absence of any explicit policy, the L^z law exists and ensures that the efficient amount of air pollution, but no more, will be created. More generally, some have used the Coase theorem to argue that whatever exists must be good since, if it was not good at the outset, subsequent trade would have made it good.

These kinds of arguments are invalid, since they simply take the Coase theorem too far. The efficient patterns of trade suggested by the Coase theorem occur only when property rights are nonattenuated. Yet, the offended receptor of air pollution is unable to purchase an exclusive right to clean air by bribing a polluter to desist: such a bribe would provide no assurance that another potential polluter would not show up, demanding bribes to desist. Without exclusive rights in air quality, efficient allocation of air resources through trade is impossible.

The possibilities that transactions costs may be positive, and in some circumstances quite high, and that income effects may exist suggest a different kind of modification to the Coase theorem. Trade among parties involved in an externality situation has an efficient outcome, but non-zero transactions costs and income effects have the result that the particular efficient outcome varies with the specification of property rights.[5]

Remember that in the analysis depicted by Figure 8.3 the allocation of resources was not influenced by the specification of property rights, but the resultant distribution of income is so influenced. Under the L^f law, the acting party pays compensation to the affected party, while, under the L^z law, the affected party pays bribes to the acting party. Thus, the specification of property rights influences the budget constraints of the involved parties. Compared with the situation under an L^z law, the budget constraint of the affected party under an L^f law is larger, while the budget constraint of the acting party is smaller. If the demand and supply of abatement of external diseconomies are influenced by the budget constraints of the demander and supplier, income effects will be observed and will be sufficient to shift the demand and supply curves for abatement. The demand curve, D^f, for abatement under the L^f law lies to the right of the demand curve D^z, for abatement under the L^z law. The supply curve S^f, under the L^f law lies to the right of the supply curve, S^z, under the L^z law (Figure 8.4). The result, in general, of non-zero income effects is that the efficient quantity of abatement under the L^f law is greater than the efficient quantity of abatement under the L^z law. The equilibrium bribe or compensation price of

FIGURE 8.4
The Coasian Market Solution: The Effect of Non-Zero Income Effects

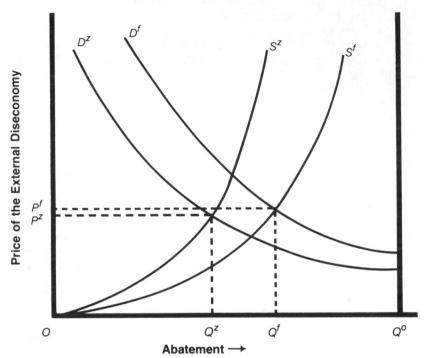

abatement under the L^f law may be higher or lower than under the L^z, depending upon the relative magnitudes of the income elasticities of demand and supply for abatement.

This finding with respect to quantity of abatement is quite general. Under an L^f law the efficient quantity of abatement will be as great as or greater than the quantity of abatement provided under the L^z law; if income effects are positive, the quantity of abatement under the L^f law will be greater.

The Coase theorem pertains to the solution of externality problems through trade, and trade commonly involves positive transactions costs. The effect of positive transactions costs is to reduce the effective value of any offer of payment. The amount paid is equal to the amount received minus the transactions costs. The effect of transactions costs may be illustrated, as in Figure 8.5, under the L^z law by a leftward shift in the demand curve for abatement to D_t^z; and under the L^f law by a rightward shift in the supply curve for abatement to S_t^f. The effect of positive transactions costs is to increase the divergence between the equilibrium quantity of abatement provided under L^z and under L^f. $Q_t^z < Q^z \leqslant Q^f < Q_t^f$.

There is a very simple method of checking on the logic of the

FIGURE 8.5

The Coasian Market Solution: The Effect of Positive Transactions Costs and Non-Zero Income Effects

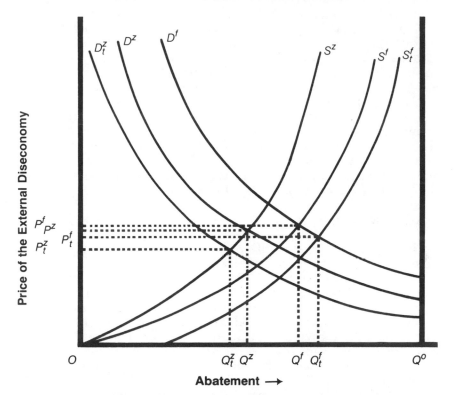

analysis used in Figure 8.5. If transactions costs (i.e., the costs of consummating trade) were larger than the potential gains from that trade, no trade would occur. If no trade occurred, equilibrium resource allocation would be exactly that allocation initially specified by the structure of property rights. Under the L^f law, the affected party has a right to total abatement; when transactions costs are so high as to prohibit trade, total abatement will be the result. Under the L^z law the acting party has a right to pollute as he pleases; when transactions costs are prohibited, zero abatement will be the result.

In the real world, the assumption of positive income effects is more realistic than the assumption of zero income effects, and the assumption of positive transactions costs is more realistic than the assumption of zero transactions costs. Under the more realistic assumptions, the efficient quantity of abatement depends upon the specification of property rights. More generally, the first part of the Coase Theorem (that an efficient solution will be achieved) remains valid, while the second part (that resource allocation is invariant to the specification of rights, provided rights are nonattenuated) does not.

This conclusion ought not to surprise those who have read Chapter 7. It is a quite general conclusion that, within the universe of nonattenuated property rights, the efficient solution varies with the specification of property rights. In general, the efficient quantity of abatement of an external diseconomy will be greater under a specification of property rights that protects affected parties, and less under a specification that protects acting parties.

It is also interesting to observe that the specification of rights determines which externalities are Pareto-relevant. With positive income effects and transactions costs, any externality lying to the right of Q_t^z is Pareto-irrelevant under L^z, while under L^f only externality lying to the right Q_t^f is Pareto-irrelevant. Thus the externalities that are considered Pareto-relevant are determined by the property rights with respect to externality.

Tax-Subsidy Solutions

The Coasian market solution relies upon trade to eliminate the inefficiencies of Pareto-relevant externality, after specification of transferable liability rules. The outcome of this trade generates efficient price ratios. Another approach to the problem of external-ity, associated with the early-twentieth-century economist A. C. Pigou, directly attacks the problem of distorted price ratios.[6] Under this approach, a government agency would calculate the efficient price ratios between $f(X_{mk})$ and all other activities, and would effectuate the calculated efficient price ratios by tinkering with the price of the externality associated with X_{mk}.

In a Pareto-relevant external diseconomy situation, a negative price would be placed by a government agency upon the external diseconomy. This could be achieved in either of two ways. Taxes could be levied upon the acting party in direct proportion to the amount of external diseconomy he creates. Alternatively, the baseline level of external diseconomy (usually, the equilibrium amount of external diseconomy when its price is zero) could be calculated and the agency could subsidize the acting party for reductions in the level of external diseconomy. The analytical differences between the tax and subsidy approaches are analogous to the differences between Coasian solutions under the L^f and L^z laws.

Consider a very simple case of a pollution tax. A straight-line tax is levied on polluting emissions. That is, the same tax is levied on each unit of emissions, regardless of the level of total emissions. The equilibrium quantity of emissions is determined by the intersection of the tax line and the supply curve for abatement (Figure 8.6).

Note that the demand curve for abatement is presented as a broken line. This is done for two reasons: (1) because the demand

FIGURE 8.6
The Pigovian Tax Solution

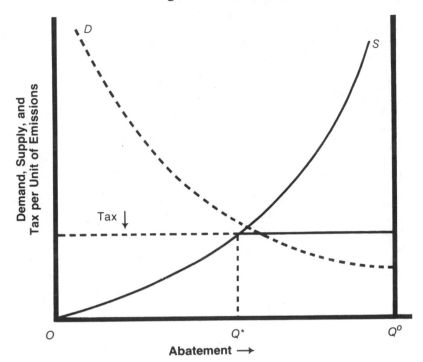

curve is ineffective, while the tax line is effective; and (2) because in the absence of nonattenuated property rights the demand curve cannot be observed, but must be estimated.

A government agency whose prime goal is economic efficiency will use all the information and expertise at its command in an attempt to set the tax such that the tax line passes through the intersection of the supply curve and the demand curve. In Figure 8.6, the tax line crosses the supply curve for abatement at a point slightly lower than the intersection between supply and demand, with the result that the equilibrium level of abatement is slightly less than the level indicated by the intersection of supply and demand. The tax line was deliberately drawn so that it failed to pass through the exact point of intersection between supply and demand. This is intended to emphasize that government agencies, facing both conceptual and empirical difficulties, are unlikely to achieve a perfectly efficient tax rate. However, it is not significant that the tax line intersects the supply curve at a point below the intersection of supply and demand; it could just as easily have intersected the supply curve at some point above the supply-demand intersection.

Given the emissions-tax rate suggested in Figure 8.6, the equilibrium level of abatement is Q^*, and a total tax equal to the tax rate multiplied by $(Q^\circ - Q^*)$ is collected. The total resource cost of obtaining abatement is the area below that segment of the supply curve for abatement that lies between zero and Q^*. However, the total expense imposed upon the industry by the pollution-tax program is equal to the total resource cost plus the total tax collected.

This kind of Pigovian tax solution uses the power of government to institutionalize a negative price for an external diseconomy. However, it leaves substantial discretion to the private sector. Each polluting firm or consumer is free to determine how best to minimize the cost imposed. Each may determine and implement the least-cost method of pollution abatement, and each may choose how much abatement to provide, subject always to the constraint that taxes must be paid for unabated pollution. These taxes provide a continuing incentive for improved abatement performance — for example, through the implementation of cost-reducing abatement technology.

In the real world, there are relatively few instances where governments have implemented the rather straightforward Pigovian solution illustrated in Figure 8.6. However, variants of the tax-subsidy idea have been tried in various places. Unfortunately, not all tax-subsidy variants have the desirable economic characteristics of the Pigovian solution. For example, policies that subsidize the use of particular pollution-control devices, directly or through special tax deductions or investment credits, are considerably less efficient. By identifying particular pollution-abatement inputs for favored tax-subsidy treatment, the market in abatement inputs is distorted and innovation of substitute inputs that are not similarly favored is discouraged.

Regulation

An alternative approach to the problem of external diseconomy is to directly regulate the quantity of external diseconomy that is permitted. For each polluting firm and consumer, a government agency will determine the maximum permissible external diseconomy. In the case of air pollution, this kind of regulation is called an emissions standard; for water pollution, it is an effluent standard. The standard may be represented by a vertical line, as in Figure 8.7. The standard indicates that the level of abatement Q^s must be provided, or the polluter will be considered in violation. Notice that there is no incentive for abatement beyond that required by the standard. The amount of pollution $(Q^\circ - Q^s)$ is permitted without charge or penalty. This is a crucial difference between a regulatory solution and the Pigovian emissions tax; in the case of the tax, all unabated emissions are taxed. On the other hand, with a regulatory approach, there is no incentive for abatement beyond that required by the standard.

Is there any assurance that polluters will comply with the standard? If there is no penalty for failure to comply, it is

FIGURE 8.7
An Emissions Standard

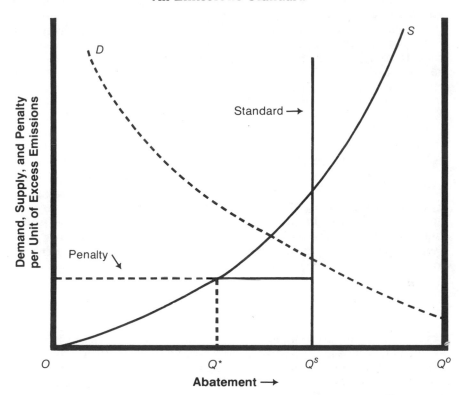

unreasonable to expect compliance. If penalties are prescribed but not enforced, it is equally unreasonable to expect compliance. Thus, the equilibrium level of compliance cannot be determined without consideration of the expected penalties for failure to comply. Penalties may take various forms: lump-sum fines; fines for each day the standard is violated; fines per unit of emissions beyond those permitted under the standard; or, perhaps, jail terms for violators. In Figure 8.7, a straight-line fine per unit of excess emissions is assumed. This kind of penalty is analytically interesting, although it does not appear to be commonly used by regulatory agencies.

The polluter will abate to the point at which the expected penalty line intersects his supply curve for abatement, if that point lies to the left of the standard, or will comply with the standard if the intersection of the expected penalty line and the supply curve lies to the right of the standard. Figure 8.7 shows the most interesting case. The polluter provides abatement to Q^*, pays expected penalties equal to the expected per-unit penalty multiplied by $(Q^s - Q^*)$, and enjoys the privilege of $(Q^o - Q^s)$ emissions without penalty.

In Figure 8.7, the standard is drawn slightly to the right of the intersection of the supply curve for abatement with the broken demand curve for abatement; the expected penalty line is drawn to intersect the supply curve for abatement at a point to the left of the standard; and the equilibrium outcome includes some abatement, the payment of some penalties for emissions, and the emission of some pollutants without penalty. While this is the most interesting case, there is no reason to expect it to be typical. On the other hand, conceptual and empirical difficulties make it unlikely that a regulatory agency could succeed in setting a standard exactly equal to the efficient level of abatement. The setting of the penalty is not conceptually difficult: it simply needs to be so high, and so well enforced, that all polluters will prefer to comply with the standard. However, government agencies have experienced substantial political pressures militating against such effective penalties.

Again, it must be noted that, in the real world, a number of quite different regulatory approaches have been tried. In particular, approaches that regulate not total emissions, but the use of particular pollution-control inputs, are likely to introduce inefficiencies and distortions in the market for pollution-control inputs while discouraging innovations in the kinds of pollution control inputs that are not required by regulation.

Emissions Taxes or Standards — Which Approach is Less Costly?

It is interesting to consider which of the governmental approaches — emissions taxes or standards — provides a given level of abatement at the lowest resource cost. Consider an industry that emits a particular kind of pollutant. For simplicity, the industry will be represented by three firms, which have the supply curves for abatement S_1, S_2, and S_3. Given a straight-line emissions tax, as shown in Figure 8.8, the tax line intersects the supply curve S_1 at point A, and supply curve S_2 at B, and the supply curve S_3 at C. The standard line intersects the supply curve S_1 at point D, S_2 at point B, and S_3 at E. To permit a simple diagrammatic analysis, the supply curves for abatement and the tax and standard lines are drawn so that:

$$Q_1 + Q_2 + Q_3 = 3Q_2, \text{ and}$$
$$Q_3 - Q_2 = Q_2 - Q_1$$

Thus, the industry provides the same total amount of abatement under the standard and the tax. For each firm, under each institutional alternative, the total resource cost of providing abatement is the area under the supply curve of abatement between zero and the level of abatement provided.

The total resource cost of abatement under the emissions tax is subtracted from the cost under the emissions standard as follows:

$$\text{standard:} \quad ODQ_2 + OBQ_2 + OEQ_2$$
$$\text{minus tax:} \quad OAQ_1 + OBQ_2 + OCQ_3$$
$$= DQ_2Q_1A + O - CQ_3Q_2E$$

Since $DQ_2Q_1A > CQ_3Q_2E$, the total resource cost under the emissions tax is less than the total resource cost under the emissions standard, for the same total quantity of abatement. Why would this be? The reason is that the emissions tax encourages the most efficient supplier of abatement, whose supply curve is S_3, to do the lion's share of the abating. The least efficient abater, whose supply curve is S_1, does the least abating.

Although the resource costs of achieving a given level of total abatement are lower with emissions taxes than with emissions standards, we observe that the representatives of polluting industries typically lobby in favor of emissions standards rather than taxes. The reason for this preference on the part of polluters is obvious. Under emissions taxes, the polluter not only meets the cost of providing his equilibrium level of abatement, but also pays the tax on unabated emissions, which amounts to the rectangle $AFQ^\circ Q_1$ for firm 1, $BFQ^\circ Q_2$ for firm 2, and $CFQ^\circ Q_3$ for firm 3. These taxes represent an additional expense to the polluter. However, they may be viewed as compensation to receptors of pollution for that pollution that remains, and receptors may thus consider the taxes perfectly fair.

The analysis in Figure 8.8 demonstrates that emissions taxes achieve a given level of total abatement at a lower resource cost than emissions standards, under conditions of static technology. Remember that emissions taxes have the additional advantage of providing continuing incentives for innovations in pollution abatement, which would reduce both the remaining emissions and the pollution-associated costs faced by the polluter.

Pollution Certificates

An interesting approach to providing incentives for pollution abatement has been proposed by the economist J. H. Dales.[7] The pollution-control agency would determine the total permissible emissions of a given pollutant in a geographic region. If the agency used an efficiency criterion, and had sufficient information at its disposal, it would decide to permit total emissions of $Q_e = Q^\circ - Q_a$ (Figure 8.9a). In the case of air pollution, the permissible total emissions would be determined after consideration of the supply curve for abatement (reductions in emissions), the demand for ambient-air quality, and the physical relationship between emissions and ambient-air quality.

Certificates permitting the exact quantity of total emissions, Q_e, that would result in the attainment of the desired ambient-air

176

FIGURE 8.8

The Resource Cost of Abatement: A Comparison of Emissions Taxes and Standards

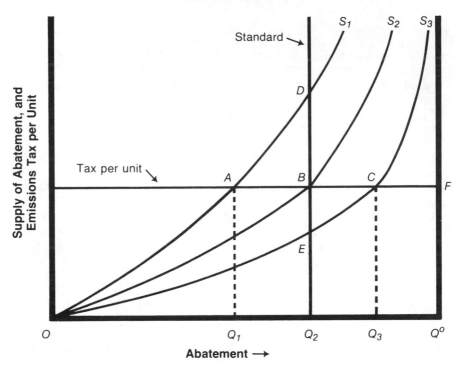

quality would be printed and auctioned to polluters. Each polluter would be permitted to emit pollutants for which he had purchased certificates, but would face prohibitive penalties for excess emissions. The demand curve for certificates, which is the mirror image of the industry's supply curve for abatement, intersects with the government-determined vertical supply line for pollution certificates (Figure 8.9b), determining the price of pollution-emission certificates. The individual polluter responds to the pollution-certificate program as though it were equivalent to a program of straight-line emissions taxes. He provides the level of abatement determined by the intersection of the price line for certificates with his own supply curve for abatement (Figure 8.9c).

The pollution-certificate program has certain advantages which it derives from its use of economic incentives. The initial certificate auction serves both to allocate emissions certificates (i.e., the right to pollute) to the highest-cost abaters, and to generate income for the public sector in much the same way as an emissions tax. This income may be viewed as compensation to the general public for the pollution emitted. In addition, the pollution certificates would be

FIGURE 8.9
A Pollution-Certificate Program

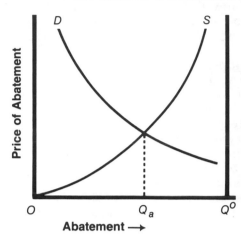

FIGURE 8.9a
Determination of the
Total Number of
Certificates to
Print
(D and S are the total
industry demand and
supply of abatement)

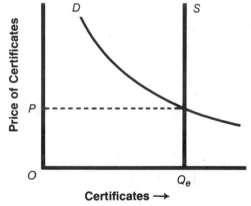

FIGURE 8.9b
Determination of the
Price of Certificates
(D and S are the total
industry demand and
supply of certificates)

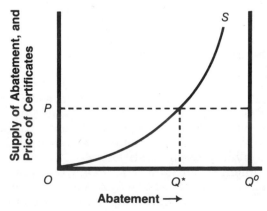

FIGURE 8.9c
Determination of the
Level of Abatement for
the Individual
(S is the individual
supply curve for
abatement)

freely transferable at any time. This would encourage innovation in pollution abatement, since innovators would be rewarded by income from the sale of certificates no longer needed. Further, industrial growth could be accommodated, as new polluters purchased unneeded certificates from established polluters in the region. This would encourage efficient pollution abatement for both new and established polluters.

A full-fledged pollution-certificate program has not yet been established in any governmental jurisdiction of which the author is aware. However, recent air-pollution-control policy of the United States Environmental Protection Agency requires that major new polluting installations (e.g., coal-burning power plants), in regions where ambient air quality is already as bad as will be permitted, may be licensed only if they can demonstrate that the new pollution they generate will be offset by reductions in the emissions of already established firms. The similarity between that policy and certain aspects of a pollution-certificate program is obvious.

Analysis of the pollution-certificate program is useful, since it draws attention to certain important problems that were glossed over in the discussion of emissions taxes and standards. In implementing a program of taxes or standards, it is necessary for the agency first to establish an ambient-air-quality standard, and then to determine the total emissions per unit time that would result in attainment of the ambient-air standard in a given region. If the agency chooses to establish an emissions tax, it must have information concerning the aggregate supply curve for abatement of each pollutant. Without that information, it cannot be reasonably sure that the tax it establishes will result in achievement of the ambient quality standards. If emissions standards are to be used, it is necessary first to determine the relationship between emissions and ambient environmental quality and then to establish an individual emissions standard for each polluter. In a dynamic economy, where polluters are free to move into and out of the region, individual emissions standards must be adjusted from time to time to ensure that the aggregate emissions of all polluters do not result in violation of the ambient environmental quality standards.

An Additional Note on Solutions to Externality Problems

The preceding analyses, while instructive, are highly simplistic. They are for the most part static, whereas the real world is dynamic. They tend to gloss over the massive informational problems that exist, especially with respect to air- and water-pollution externalities, given our ignorance of basic environmental processes, and the vagaries of climatic and hydrological conditions.

The analyses of governmental solutions — for example, emissions taxes, standards, and pollution certificates — ignored the important issue of transactions costs. Yet, common sense and casual observation tell us that the transactions costs borne by individuals, firms, and government agencies will be substantial. Transactions costs will be incurred in establishing specific policies, implementing those policies, and enforcing them. The analyses of both governmental solutions and Coasian solutions tended to gloss over the issue of enforcement. Regardless of the mechanism chosen for solution of externality problems, the solution finally chosen must be enforced. The creation of external diseconomies must be monitored, to determine that each polluter is abiding by the provisions of the solution ultimately agreed upon. Is each providing the level of abatement determined by the market solution, the emission standard, or the number of pollution certificates he holds? Is each paying the tax for remaining emissions, or the penalty for violating a market solution, an emission standard, or a pollution-certificate arrangement?

INDIVISIBILITY IN CONSUMPTION

Consider a good that, once produced, is available to all consumers without rivalry. The total quantity of the good is determined in the production process, but it is not necessary to divide the total output of the good among the various consumers. Each effectively has access to the total quantity of the good. Consumption by one individual does not reduce the amount remaining for other consumers.

Most goods are not like that. The bread and wine of Chapter 6 were perfectly divisible in consumption. The individual 1 was able to consume exactly the total production of each good minus the amount consumed by the individual 2.

However, there are some goods, services and amenities that are indivisible in consumption. And many of these are of vital importance to natural-resource and environmental policy. If ambient air of a given quality is provided, each and every one of us may breathe that air and use it as a visual medium, without effectively reducing the amount of it available for others. If I am viewing an attractive scene alone, the scenic beauty available to me is not diminished by 50 percent when I am joined by another observer. If I obtain utility from the simple knowledge that a previously endangered species, somewhere in the world, is flourishing, the utility I gain is not diminished if others also gain utility from similar knowledge.

Since the necessary and sufficient conditions for Pareto-efficiency were established for private goods (which are strictly divisible and for which there is strict rivalry in consumption), it is not surprising that indivisibility in consumption provides impediments to the achievement of efficiency. For an economy containing two perfectly divisible goods, the summary necessary condition for Pareto-efficiency is:

$$RCS_{Z_1 Z_2} = RPT_{Z_1 . Z_2}$$

for all consumers and all firms. The production of perfectly divisible goods should proceed until:

$$P = MC;$$

that is, until its price is equal to the marginal cost of producing it.

For an economy containing a divisible good, Z_1, and an indivisible good, Z_p, the summary necessary condition for Pareto-efficiency is:

$$\sum_{j=1}^{n} (RCS_{Z_1 . Z_p})_j = RPT_{Z_1 . Z_p} \qquad j = 1,....,n$$

that is, the sum of the rates of commodity substitution for all consumers, j, must be equal to the rate of product transformation for each producer. The efficient total output of an indivisible good is determined by:

$$\sum_{j=1}^{n} MV_j = MC;$$

that is, the money value of utility provided by the marginal unit of the good, summed over all consumers, should be equal to the marginal cost of producing an additional unit of the indivisible good.

PRICING AND RATIONING OF INDIVISIBLE GOODS

Is there any nondiscriminatory pricing system that will result in the efficient production and rationing among consumers of an indivisible good? Consider the *marginal cost of adding an additional consumer* for an indivisible good, once it has been produced. Since consumption is nonrival, the marginal cost of adding an additional consumer is zero. Thus, it would be inefficient to exclude any consumer whose money value for the good is any positive amount. Prices greater than the smallest conceivable positive amount would inefficiently exclude consumers.

The revenue available to the producer of an indivisible good is the price collected from each user summed over all users. If the efficient price to consumers is some infinitesimally small positive amount, it is quite likely that the total revenue to the producer will be insufficient to permit him to recoup the costs of producing the good. Thus, very low positive prices will most likely fail to result in collection of sufficient revenue to cover the costs of providing the good, while higher positive prices will inefficiently exclude potential consumers whose valuation of the good is positive but low. There is no nondiscriminatory pricing system that will permit the achievement of Pareto-efficiency in private-sector production of indivisible goods.

Under certain circumstances, it is possible that an indivisible good may be provided by the private sector. If it is possible to exclude users who do not pay, a private-sector producer of an indivisible good may be able to collect sufficient revenue to provide him the incentive to produce the good. If there is open entry into the industry of producing that good, competition among producers may drive down the price until the total costs of production are equal to total revenue and no pure profits exist. Such a solution is inefficient, because consumers with positive but low valuations of the good are excluded. However, it may well be a second-best solution that permits the private sector to provide the good and ration it among consumers without recourse to price discrimination and without enjoying excessive profits. Unfortunately, open entry into the business of producing an indivisible good is often an unrealistic assumption. In such circumstances, price regulation often replaces open entry as the device to ensure that the producer does not enjoy excessive profits. As is well known, such regulation meets with varying degrees of success, but is seldom completely satisfactory.

The conditions for Pareto-efficiency in an economy that includes indivisible goods can be satisfied only if there is perfectly discriminatory pricing of the indivisible good. Some mechanism must be found to charge each user of the indivisible good the money value of utility he derives from the good. It is nearly impossible for an outsider to objectively determine the money value of the marginal utility each individual derives from consuming the good and, in the absence of a method of objective determination, the individual has obvious incentives to understate his valuation of the good. Therefore, it has generally proven impossible to implement Pareto-efficient, perfectly discriminatory pricing systems for indivisible goods.

Indivisible goods may, of course, be provided by the public sector. The public sector may choose to finance provision of these goods out of general revenues, and make them available to all comers. Alternatively, the public sector may choose, if it is possible to exclude those who do not pay, to charge a nondiscriminatory price for the enjoyment of the indivisible good. Under this latter approach, the public sector has the option of setting the price so that the revenues it receives will exactly recover the cost of providing the good, or at some higher or lower level.

THE "DEMAND" FOR AN INDIVISIBLE GOOD

The total value of the utility any individual obtains from a good that is indivisible in consumption is a function of the quantity of that good which is produced. The total value curves of three individuals for the indivisible good, Z_p, are illustrated in Figure 8.10. The total value curve typically passes through the origin (since the zero level of provision of an indivisible good would have zero value) and has positive but decreasing slope as the level of provision of Z_p increases. One would expect to observe diminishing marginal utility for indivisible goods, just as for divisible goods. It is possible that, at very high levels of provision, marginal utility may become negative and the total value curve may turn downward. To determine the total value, to all actual and potential users of an indivisible good, individual values are summed vertically. Thus the aggregate total value curve for the indivisible good, in a society consisting of three persons, is derived by vertical summation of the three individual total value curves (Figure 8.10).

The concept of a demand curve is not meaningful for an indivisible good. The consumer is not confronted with the choice of how many homogeneous units to purchase at a given unit price. Rather, he must determine his total valuation for each given level of provision of the indivisible good. The total value curve is the locus of total value as the level of provision rises. In order to focus upon the marginal value of increments in the level of provision of an indivisible good, it is possible to derive individual marginal value curves by taking the first derivative of the individual total value curves. Individual marginal value curves may be summed vertically, to derive the aggregate marginal value curve that, for an indivisible good, is analogous to the industry demand curve for a divisible good. This provides the basis for the often used, but rather imprecise, statement "the industry demand for an indivisible good is derived by vertical summation of individual demand curves, whereas the industry demand curve for a divisible good is derived by horizontal summations of the individual demand curves."

The efficient level of provision of an indivisible good, the level at which the sum of the individual marginal valuations is exactly equal to the marginal cost of an increment in the level of provision, is determined by the intersection of the aggregate marginal value curve with the marginal cost curve (Figure 8.11). As indicated above, the efficient level of provision, alone, is insufficient to ensure Pareto-efficiency. Pareto-efficiency will not be achieved unless each individual consumer can be charged an amount equal to his total valuation of the good.

CONGESTIBLE GOODS

There is a class of goods that behave like indivisible goods, as the number of users increases from zero to some positive number that may be quite large. Over this range, additional consumers may be

FIGURE 8.10

Individual and Aggregate Total Value of an Indivisible Good

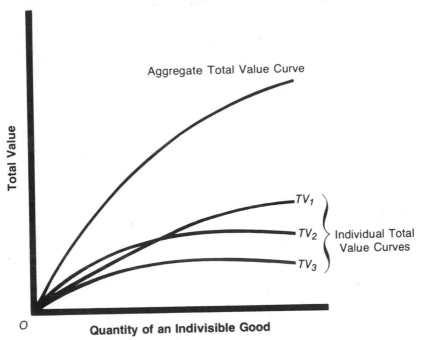

added, without any rivalry. Eventually, however, congestion of users sets in and the addition of more users reduces the utility of all users. For a given level of provision of a congestible good, the marginal cost of adding additional users is zero until congestion sets in; as users are added beyond this range, however, the marginal cost of adding additional users commences to rise. Eventually, the marginal cost of adding additional users approaches infinity, as an absolute capacity constraint is reached (Figure 8.12). Any good that can be enjoyed by many individuals, but subject to a capacity constraint, and for which the fixed cost of provision far exceeds the marginal cost of adding additional users until the capacity constraint is approached, has the characteristics of a congestible good.

Congestible goods include roads, bridges, and almost anything that is provided to the public within walls — e.g., restaurant services, concerts, spectator sports, etc. Many natural and environmental amenities have the characteristics of congestible goods: for example, campgrounds, scenic-view points, hiking trails, hunt areas, and fishing and boating sites.

The basic economic questions with respect to congestible goods are: (1) how should the capacity constraint be determined? and (2) how should access to the congestible good be rationed among

FIGURE 8.11
The Efficient Level of Provision of an Indivisible Good

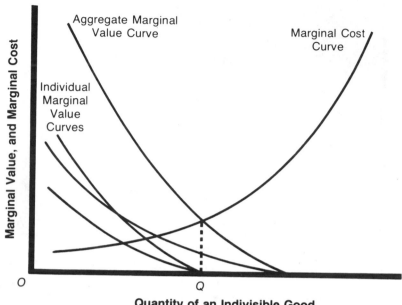

Quantity of an Indivisible Good

individuals? The economists O. A. Davis and A. Whinston address these questions.[8] They consider an economy with one divisible and one congestible good, and solve the following problem: Maximize the sum of the money value of the individuals' utility, subject to (1) a constraint on available resources, (2) the production functions for the divisible and congestible goods, (3) a constraint that no more of the divisible good can be consumed than is available in each time period, and (4) a constraint that no more of the congestible good can be consumed than is available in the first time period.

The solution of this problem permits the following conclusions. (1) Production and consumption of the divisible good can satisfy all the necessary and sufficient conditions for Pareto-efficiency. (2) Pareto-efficiency in provision of the congestible good is impossible, without resort to perfectly discriminatory pricing. (3) A workable second-best solution for provision and pricing of a congestible good has the following characteristics: individuals should consume the congestible good in each time period so that the money value of their marginal utility is equal to $p(t)$, which is the shadow price of access to the congestible good in the time period, t; and, if the net revenue from the congestible good is to be maximized, the capacity should be chosen in the initial period so that:

$$\sum^{T} p(t) \cdot X(t) = MC$$

where there are T total time periods

$X(t)$ = 1, if the marginal unit of capacity (i.e., the last seat in a concert hall) is occupied in time t,

    = 0, if not; and

MC = the marginal costs of increments in the capacity of the congestible good in the initial time period.

All of this implies the following. If the demand for a congestible good is variable over time, while the supply is fixed by a decision in the initial time period, the most appropriate access fee, $p(t)$, may be zero in periods of light use. However, the capacity of the congestible good should not be so large that the capacity constraint is never binding. If the cost of provision of the congestible good is to be covered by revenue raised from access fees, $p(t)$ must be greater than zero in some time periods. If the access fee is to serve as a rationing device, $p(t)$ should be set equal to the marginal cost of adding an additional user during periods of great demand and heavy congestion. Further, if the access fee is to serve the purpose of rationing the congestible good, when demand is variable across time periods, $p(t)$ should be published in advance for each time period, so that users may choose not only how often but also at what times to use the congestible good.

If there is no mechanism for excluding those who do not pay, it is impossible to use varying prices over time to ration the demand, and to generate revenue with which to provide the congestible good. In

FIGURE 8.12

The Marginal Cost of Adding Additional Users of a Congestible Good

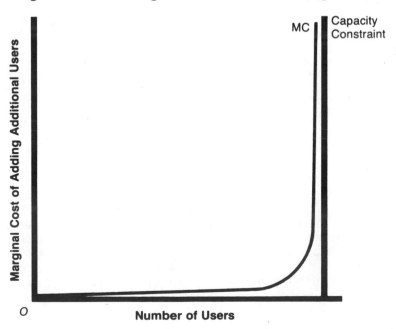

such cases, the congestible good is provided by the public sector using general revenues, by private philanthropy, or not at all. The only effective rationing device is the crowding itself: the disutility from congestion is sufficient to discourage some potential users.

Even where exclusion and, thus, the use of access fees to ration the congestible good is feasible, public agencies may choose to provide congestible goods, using general revenues and setting $p(t)$ equal to zero or to some amount much lower than the market would bear during periods of high demand. The typical result of such a policy is that time in queue and tolerance for inconvenience are partly or totally substituted for price, as rationing devices.

Where price is used to ration congestible goods and to generate revenues for their provision, one or another variation of the pricing strategy wherein $p(t)$ varies across time periods is often observed. Public-transportation facilities may offer reduced charges during off-peak hours. The authorities that operate toll roads and bridges could, if they chose, follow a similar policy. However, it seems that they rarely do. In many parts of the world, publicly or privately owned electric utilities offer time-variable charges; utility regulatory commissions in the United States are currently encouraging such pricing strategies. Vacation resorts often offer off-season rates. But perhaps the best example of time-variable charges for congestible goods is provided by the telephone companies in the United States and Canada, where the tolls for long-distance calls vary very substantially with time of day and day of the week.

The observant reader may have noticed that several of the above examples of pricing strategies for congestible goods concerned goods and services that are typically provided by privately owned utilities with franchised monopolies in their service areas. While the public, in general, may benefit from judiciously selected, variable time-of-service charges, the public is usually anxious to ensure that the total revenue of these firms is not so large as to permit substantial "pure profits." Many of the firms that provide congestible goods and services are, therefore, subject to public-agency regulation of the prices they charge. Such regulation may be, in varying degrees, effective, but it is seldom entirely successful.

NONEXCLUSIVE GOODS AND RESOURCES

There are a number of quite different goods, services, amenities, and resources that are nonexclusive. Nonexclusiveness is an attenuation of property rights and results in inefficiency. Without exclusion, it is impossible to collect a price for use. Under such circumstances, price serves neither to ration the good or resource among users, nor to provide revenue for the production of the good or the maintenance and conservation of the resource. The typical allocative results of nonexclusiveness are underprovision of a good, service, or amenity relative to the efficient level of provision;

excessive levels of discommodities and disamenities, relative to the efficient level; overexploitation of a resource, relative to the efficient level of exploitation; and underinvestment in the management, conservation, and productive capacity of a resource.

The solution to the problems engendered by nonexclusiveness is obvious, especially in a society that values individual initiative. Exclusive, nonattenuated property rights ought to be established and enforced. Then, the entirely self-motivated actions of independent individuals will be sufficient to ensure efficient outcomes. Many societies, in many places, have specified exclusive property rights with respect to some previously nonexclusive goods and resources. For example, the abuses that result from nonexclusive use of grazing land were halted by the establishment of private property in land.

Nevertheless, some goods and some resources remain nonexclusive, even in those societies that place the highest value on private property and individual enterprise. Why? There are two broad classes of reasons. The first is cultural and political. All societies identify some goods, services, amenities, and resources that, it is thought, ought to be beyond the reach of commerce. There are many different ways of expressing this idea: "the best things in life are free"; "some things ought not to be bought and sold, but should be considered everyone's birthright"; and "some things are too important to be left to the market." Different cultures have entirely different notions as to which goods, amenities, and resources ought to be immune from market influences, and some societies place many more items in that category than do others. In the United States, natural environments, wild rivers, and historical sites are often considered to be in that category.

The second reason why some goods and resources are nonexclusive lies not in the arenas of culture, tradition, and politics, but in the basic characteristics of the goods and resources themselves. Why are there oyster farms, but no salmon farms? Oysters are sedentary and grow to maturity while attached to a particular rock. Thus, societies that choose to define exclusive property rights in oyster beds have little difficulty in so doing. Oyster beds can be clearly and easily delineated, and the oysters will remain in place. Exclusive property rights in oysters, once established, are easily secured and enforced. Thus, oysters can effectively be produced in efficient, private-sector operations similar to farming on dry land.

On the other hand, Pacific salmon hatch in the upper reaches of the coastal streams in the western United States and Canada. At various stages in their life cycle, they swim downstream, travel huge distances in the Pacific Ocean to feeding grounds in the general vicinity of the Aleutian Islands, travel back down the West Coast and eventually return to the stream in which they were hatched and travel upstream to spawn. The huge distances salmon travel over their life cycles, and the infeasibility of delineating and enforcing exclusive property rights over specific fish or, alternatively, specific small sections of the Pacific Ocean, estuaries, and coastal streams, militate against the establishment of exclusive property rights in salmon. Thus, ownership in salmon is established not throughout the life cycle as in a typical livestock-farming operation, but at the point of capture by the fisherman. More generally, there are many goods and resources that, because of their physical characteristics, are not well adapted to the specification of exclusive property rights therein. The costs of specifying, securing, and enforcing exclusive rights in such goods and resources exceeds any benefits that may be gained.

In the case of goods and resources for which exclusion is infeasible, the economist's advice that efficiency can be achieved through the establishment of nonattenuated property rights is unhelpful. A number of important natural resources and environmental amenities fall into this category. These include ambient air; water in streams, lakes and the ocean; migratory species of wildlife; and species that have little commercial value. They also include fish in the ocean and in lakes and streams too large for individual private ownership, and oil, natural gas, and groundwater pools that lie beneath lands owned by many different individuals. There are also disamenities and negatively valued resources for which effective exclusion is infeasible. These include pest populations, disease-causing organisms for which there is no known method for obtaining immunity, and pollutants carried by ambient air or nonexclusive hydrological systems.

Where exclusion is feasible, the specification of exclusive property rights is a political decision. However, where the establishment of exclusive, nonattenuated property rights is infeasible, the range of political choice is more limited. The totally nonexclusive, *res nullius,* situation has some very undesirable properties from the perspective of economic efficiency. Often, however, a society has options within the set of *res communis* kinds of rights. Rules that specify who shall have access to the good or resource, and under what conditions, may be established and enforced. Hunters and anglers may be subject to licensing requirements, restrictions on the hunting and angling seasons, bag limits, and the methods that may be used for hunting and angling. The farmer drawing from a groundwater pool may be subject to restrictions on the capacity of his pump, the days on which it operates and the number of hours it operates on a given day, or the total quantity of water withdrawn in a given time period.

These kinds of rules of access do not have all of the efficient characteristics of nonattentuated property rights. However, they may provide a system of workable rights, where exclusive property rights are infeasible.

There is a wide variety of possible specifications of these kinds of rules of access, within the realm of *res communis.* Consider, for example, an ocean fishery. With increasing demand for seafood, and improved fishing technology, open access to the fishery has resulted in overfishing. Fish are harvested at a rate that threatens the biological capacity of the fish population to replenish itself. The current level of fish harvests cannot be sustained indefinitely. This problem is quite typical of those encountered where property rights are nonexclusive. Yet the establishment of nonexclusive property rights in an ocean fishery would be prohibitively expensive. What can be done? There is a substantial demand for seafood. The fishery represents a renewable resource, which ought not be allowed to deteriorate through mismanagement. A fishing industry has been established, for many years, and the resources invested in that industry (fishing boats and equipment, and fishing skills) are not especially mobile. For these various reasons, it seems that something should be done to preserve and perpetuate the fishery.

In addition, there is the problem of overinvestment in inputs used for the capture of fish. It seems that too many fishermen are pursuing too few fish, and that each is investing in innovative technological equipment to make him more effective in the chase for the ever-diminishing stock of fish.

In a situation such as this, various, quite different, types of rules of access could be used. It is useful to consider the relative efficiencies of the outcomes that would be expected to result from different kinds of rules. To implement any rules of access, an agency with authority over the fishery would have to be established. The agency could choose to limit the fishing season. Surely, with fewer days of fishing permitted, the reproductive stock of fish could be maintained. However, this approach would be relatively ineffective in maintaining the reproductive stock, while it would likely have a perverse effect on the problem of overinvestment in fishing inputs. With a restricted fishing season, fishermen would compete with one another to purchase and use the biggest and fastest fishing boats and the most effective technology to locate and capture fish.

Another approach would be to restrict entry into the occupation of fishing. This would likely be done by licensing fishermen and granting licenses only to those who are presently occupied as fishermen and their heirs. While such a licensing strategy would create valuable property for fishermen (i.e., their licenses, which would acquire a capital value), it would do little to conserve the fishery.

The agency may choose to restrict other kinds of fishing inputs. It may limit the size of fishing boats, or their capacity to store and refrigerate fish; or, it may restrict or prohibit the use of particularly effective devices for locating or capturing fish. These kinds of input restrictions would be relatively ineffective in conserving the fishery, since astute fishermen would soon substitute other kinds of inputs for the restricted kinds. This process of input substitution, however, would result in inefficient investment of resources in fishing.

The agency could try a quite different approach. It could establish marketing quotas for fish and distribute those quotas among fishermen. Fish caught in excess of the marketing quota could not be sold. Each fisherman, once his marketing quota is established by the agency, would be free to determine his least-cost combination of inputs (capital, technology, labor, and time) to produce his given quota of fish. If the fish-marketing quotas were transferable (i.e., could be sold to other fishermen), the process of dynamic adjustment in the fishing industry would be encouraged. More productive fishermen could expand their operations, and technologically advanced firms could enter the industry. Exiting fishing firms would enjoy additional capital liquidity, when they sell their fish-marketing quotas to entering or expanding firms.

This example illustrates some quite general principles pertaining to the relative efficiency of various kinds of rules of access. If the problem is overexploitation of a resource, the preferred solution involves direct restriction of the rate of exploitation (e.g., the rate at which fish are captured and marketed), rather than restriction of various inputs used in the process of exploitation. Where restrictive rules are necessary, efficiency will be served if the rights created by those rules are transferable. Finally, it should be reiterated that even the more efficient kinds of *res communis* rules of access will not result in the attainment of Pareto-efficiency. However, where exclusion is infeasible, intelligently devised rules of access may result in workable, second-best solutions that sustain productivity in the long run, discourage waste of inputs, and permit firms in the industry to earn reasonable and secure incomes.

A NOTE ON "PUBLIC GOODS"

Much of the literature in welfare economics, public finance, and resource economics addresses itself to something called "public goods." In this book, that term has been avoided, because the "public good" is a concept which, due to inconsistent definition, has generated substantial confusion. In his classic article, Paul A. Samuelson defined a "public good" in exactly the same way as indivisible goods were defined in this chapter.[9] A "public good" is a good that is consumed without rivalry. However, Samuelson's paper and much of the subsequent literature implied that "public goods" are nonexclusive, in addition to being indivisible in consumption.

I find it useful to conceptualize indivisibility in consumption and nonexclusiveness as entirely distinct phenomena, which may or may not be observed together. Therefore, I do not use the term "public good." Instead, four categories of goods are identified: divisible, exclusive goods; divisible, nonexclusive goods; indivisible, exclusive goods; and indivisible, nonexclusive goods. Each of these four categories of goods has its distinguishing characteristics with respect to the possibility that the good may be provided by markets, and the possibility that its provision may be Pareto-efficient.

Divisible, Exclusive Goods. This is the category of goods (termed "private goods" by those who use the term "public goods" to describe indivisible goods) that includes the bread and wine, for which the conditions for efficient production, distribution, and consumption were examined in Chapter 6. Such goods may be provided by markets, and, given perfect markets, Pareto-efficiency in their provision may be achieved.

Divisible, Nonexclusive Goods. Since it is impossible to collect payments for the provision of such goods, they cannot be provided in private markets. Such goods may be provided by private philanthropy (but usually in suboptimal quantities) or by the public sector, which would finance them from general revenues. If it were physically and economically feasible, exclusion could be introduced into the market for such goods. Then the public sector could provide such goods, and charge a fee for their use and enjoyment. Alternatively, the private sector could provide these kinds of goods. If exclusive and nonattenuated property rights were specified and enforced, the private sector could then provide these kinds of goods in a Pareto-efficient manner.

Indivisible, Exclusive Goods. These goods can be provided either by the public sector, which could choose to charge a fee for their use and enjoyment, or by the private sector. Second-best solutions may be achieved, but the indivisibility precludes the attainment of Pareto-efficiency in the absence of perfectly discriminatory pricing.

Indivisible, Nonexclusive Goods. These goods may be provided only by private philanthropy (usually in suboptimal quantities), or by the public sector, which would finance their provision from general revenues. If exclusion were physically and economically feasible, and politically acceptable, exclusive rights could be specified and the goods could be provided through the market or by the public sector on the basis of user charges. If this occurred, Pareto-efficiency would be impossible, but second-best solutions may be attainable.

MONOPOLY

The analyses of sources of inefficiency in this chapter have been concentrated upon externality, indivisibility in consumption, and nonexclusiveness. These particular sources of inefficiency are characteristic of many important problems confronted by contemporary resource economists. However, it is well to remember that the classical source of inefficiency is the absence of competition that is manifested, in its most extreme form, by monopoly. And monopoly is of substantial concern to the resource economist. It is always possible that a monopolist may gain control of the stock of an important resource. In recent years, nations controlling very substantial proportions of the earth's reservoirs of particular resources, especially petroleum, have formed cartels that have acted in a monopolistic manner. There is an additional reason for the resource economist to be concerned about monopoly. As the analysis of the congestible good suggested, there are certain kinds of congestible goods (for example, sewer systems, water systems, rail systems, oil and gas pipelines, and electricity-transmission systems) which tend to be "natural monopolies" in the geographic regions they serve.

The simple, textbook analysis of monopoly proceeds as follows. Assume that an industry, consisting of one monopolistic firm, has constant marginal and average costs, at the level MC = AC = R. The demand curve for its product is DD'. Under perfect competition, the industry would produce an output of Z'', and that output would be priced at R = MC. However, the marginal revenue curve of the monopolist is DM. Setting marginal revenue equal to marginal cost, the monopolist selects the level of output Z', which he sells not at the price R, but at the price P, which is the demand price for Z' units of output (Figure 8.13).

The monopolist restricts output at the level Z', and enjoys an excess profit equal to PBAR. The triangle BCA provides an approximate estimate of the economic loss that results from the monopolization of the industry. Under the assumptions of this analysis, monopoly is most certainly a source of inefficiency.

As stated above, in the discussion of congestible goods, it is common for public agencies or commissions to regulate the prices established by firms that are franchised "natural monopolies" in their service regions. There is a substantial literature on the

FIGURE 8.13
Price and Output, for a Monopolist

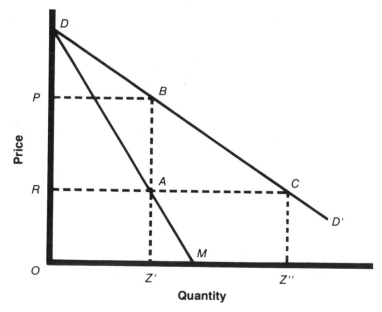

economics of this kind of regulation. Suffice it to say that, due to fundamental difficulties in the economics of "natural monopolies," to the lack of adequate information and of adequate regulatory tools, and to political pressures, there is some doubt that the regulation of this kind of monopoly is especially effective in ensuring adequate service to consumers at reasonable prices.

It has been long believed that many "natural monopolies" face *declining long-run marginal cost* curves. In such circumstances, economic analysis would suggest that price should be set equal to marginal cost. However, given continually declining marginal cost curves, marginal cost is always less than average cost. Thus, total revenues, when price is equal to marginal cost, are insufficient to recover total costs. There is a substantial literature on "marginal cost pricing"; typically, it concludes that price should be set equal to marginal cost, in order to encourage the efficiencies that can be achieved by large-scale production under declining cost curves, and that any deficit in revenues ought to be made up by lump-sum subsidies.

This kind of analysis has provided the economic logic justifying declining block rates for electricity, domestic and industrial water, etc.

In recent years, this logic has seemed less compelling. While the congestible good nature of a water-delivery system suggests that the costs of delivery decline when more water is provided, increasing demands for, and threatened shortages of, water have led to the realization that the marginal cost of water is not declining (only the marginal cost of water delivery, itself, is declining). The rapidly increasing costs of construction of new electric generators, the increasing awareness of the environmental costs of electricity generation, and the increasing scarcity of feedstock fuels for electricity generation, in recent years, have led to a reassessment of the idea that the electricity industry faces decreasing marginal costs.

Accordingly, in recent years, emphasis on marginal cost pricing has shifted, away from the case of continually decreasing marginal costs and the need to provide lump-sum subsidies, to the case of increasing marginal costs. In this latter case, marginal cost pricing seems desirable, to discourage increases in the quantity demanded. However, marginal cost pricing of the output of a monopoly facing an increasing marginal cost curve threatens the possibility that the monopoly may enjoy excess profits. For this reason, the discussion of monopoly in the natural-resource-related industries, in recent years, has become more concerned with using marginal cost pricing to restrain the growth of quantity demanded, while regulating industry profit margins. The previous concern, with marginal cost pricing to encourage consumption and with lump-sum subsidies to ensure that total revenue equals total costs, now seems less relevant.

QUESTIONS FOR DISCUSSION

1. "We observe in the real world actions that are taken not because the benefits from the action exceed the total costs, but because the actor finds it possible to impose some or all the costs upon others." Compile a list of various types of such actions, identifying in each case the circumstances that permit the actor to impose some of the costs upon other people.
2. Is it conceivable that there could be too little pollution? Explain.
3. "When a Pareto-relevant external diseconomy in production exists, the price of the product will be too low." Is this statement consistent with the idea that pollution controls are inflationary?
4. "The Coase Theorem proves that government has no business getting involved with pollution-control regulations." Evaluate this statement critically.
5. Do you think that emissions taxes on pollutants from automobile exhausts would result in achievement of a given level of ambient-air quality at lower resource cost than the current program that regulates emissions from new cars? Would any unusual difficulties be encountered in administering an emissions tax for automobile-exhaust pollutants? How might these be overcome?
6. Given that ambient air is indivisible in consumption and nonexclusive, how might the demand curve for air-pollution abatement be estimated?
7. "Emissions taxes on industrial polluters, if imposed, would be passed on entirely to the consumer." Is this statement always true? Does it make any difference whether the industry is competitive, or a regulated public utility with a spatial monopoly in its franchise area?
8. "If government insists upon regulating, then surely it should regulate performance rather than inputs." Do you agree? Explain. With this discussion as background, evaluate the economic efficiency of programs which:
   (a) mandate the use of scrubbers on coal-burning electric generating plants in order to control air pollution, and
   (b) restrict the design of fishing nets in order to maintain the fish resource.
9. Simple, partial equilibrium analyses tell us that (1) a monopolist inefficiently restricts output, and (2) a polluter inefficiently expands output. What can we say about the level of output of a polluting monopolist? Is the case of a polluting monopolist an application of the *theory of second-best*?

FURTHER READINGS

Agnello, R. J., and L. P. Donnelly. 1976. "Externalities and Property Rights in the Fisheries," *Land Economics.* 52: 518-529.

Barkley, Paul W., and David W. Seckler. 1972. *Economic Growth and Environmental Decay; The Solution Becomes the Problem.* New York: Harcourt Brace Jovanovich. (Chapters 8 and 9.)

Baumol, William J., and Wallace E. Oates. 1975. *The Theory of Environmental Policy.* Englewood Cliffs: Prentice-Hall. (Chapters 2 and 3.)

Christy, F. T., Jr., and A. Scott. 1965. *The Common Wealth in Ocean Fisheries.* Baltimore: The Johns Hopkins University Press.

Christy, F. T., Jr. 1975. "Property Rights in the World Ocean," *Natural Resources Journal.* 15: 695-712.

Coase, R. 1960. "The Problem of Social Cost," *Journal of Law and Economics.* 3: 1-44.

Davis, O. A., and A. B. Whinston. 1967. "On the Distinction Between Private and Public Goods," *American Economic Review.* 57(May): 360-373.

Freeman, A. Myrick III. 1971. *The Economics of Pollution Control and Environmental Quality.* Morristown: The General Learning Press.

Head, John G. 1976. "Mixed Goods in Samuelson Geometry," *Public Finance.* 31: 313-337.

Quirk, James P. 1976. *Intermediate Microeconomics.* Chicago: Science Research Associates. (Chapters 14 and 17.)

Randall, Alan. 1972. "Market Solutions to Externality Problems: Theory and Practice," *American Journal of Agricultural Economics.* 54(May): 175-183.

Samuelson, Paul. 1954. "The Pure Theory of Economic Expenditure," *Review of Economics and Statistics.* 36: 387-389.

Samuelson, Paul. 1955. "A Diagrammatic Exposition of a Theory of Public Expenditure," *Review of Economics and Statistics.* 37: 350-356.

ADVANCED READINGS

Baumol, William J., and Wallace E. Oates, 1975. *The Theory of Environmental Policy.* Englewood Cliffs: Prentice-Hall. (Chapters 4 through 10.)

Maler, Karl-Gordan. 1974. *Environmental Economics.* Baltimore: The Johns Hopkins University Press.

ENDNOTES

1. See, for example, Day, Richard H. 1978. "Adaptive Economics and Natural Resources Policy," *American Journal of Agricultural Economics.* 60(May): 276-283.
2. The definitions that follow are those of Buchanan and Stubblebine. 1962. "Externality," *Economica.* 29: 371 384.
3. Coase, R. 1960. "The Problem of Social Cost," *Journal of Law and Economics.* 3: 1-44.
4. See, for example, Demsetz, H. 1964. "The Exchange and Enforcement of Property Rights," *Journal of Law and Economics.* 7: 11-26.
5. The following analysis is based on Randall, A. 1972. "Market Solutions to Externality Problems: Theory and Practice," *American Journal of Agricultural Economics.* 54(May): 175-183.
6. Pigou, A. C. 1940. *The Economics of Welfare.* London: Macmillan.
7. Dales, J. H. 1968. *Pollution, Property and Prices.* Toronto: University of Toronto Press.
8. Davis, O. A., and A. B. Whinston. 1967. "On the Distinction Between Private and Public Goods," *American Economic Review.* 57(May): 360-373.
9. Samuelson, Paul. 1954. "The Pure Theory of Economic Expenditure," *Review of Economics and Statistics.* 36: 387-389.

III. INTERTEMPORAL PRODUCTION AND CONSUMPTION: SOME ECONOMIC THEORY FOR THE FUTURE

This section is about time. In Section II, the concept of time was recognized, but only in a most limited manner. The producing firm was permitted to distinguish between the short run and the long run, the long run being a time period sufficiently long to permit the adjustment of all factors of production to market conditions. The "long run" is merely a convenient fiction: a single time period sufficiently long to permit all adjustments, but sufficiently short that all underlying market conditions remain unchanged. In this section, we encounter for the first time an economic theory that admits the existence of separate, consecutive time periods. At last, we take seriously the possibility that decisions made in one time period help to shape the opportunity sets in later time periods.

The decision to save money, to conserve resources, or to exercise restraint in the creation of persistent and hazardous wastes is undertaken with a view to increasing opportunity sets in future periods. The decision to borrow money, to delay maintenance and replacement of durable goods, to extract exhaustible resources, to harvest biological resources without restraint, or to create wastes now that may cause hazards in the future is undertaken in order to increase present opportunity sets, even at the expense of reduced opportunity sets in future time periods. There may be good reasons for a decision to expand current opportunity sets at the expense of future opportunity sets. The needs and desires of the moment may seem pressing. There may be good reasons to expect that future opportunity sets will be so large that the future can well afford to transfer some opportunities to the present: during the Four Hundred Year Boom, in the modern economies, measurable wealth *has* increased over time.

In this section, the economics of intertemporal production and consumption decisions is examined. In Chapter 9, the economic theory of saving and investment decisions is developed. Private saving and investment decisions are examined, and it is found that capital markets function, ideally, in accordance with principles of economic efficiency that are not logically different from those that govern resource allocation in the static context. Then, the theory of public investments is considered.

Chapter 10 examines the allocation of natural resources over time. For exhaustible resources (e.g., minerals), the economic principles governing the rate of extraction and the rate of recycling are examined. Can optimal rates of extraction and recycling be determined? Are there good reasons to expect that private and social optima may diverge? Then, we turn to the allocation of biological resources. It is useful to distinguish between "managed" biological resources (e.g., timber, which may be planted, tended, and harvested in accordance with a schedule set by man) and "unmanaged" biological resources (e.g., an ocean fishery, where only the rate of harvest may be directly controlled by man).

In the case of the timber resource, the economic question is to determine the optimal rotation, the time period between planting and harvest that will maximize the economic productivity of timberland. In the case of the ocean fishery, the economic question is to determine the optimal rate of catch in order to maximize the long-term economic value of the fishery. In both the timber and the fishery cases, man may determine the timing and the extent of the harvest; but in the fishery case, the reproduction and growth of the fish resource is beyond the direct control of man.

In Chapter 11, the logic of conservation is examined. Special difficulties arise in conservation decisions, particularly those that involve the perpetuation of unique resources and the exercise of restraint in the creation of hazardous and virtually indestructible wastes. The time horizons are very long, much longer than the time horizons for typical business investments. Decisions in one time period may literally remove particular options from all future opportunity sets. In other words, some decisions, if taken, are irreversible. The future is intrinsically uncertain, and that uncertainty increases exponentially as the time horizon becomes very long. These concerns are paramount in decisions with respect to the preservation of unique environments and endangered species and the creation of hazardous and persistent wastes.

9

Investment Decisions

Life goes on. Although nothing is certain, it behooves each of us to act today as though there will be a tomorrow. Each individual gains utility, to some degree, from present consumption, the expectation of future consumption, the accumulation of wealth, and the sense of having provided for one's heirs. How does the individual make production and consumption decisions that influence his opportunities in the present and in future time periods?

PRIVATE DECISIONS

Following the procedure established in Chapter 5, we analyze, first, individual decisions and, then, the operation of markets (in this case, long-term capital markets).

SAVING, BORROWING, AND INVESTMENT

Consider a single individual who must solve the problem of allocating his consumption activities across two time periods, which we will designate, with great imagination, period 1 and period 2. We will address only the issue of his total consumption in each period, and will assume that his total consumption in each period can be defined by the size of his budget in each period — i.e., Y_1 in period 1, and Y_2 in period 2.

First, assume that the individual receives an income of $\bar{Y}_1$ in period 1, and $\bar{Y}_2$ in period 2, such that $\bar{Y}_1 = \bar{Y}_2$. There is no way to transfer income from one period to another. Consider three different individuals, A, B, and C, from whose utility functions may be derived, respectively, the indifference curves I_a, I_b, and I_c. These indifference curves define the preferences of the three individuals as to the timing of their consumption activities. Since the individuals are unable to reallocate consumption across time periods, each of the three indifference curves passes through a common point that represents $\bar{Y}_1$ and $\bar{Y}_2$, the only feasible allocation of consumption across time (Figure 9.1).

If it were possible to reallocate consumption across the time periods, individuals B and C would do so. Consider the broken line WW, where $W = \bar{Y}_1 + \bar{Y}_2$. This is an intertemporal budget line. If the individual could transfer all of his consumption to period 1, his total consumption would be W. Similarly, W could be consumed in period 2 if consumption in period 1 were zero. If it were possible to transfer consumption across time periods (i.e., if the intertemporal budget line existed), the individual B would transfer consumption from period 2 to period 1 so that his total consumption is $Y^*_{1b} + Y^*_{2b}$, and he achieves the higher indifference curve I^*_b. Individual B has a *positive time preference:* that is, he values immediate consumption more highly than consumption in later time periods. The individual C would transfer consumption from the immediate time period to the later time period, so that his total consumption was $Y^*_{1c} + Y^*_{2c}$ and he achieves the higher indifference curve I^*_c. Individual C has a *negative time preference:* he values consumption in a later time period more highly than immediate consumption. Individual A, who has a *neutral time preference,* would prefer the same total consumption in each time period. Since, by assumption, his income in each period is equal, he would not choose to make any transfers across time periods.

Now, let WW be unbroken. That is, we now assume the intertemporal budget line WW (designated intertemporal budget line 1 in Figures 9.2a and b) actually exists. This line has a slope of -1. Individual A would choose to make no transfer of income across time periods (Figure 9.2a). On the other hand, individual B would transfer income from the second time period to the first. He would *borrow* a portion of his second period income in order to spend it in the first period. His total consumption would be $Y^{*\prime}_1 + Y^{*\prime}_2$ (Figure 9.2b).

The intertemporal budget line WW, of slope -1, assumes that income may be transferred across time periods on a one-for-one basis. In such a case, the individual with neutral time preference would equalize consumption in each period, while the individual with positive time preference would transfer consumption to the immediate time period.

College students, of all people, are aware that it is seldom possible to transfer consumption from the future to the present on a one-for-one basis. Customarily, future income undergoes some diminution when transferred to the present, while present income, when saved for the future, tends to grow. In other words, the borrower pays *interest,* while the saver receives interest. The budget line WW assumes that the interest rate, for both saving and borrowing, is zero.

FIGURE 9.1
Neutral, Positive and Negative Time Preferences

Total Consumption (Income) in Year 2
W
$\overline{Y}_2 = Y^*_{2a}$
$I_a = I^*_a$
45°
O
$\overline{Y}_1$
$= Y^*_{1a}$
W
Total Consumption (Income) in Year 1

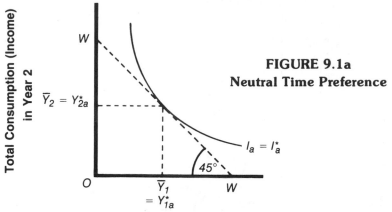

FIGURE 9.1a
Neutral Time Preference

Total Consumption (Income) in Year 2
W
$\overline{Y}_2$
Y^*_{2b}
I^*_b
I_b
45°
O
$\overline{Y}_1$
Y^*_{1b}
W
Total Consumption (Income) in Year 1

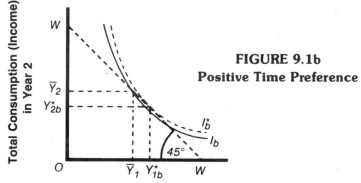

FIGURE 9.1b
Positive Time Preference

Total Consumption (Income) in Year 2
W
Y^*_{2c}
$\overline{Y}_2$
I^*_c
I_c
45°
O
Y^*_{1c}
$\overline{Y}_1$
W
Total Consumption (Income) in Year 1

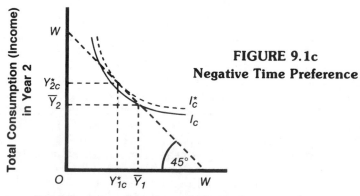

FIGURE 9.1c
Negative Time Preference

FIGURE 9.2a

Intertemporal Consumption Decisions, for a Consumer with Neutral Time Preference

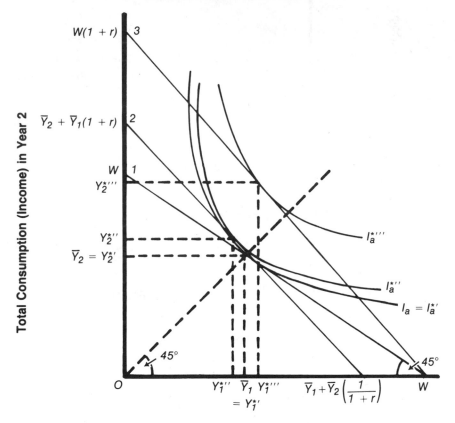

Total Consumption (Income) in Year 1

Now, assume that the individual will receive the incomes $\bar{Y}_1$ and $\bar{Y}_2$, respectively, in each time period; however, he may save a portion of the income for period 1 and spend it, plus interest, in period 2; or he may borrow a portion of his period 2 income and spend it, less interest, in period 1. If we assume, unrealistically, that the interest rate, r, is equal for saving and for borrowing (i.e., that financial-transactions costs are zero), the budget line 2 becomes relevant. If all income, for both periods, was spent in period 1, $\bar{Y}_1 + \bar{Y}_2(1/1+r)$ could be spent. If consumption in period 1 were zero, $\bar{Y}_2 + \bar{Y}_1(1 + r)$ could be spent in period 2. The slope of the intertemporal budget line 2 is $-(1 + r)$, where r is the *interest rate*. The higher the interest rate, the steeper the intertemporal budget line. The existence of a positive interest rate is sufficient to induce individual A, who has neutral time

FIGURE 9.2b
Intertemporal Consumption Decisions, for a Consumer with Positive Time Preference

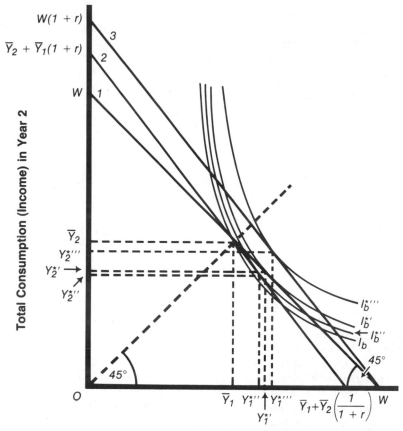

Total Consumption (Income) in Year 1

preference, to become a saver: his total consumption becomes $Y^{*\prime\prime}_1 + Y^{*\prime\prime}_2$. Individual B remains a borrower, but the positive rate of interest is sufficient to reduce the amount that he borrows.

Finally, consider the intertemporal budget line 3, which would be relevant if the individual were able to receive his total income for the two periods — i.e., $\overline{Y}_1 + \overline{Y}_2 = W$, in the first period. The slope of budget line 3 is $-(1 + r)$; i.e., the same as the slope of budget line 2. Yet, given a positive rate of interest, both individuals, A and B, are able to achieve higher total utility and greater total consumption in *each* time period under intertemporal budget line 3 than under intertemporal budget line 2. The present value of $\overline{Y}_1 + \overline{Y}_2 = W$, received in period 1, is greater than the present value of an income stream consisting of $\overline{Y}_1$ in period 1 and $\overline{Y}_2$ in period 2.

The foregoing analyses make a number of important points. (1) Individuals have preferences as to the timing of consumption; they may have positive, negative, or neutral time preference. (2) The existence of capital markets, which permit intertemporal transfers of consumption, increases — or, at least, does not decrease — utility. (3) Positive rates of interest tend to encourage saving and discourage borrowing. The individual consumer will determine his preferred rate of saving or borrowing by identifying the point of tangency between his intertemporal indifference curve and the intertemporal budget line he faces. The necessary condition for intertemporal efficiency in consumption is:

$$RCS_{Y_1, Y_2} = \frac{P_{Y_1}}{P_{Y_2}} = \frac{1}{1 + r} \, ,$$

where 1 and 2 are consecutive time periods.
(4) When interest rates are positive, the present value of $\$W$ in time period 1 is greater than the present value of the income stream $\$w_1 + \$w_2 + ... + \$w_n$, where $1, 2, ..., n$ represent successive time periods and $w_1 + w_2 + ... + w_n = W$.

The above analyses have been confined to the decision problem of a consumer who may transfer income among time periods using capital markets. Now, we consider an individual who has no *market opportunities* for the intertemporal transfer of capital, but who has *productive opportunities*. That is, he may take part of his income $\bar{Y}_1$, in period 1, and *invest* it in productive opportunities. Given the concave intertemporal production possibilities curve, $P_2 P_1$, he would choose to invest the amount $\bar{Y}_1 - Y_1$ in the first period, which would permit his consumption to increase by $Y_2 - \bar{Y}_2$ in period 2. By taking advantage of this productive opportunity, he is able to move from the indifference curve $\bar{I}$ to the higher indifference curve I (Figure 9.3). The efficiency condition for investment, for an individual who faces only productive opportunities, is:

$$RCS_{Y_1, Y_2} = RPT_{Y_1, Y_2} .$$

Now, consider the individual who enjoys both market and productive opportunities for intertemporal transfer. He invests $\bar{Y}_1 - Y_1^i$ (an even greater amount than $\bar{Y}_1 - Y_1$), in year 1. This raises his potential income in year 2 to Y_2^i. His efficiency condition for investment is:

$$RPT_{Y_1, Y_2} = \frac{1}{1 + r} .$$

Having a positive time preference, he would prefer a relatively

FIGURE 9.3

Investment and Borrowing: The Intertemporal Decision of an Individual with Productive and Market Opportunities

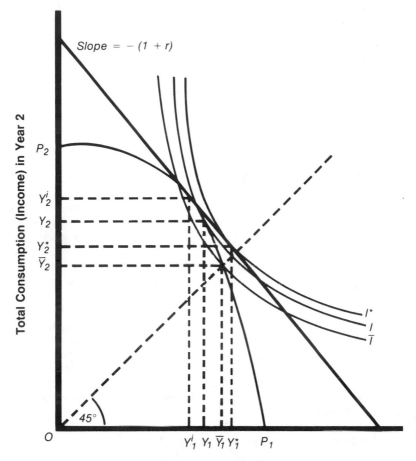

Total Consumption (Income) in Year 1

higher consumption in period 1. Using the market opportunities available to him, he borrows the amount $Y_1^* - Y_1$, thus permitting him the level of consumption Y_1^* in year 1 and Y_2^* in year 2 (Figure 9.3). His efficiency condition for borrowing is:

$$\text{RCS}_{Y_1, Y_2} = \frac{1}{1 + r}.$$

By using both the productive opportunities and the market opportunities available to him, he is able to attain the indifference curve I^*, which is the highest feasible indifference curve. The intertemporal efficiency condition for an individual facing both productive and market opportunities is:

$$RCS_{Y_1,Y_2} \;=\; RPT_{Y_1,Y_2} \;=\; \frac{1}{1+r} \; .$$

MARKET EQUILIBRIUM, INTEREST RATES AND AGGREGATE INVESTMENT

The above analyses were adequate to determine intertemporal efficiency conditions for an individual facing a given interest rate. Now it is necessary to examine intertemporal capital markets, and the determination of the interest rate. It is reasonable to assume that, as investment increases, successive marginal investment opportunities generate successively lower returns to investment. That is, the *marginal efficiency of investment* (MEI), which can be taken as the demand for investment capital, falls as total investment becomes larger. It is equally reasonable to assume that, as saving increases and successively larger amounts of present consumption are foregone, the *marginal rate of time preference* (MTP) increases. That is, successively higher interest rates are necessary to induce successively greater savings. The supply curve for savings is thus positively sloped.

The intersection of MEI and MTP (Figure 9.4) determines the equilibrium rates of saving and investment, and the equilibrium interest rate, r, in a static analysis. The reader is left to perform, for himself, simple analyses to determine the effects of various shifts and slope changes in the MEI and MTP curves. For example, an improvement in technology is likely to shift MEI rightward and to increase its slope. *Ceteris paribus,* this would increase interest rates, saving and investment.

Money, the Price Level, and Interest Rates

Regard money as simply a counting device that has no purpose other than to facilitate trade by reducing transactions costs. Money, then, is worth what one can buy with it. If the quantity of money were to increase, without any change in the available quantities of all goods, services, and resources, money incomes and the money prices of all goods, services, and resources would rise proportionally: that is, the price of any item, i, initially P_i, would increase to aP_i. The rate of price increase, a, is called the *rate of inflation*.

If a is positive, the "money rate of interest" will be greater than the real rate of interest. With continuous compounding,

$$r^m = a + r$$

where r^m = money rate of interest,

FIGURE 9.4
Market Equilibrium Investment, Savings and Interest Rate

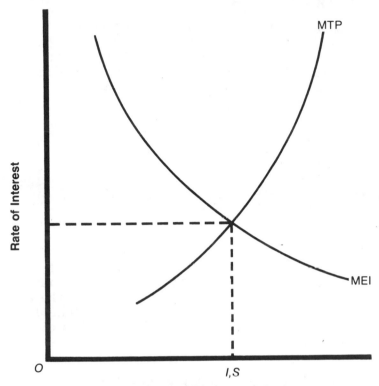

Aggregate Investment and Savings

a = inflation rate, and
r = real rate of interest.
Observed interest rates thus reflect both the real interest rate and the
anticipated rate of monetary inflation.

CAPITAL ACCUMULATION

A *capital good* is a physical object existing in the present but
providing a source of income or consumption opportunities in the
future. Capital goods are thus intermediate goods valuable not for
their own sakes but only insofar as they represent the potential of
generating consumption goods. *Capital value* is the present market
value equivalent of the future stream of income, or consumption,
that may be produced with a particular capital good. In this sense,
endowed wealth, W_o is equal to current income or consumption, Y_o,

plus capital value, K_o. Note that Y_o and K_o are not individually fixed, but are subject only to the constraint:

$$W_o = Y_o + K_o.$$

The process of *investment* involves diverting some of Y_o to K_o; the process of *disinvestment* involves converting some of K_o to Y_o.

For the individual investor who, presumably, wishes to maximize the present value of his current and future consumption possibilities, the optimal investment strategy is that strategy $P*$ which maximizes wealth W_o^{p*}, where:

$$W_o^{p*} = p_o + \frac{p_1}{1 + r} + \frac{p_2}{(1 + r)^2} + \ldots + \frac{p_T}{(1 + r)^T} \, ,$$

where p_t = revenue in year t, and
    $t = 0, 1, 2, \ldots, T$.
This solution maximizes the *present value of wealth*, W_o^{p*}, and is exactly equivalent to the solution:

$$W_o^{p*} = p_o + K_o^P,$$

where the attained *capital value,* K_o^P, equals the present value of all revenue beyond year 0. An additional project should be undertaken, so long as the resultant change in W_o^P is positive. The marginal condition for investment states that the value of capital formed by an incremental investment should be just equal to the value of consumption sacrificed.

PUBLIC INVESTMENTS

The natural resource economist needs to understand the economics of private investment since, in a modern mixed economy, significant categories of natural resources are typically privately owned: mineral deposits, agricultural and forest land, and the biological resources that make that land productive. In addition, the firms that use natural resources as inputs into the production of commodities and amenities are typically privately owned.

Nevertheless, many important natural and environmental resources remain, wholly or partly, in the public domain: air; water in streams, lakes and the ocean; groundwater; and public lands (which may include forest land, range land, scenic attractions and natural treasures, and riparian, estuarine and beachfront lands). In addition, the public sector is a major investor in the management, development, and conservation of natural and environmental resources.

The public sector is, in some significant ways, a uniquely favored investor. Unlike private investors, the public sector is not always required to raise capital on the market, where it would compete with other investors for the savings of consumers, who must be induced to delay consumption. Although the public sector *may* compete in capital markets, it has other means of raising capital. The power to raise revenue permits it to gather investment funds by taxation, diverting income and wealth from private investment and from individual consumption. Control of the money supply permits it to raise capital by merely creating additional money: the resulting inflation is a form of tax upon private investors and individual consumers.

The public sector enjoys its uniquely favored position with respect to the raising of capital because (in democratic societies) it is believed that the public sector is better able to undertake certain socially desirable investments that are unattractive to the private sector. The private sector may be unwilling to undertake certain investments that require massive amounts of capital and for which the payoff is risky and likely to accrue in the distant future. Perhaps more important, the public sector is able to undertake investments in the management, development, and conservation of resources where nonexclusive rights to the resources themselves, or the commodities and amenities produced as a result of investment, would discourage private investment.

Unfortunately, the fact of democratic government, alone, is insufficient to ensure that all public-sector investments are in the best interests of society. There are at least two important reasons for this: (1) the long-standing practice (a form of logrolling) wherein each legislator is inclined to vote in favor of another legislator's "pet" project, in return for similar consideration; and (2) the growth of the bureaucracy in modern democratic societies has established a powerful and effective force favoring continual increases in public-sector activity in general, and investment in particular. A major function of the natural resource economist, in his professional role, is the economic evaluation of public-sector investments. In this activity, the natural resource and environmental economist, while as always cognizant of the imperfection of efficiency as a criterion, is mostly concerned with ensuring that those proposed public investments that are undertaken are efficient.

The efficiency conditions for public-sector investment are, obviously, identical to the efficiency conditions of private-sector investment. The optimal public investment strategy, P^*, is that which maximizes W_o^p. An additional project should be included in the efficient public-sector investment strategy if the resulting change in W_o^p is positive; and, at the margin, the value of capital formed by incremental investment should just equal the value of consumption sacrificed. Remember that:

$$W_o^p = p_o + \frac{p_1}{1 + r} + \frac{p_2}{(1 + r)^2} + \ldots + \frac{p_T}{(1 + r)^T} ;$$

i.e., the present wealth, or *present value* of a stream of revenue p_o,

$p_1,...p_T$ is determined by *discounting* revenue accruing in all but the initial time period. Discounting is performed by dividing the revenue, p_t, accruing in the period t, by $(1 + r)^t$. The real rate of interest, r, is crucial to the outcome of the discounting procedure for determining the present value of a stream of revenue; r is called the *discount rate*. Examination of the formula for determining present value, W_o^p, suggests immediately that the empirical magnitude of r has a substantial influence on (1) the calculated magnitude of W_o^p, and (2) the relative influence of revenues accruing in distant time periods upon the calculated magnitude of W_o^p. The greater the magnitude of r, *ceteris paribus*, the smaller the calculated W_o^p and the smaller the relative contribution of revenues accruing in distant time periods.

THE SOCIAL DISCOUNT RATE

There is a continuing controversy, with a long history, concerning the appropriate magnitude of r for use in evaluating public investments. Some have argued that the public sector, in undertaking investments, often seeks the attainment of goals other than economic efficiency. Therefore, so the argument goes, it is appropriate to use estimates of the social discount rate that are considerably lower than market-generated estimates of the magnitude of r. For the purpose of evaluating the efficiency of proposed public-sector investments this argument must be rejected. Diverting funds from the private sector to the public sector, in order to achieve a rate of return lower than the real r, is clearly an inefficient undertaking and, in any competent evaluation, must be identified as such. There may be good reasons to undertake an inefficient public-sector investment, but the inefficiency of such an investment should be recognized. It serves no useful purpose to bias the efficiency evaluation of such a project, through manipulation of the social discount rate, in order to make the inefficient appear efficient.

To this point, we have concluded that the social discount rate should be set equal to the real efficient rate of interest, r. In a perfect economy, with costless capital markets, the social discount rate should be set equal to:

$$MEI = MTP = r.$$

Unfortunately, capital markets are seldom perfect, and are never costless to operate. The interest rate facing the saver is not equal to the interest rate facing the borrower. More important, observed interest rates reflect three quite different economic parameters: (1) r; (2) the anticipated rate of monetary inflation, a; and (3) lender's risk, which reflects the possibility that, for various reasons, the principle and the accrued interest may not be repaid by the borrower. In addition, if one examines the private-sector return on investment, in order to learn about the empirical magnitude of MEI = r, a further element of confusion arises: in countries (e.g., the United States) that tax corporate income, one must examine not after-tax corporate returns but pre-tax returns.

Given all these elements of confusion, how can one estimate the magnitude of r by observation, in an economy where (for example) the savings banks pay five percent interest on depositor's funds; municipal bonds pay seven percent (untaxable) interest; government treasury bonds may pay relatively low rates of interest (but, if so, are traded in financial markets at substantially below face value); the prime rate of interest (the rate which large banks charge their most favored borrowers) is nine percent; interest charged on home-mortgage loans is ten percent; credit unions charge twelve percent interest on consumer loans; retailers and credit-card companies typically charge eighteen percent; and finance companies offering consumer loans to poor credit risks may charge up to forty-two percent; the rate of inflation is 7.5 percent; and corporate incomes are taxed at the rate of forty-eight percent? No wonder the magnitude of the social rate of discount remains controversial.

The author has personally come to terms with the controversy in the following way, which seems reasonable to him. Beyond saying that it "seems reasonable to him," he makes no definitive claims on behalf of his approach, recognizing that well-trained and reasonable economists may sincerely and vigorously debate it.

1. The social discount rate should reflect MEI. The banks' prime lending rate is a reasonable indicator of MEI, if it is adjusted for the rate of inflation, a, and for the corporate income tax.
2. Although the public sector is large and diversified, public investments are *not* risk-free. They are, perhaps, about as risky as the loans made by large banks to favored corporations. Thus, the risk premium inherent in the banks' prime lending rate is appropriate for public investment.
3. *So long as future revenue streams from public investments are valued at current prices,* the social discount rate should be the real rate of interest, r, not the monetary rate of interest, $r + a$. Thus, it is necessary to adjust the prime rate of interest to account for the influence of inflation. This is not as easy as it sounds. The prime rate of interest reflects anticipated inflation during the period of the loan, not the actual rate of inflation at the time the loan is made. Accordingly, there are times (usually of high inflation, which is expected to be of short duration) in which the rate of inflation exceeds the prime interest rate, and real r is negative. The best approach is to examine the real rate of interest, over a sufficiently long period that short-run business cycles do not unduly influence the result. In the long run, it appears, the real rate of interest, r, in the United States, as reflected by the prime lending rate, is about 2.5 to 3 percent.

4. Where corporate income taxes approach fifty percent, a private corporation undertaking a low-risk investment needs to earn approximately twice the prime interest rate. This suggests that MEI in the private sector is about six percent in real terms, in the United States.

Accordingly, the author suggests that public investments should be evaluated using a social discount rate of about six percent. If social discount rates of about this magnitude are to be used in evaluating public investments, it is essential that all revenues (benefits minus costs) in each future time period be estimated at current, rather than inflated future, prices.

PUBLIC-SECTOR INVESTMENT CRITERIA

So far, we have concluded that public investment strategies should be chosen so as to maximize the present value of future revenues (i.e., W_o^p), given that discounting is performed using the real rate of interest, $r = \text{MEI} = \text{MTP}$. In addition, an incremental project should be added to the public-investment package, so long as the resulting change in W_o^p is positive: and, at the margin, the value of capital formed by an incremental investment should just equal the value of consumption sacrificed. Now, we examine the various public investment decision criteria that have been proposed in order to implement these efficiency conditions. Of the many proposed criteria, we examine three, all of which have considerable support, as indicated by the recommendations of professional economists and by their acceptance by various public-sector decision-making institutions: maximum present value, the benefit/cost ratio, and the internal rate of return.

Maximum Present Value

If the availability of funds for public-sector investment is unconstrained, the set of projects that maximizes W_o^p should be selected. In evaluating a single project, that project should be included in the public-sector investment strategy if its incremental effect on W_o^p is positive. That is, if its present value V_o is positive; i.e.:

$$V_o = (b_o - c_o) \ + \ \frac{b_1 - c_1}{1 + r} \ + \ \frac{b_2 - c_2}{(1 + r)^2} \ + \ \ldots \ + \ \frac{b_T - c_T}{(1 + r)^T} > 0,$$

where b_t = benefits accruing in time period t, and
$ c_t$ = costs accruing in time period t.
Given that the funds available for public-sector investment are unconstrained, the maximum present value criterion may be easily implemented in a manner entirely consistent with the conditions for efficiency in investment.

Where the availability of funds for public-sector investment is constrained, the optimal investment strategy is to maximize W_o^p

subject to the constraint on total funds invested. Where different projects must be implemented in different, discrete-sized undertakings, or not at all, the selection of the project package that maximizes W_o^p subject to a funds constraint is an integer-programming problem.

Where different projects have different, discrete sizes, and different values for V_o, there is no simple decision rule to determine, in isolation, whether a particular proposed project should be included in the optimal public investment strategy. All proposed projects must be considered together, in terms of V_o and the total investment required in the initial time period, and the package of projects that maximizes W_o^p subject to the funds constraint in the initial time period must be selected simultaneously.

The Benefit/Cost Ratio

The maximum present value criterion, maximize W_o^p, is equivalent to a criterion requiring the maximization of $B_o^p - C_o^p$ (where B_o^p is the present value of the stream of benefits from the selected package of projects, and C_o^p is the present value of the stream of costs). The maximum present value criterion simply maximizes the difference between B_o^p and C_o^p.

The benefit/cost ratio criterion differs from the maximum present value criterion in that it focuses upon the benefit/cost ratio, B_o^p/C_o^p. If public-sector investment funds in the initial time period are unconstrained, all projects for which $B_o/C_o \geqslant 1.0$ (where B_o is the present value of the stream of benefits b_t in each year $t = 0, 1, ..., T$, and C_o is similarly defined for costs) are included in the optimal public-sector investment strategy. The set of projects so chosen is identical to the set chosen by maximizing W_o^p. A particular project is included in the set if its benefit/cost ratio is equal to or greater than 1, which is identical to the result obtained by selecting projects whose $V_o \geqslant 0$. In the case where there is no constraint on funds for investment in the initial period, the benefit/cost ratio criterion and the maximum present value rule yield identical results.

When there is a constraint on investment funds in the initial time period, the following benefit/cost ratio criterion is satisfactory under certain conditions but not others: select discrete-sized projects, one by one, starting with that project whose benefit/cost ratio is highest, and working down, until the investment funds constraint in the initial time period is exhausted. That strategy will be quite effective when the candidate projects are of approximately similar size and when the total investment funds far exceed the investment cost of any project. Such a decision strategy will be inadequate, however, when candidate projects are of vastly different discrete sizes and when the size of some candidate projects is quite large relative to the total investment budget. In that case, it is best to revert to a procedure that maximizes the present value of the set of discrete-sized projects, given a constraint on the availability of investment funds in the initial time period.

Maximum Present Value and the Benefit/Cost Ratio:
A Note on the Selection of Optimal Project Size

The discussion thus far has implicitly assumed either (1) all possible projects may be built at a given specific size or not at all, or (2) that the optimal size of each project has been determined in advance of the selection of the optimal package of projects. In the real world, there are many kinds of projects that may be built at various sizes. Thus, it is essential, for efficiency in public investment, to determine the optimal size of each project, in addition to determining the optimal package of projects.

When there is no constraint on the availability of public investment funds in the initial time period, the size of each project should be determined so as to maximize V_0 or $B_0 - C_0$. So long as the present value of the project is equal to or greater than zero, or its benefit/cost ratio is equal or greater than one, each project should be incremented in size until $V_0^i = 0$ or $B_0^i/C_0^i = 1$ (where V^i, B^i, and C^i refer, respectively, to the incremental present value, benefits, and costs, associated with each increment in project size).

Where there is a constraint on funds for public investment in the initial time period, there is no simple, noniterative procedure for determining the optimal size of individual projects. It is possible, using integer programming, to select the optimal package of projects, subject to the constraint on investment funds, where each project may be implemented at an array of different sizes. It is necessary, of course, to constrain the computer program so that the selection of a particular project at any given size eliminates the possibility of simultaneously implementing the same project at a different size.

Internal Rate of Return

The internal rate of return, for a project or a package of projects, is defined as the rate of discount that makes its present value equal to zero. The internal rate of return, ρ, is determined implicitly by:

$$0 = p_0 + \frac{p_1}{1 + \rho} + \frac{p_2}{(1 + \rho)^2} + \ldots + \frac{p_T}{(1 + \rho)^T}.$$

Where the availability of public-sector investment funds is unconstrained, projects are selected for implementation, starting with the project whose ρ is highest, and working downward, until ρ for the last-selected project is exactly equal to the social rate of discount. Project size, where variable, may be optimized by incrementing project size until ρ for the last acceptable increment is equal to the social rate of discount. These rules are, conceptually, identical to the maximum present value criterion.

Where public-sector investment funds are limited in the initial time period, it is meaningful to select the package of projects that maximizes ρ, only if one imposes the constraints that the total public-sector investment budget for that time period must be exhausted and no project whose ρ is less than r may be selected.

The internal rate of return criterion has fallen into disfavor, for three reasons. (1) Internal rates of return are not easy to calculate, without the use of computers. (2) More important, the internal rate of return criterion may derive ambiguous results, when used in comparing projects whose time streams of benefits and costs are quite different. For projects in which (without discounting) benefits are less than costs in the early time periods, greater than costs in intermediate time periods, and less than costs in later time periods, it is impossible to calculate a unique internal rate of return. (3) When a project may be built at any one of several sizes, the optimal size is *not* the size that maximizes ρ. When capital funds are unconstrained, the optimal size is that for which incremental ρ equals the social discount rate. When capital funds are constrained, optimal size for each acceptable project is that for which incremental ρ equals incremental ρ for all the other acceptable projects; and the determination of optimal size is no simple calculation.

Summary

For these reasons, the maximum present value criterion is the preferred decision rule for public-sector investments. The benefit/cost ratio criterion, being fundamentally similar to the maximum present value criterion, provides a workable decision rule in many circumstances. The internal rate of return rule has fallen into disfavor for evaluating domestic natural resource and environmental investments; however, it remains in use in some international development agencies.

QUESTIONS FOR DISCUSSION

1. Under what conditions could a rational individual be simultaneously:
   a) an investor and a borrower?
   b) a saver and a borrower?
2. During the 1970's there were periods when observed interest rates facing borrowers were less than the actual rate of inflation. How could this be?
3. Some have argued that the discount rate used in evaluating public-sector investments should be lower than the real opportunity cost of capital in the private sector. Critically evaluate this argument.
4. Compare and contrast *maximum present value,* the *benefit/cost ratio,* and *internal rate of return,* as criteria for public investment decisions.
5. What difficulties are likely to arise in estimating, in advance, the

present value of a proposed public-sector investment in research aimed at development of a new production technology?

FURTHER READINGS

Barkley, Paul W., and David W. Seckler. 1972. *Economic Growth and Environmental Decay; The Solution Becomes the Problem.* New York: Harcourt Brace Jovanovich. (Chapter 7.)

Baumol, William J. 1968. "On the Social Rate of Discount," *American Economic Review.* 58: 788-801.

Fisher, Anthony C., and John V. Krutilla. 1975. "Resource Conservation, Environmental Preservation, and the Rate of Discount," *Quarterly Journal of Economics.* 89: 348-370.

Herfindahl, Orris C., and Allen V. Kneese. 1974. *Economic Theory of Natural Resources.* Columbus: Charles E. Merrill Publishing Company. (Chapter 5.)

Hirschleifer, J. 1970. *Investment, Interest and Capital.* Englewood Cliffs: Prentice-Hall.

Sassone, Peter G., and William A. Schaffer. 1978. *Cost-Benefit Analysis; A Handbook.* New York: Academic Press, Inc. (Chapters 2 and 6.)

Seagraves, J. 1970. "More on the Social Rate of Discount," *Quarterly Journal of Economics.* 84: 430-450.

Singer, Niel M. 1972. *Public Microeconomics.* Boston: Little, Brown and Company.

ADVANCED READING

Sjaastad, Larry, and Daniel Wisecarver. 1977. "The Social Cost of Public Finance," *Journal of Political Economics.* 85: 513-547.

10

The Allocation of Natural Resources Over Time

Decision problems concerning the management, development, and conservation of natural and environmental resources over the long haul exhibit the characteristics of the investment-decision problem. Decisions in one time period help shape opportunity sets in later time periods. The decision to conserve a natural resource involves a transfer of consumption from immediate to later time periods, and is thus similar to the saving decision. A decision to exploit a natural resource involves a transfer of consumption from later time periods to the immediate period, and is thus similar to a decision to borrow. The decision to develop a natural resource for productive purposes and to maintain its productivity in those uses is similar to the investment decision. Accordingly, the logic of investment-decision theory can be applied directly to the management of natural resources. In so doing, the most difficult problem arises not in the application of investment-decision theory, but in the adequate representation of the physical productivity of natural resources over time and the way in which management decisions influence the time pattern of physical productivity.

EXHAUSTIBLE RESOURCES

Consider a resource that exists in a given quantity and quality, and in a given place. Assume that, over any time period meaningful to man, resource quality will remain unchanged and the quantity of the resource will not increase, but will decrease by exactly the amount taken by man. Such a resource is called an *exhaustible resource*. Mineral deposits quite closely approximate the above-stated concept of exhaustible resources, and will be used as the example in analyzing the economics of exhaustible resources.

THE CONCEPT OF EXHAUSTION

Exhaustion may be viewed as both a process and a state. Continuing extraction of an exhaustible resource constitutes the process of exhaustion. The state of exhaustion is reached when literally none of the resource remains or, more realistically, when the remaining resource is so inconveniently situated that the cost of extraction becomes so high that the quantity demanded is zero. The simplest analytical concept of exhaustion is one in which extraction costs are constant until the point of exhaustion is reached, at which point they suddenly become infinite. A more realistic conceptual model visualizes a gradual rise in the cost of extraction over time, as less and less accessible deposits are exploited, until eventually the cost of extraction is so high that the quantity demanded is zero. Given this latter concept, the state of exhaustion is determined by extraction cost and demand; e.g., a rightward shift in the demand for the resource would induce further extraction of a resource that was previously considered exhausted.

THE OPTIMAL RATE OF EXTRACTION

Consider the decision problem of the owner of an exhaustible mineral deposit. He seeks to maximize V_o, the present value of the stream of net revenues from extracting the resource, where:

$$V_o = (P_o - C_o) \; + \; \frac{P_1 - C_1}{1 + r} \; + \; \frac{P_2 - C_2}{(1 + r)^2} \; + \; ... \; + \; \frac{P_T - P_T}{(1 + r)^T} \, ,$$

where P_t = the price of the resource extracted in period t,

$\quad C_t$ = the unit cost of resource extraction in period t, and

$\quad T$ = the time period at which exhaustion occurs.

In this formulation, $P_t - C_t$ is equal to R_t; i.e., the unit *royalty* in time period t.

The resource owner converts wealth — i.e., minerals in the ground — to current income by extracting and selling the resource. His decision problem is similar to any other investment decision problem. He may invest in conserving the mineral deposit; he may liquidate the mineral deposit and invest in financial securities that yield interest at the rate, r; he may liquidate some portion of either the mineral deposit or the financial securities, to pay for current consumption; or he may borrow money for current consumption, while conserving the mineral deposit.

If he expects R_t to be the same in each time period, t, he would extract all of the minerals in the initial period, devoting a part of his receipts to current consumption and the remainder to investments that yield interest at the rate, r. If he expects R_t to grow in each succeeding time period at a rate that exceeds r, he will hold the mineral deposit "in the ground" indefinitely: its net present value in the ground is greater than the net present value of the financial securities he could purchase with the royalties from extraction. But, surely, he would extract enough of the mineral in each time period to pay for his current consumption. No! If he could borrow at the interest rate, r, he would pay for current consumption by borrowing: the royalty (i.e., the undiscounted net value of his mineral deposit) is growing faster than his interest bill. However, if he expects the rate of growth of royalties to be equal to r, he will always be indifferent between holding mineral deposits or financial securities as investments. Thus, he will extract exactly enough minerals in each time period to pay for his chosen level of consumption.

One result of maximizing V_o, in the preceding equation, is:

$$R_o = \frac{R_1}{1 + r} = \frac{R_2}{(1 + r)^2} = \ .... \ = \frac{R_T}{(1 + r)^T}$$

that is, the present value of unit royalties must be equal in each time period. Otherwise, resource owners could increase the present value of their mineral deposits by shifting extraction among time periods. Only under this condition — i.e., that R_t grow at the rate r, or the *present value* of R_t remain constant over time — will some extraction occur in each time period.

This condition would appear to provide a threat of instability in the markets for exhaustible resources. If resource owners expected a fall in the price of extracted resources, they would be induced to increase the rate of extraction, thus *contributing to* the expected price decrease. If they expected a considerable increase in the price of extracted resources, they would be induced to leave the resources in the ground, thus exacerbating the expected price rise.

However, remember that mineral deposits are capital resources. Thus,

$$V_o = (P_o - C_o) + K_o,$$

where K_o = the capital value of resource deposits remaining at the end of time $t = 0$.

Future expectations of P_t, the market price of extracted resources, result in changes in the resource owner's estimate of K_o. The continual re-evaluation of K_o, as price expectations change, tends to restore the equality between r and the growth rate of R_t and thus introduces an element of stability into the market for extractive resources. Thus, the conclusion with respect to the stability of these markets is problematical, since both stabilizing and destabilizing influences have been identified.[1]

Do Private and Social Optima Diverge?

The optimal condition for extraction of privately owned exhaustible-resource deposits is a pure efficiency condition, and the market rate of interest, r, plays a crucial role in this condition. Thus, two questions arise: (1) is the market rate of interest, r, a reasonable estimate of the social discount rate, and (2) does the social discount rate reflect both intertemporal efficiency and equity, or only efficiency concerns for a relatively short time horizon?

In Chapter 9, it was argued that the social discount rate should be equal to the MEI, as determined in private capital markets. This conclusion is reasonable if, and only if, one is comparing private and public investments with similar time horizons. However, the time horizon for private investments is relatively short, ranging from overnight deposits to investment in plant and equipment that are seldom expected to be serviceable for more than twenty to forty years. On the other hand, a society that expects to survive and prosper into the indefinite future must be concerned that its exhaustible resources continue to provide services for many, many generations or, at least, until technological developments permit the substitution of new exhaustible or flow resources for the exhaustible resource under consideration. Given that a discount rate of, say, six percent results in the attachment of only trivial weight to outcomes two, three, or more generations in the future, there is a reasonable basis for concern that market-determined discount rates for extractive resources may be considerably higher than longer-term social discount rates.

The efficiency condition for resource extraction allows a crucial role for r, the market rate of interest, which is determined by the current generation. Thus, the efficiency condition allows a dictatorial role for current generations in the establishment of criteria that determine the quantity of extractive resources "saved" for future generations. Thus, there is no reason to believe that the efficiency condition for resource extraction is sufficient to provide for *intergenerational equity.*

There are a number of additional reasons to suspect that private resource markets may not provide a socially optimal rate of resource extraction. Where stocks of exhaustible resources are effectively monopolized, or cartelized (as has been achieved by the Organization of Petroleum Exporting Countries), the market-determined rate of resource extraction may be too low. Where resource extraction involves Pareto-relevant external diseconomies (such as may result from the surface mining of coal, or the release of atmospheric pollutants when coal is burned), the market-determined rate of resource extraction may be too high. Finally, private resource owners face several sources of risk and uncertainty: technological uncertainty, which leaves the resource owner uncertain as to future demands for the resource, and future costs of extraction; uncertainty with respect to property rights, such as may occur when resource owners fear the prospect that resource deposits may be expropriated by national governments; and uncertainty as to resource prices, which is exacerbated by the general absence of forward markets in resources. Although these uncertainties loom large in the mind of the private resource owner, with his relatively short life expectancy, they are less important to a society that expects to survive indefinitely.

What can a society, operating through its governmental institutions, do in a situation where it expects that market-determined rates of resource extraction are not socially optimal? It may attempt to directly determine extraction rates by restricting resource-extraction inputs or, more effectively, by restricting the quantity of the resource that may be marketed in each time period. Alternatively, it may attempt to influence unit royalties, $P_t - C_t$, through taxation policy, thus influencing rates of extraction while leaving the resource owners to determine their optimal extraction strategies in the face of government-influenced price incentives. Below, we briefly consider the economic results of two resource-taxation strategies: property taxes and severance taxes.

Property Taxes

Exhaustible resource deposits may be taxed as real property. For a given rate of property taxation, the resource owner's tax payments vary directly with the value of the remaining, unexploited deposits. The smaller the remaining deposits, the smaller the resource owner's property-tax payments. Thus, when a property tax is imposed upon resource deposits, the resource owner may then maximize V_0 by *increasing* the rate at which he exploits the resource. The larger the property tax, the greater the increase in the rate of extraction.

Severance Taxes

Governments may impose a severance tax, which is a unit tax on extracted resources. In effect, a severance tax is a predetermined royalty collected by government before the resource owner may collect royalties. A severance tax increases c_t, the unit costs of extraction facing the resource owner, and *ceteris paribus* decreases the rate of resource extraction in the present time period. Severance taxes tend to reduce the rate of resource extraction, and the higher the severance tax, the greater the reduction in extraction rates.

Some governmental jurisdictions have instituted *depletion allowances,* which are, in effect, negative severance taxes. The effect of a depletion allowance is to *increase* extraction rates.

THE RATE OF RECYCLING

It is often possible to *recycle* metal resources (and also paper, which is a manufactured product using biological, rather than exhaustible, resources as the basic input). Resource recycling is often regarded, by its enthusiasts, as mankind's best hope for extending the availability of natural resources into distant time periods. It must be recognized, however, that recycling is not a costless process. The Second Law of Thermodynamics indicates that, in a closed system, infinite recycling is impossible. Even with a continuous flow of inputs from outside the system (e.g., the effective use of solar energy), infinite recycling is not possible. Some loss of the resource occurs each time it is recycled. Each complete resource cycle (i.e., manufacturing, use, and recycling) involves some degradation of the resource, and requires inputs of energy. Given that recycling is a costly process, the resource user will choose between newly extracted resources and recycled resources on the basis of relative cost. In any time period, recycled resources will be used only if they are cheaper than newly extracted resources. The privately owned resource-using firm will seek to minimize C, the total cost of resource use, where:

$$C = TC_E(Z) + TC_R(Z),$$

subject to $Z = \bar{Z}$,

where $\bar{Z}$ is the desired quantity of output, and
$\quad$ TC_E and TC_R are the total costs of extracted and recycled resources, respectively, each shown as a function of output, Z.

Minimum cost to produce a given level of output is achieved when the marginal cost of newly extracted resource use is equal to the marginal cost of recycled resource use.

Do Private and Social Optima Diverge?

If the market-determined r facing the owner of the extracted resource is higher than the social discount rate, the unit price of newly extracted resources will be lower than the socially optimal price. Thus, the social cost of using newly extracted resources will be higher than the price faced by the resource-using firm. If, in addition, the process of resource extraction involves Pareto-relevant external diseconomies in excess of those involved in the recycling process, the private costs of using newly extracted resources will further understate the social costs. Therefore, if these two conditions hold, the socially optimal rate of recycling will be greater than the recycling rate determined by private markets.

In such a situation, severance taxes on newly extracted resources and pollution taxes on the external diseconomies from resource extraction would encourage a recycling rate nearer to the socially optimal rate.

BIOLOGICAL RESOURCES

Biological resources differ from exhaustible resources in that they have the capacity to reproduce themselves over time. Biological resources tend to be much more complex than extractive resources.

They typically utilize flow resources (e.g., sunlight) and fund resources (e.g., water and soil fertility). In addition, they may use extractive, exhaustible resources; e.g., in cases where fertilizer made from mineral deposits and cultivation practices using fossil fuels are employed to increase their productivity.

In the economic analysis of problems of biological-resource management, the question of property rights is paramount. Where property rights are nonattenuated, as may occur where crops, forest products, and livestock are produced on privately owned land, biological resources may be *managed* much as inorganic inputs are typically managed in production processes. If, on the other hand, the establishment of exclusive property rights in biological resources is infeasible (e.g., in the case of ocean fisheries), biological resources must be *unmanaged*: management throughout the life cycle is impossible. A degree of control over the long-run productivity of this kind of biological resource is attainable only by manipulating the rate of harvest.

MANAGED RESOURCES

Consider the decision problem facing the owner of a newly planted tract of trees, who wishes to determine the optimal time at which the trees should be harvested. When very young, the trees, if harvested, would have little value. As they grow older, the harvest value of the trees will increase rapidly. However, the trees cannot continue indefinitely to increase in harvest value; eventually, the trees will grow old and die, becoming useful only as firewood, which is of lesser value than lumber.

Assume that the landowner wants only to maximize the present value of this current stand of trees. He seeks to select a harvest time, t^*, such that W_0 is maximized, where:

$$W_0 = \frac{P_t - C_t}{(1 + r)^t} \quad - \quad k_o \quad = \quad V_0 - k_o$$

where P_t = the sale value of the lumber at time t,
C_t = the cost of harvest at time t, and
k_o = the initial investment in purchasing the tract of trees, and
V_0 = the present value of harvested trees.

The solution to this decision problem is illustrated in Figure 10.1. The curve labeled $P_t - C_t$ represents the (undiscounted) sale price minus harvest cost of the trees in each time period, t. The curve, labelled k_t^r, which intersects the vertical axis at point k_o, represents the initial purchase cost of the trees, *compounded* at the rate of interest, r. The broken line passing through point k_o represents the initial purchase cost of the tract of trees compounded at a zero interest rate. The curve intersecting the vertical axis at V_0^r represents the maximum present value of harvesting the trees,

FIGURE 10.1

The Optimal Harvest Date for a Managed Biological Resource

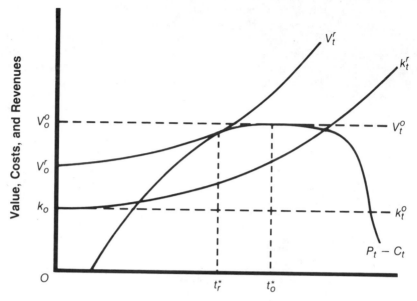

Number of Time Periods to Harvest

when the interest rate is r. The broken line intersecting the vertical axis at V_0^o represents the maximum present value of the harvested trees when the interest rate is zero. The optimal harvest period at the interest rate r is t_r^*; while the optimal harvest time at a zero interest rate is t_0^*. Only if the interest rate is zero will the owner choose to harvest the trees when $P_t - C_t$ is at a maximum. At positive interest rates, harvest will occur at some time before the (undiscounted) $P_t - C_t$ reaches a maximum.

The Optimal Rotation

It is unrealistic to assume that the owner of a tract of newly planted trees seeks to maximize only the net value of the harvested trees. More realistically, he seeks to maximize W_0, where:

$$W_o = \frac{P_t - C_t}{(1 + r)^t} - k_o + K_o,$$

where k_o = the cost of planting the trees, and
K_o = the present value at time 0 of the capital asset embodied in the land upon which the trees grow.

Since the land can be used, in any time period, either for continuing the growth of the existing stand of trees or for replanting (i.e., initiating the growth of a new stand of trees), the landowner is interested not in maximizing the present value of a given stand of trees, but in maximizing the present value of all future productivity from his land. His problem is to determine the *optimal rotation* of trees on his land.

Assume, first, that $K_0 = 0$. That would necessarily imply that the (undiscounted) $P_t - C_t$ was growing at exactly the rate of interest, r. In this case, the optimal length of rotation is exactly equal to t_r^*, which is the optimal harvest time for the problem, examined above, in which a single stand of trees is to be harvested.

However, examination of Figure 10.1 indicates that there are periods in which the rate of growth of $P_t - C_t$ is greater than the rate of interest, r. This occurs at any time when the $P_t - C_t$ curve is sloped more steeply than the V_t curve. In such a case, K_0 is positive. Then, the optimal rotation period t_r^{**} is shorter than t_r^*. The opportunity to replant and enjoy a period at which the (undiscounted) growth of $P_t - C_t$ is greater than the rate of interest, r, is sufficiently attractive to induce the landowner to enter an indefinite rotation sequence where each harvest period t^{**} is shorter than t_r^*, the harvest time when that opportunity does not exist.

There is another interesting version of the rotation problem. Assume that the landowner wishes to establish a constant rate of harvest in each time period. Thus, he must plant the same number of new trees in each time period. Given a finite amount of land, and a constant amount of land per tree, his problem is to determine the planting rate and the harvest rate simultaneously with the optimal time period from planting to harvest.

The process of solving this problem is mathematically complex, but the solution makes sense at an intuitive level. Planting begins at time 0 and continues at a constant rate; harvesting begins at time t_i^* and continues at a constant rate. After this time, the number of trees harvested is equal to the number planted in each unit of time. How long is t_i^*? The optimal t_i^* occurs when the following condition is satisfied: the increment in the net harvest value per tree, $p_t - c_t$, per year of additional tree life must be equal to the increment in interest on $p_t - c_t$ per year of additional tree life minus the marginal savings in planting cost resulting from extension of tree life.

"UNMANAGED" BIOLOGICAL RESOURCES

Now, consider a nonexclusive resource like the ocean fishery, in which it is infeasible to establish exclusive property rights to individual fish. For this reason, the ocean fishery cannot be privately managed as can the forest on privately owned land. In the case of the forest, the landowner controlled the number of trees per acre of land, the time of planting, and the time of harvest, thus exercising substantial control over the forest throughout its life cycle. In the case of the ocean fishery, however, only the rate of harvest can be controlled. Controlling the rate of harvest, in an ocean fishery, is not so simple as controlling the rate of harvest in a privately owned forest: since no single private individual controls access to the ocean fishery, control of the rate of harvest must be established through the use of policy tools implemented at the institutional level.

The Production of Fish

Assume that the fishery is circumscribed in space, and constrained in terms of several biologically relevant parameters — e.g., total nutrients, water temperature, etc. Then, there will be a maximum mass of fish, $\bar{X}$, that it can support. In any given time period, growth in the total mass of fish is the net result of births, deaths, and changes in the average size of individual fish in the mass. Quite likely, there is a critical level of fish population, X_e, below which growth will be negative until extinction occurs. Thus, the mass of fish is effectively bounded by X_e and $\bar{X}$. As the mass approaches $\bar{X}$, the individual units begin to compete with each other for available nutrients, and the relative growth in the fish mass slows down.

Define $\dot{X}$ as the absolute rate of growth of the fish mass. Then, $\dot{X} = f(X)$; i.e., the absolute rate of growth in the fish mass is a function of the size of the fish mass. The production relationships for fish are illustrated in Figure 10.2, which plots X as a function of time, and Figure 10.3, which plots $\dot{X}$ as a function of X. In Figure 10.3, $\dot{X}$ is maximized when the total fish mass is X_m; the relative rate of growth in fish mass, $\dot{X}/X$, is maximized when the total fish mass is X_g, is 0 at X_m, and is negative thereafter.

FIGURE 10.2
Fish Mass, as a Function of Time

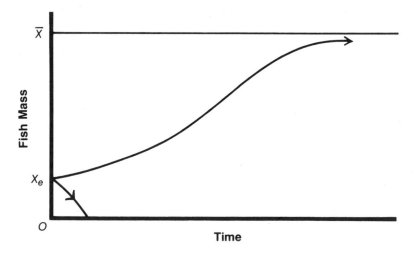

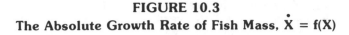

FIGURE 10.3
The Absolute Growth Rate of Fish Mass, $\dot{X} = f(X)$

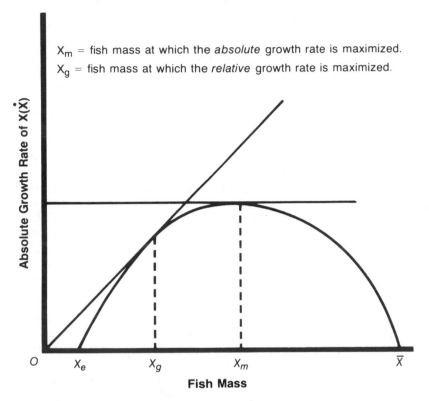

X_m = fish mass at which the *absolute* growth rate is maximized.
X_g = fish mass at which the *relative* growth rate is maximized.

Absolute Growth Rate of $X(\dot{X})$

O X_e X_g X_m $\overline{X}$

Fish Mass

The Competitive Fishery[2]

Assume that an ocean fishery, where fish-production relationships are as described immediately above, is worked by competing fishermen with no effective limit on total catch. The production function for fish caught, Z, is $Z = h(X,E)$, where E is fishing effort. Assume that E has a constant cost per unit (i.e., fishing effort is homogeneous; thus, this simplified model does not permit substitution among inputs in the creation of fishing effort). If we further *assume that catch in any time period must be equal to the absolute growth of fish mass in that time period,* we can derive an average cost function for fish caught.

The average cost function for fish caught has two branches, divided by the zero catch, and the maximum sustainable catch, Z_m, which is associated with the fish mass X_m. The lower branch of this average cost function is attained when total fishing effort is so small that the fish mass is equal to or greater than X_m; the upper branch is attained when fishing effort is so great that total fish mass is equal to or less than X_m.

Now superimpose a demand curve for fish caught, DD' which passes through the branched average cost curve and points A and B (Figure 10.4). If we assume, reasonably, that each fisherman behaves as though his own fishing effort has no impact on the total fish mass, X, the fishing industry will behave as though the supply curve for fish caught, at any point on the branched average cost curve, is a straight line passing from the origin through that point. At the point A, the industry behaves as though the supply curve for fish caught was "S_A"; while, at point B, it behaves as though the supply curve for fish caught was "S_B".

It can be demonstrated that the point A represents an unstable equilibrium: if the fish stock were to autonomously change, the decisions made by independent fishermen would not, in aggregate, return the stock to the level associated with A, but would result in further divergence of the total fish mass. On the other hand, B is a stable equilibrium. Note that it is not necessary that stable equilibria be located on the lower branch of the average cost curve. For example, if demand for fish caught were to shift to $D''D'''$, the point C would represent a stable equilibrium. In general, the rule is that if the demand curve intersects the average cost curve at only one point, that point is a stable equilibrium; whereas if the demand curve intersects the average cost curve at two points, the lower point of intersection will represent a stable equilibrium. These stable equilibrium points have several virtues: (1) they are stable; (2) price is equal to average cost, and there are no "pure profits"; and (3) the market for fish caught is cleared at the lowest possible unit price.

There is, however, a serious problem with these stable-equilibrium solutions. In our analysis, we derived these solutions using a model that *assumed* that in any given time period, total catch must equal the absolute growth of fish mass. Unfortunately, with open entry into the fishing industry, there is no reason to expect this condition to be satisfied. In all likelihood, in the real world, open entry of competing fishermen will result in instability in fish markets, and operation on the upper branch of the curve depicting average cost per unit of fish caught. Operation on the upper branch implies that the fish mass is uneconomically low, and excessive fishing effort is expended in the industry. Depending on the production conditions in the fishery (which are, in the real world, much more complex than has been depicted here), there is no assurance that an open-access, competitive fishing industry will not result in extinction of the fishery. Without effective control of the total fish harvest, stable and efficient solutions optimizing the exploitation of the fishery cannot be achieved.

These conclusions with respect to the open-access, competitive fishing industry may be derived intuitively, as we have done here, or more rigorously, using static models that focus upon the attainment of equilibria without very much regard to the time path of progress toward those equilibria. Accordingly, the above treatment did not conceptualize the decision about fish harvest as an investment

FIGURE 10.4
Average Cost of Fish Caught

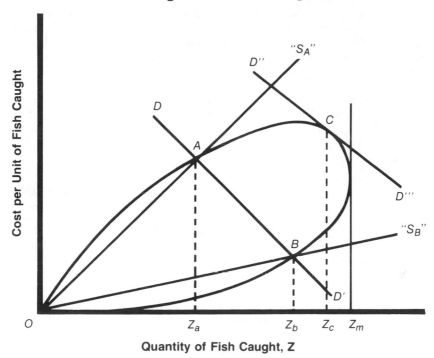

Quantity of Fish Caught, Z

problem. It is useful, however, to conceptualize the problem of fishery management, given control over the total harvest, as an investment problem.

Optimal Control of Fish Harvest

Given that $\dot{X} = f(X)$, in the absence of fishing, and $\dot{X} = f(X) - Z$, in the presence of fishing effort, where $Z = h(X,E)$, the fishery manager (either a single owner of the whole fishery, if that is possible, or an institution exercising control over the exploitation of the fishery) may seek to manage the fishery by controlling Z, either directly, or indirectly through control of E. Given information on the unit price of fish caught, the unit cost of fishing effort, E, and the rate of interest, r, it is possible to set up the following problem: maximize the net present value of fishery services (i.e., the amount by which the value of fish caught exceeds the cost of fishing effort) over an infinite number of time periods, subject to $\dot{X} = f(X) - h(X,E)$. The decision problem could be set up as an *optimal control model*, where either Z or E would be used as the control variable. This is a particular form of multiperiod investment decision model, in which the fishery itself would be regarded as a capital resource. In addition, capital inputs subsumed under our catchall category E (i.e., any capital inputs that contribute to the production of fishing effort) would also be treated as capital investments.

Optimal control models are mathematically complex, and neither the setting up of such models nor their solution is within the scope of this book. However, some characteristics of the kinds of solutions that may be derived from optimal control models of the fishery are briefly discussed immediately below.

(1) Where $f' = d\dot{X}/dX$ (i.e., the rate at which relative growth in fish mass increases as fish mass itself increases), r must be greater than f', for some values of X, in order to achieve a bounded steady-state solution. Of course, it is also necessary that, at some points, f' be greater than r: if f' is never greater than r, present value of the fishery will be maximized by deliberately exploiting it at a rate that will lead to its eventual extinction. That is, if the natural productivity of the fishery is too low, exhausting it will be preferred to maintaining it.

(2) Depending on the empirical specification of $X = f(\dot{X}) - h(X,E)$, the unit price of fish caught, the unit cost of fishing effort, and the rate of interest, the steady-state solution (if attainable) may involve either a greater or a lesser fish mass than existed in the initial time period. If the functions that determine $\dot{X}$, the price of fish, the cost of fishing effort, or the rate of interest were to change from one time period to another, the pre-change steady-state solution would no longer be appropriate, and the system would move toward a new steady-state solution (if attainable).

(3) Assuming a steady-state solution is attainable, it may be institutionally implemented as follows: (a) the amount of fish caught, Z, may be directly controlled in each time period, preferably through the use of marketable rights to sell fish; or, (b) if fishing effort, E, is to be the control variable, it may be controlled in each time period by the imposition of *two* taxes — a tax on fish caught *and* a tax on capital inputs into fishing effort.

(4) Given the wide range over which the relevant prices, fish-mass production functions, costs of E, and interest rates may vary in the real world, there is no *a priori* assurance that a steady-state (i.e., stable sustained yield) solution will be attainable for each fishery. Other outcomes, each distinctly possible, include solutions that lead to extinction of the fishery, solutions in which fishing activity is unprofitable and the fishing industry eventually goes out of business, solutions in which the production of fish caught is cyclical and fluctuates across time periods, and solutions that involve multiple equilibria as opposed to a unique and stable equilibrium.

BIOLOGICAL RESOURCES:
DO PRIVATE AND SOCIAL OPTIMA DIVERGE?

In the case of "managed" biological resources, the possible

answers to this question cover much the same range as was covered in the case of exhaustible resources. If the market interest rate diverges from the social discount rate, private and social optima will diverge. If the market rate of interest is higher than the social discount rate, private optima may involve premature harvest and underinvestment in the maintenance of the productive capacity of the resource, when compared to social optima. Monopolistic ownership of managed biological resources may lead to inefficient restriction of current output of commodities and services produced using the resource. Uncertainty and insecurity of resource ownership may lead to premature harvest and underinvestment in the maintenance of productive capacity. If there exist Pareto-relevant external diseconomies associated with the production or harvesting of the resource, or with its use as an input in production processes, the output of resource products and amenities that is privately optimal will exceed that which is socially optimal.

Public institutions may seek to control the rate of exploitation of managed biological resources through judicious application of severance taxes (called "stumpage" taxes, when applied to harvested lumber) and pollution-emissions taxes.

In the case of "unmanaged" biological resources, all the above kinds of divergences between private and social optima are possible. In addition, the overexploitation and underconservation that typically result from nonexclusive property rights will occur unless the rate of harvest can be effectively controlled at the socially optimal rate. Control of the rate of harvest may be attempted, through public institutions, by controlling the inputs used in harvest or, preferably, by establishing transferable marketing quotas for the harvested resource. Transferable marketing quotas leave the individual firm free to choose the efficient combination of inputs, while providing an avenue through which more efficient firms can enter the industry, or expand their output. Less efficient firms, forced to exit the industry or contract their output, would be compensated (in part) by a one-shot receipt of capital from the sale of marketing quotas no longer needed.

QUESTIONS FOR DISCUSSION

1. There was a time, not so long ago, when the U. S. simultaneously pursued the following policies with respect to oil: the amount of oil permitted to be imported was restricted by quotas, and an oil-depletion allowance was applicable to domestic production. What effects would you expect this combination of policies to have on the consumption of oil, the domestic production of oil, and the rate of discovery of new domestic oil reserves?
2. What are the economic limits to recycling, in a market economy?
3. In this chapter, the economics of recycling was discussed, in terms of exhaustible resources. Can you develop an economic analysis of recycling paper products?

4. A wine-lover has a given cellar capacity, a budget constraint, and a utility function that includes preferences with respect to the quantity and quality of wine he consumes. Quality of wine at the time of consumption is a function of initial quality and time spent aging in the cellar. He wants to optimize the initial quality of wine purchased and the time each bottle is aged, subject to a constraint that his total consumption equals Q in each period.

   Which, if any, of the intertemporal resource-allocation decision models presented in this chapter is adaptable for solving his problem? How should it be adapted?

5. Under what, if any, conditions would it be the preferred policy to consciously permit the extinction of a biological resource?

6. We have seen some of the difficulties that arise in attempting to optimize the long-term management of a fishery, where a single resource manager (or management institution) has control over fishing inputs or the rate of fish harvest. What problems might arise in the long-term management of fish resources in international waters? How might these problems be overcome?

FURTHER READINGS

Anderson, Lee G. 1977. *The Economics of Fishery Management.* Baltimore: The Johns Hopkins University Press.

Gaffney, Mason M. 1957. "Concepts of Financial Maturity of Timber and Other Assets," American Economics Information Series Number 62, Department of Agricultural Economics, North Carolina State College, Raleigh.

Herfindahl, Orris C., and Allen V. Kneese. 1974. *Economic Theory of Natural Resources.* Columbus: Charles E. Merrill Publishing Company. (Chapter 4.)

Hirschleifer, J. 1970. *Investment, Interest, and Capital.* Englewood Cliffs: Prentice-Hall. (Chapter 3.)

Hotelling, H. 1931. "The Economics of Exhaustible Resources," *Journal of Political Economics.* 29(Apr): 137-175.

Pearce, D. W. 1976. *Environmental Economics.* New York: Longman, Inc. (Chapters 7 and 8.)

Solow, Robert M. 1974. "The Economics of Resources or the Resources of Economics," *American Economic Review.* 64(May): 1-14.

ADVANCED READINGS

Dasgupta, P., and G. Heal. 1974. "The Optimal Depletion of Exhaustible Resources," *Review of Economic Studies. (Symposium):* 3-28.

Smith, Vernon L. 1968. "Economics of Production From Natural Resources," *American Economic Review.* 58(June): 409-431.

ENDNOTES

1. See Solow, Robert M. 1974. "The Economics of Resources or the Resources of Economics," *American Economic Review*. 64(May): 1-14.
2. Materials on the competitive fishery summarize the results of models presented in Herfindahl, Orris C., and Allen V. Kneese. 1974. *Economic Theory of Natural Resources*. Columbus: Charles E. Merrill Publishing Company. (Chapter 4.)

11

The Logic of Conservation

There are, I fear, roughly as many definitions of "conservation" as there are individuals who use the term. One hears conservation equated with preservation, although not by the more sophisticated commentators. The latter are more likely to speak in terms of "wise use" and "protection from waste," but these are hardly precise, without further definition: what is meant by "wise use" and "waste"? Nevertheless, in spite of all this uncertainty with respect to its precise meaning, the term "conservation" tends to generate an emotional response on the part of those who see the insufficiency of conservation effort as the greatest failing of "myopic capitalism," and those who see "conservationist sentiment" as a major roadblock to economic progress.

Let me attempt a definition which, I hope, will seem reasonable to some: conservation is synonymous with the socially optimal allocation of natural resources over time. Those who, upon reflection, find themselves in agreement with this definition may be pardoned for wondering why, immediately following a chapter on the allocation of natural resources over time, it is necessary to present a chapter on conservation. My answer is as follows. In Chapter 10, a number of circumstances were identified in which private optima may be expected to diverge from social optima. In such cases, private markets cannot be trusted to optimally allocate natural resources over time. This chapter on conservation, then, has the specific purpose of addressing those circumstances in which the divergence between private and social optima is expected to be most pronounced; that is, those circumstances in which the conservationist approach, emphasizing (as it does) the long-term view, a concern for the welfare of generations whose "day in the sun" lies in the distant future, and a concern for the avoidance of risk, especially catastrophic risk, seems most appropriate.

SPECIAL PROBLEMS IN INTERTEMPORAL ALLOCATION

In a world of attenuated property rights, there is always a reasonable concern that private optima for the intertemporal allocation of resources will diverge from the socially efficient allocation. In addition, there is no reason to assume that a socially efficient intertemporal allocation of resources will result in intergenerational equity, the "fair" or "just" distribution of opportunity sets among different generations. But the focus of this chapter is upon those kinds of intertemporal resource-allocation decision problems that involve special difficulties: very long time horizons, extreme risk and uncertainty, and irreversibility.

VERY LONG TIME HORIZONS

In dealing with resource-allocation problems that involve several consecutive time periods, and where actions taken in a given time period influence the opportunity sets in later time periods, traditional economic theory assigns a crucial role to r, the rate of interest. It generally concludes that intertemporal efficiency requires that r = MTP = MEI, and that the empirical magnitude of the social discount rate is best determined through judicious observation of market interest rates and their manipulation to correct obvious sources of the failure of market interest rates to reflect the social opportunity cost of capital. Yet, market interest rates are determined in the market for capital investments that vary in duration from overnight to periods of seldom more than twenty to forty years. Revenues accruing only two or three generations hence are reduced to trivial amounts when their present value is determined using social discount rates derived from market interest rates.

Some of the most serious, and most intractable, difficulties confronting society as it wrestles with intertemporal resource-allocation problems are those in which the relevant time horizon is much more than a few years or decades. The half-life of certain kinds of nuclear residues is measured in the thousands of years. When a mineral deposit is entirely exhausted, it cannot be replaced in time periods less than geological eras (which are measured in the millions and billions of years). It is reasonable to assume that when a living species becomes extinct, it is gone forever. More generally, the desire of human societies and civilizations to perpetuate themselves and their culture into the indefinite future is not easily analyzed with an economic theory that thinks in terms of years, or decades, at most.

RISK AND UNCERTAINTY

The future is inherently uncertain. The uncertainty is exacerbated when the period under consideration spans many generations into the future, and when man's ability to develop and implement new technologies outstrips his capacity to predict, monitor, and mitigate the adverse effects of those technologies.

When considering the long-term future, several types of uncertainty are significant. *Technological uncertainty* involves lack of knowledge of the adverse impacts of new technologies (which may encourage their premature implementation), and the inability to foresee the new technologies that will be developed in the future. As an example of this latter kind of technological uncertainty, consider technologies that would permit more-readily-available resources to substitute for those exhaustible resources whose supplies are dwindling. Excessive optimism about the development of new technology will encourage excessively high rates of extraction of the exhaustible resource and its premature exhaustion, which would impose a high cost on future generations. On the other hand, excessively pessimistic expectations about future technology will result in extraction rates of exhaustible resources that are inefficiently low.

An additional type of technological uncertainty concerns the development of resource-using technologies. In Chapter 2, a resource was defined as something that is valued because it is both useful and scarce. Thus, the possibility always exists that technological developments will find valuable uses for things not currently considered resources, and new and valuable uses for those resources that are currently low-valued. For example, the history of mankind has been marked by the discovery of new medicinal uses for chemical compounds found in particular biological species — a process that continues to this day and can be expected to continue in the future. This provides one of the reasons for a concern with the preservation of endangered species in order to maintain the world's "gene pool" (the reservoir of global genetic diversity): the possibility exists that, by permitting the extinction of species that currently seem worthless, yet-to-be-discovered uses (medicinal and other) may be forever foreclosed.

The definition of a resource as that which is valued because it is useful and scarce suggests that, in addition to technological uncertainty, *demand uncertainty* is a serious concern. The tastes and preferences of individuals in future generations may be quite different from those of current generations. In addition, it is not easy to predict the populations and per capita incomes of future generations. For these reasons, there exists substantial uncertainty as to how future changes in patterns of demand will influence future scarcity relationships. Scarcity, of course, is influenced by both demand and supply conditions, and technology influences demand as well as supply. Technology introduces new commodities and amenities into opportunity sets, and effective demand for those new commodities and amenities cannot arise until they exist.

IRREVERSIBILITY

Many kinds of decision problems provide the decision maker with the comfort and security of knowing that, should he make in this time period a decision he later regrets, he can minimize his losses over the long haul by changing directions, at some cost, in a future time period. Many of the items in today's opportunity set, even if not selected today, will remain in future opportunity sets.

However, there are some items that, if not selected from today's opportunity set, will be eliminated from future opportunity sets. The decision to eliminate these items from today's choice bundle is *irreversible*.

Although it provides a convenient shorthand to speak, dichotomously, of decisions as being either reversible or irreversible, such language is highly imprecise. The Second Law of Thermodynamics indicates that the reversible-irreversible dichotomy is really a continuum, and that the endpoints on that continuum will seldom be observed. No choice is reversible at zero cost, and many choices called irreversible may be reversed at some less than infinite cost. Nevertheless, the idea of irreversibility is useful because it draws our attention to those choices that can be reversed only at extremely high cost.

The extinction of a biological species is, in this sense, irreversible. So is the creation, through genetic manipulation, of some new destructive (e.g., disease-causing) organism that proves to be near indestructible. Similarly, the generation of hazardous wastes (e.g., nuclear wastes, and also various kinds of toxic synthetic chemicals) is irreversible: future generations may find effective ways of isolating these wastes and rendering them harmless, but they will always be obliged to bear the costs of so doing. The large-scale destruction of geological, hydrological and ecological systems is also irreversible, in the pragmatic sense in which we have been using that word. The vanishing wilderness is not inexpensively re-created. If a decision were made to divert that piece of real estate known as the Grand Canyon to some entirely different use, thereby effectively eliminating the Grand Canyon as we know it, its re-creation in some later time period would be extremely, if not prohibitively, expensive.

THE CONTRIBUTION OF ECONOMICS

Traditional economics, when confronted with problems involving multiple-period time horizons and uncertainty, offers the concepts of *present value* and *expected value*. The concept of present value is fundamental to the analysis of investment decisions, and the conservation decision is an investment decision. The calculation of present value involves discounting procedures, the inadequacies of which, for decisions affecting the long term, have already been discussed. The expected value approach relies upon probabilities and is, therefore, applicable to decisions involving risk but not to those involving uncertainty. Where both the value of each possible outcome from a decision and the probability of each outcome actually occurring are known, the expected value of a decision may be determined by multiplying the value of each outcome by its probability and summing over all possible outcomes. Where time horizons are fairly short and the values of each of the possible outcomes are of roughly the same order of magnitude, the concepts of present value and expected value are quite serviceable.

However, economics is all but silent when confronted with the need to analyze a decision involving, say, a truly catastrophic outcome with very low probability at some future time. In recent years, economists have suggested several rather tentative approaches to the analysis of decision problems involving very long time horizons, extreme uncertainty, and/or irreversibility.

EXTENSIONS OF THE BENEFIT COST APPROACH

Working with the traditional present value, or benefit cost, approach, some resource economists have attempted to expand or, if you will, perfect that approach. In application, the benefit cost approach has typically resulted in quantification and valuation (and, therefore, explicit economic consideration) of only those benefit and cost items that are readily quantified and valued. In the last two decades, considerable progress has been made in incorporating benefits and costs associated with "non-market" goods and amenities (i.e., those that are not marketed, because of externality, indivisibility in consumption, and nonexclusiveness problems, individually, or in some combination) into the quantitative benefit cost analysis framework. This kind of approach has recently been extended to the valuation of fears, concerns, and sentiments individuals in the current generation may have for the future. Care is taken to ensure that evidence of growing demand for recreational and aesthetic amenities[1] and for health and personal safety[2] is recognized in benefit cost analyses.

Two additional sources of economic value have been recently recognized: option value and existence value.

Option Value

An individual who is not currently observed to be using a particular commodity or amenity may, nevertheless, place some positive value on the option to use it in the future. The purchase of options is a long standing practice in the real-estate and securities markets, where quite efficient markets in options are in operation.

The idea behind the concept of option value is that, although options markets in natural and environmental resources and the commodities and amenities they provide seldom exist, the same kind of individual motivations effectuated in real-estate and securities options markets are likely to exist with respect to natural and environmental resources. Since this contention is reasonable on its face, it makes sense to identify the sources of option value that are relevant to intertemporal allocation decisions, to quantify those values, and to include them in benefit cost analyses.

Existence Value

Individuals with an understanding and appreciation of natural systems and the important role diversity plays in those systems may derive utility from the mere knowledge that those systems exist intact. The disappearance of a natural environment or the extinction of an individual species may, therefore, cause disutility for an individual who has never been observed "using" those natural resources. This utility from existence, or disutility from extinction or disappearance, provides the source of existence value. Existence, as a commodity or amenity, is indivisible in consumption: the utility that an individual gains from knowing that a species or ecosystem exists is not diminished merely because others also enjoy that knowledge. Efforts are currently being made by researchers in natural resource and environmental economics to develop effective methods of quantifying existence values, so that they may be incorporated into benefit cost analysis of any proposed undertaking that threatens the continued existence of particular species or environments.

The extension of the benefit cost framework to include "non-market" goods, and option and existence values, is clearly a contribution to the perfection of that framework. Nevertheless, the perfection of the benefit cost framework would fail to satisfy those who are concerned with the very-long-run future of natural and environmental resources. Why? Because the benefit cost framework is dependent on discounting procedures that are much more defensible when used to evaluate proposals whose effects would be confined to the near-term future than when used to evaluate proposals with very-long-term consequences.

THE SAFE MINIMUM STANDARD

The concept of the safe minimum standard (SMS) was developed for analysis of problems concerning endangered species, but, it seems, could be adapted to many problems involving very long time horizons, massive uncertainty, and/or irreversibility. The SMS concept represents a partial retreat from the benefit cost framework. It recognizes that, regardless of the conceptual validity of the benefit cost framework it is, in application, often very incomplete. Thus, the

SMS concept offers a decision criterion that is admittedly incomplete, but that has the virtue of claiming no more completeness than it can deliver (a virtue that is not always apparent in applied benefit cost analyses). The safe minimum standard of preservation for a given species is identified in terms of a population just large enough to ensure survival of the species. The safe minimum standard is, therefore, set just a little higher than X_e (as defined in the section on "Unmanaged Biological Resources," Chapter 10). In other words the SMS is a level of conservation sufficiently high to reduce the probability of extinction (or irreversible loss) to a very low level. The expected costs of maintaining the safe minimum standard are then estimated, usually in terms of the present value of economic opportunities that would be foregone. Although there is often no direct, dollar for dollar, comparison of the economic value of maintaining the SMS versus the value of economic opportunities thus foregone, the decision maker is encouraged to choose a risk-averse strategy. For any species, population should be permitted to fall below the SMS only if the value of economic opportunities foregone by maintaining the SMS is "too high," or "very high." The SMS decision criterion is clearly incomplete, but it is useful in that it draws attention to the huge and often unquantifiable uncertainties involved in irreversible change, and to the desirability of a risk-averse decision strategy when considering such changes.

INTERGENERATIONAL EQUITY

Drawing on concepts of social choice (developed by Kenneth Arrow,[3] among others) and distributional justice (developed by John Rawls [4] and James M. Buchanan,[5] among others), a new line of conceptual inquiry into the intergenerational choice problem has been initiated by Talbot R. Page.[6] This line of inquiry recognizes the discounting concept as entirely an efficiency concept. As is well known (Section II), the empirical specification of what is efficient depends on the distribution of endowments. In intertemporal resource-allocation problems, where the opportunities of many generations are at stake, the endowments, at any given time, are all in the hands of living generations. Thus, viewed from the theories of social choice and distributive justice, the discount rate that is determined entirely by living generations is, when used as the basis for a decision rule to adjudicate conflicts between living and unborn generations, dictatorial. That is, the present generation dictates to all future generations. Page has begun an inquiry designed to discover intergenerational and intertemporal decision rules that meet the criteria for distributive justice in that, among other things, they do not permit a dictatorial role for any particular generation. This line of inquiry represents a fundamental attack on discounting procedures as decision rules. Its eventual outcome will be of great interest to natural-resource and environmental economists.

However, as of this writing, no firm conclusions that could be translated into operation decision rules have been achieved.

A CONCLUDING COMMENT

The present-value and expected-value concepts derived from traditional economics have proven to be of little use for the solution of decision problems involving very long time horizons, massive uncertainty, and/or irreversibility. Natural resource and environmental economists are interested in developing and refining the logic of economics, to make it more pertinent to these kinds of problems. Economics, alone among the social sciences, seems able to generate precise decision rules and to rigorously analyze their foundations. Thus, there is much at stake for the future of society in the outcome of this process of economic inquiry.

In the interim, common sense, combined with the little that economics can tell us, suggests caution, restraint, and risk aversion as appropriate responses to decision problems involving very long time horizons, massive uncertainty, and/or irreversibility. Options that involve even very low probabilities of catastrophic disaster at some future time should be approached with great caution and restraint.

These words, "caution," "risk aversion," and "restraint" are not precise economic terms. In fact, they sound suspiciously like some of the terminology used by those who take "conservationist" positions. This author concludes that, for those intertemporal resource-allocation problems whose outcomes will affect only the near-term future and where the values of the various possible outcomes are of roughly the same order or magnitude, the intertemporal decision rules derived, or alluded to, in Chapter 10 are viable. In these circumstances, conservation for conservation's sake is of no compelling importance. However, for intertemporal decision problems involving very long time horizons, uncertainty, and/or irreversibility, the caution, risk aversion, and restraint inherent in the conservationist approach has much to offer.

QUESTIONS FOR DISCUSSION

1. Distinguish carefully between "conservation" and "preservation."
2. If there were available an acceptably reliable estimate of the *cost* of ensuring the survival of an endangered species (e.g., the California condor or the bald eagle) of which the typical citizen is very much aware, how could the *desirability* of such an investment be determined? What kinds of information should be collected, and how should it be used? Is it likely that a reliable analysis of the *benefits* of such an investment could be performed?

3. Consider now, an endangered species such as the snail darter, which was unknown to biologists, let alone the typical citizen, until recently. For such a species, try to answer the questions posed in 2 (above). How would your answer vary from that appropriate for 2?
4. The author has argued: "Common sense, combined with the little that economics can tell us, suggests caution, restraint, and risk aversion as appropriate responses to decision problems involving very long time horizons, massive uncertainty, and/or irreversibility."

Others have argued that excessive caution may be the most risky policy of all, since it would deprive society of the necessary capital to develop substitutes for resources approaching exhaustion and technology for environmental protection.

The issues have been delineated. Proceed with the debate!

FURTHER READINGS

Bishop, R. C. 1978. "Endangered Species and Uncertainty: The Economics of a Safe Minimum Standard," *American Journal of Agricultural Economics.* 57: 10-18.

Ciriacy-Wantrup, S. V. 1968. *Resource Conservation: Economics and Politics.* Berkeley: University of California Press. 3rd edition.

Krutilla, J. V. 1967. "Conservation Reconsidered," *American Economic Review.* 57: 777-786.

Krutilla, J. V., and A. C. Fisher. 1975. *The Economics of Natural Environments.* Baltimore: Johns Hopkins University Press.

ADVANCED READINGS

Arrow, K. J., and A. C. Fisher. 1974. "Environmental Preservation, Uncertainty and Irreversibility," *Quarterly Journal of Economics.* 88: 312-319.

Fisher, A. C., J. V. Krutilla, and C. J. Cicchetti. 1972. "The Economics of Environmental Preservation: A Theoretical Empirical Analysis," *American Economic Review.* 62: 605-619.

Page, Talbot, and John Ferejohn. 1978. "On the Foundations of Intertemporal Choice," *American Journal of Agricultural Economics.* 60(May): 269-275.

ENDNOTES

1. See Krutilla, J. V., and A. C. Fisher. 1975. *The Economics of Natural Environments.* Baltimore: John Hopkins Press; and Fisher, A. C., J. V. Krutilla, and C. J. Cicchetti. 1972. "The Economics of Environmental Preservation: A Theoretical and Empirical Analysis," *American Economic Review.* 62: 605-619.
2. See, for example, Thaler, Richard H., and Sherwin Rosen. 1975. "The Value of Saving a Life: A Market Estimate," in *Household Production and Consumption,* Nestor Terleckyj, ed. *National Bureau of Economic Research Studies in Income and Wealth.* 40. New York.
3. Arrow, Kenneth J. 1951. *Social Choice and Individual Values.* New York: John Wiley and Sons.

4. Rawls, John. 1971. *A Theory of Justice*. Cambridge: Harvard University Press.
5. Buchanan, James M. 1975. *The Limits of Liberty: Between Anarchy and Leviathan*. Chicago: University of Chicago Press.
6. Ferejohn, John, and Talbot Page. 1978. "On the Foundations of Intertemporal Choice," *American Journal of Agricultural Economics*. 60(May): 269-275.

IV. RULES OF THE GAME: THE INSTITUTIONAL FRAMEWORK

The theoretical analyses of Sections II and III made clear, time and time again, the crucial role of institutions in shaping individual opportunity sets and the outcomes of economic interaction. Nonattenuated property rights were found to be essential, if the independent economic activities of individuals were to result, in aggregate, in economic efficiency. The particular specification of property rights was found to influence resource allocation, commodity distribution and consumption, the prices at which trade takes place, and the incomes of individuals. Regulatory and public-finance institutions were found to provide mechanisms for the collective control of externality and the management of nonexclusive resources. Public-sector economic activity provided the only means by which those goods that are nonexclusive because the costs of exclusion are prohibitive may be provided in efficient quantities. Price regulation was seen to be a commonly used, if not especially effective, method of discouraging the generation of "pure profits" in those industries where declining marginal costs and the absence of spatial competition lead to "natural monopolies." Taxation policy was seen to provide a means whereby a degree of collective control can be exercised when private decisions lead to intertemporal resource misallocation (under- or over-exploitation). In these ways, the role of institutions in influencing economic outcomes, in an economic system that relies principally on individual action motivated by individual interests, was recognized.

While the role of public institutions was thus recognized, institutions themselves were presented in a rather abstract form. From Sections II and III, there fails to emerge a comprehensive picture either of the role of governmental and other collective institutions in a modern mixed economy, or of the complex framework within which institutional decisions influencing the utilization of particular resources arise. The purpose of this section is to provide the rudiments of such a picture.

Chapter 12 provides a discussion of the loci of economic decision making in a mixed economy. First, the roles of private and public decision making are examined; then, the interactions among public-sector institutions at various levels are considered. The materials in Chapter 12 are broadly applicable to any modern mixed economy. Chapters 13 and 14 look, more specifically and in more detail, at institutional structures that influence the management of natural and environmental resources. The focus is upon the institutions that exist in the United States, but the perceptive reader will observe that, while countries with modern mixed economies may choose somewhat different configurations of institutions to address particular problems in the interaction between the private and public sectors and in resource management more specifically, each country must find some way to handle the various problems that give rise to a felt need, or "demand" if you will, for institutions. Careful observers have noticed that the similarities among the institutional structures of countries with modern mixed economies far outweigh the differences.

Chapter 13 introduces, in layman's terms and without any great precision, some important legal concepts that are essential to an understanding of the mechanisms for and the constraints upon public-institutional influence on resource and environmental policy in the United States. Chapter 14 uses two case studies (of surface-mining control and reclamation regulations, and federal investments in water projects) to illustrate the complex interrelationships among the private sector and government at all levels.

12

The Loci of Economic Decision Making

A modern mixed economy allows individuals, acting independently and in pursuit of their own self-interest, a major role in the making of economic decisions. However, not all economic outcomes are entrusted to the private markets that arise from the interaction of independent individuals. While individuals influence economic outcomes through the allocation of their budgets, they seek, in addition, a different kind of influence through the use of their political and legal endowments: the rights to vote, to speak and write in order to persuade others, to work in political parties, interest groups and issue-oriented organizations, and to litigate. The very same individuals pursue their self-interest through economic, political, and legal means. Thus, there exists a significant role for government in economic activity, and individuals seek to use both the market and the government in pursuit of their private goals. Individuals who sense that their comparative advantage lies in the political and/or legal arenas seek to expand the economic influence of government, while those whose comparative advantage is in the market seek to maximize the economic role of markets. Regardless of which group is in the ascendancy in a particular country at a particular time, the interactions between government and the market are pervasive.

Given that each individual seeks to use both the market and the government to achieve his ends, the terms "government interference" and "government intervention," in common usage among certain groups of economists, appear remarkably naive.

INTERACTIONS AMONG PRIVATE
AND PUBLIC SECTORS

A useful way to approach the issue of private/public-sector interactions is to consider, first, the minimal state (i.e., the most confined role for the political-legal sector that is compatible with economic productivity and social harmony). Then, the forces that may lead the political-legal sector to grow beyond the minimal state can be examined.

THE MINIMAL STATE

What is the most confined role for collective political-legal activity that is compatible with economic productivity and social cohesion, in a system that seeks to maximize the scope for private initiative while providing the basis for political stability and socio-cultural continuity? In order to consider this question, it is helpful to introduce the term "the state," to denote the whole range of political-legal institutions and activities a society collectively establishes and undertakes in order to achieve those ends it believes are not best served by purely private initiative. The question then is: what are the roles and functions that must be undertaken by the minimal state?

The minimal state must establish and enforce rights, preferably nonattenuated rights, defining the relationships among individuals with respect to each other, their government, and property objects (human rights, civil rights, and property rights). Without a comprehensive system of rights, interpersonal relationships would be highly insecure and conflicts would tend to be adjudicated by force (plunder and war), rather than through trade.

In order to establish such a system of rights, it is necessary for the state to undertake *legislation,* in order to specify rights; *policing and enforcement,* in order to enforce the rights specified; the operation of a *judicial system,* to resolve conflicts among individuals, between individuals and the police, between individuals and the legislature, and between legislation and "higher" (e.g., constitutional) law; and *military defense,* to protect the rights of individuals within the society when these are threatened by alien hordes.

The minimal state must "do something about" situations where exclusive rights are infeasible, and where "natural monopoly" exists. Without state action, nonexclusive resources would be abused and overexploited, and nonexclusive goods, services, and amenities would be seriously underprovided. These situations would soon become intolerable to the society. "Natural monopoly," which arises in industries that face continually declining marginal cost curves and, therefore, tends to result in spatial monopoly (the establishment of a single firm to provide services to a given region), would, if entirely uncontrolled, lead to excessive profits (which may possibly be tolerable to the society) and territorial wars among predatory firms seeking to expand their spatial monopolies (which would surely be intolerable). These needs to "do something" would lead the state into some kind of *regulation* of access to nonexclusive resources, or some kind of *taxation* policies to influence the pattern of their exploitation; to some form of *state economic activity* either to provide nonexclusive goods, services, and amenities or to subsidize their provision by the private sector; and to some form of state *licensing, franchising,* and/or regulation of spatial monopoly.

In order to perform the above-mentioned services, the state would need to *procure materials and services* and to *collect revenues* with which to pay for them.

To permit *coordination of state activities,* an administrative structure within the state (i.e., a bureaucracy) would need to be established.

Thus, even the minimal state exerts substantial influence on the patterns and outcomes of private economic activity. Through procurement and revenue collection, the minimal state influences the demand for goods and services, their prices, and the incomes of those who provide them. By the act of establishing and enforcing rights, the state influences resource allocation, commodity distribution, prices, and the distribution of income and wealth. The undertaking of legislative, policing, judicial, military, licensing, franchising, taxation-policy, and regulatory activities by the minimal state establishes the state as both a modifier of economic activity and an economic force in its own right. The ways in which it chooses to carry out its role as an economic unit will influence, directly or indirectly, all other economic units in the society.

BEYOND THE MINIMAL STATE

The economic influences of even the minimal state are, in themselves, quite pervasive. In addition, they provide the seeds for the growth of the state as an economic, as well as a political and legal, institution.

Since the state establishes and enforces interpersonal rights, it will attract the attention of all those citizens who have a personal interest in the particular kinds of rights specified, all those who have a personal interest in the degrees of severity and selectivity of enforcement, and all those who seek to pursue legislative, law-enforcement, legal, judicial, and military careers. Thus, we see the growth of the bureaucracy and the establishment of public-employee interest groups and private lobbies designed to influence the pattern and direction of state activity.

The obvious need for some state activity in regulation, direction through tax policy, or direct provision of goods and services, which arises from the prohibitive costs of exclusion with respect to certain goods and resources and from the existence of spatial monopoly, sows the seeds of more pervasive government influence on private activity. If nonexclusive goods and resources and spatial monopoly provide sufficient rationale for direct government activity or government influence through regulatory and taxation policy, surely externalities, indivisibility in consumption, monopoly in general, and the need to provide "merit goods" (those goods that are thought to be socially desirable in quantities larger than are purchased in the market) provide equally good reasons for activist governmental policy. Thus, we find governments in modern mixed economies regulating land use, public health and safety, and environmental quality; providing education, public health services, flood control, irrigation water, drainage, outdoor recreation, ballet, opera, literature and the fine arts, and protection of cultural, historical and natural monuments and treasures; and controlling the prices charged by monopolies, oligopolies and cartels, or regulating mergers among firms, with a view to limiting the formation of firms that may eventually attain monopolistic or oligopolistic positions in their particular markets.

The need to procure materials and services provides opportunities for the state to use its procurement policies to encourage the economic progress of particular industries, particular regions of the country, or particular, identifiable groups of citizens. The need to collect revenue provides the state the opportunity to use taxation policy to discourage economic activities it dislikes and encourage those it likes, and to redistribute income and wealth among its various citizens. Thus we see excise taxes, sales taxes, property taxes, taxes on imports and exports, user taxes, taxes on luxury items, and progressive income taxes, all of which are intended to influence economic outcomes, as well as to collect revenues.

As individuals and interest groups perceive the actual and potential economic importance of the state, they will invest in influencing the state according to the same decision criteria used to determine their private-sector investments. Thus, while there are forces encouraging the growth of the state and its expansion into new areas of activity, there are also forces seeking to restrain the growth of the state, to discourage its expansion into different kinds of activities, and to encourage an actual retrenchment in total state activity. The political and legal battles that almost always arise when the state enters a new economic arena are battles between those individuals who expect the proposed state activity to make them better-off and those who expect it to make them worse-off.

LOCI OF DECISION MAKING WITHIN THE STATE

The above discussion may have left the impression that the state is a monolith. Nothing could be further from the truth. At the most atomistic level, the state is composed of every individual who votes, pays taxes, contributes to political causes, pleads his case before the judiciary, petitions administrative agencies, or is employed in any state function. In this sense, almost every individual plays a role in the state, and each makes individual decisions as to how he shall play that role.

At a more functional level of analysis, the state may be seen as consisting of many different units, each having different kinds of responsibilities, each exercising different kinds of authority, and each having jurisdiction over different subpopulations of society, defined in terms of geographic, occupational, industry, or interest-group constituencies. These different organizational units of the state may find themselves in conflict, one with another. In addition, while each unit may be able to establish rules and incentives to encourage a common purpose among its employees and constituencies, each individual employee, constituent or client pursues his own self-interest within that structure of incentives, and seeks to modify that structure of incentives to make it more to his liking. Given this view of the structure of the state, it is important and meaningful to explore the loci of economic decision making power, not only between the private sector and the state, but also within the state.

To get this latter inquiry underway, it is useful to consider both the functional and the jurisdictional division of powers within the state. What kinds of things may each unit of the state undertake, and over what regional jurisdiction may each unit exercise its powers?

THE DIVISION OF STATE FUNCTIONS

It is common to divide the functions of the state into three fundamental categories: legislative, administrative, and judicial. These arc the famous "three branches of government" under the "separation of powers" doctrine that is basic to the republican democracy practiced in the United States. In parliamentary democracies, it is also necessary to take care of these three fundamental activities of government. However, under that form of government, the legislative and administrative functions are more nearly merged, through the devices of party responsibility and the selection of cabinet ministers (heads of administrative departments) from among legislators of the majority party or coalition.

While it is useful to talk about the legislative, administrative, and judicial functions of the state, there is a substantial variety of quite different undertakings within each of these broad functions, considerable interaction among the three functions, and a number of activities of the state that are not conveniently categorized in any one of these three functions. Some examples from the United States should help clarify these points.

Legislation seems to be a straightforward function: the making of laws. However, there is very substantial interaction among units of government in the field of legislation. The constitution restricts the items and activities that may be legislated, and the judiciary interprets the constitution. With the ever-increasing economic, social, and technological complexity of society, and of the state itself, legislatures find it impossible to write laws with sufficient precision and detail to permit their direct implementation. So, legislation, more and more, takes the form of enabling legislation. The legislature, in effect, states in fairly general terms those things it wants to see achieved with respect to a particular problem situation. It assigns to some administrative agency the duty of carrying out its wishes. The first task of the administrative agency is to draft, submit to public review and comment, and eventually promulgate detailed regulations for the implementation of the legislation. Thus, to a significant extent, administrative agencies legislate. The regulations promulgated by administrative agencies are then subject to judicial review, in order to determine that they fulfill the legislative mandate without exceeding the authority granted the agency under the legislation. The legislature may summon members of the agency's staff to appear before it in legislative hearings, to explain and defend the agency's performance in implementing the legislation.

The workaday function of the *judiciary* is to dispose of criminal trials and civil litigation, thus enforcing the system of rights specified by the legislature. However, the judiciary gains the greatest public notice when it adjudicates disputes about the scope and functions of the state itself, by deciding the constitutionality of legislation, regulations, or administrative action, and by reviewing regulations and administrative actions intended to implement laws passed by legislatures.

The primary role of the *administration* is to implement laws passed by the legislature, subject to judicial review. In this role, the administration is sufficiently complex. There are agencies to collect revenues, agencies to spend revenues, agencies to oversee budgetary matters, and agencies to prevent financial shenanigans within other government agencies and to apprehend the perpetrators thereof; there are agencies to encourage production, to control pollution, to enforce product-safety and industrial-safety regulations, and to combat inflation; there are agencies to encourage the exploitation of resources, and agencies to conserve resources; there are agencies to provide services through the public sector, and agencies to encourage the vigor of the private sector; and, above all, there are agencies to coordinate the relationships among agencies, agencies to adjudicate disputes between agencies, and agencies to enforce the law as it pertains to other agencies. In addition, the administration plays a significant part in legislation, by proposing legislation, by approving or vetoing (subject to possible legislative override) bills passed by the legislature, and by appointing the members of the judiciary who review legislation.

In addition, there is a substantial array of state activities that do not fit easily into the legislative, administrative, or judicial categories. There are quasi-independent, but wholly government-owned, corporations such as the U. S. Postal Service and the

Tennessee Valley Authority. There are undertakings that combine private-sector and government initiative, such as COMSAT. There are all kinds of boards and commissions, to which citizens are appointed as members, to decide such things as what uses shall be permitted of particular tracts of land, which beauticians shall be licensed to provide services for fee, and what rates for service will be charged to the customers of electric utilities.

JURISDICTION

Over what populations do the various units of the state have jurisdiction? There are some governmental units whose jurisdictions are determined by occupational or interest-group categories. However, the jurisdiction of governmental units is most commonly determined by geographic boundaries. The broadest subdivisions of jurisdiction are national versus local or, in those countries with federal systems of government, federal, state, or local. Since each citizen, consumer, and firm is simultaneously a constituent of a locality, a state, and a country, it is necessary to systematically assign the functions of government among the various geographically based jurisdictions.

In the United States, the states are the primary units of government, holding all those powers not specifically assigned to the federal government. The federal government, however, has been very adept at expanding its effective jurisdiction, in a number of significant ways. Various parts of the federal constitution specifically constrain the states from undertaking certain actions, and the federal courts have, in recent years, tended to interpret the rights of the federal government vis-à-vis the states, more broadly. The federal right to supervise interstate trade has provided, under judicial interpretation, an excuse for the federal government to regulate, if it so chooses, just about anything that crosses state boundaries. More creatively, the federal government has learned to use its substantial financial clout to regulate indirectly many of those things it has no constitutional right to regulate directly. The federal government is, far and away, the major collector of revenues, a substantial proportion of which it returns to the states. More and more, the federal government mandates specific actions on the part of the states in order to qualify themselves for federal financial assistance. In that way, the federal government effectively regulates many activities the regulation of which is, constitutionally, the responsibility of the individual states.

The state governments are the primary units of government, in the United States. They enjoy the police power (the power to regulate), and they are expected to provide most of the services citizens expect from their government (except for such obviously national undertakings as national defense). Local governments (i.e., city and county governments) are literally creatures of state government. They are established by state government, their geographic boundaries are determined by state government, and the powers they exercise are granted to them by state government and could be revoked, if state government so chose. States typically delegate to local governments the provision of many kinds of services that are conveniently provided at the local level, and many regulatory functions, such as planning and zoning, building codes, and health and safety regulations. In recent years, however, states have been more inclined to specify the performance expected of local governments, under the very credible threat of revoking the powers delegated to local governments.

The federal-state-local trichotomy is insufficient to fully categorize the geographic boundaries of jurisdiction of governmental units. There are a significant number of interstate and multistate governmental units (e.g., interstate rivers commissions and compacts). Within states, there is a variety of regional governmental units spanning several local jurisdictions: e.g., regional planning districts, soil and water conservancy districts, public-utilities districts, and river-basin commissions. This brief listing is sufficient to suggest that many of these regional (i.e., multi-locality) units are established at the initiative of federal, rather than state, governments.

SUMMARY AND PERSPECTIVE

The above discussion is intended to flesh out, a little, the previous somewhat abstract concept of institutions. In addition, it is intended to make, directly or by way of illustration, the following points. Government activities and undertakings (in the "minimal state," as well as under the kinds of governments found in modern mixed economies) have a pervasive influence on private activity. Further, there is no clear and absolute distinction between "government" and "the economy." Government activity influences economic interaction. More fundamentally, each individual is simultaneously an individual, a member of some kind of economic unit, and a constituent of many governmental units. He has endowments that are useful in the market and endowments that are useful in the political-legal arena, and he uses both kinds of endowments to further his own interests. Thus, individuals seek to use government, just as they seek to use the market, to further their own objectives.

Further, government is not a monolith. It is divided into many different units, along both functional and jurisdictional lines, and the interactions among these units are complex. It is unreasonable to expect government always to act consistently and cohesively, as if with a single will. Government, while it exists to resolve conflicts, is itself an arena of conflict. Different units of government exist for different purposes, are authorized to use different mechanisms in order to achieve their objectives, and receive support from different segments of the citizenry and the private sector.

Individual economic actors and the markets that result from their interaction are influenced substantially by the incentives that emerge from "government" (the political-legal arena), and it is the outcome of conflict between individuals and government units, and among government units themselves, that determines those incentives.

QUESTIONS FOR DISCUSSION

1. Webster defines anarchy as "a Utopian society having no government and made up of individuals who enjoy complete freedom." Compare and contrast anarchy with "the minimal state." Is anarchy feasible? If so, would that contradict the idea of "the minimal state"?

2. "Rules simultaneously restrict the individual and liberate him." What does this statement mean? Does it offer an important insight, or is it merely internally contradictory?

3. Some have argued that, in democracies, the public sector tends always to grow relative to the private sector. Using concepts presented in this chapter, construct an argument that would reach this conclusion. Then, critically evaluate your argument.

4. In the U. S., some have complained about "the increasing tendency of the judiciary and the bureaucracy to legislate." Assuming that this tendency exists, it is desirable? Is it inevitable?

5. The U. S. Department of the Interior and the departments concerned with resource management in some states include, under a single cabinet-level department, agencies whose purposes are to promote "resource development" *and* agencies to promote "resource conservation and environmental protection." In such an institutional environment, "development versus conservation" conflicts tend to be resolved within the department, with the result that the department secretary presents a single recommendation to the cabinet and the chief executive. Some observers have recommended that the "resource development" and "resource conservation and environmental protection" functions be assigned to separate cabinet-level departments. Then conflicts would be resolved in the cabinet, with the chief executive presiding. Discuss the pros and cons of this recommendation.

FURTHER READINGS

Ackerman, Bruce A., Susan Rose-Ackerman, James W. Sawyer, Jr., and Dale W. Henderson. 1974. *The Uncertain Search for Environmental Quality*. New York: The Free Press, Macmillan.

Breton, Albert, and Anthony Scott. 1978. *The Economic Constitution of Federal States*. Toronto: University of Toronto Press.

Buchanan, James M., and Gordon Tullock. 1962. *The Calculus of Consent*. Ann Arbor: University of Michigan Press.

Buchanan, James M. 1977. *Freedom in Constitutional Contract.* College
   Station: Texas A&M University Press. (Especially parts I and V.)
Patterson, Davidson Ripley. 1979. *A More Perfect Union: Introduction to
   American Government.* Homewood, Illinois: Dorsey-Irwin.

13

Some Important Legal Concepts

Any system of laws defines the rights of people with respect to each other, and with respect to their government. In any society with established procedures and traditions, and where citizens have some rather definite expectations concerning the broad configuration of laws, there are some basic legal constructs that are quite durable. These basic constructs form the building blocks of the system of rights. The process of institutionalizing and implementing policy is, for the most part, a process of utilizing these basic constructs, in ways that are more or less creative, rather than the more revolutionary process of creating and establishing whole new legal constructs.

Given that certain basic legal constructs form the building blocks of both individual rights and public-policy instruments with respect to natural and environmental resources, the study of resource and environmental policy cannot proceed in a legal vacuum. In this chapter, a small number of basic legal constructs and concepts are introduced and explained, rather imprecisely, in layman's language. The discussion proceeds in terms of the laws of the United States, but since much of American law had its origins in English tradition and, especially, English common law, many of these legal concepts will be applicable with fairly minor modification to other countries whose legal traditions are based on English law.

PRIVATE-LAW CONCEPTS OF PROPERTY

The private-law property concept that corresponds most closely to the abstract notion of ownership is *fee-simple title*. Property is "owned" and the owner may use it in any way he sees fit, subject only to any existing deed restrictions (see below) and to the other provisions of private and public law (which may restrict the rights of the owner). The owner may dispose of his property in any way he sees fit: by transferring it to another, in voluntary exchange; by making a gift; or by willing it to his heirs, upon his death.

The rights of fee-simple titleholders may be limited by *deed restrictions* that are private agreements voluntarily entered into. These may include *contracts* or *estates in land.* Contracts are personal agreements, and therefore, in the case of land, do not "run with the land." The beneficiary of a contract is left without protection, in the event that the grantor sells the land. Estates in land "run with the land." The beneficiary remains the dominant party, even if the grantor transfers the land to another. Deed restrictions are generally enforceable by the courts, upon complaint by a plaintiff, who must be a party to the agreement. There are some limits to the kinds of deed restrictions that will be enforced by the courts. For example, if a deed restriction has been consistently violated over time, courts will usually refuse to enforce it. Deed restrictions that violate other, dominant provisions of private or public law are not enforceable. For example, racially discriminatory deed restrictions are not enforceable.

Easements provide an arrangement whereby the property owner sells some of the rights in that property to another party, the beneficiary, who becomes the dominant party with respect to those rights. Easements are estates in land, and "run with the land" in perpetuity. An easement can be removed only if the dominant party voluntarily transfers it to the property owner. In the case of *positive easements,* the dominant party buys the right to do something with another's property. Examples of rights transferred as positive easements include: the right to travel across another's land in order to gain access to one's own lands; the right to construct utility lines or a canal across another's land in order to provide service to one's own land; and the right of access for hunting, fishing, or recreational uses. In the case of *negative easements,* the dominant party buys from the owner his right to do something, thereby foreclosing some of the owner's options. Negative easements may foreclose an owner's right to convert land to some different use, or to degrade the aesthetic qualities of land.

Private-property rights are subject to, and therefore protected by, the *laws of nuisance, trespass, etc.* These laws define the rights of owners inconvenienced by the actions of others. They are enforceable, under private law, in civil litigation. These laws offer property owners some protection against external diseconomies imposed upon them by others. However, this protection has been continually eroded, since the onset of the industrial revolution, by courts that have failed to enforce them in cases where, in the judgment of the court, enforcement would preclude or impede economic progress. The laws of nuisance, trespass, etc., provide no protection for a damaged party who cannot identify the party responsible for the damage and cannot demonstrate that the damage is creating an *economic* loss. These laws have been notoriously inadequate to deal with degradation of nonexclusive resources (e.g., ambient air, or water in streams, lakes, or the ocean).

STANDING TO SUE

The concept of *standing to sue* is pertinent to both private and public law. Litigation under private or public law will be dismissed by the courts if it is ruled that the plaintiff has no standing to sue. Under private law, in order to obtain standing, a plaintiff must usually establish that he has a significant economic interest in the protection he is seeking the courts to provide. This economic interest is usually established through property ownership. Thus, parties offended by degradation of nonexclusive resources have generally been unable to obtain standing to sue under private law. Public laws customarily specify who, and under what conditions, has standing to sue. Different public laws may define standing quite differently.

PUBLIC LAW

The fundamental concepts of public law that define the tools available to governments for use as instruments in implementing natural resource and environmental policy are the power of eminent domain, the police power, and the power to tax.

EMINENT DOMAIN

Eminent domain is the power of the "sovereign" (originally, under English common law, the King of England) to condemn property for the public purpose. The power of eminent domain is vested in the federal and state governments, and the latter may delegate it to local governments. Governments may choose to extend the power of eminent domain to certain quasi-public and even privately owned units: e.g., urban-renewal commissions, and investor-owned utilities.

Since condemnation involves the appropriation of property objects, *just compensation* must be paid. More than 150 years ago, the U. S. Supreme Court defined just compensation as *fair market value* — i.e., the price that would be agreed upon by a willing buyer and a willing seller. Note that this is not Pareto-safe compensation: the power of eminent domain is invoked only when the seller is unwilling. Just compensation is usually determined in negotiations between the unit exercising the power of eminent domain and the property owner, but the courts stand ready to determine just compensation in the absence of an out-of-court compensation settlement. If an out-of-court settlement is made, an interested party, provided he obtains standing, may sue the governmental unit, claiming that it has exceeded its authority by paying excessive compensation. For this kind of suit, standing may pose a problem. However, in many states, a taxpayer has standing.

The power of eminent domain, vested in the sovereign, is not unlimited. Condemnation must be "for the public purpose." Gradually, the courts have expanded the definition of the public purpose. For example, after much litigation, urban renewal was accepted as a public purpose.

THE POLICE POWER

The police power is the power of government to regulate the behavior of citizens in order to protect the public health, welfare, safety, and morals. The police power is vested in state government, which may delegate it to local governments. In America, the federal government does not enjoy the police power. However, the federal government, which customarily collects more taxes than it can directly spend and returns considerable funds to state and local governments in the form of various kinds of grants, has successfully used the police power by establishing regulations and denying funds to states that do not enact and enforce regulations consistent with the federal regulations.

Since the police power is the power to regulate behavior, rather than to appropriate property objects, compensation is not required. This is clearly a legalistic, rather than an economic, distinction: regulation can reduce the value of property objects, by restricting the uses that can be made of them.

The police power is not unlimited. The fifth and fourteenth amendments to the U. S. Constitution guarantee equal protection under the law and protect property against "taking without due process." Where police-power regulation substantially reduces the value of property objects *and* leaves the property owner with essentially no way to derive economic benefits from his property, courts may declare it an unconstitutional taking of property. Almost every time a governmental unit invokes a new form of regulation under the police power, a spate of litigation involving the "takings" issue follows. In recent decades, American courts have been noticeably more sympathetic to governmental units in their attempts to use the police power to control external diseconomies in the use of natural and environmental resources.

Police-power regulation takes many forms, a goodly number of which provide tools for governments in the implementation of natural-resource and environmental policy. These include land-use zoning, building codes, health and safety codes, subdivision controls, air- and water-quality regulations, and surface-mining and reclamation regulations.

Police-power regulations may be enforced under criminal law, and also under civil law. In the latter case, the solution is often an "equitable remedy"; for example, the violator is ordered to cease the offending behavior or, in the case of zoning and building regulations, remove the offending structure. Police-power regulations are often implemented by various specially constituted boards and commissions, whose members are appointed by governments. These boards and commissions are responsible to some governmental unit, but often they exercise substantial discretion. For example, they may grant variances and special exceptions to the regulations.

The Economics of Police-Power Regulation

Police-power regulation provides a mechanism whereby citizens, exercising political power through governmental units, may seek to control the uses owners make of their property without bearing the expense of just compensation under the power of eminent domain. It is therefore not surprising that the police power is a preferred tool of governments, and that property owners often find themselves in the position of attempting to defend their pre-existing rights against a proposed expansion of the police power. Currently controversial examples include the various Wild Rivers programs, which use the police power to limit the uses that may be made of land bordering "wild rivers" (usually to quite primitive agricultural uses), and programs that limit the extraction of minerals on certain classes of public lands. In both of these cases, the "taking" issue arises. Landowners may claim that Wild Rivers programs leave them with no economically feasible use of their land. Where mineral rights are privately owned, mineral owners may claim that regulations restricting or forbidding mineral extraction on public lands leave them with no economically feasible use of their mineral resources.

While it is clear that the police power provides government with a relatively inexpensive method of controlling the uses made of privately owned property, it is equally clear that the use made of the police power may very substantially influence the income and wealth of property owners. In some cases, economic injustice may be perceived, when a newly imposed regulation "wipes out" a property owner's prospects of income and wealth. In other cases, a change in police-power regulation may provide "windfall gains" for property owners. This may often be the case when land-use zoning regulations are changed, in the face of growing demand for land in more intensive uses, to permit a previously prohibited high-valued use of land. Thus, planning and zoning commissions, for example, have substantial powers to confer economic benefits and losses upon individuals. The public must be constantly alert for arbitrary and capricious uses of zoning authority, and for attempts by prospective beneficiaries to offer inducements, which are illegal or of dubious morality, for zoning authorities to change zoning regulations in ways that would confer windfall gains on the beneficiary.

THE POWER TO TAX

The power to tax is the power to raise revenues, for the purposes of government. While it is perfectly clear that taxation provides government a tool to influence the economic incentives facing individuals and thus implement allocative and distributional policy, the primary constitutional purpose of taxation is to raise revenues, rather than to provide a policy tool. The power to tax is vested in federal and state governments, and the latter may delegate that power to local governments. New taxes may be introduced, and rates of taxation may be increased without compensation.

The power to tax is not unlimited. The fifth and fourteenth amendments to the U. S. Constitution guarantee equal protection under the law. Thus, people must be treated equally, under taxation law, unless there is a basis for classification, in which circumstance like cases must be treated alike. The equal-protection clauses may limit the power of governments to use taxation as a policy tool. In addition, constitutional prohibitions on interference with interstate trade limit the use, by a state, of taxation as a policy tool (e.g., to provide a state with some protection against external diseconomies imposed upon it from out of state).

Rates of taxation must be determined by legislative bodies. It is unlawful for a legislature to permit administrative discretion in the establishment of tax rates. Therefore, a legislature cannot, for example, establish a system of effluent taxes, leaving the precise definition of effluent-tax schedules to an administrative agency. It has been speculated that this may in part explain the obvious American preference for the use of the police power, rather than the power to tax, as a policy tool for the control of external diseconomies. A legislature may pass enabling legislation for police-power regulation, assigning to an administrative agency the task of specifying and adopting precise regulations. However, a legislature may not use the power to tax in an analogous fashion. Since the constraints on manpower and expertise that face legislative bodies are much more severe than those facing administrative bodies, it is understandable that legislatures seem to prefer the regulatory route, whereby programs enabled by legislatures may be "fleshed out" by administrative agencies.

The Economics of Taxation

It is clear, to anyone with a rudimentary understanding of microeconomic theory, that the power to tax involves the power to modify prices, thus reallocating resources and redistributing income and wealth. A whole subdiscipline of economics, public finance, has been developed in order to analyze the economics of taxation. In natural-resource and environmental economics, a large number of theoretical analyses have been developed, each demonstrating that, for some particular resource or environmental problem, the modification of incentives via taxation is more effective, or less likely to result in inefficiency, than regulation. However, constitutional restrictions on the power to tax, which include the equal-protection clauses and the provisions that prohibit legislatures from assigning to administrative agencies the task of determining taxation rates, make taxation a rather blunt policy tool.

QUESTIONS FOR DISCUSSION

1. Some writers have conceptualized the rights pertaining to, say, land as "a bundle of sticks." By this, they mean that rights are not monolithic, but instead consist of many different kinds of rights that may be severed and assigned separately or in various combinations. Does this analogy make sense? Support your conclusion with examples.
2. Legislative actions and judicial decisions sometimes redefine *standing to sue*. What relationship would you expect between the definition of standing to sue and the time and transactions costs expended in litigation?
3. "Just compensation under eminent domain is not Pareto-safe compensation." Carefully develop this argument.
4. Under eminent domain, just compensation prevents "wipe-outs." However, "wipe-outs" may result from police-power regulations, or changes in taxation policy. Does this give the economist reason to conclude, along with Dickens,[1] that "the law is an ass, an idiot"? Explain.
5. It has been observed that the rationale for effluent taxes was developed largely in the United States, yet they have been implemented more often in Western Europe than in the U. S. How could this be? Might the restrictions placed upon taxation in the U. S. Constitution be a contributing factor?

FURTHER READINGS

Babcock, Richard F. 1966. *The Zoning Game.* Madison: University of Wisconsin Press.

Bosselman, Fred, David Callies, and J. Banta. 1973. *The Taking Issue.* Washington: Council of Environmental Quality.

Michelman, Frank L. 1967. Property, Utility, and Fairness: "Comments on the Ethical Foundations of 'Just Compensation' Law," *Harvard Law Review.* 80: 1165-1258.

Niskanen, William A. 1971. *Bureaucracy and Representative Government.* Chicago: Aldine-Atherton.

Pechman, Joseph A. 1977. *Federal Tax Policy.* Washington: Brookings Institution. 3rd edition.

Reich, Charles A. 1963. "The New Property," *Yale Law Journal.* 73: 733-787.

Whyte, William H. 1968. *The Last Landscape.* New York: Anchor Doubleday.

Wilcox, Clair. 1966. *Public Policies Toward Business*. Homewood: Irwin.
Wunderlich, Gene L., and W. L. Gibson, Jr. 1972. *Perspectives of Property*. University Park: The Pennsylvania State University.

ENDNOTE

1. Dickens, Charles, *Oliver Twist* (Ch. 10).

14

Natural Resources and the State: Legislative, Administrative, and Judicial Processes as They Apply to Natural and Environmental Resources

The role of the state, through its legislative, administrative, and judicial functions, in the public management of natural resources and the establishment of incentives to influence their private management, is extremely complex. It is said, only half jokingly, that no man lives who can comprehend the entirety of the governmental role in the management and conservation of natural resources. In such a context, it seems of little use to provide the student with a catalog of governmental agencies concerned with natural and environmental resources, complete with organization charts, statements of duties and jurisdictions, active and proposed programs, avenues of communication with other agencies, and the provisions that exist for legislative oversight and judicial review of the agencies' activities. Such a catalog would represent information overload.

Instead, presented below are two simplified case studies designed to illustrate the legislative, administrative, and judicial processes through which political-legal influence is brought to bear on the markets in natural and environmental resources. These case studies concern the environmental impacts of surface mining for coal, and the construction of federal water projects.

CONTROLLING SURFACE MINING FOR COAL

Large-scale surface mining for coal has become highly visible in the last three decades. While it provides an inexpensive method of exploiting certain kinds of coal deposits, its environmental impacts are quite massive and, being quite spectacular, have attracted considerable public attention.

THE PROBLEM

Surface mining involves the removal of vegetative cover and overburden, in order to extract the underlying coal. The overburden must be stored and, if reclamation is planned, eventually replaced at the mine site. The mining process may inconvenience the owner of surface rights to the land, and it may involve blasting, rock falls, etc., which inconvenience neighboring landowners. If reclamation is inadequate, the inconvenience to the landowner and his neighbors may continue long after mining has been completed.

Soil is disturbed during mining, overburden storage, and the replacement of overburden at the mine site, often resulting in increased runoff and sedimentation. Water quality is thus damaged, and the frequency and severity of floods increased; both of these effects may be felt by citizens, who may or may not be landowners, many miles from the mine site.

The surface-mining site is considered aesthetically unpleasant, and, depending upon the reclamation procedures followed, aesthetic damage may continue long after mining has ceased. The inevitable disturbance of soil structure during mining and reclamation may damage the surface and underground hydrological patterns, and may diminish future soil productivity in agricultural and other uses.

Several quite different categories of individuals may be adversely affected by the environmental damage resulting from surface mining. These include the surface landowner; the owners of neighboring land; those who use water for any purpose, anywhere downstream in the disturbed watershed; and a broad "general public" group of citizens who are offended by the aesthetic effects of surface mining and the prospect of reduced productivity from the nation's soils. Historically, the claims of these various groups have been weighted quite differently: the rights of surface and neighboring landowners have been accorded considerable respect; the rights of water users have been more limited; and the rights asserted by citizens who claim to be offended by the way in which others use land that they own have held little sway.

REMEDIES IN PRIVATE LAW

A landowner who holds fee-simple title to both the surface and mineral estates has very substantial protection. Surface mining may not take place without his consent, and, it is reasonable to presume, he will not permit the extraction of coal by surface mining unless he is fully compensated for the value of the minerals extracted and for any damage that occurs to the surface land. However, in the Appalachian states, where coal mining has a long history, mineral rights were severed from surface rights and made dominant to them, sixty to one hundred years ago, under the "broad-form deed." This arrangement left many surface landowners exposed to damage of a kind and on a scale they could scarcely have anticipated at the time the mineral rights were severed and sold. Since the development of modern surface-mining methods, the courts of most Appalachian states (but not Kentucky) have modified the broad-form mineral deed, requiring that a surface miner first obtain the consent of the surface landowner.[1]

Private law provides remedies for neighboring landowners who may be damaged, under nuisance law. Neighboring landowners may obtain injunctive relief from practices that damage them and, perhaps, compensation for damage that has already taken place. Users of water whose quality is impaired by surface mining have less effective remedies, under private law. To obtain relief, they must prove that the impairment of water quality has been economically damaging to them, and that it was caused by a particular surface-mine operator. The general citizen, concerned with deterioration in the productivity of soil, and aesthetic qualities of the landscape, is without remedy under private law.

LOCAL GOVERNMENT

Local government may exercise only those powers specifically delegated to it by state government. These often include the power to zone under the police power, and the power to tax. However, there have been only a few instances in which local governments have effectively used these powers to control the external effects of surface mining for coal.

STATE GOVERNMENTS

The judiciary, in many Appalachian states, has provided some protection for surface landowners through its interpretation of private contract law. Broad-form mineral deeds sold many years ago have been modified, either on the grounds that their original sale represented a transaction between grossly unequal parties (wealthy and knowledgeable buyers of mineral rights, and poor and ignorant landowners) or, more commonly, on the grounds that a landowner severing and selling his mineral rights many years ago could not reasonably have been expected to foresee the development of modern surface-mining methods.

Police-power regulation represents a major tool by which state government may attempt to control the external effects of surface mining. During the 1950's, 1960's, and 1970's, most states where surface mining for coal is a significant activity have undertaken some form of regulation under the police power. In order to undertake surface mining, an operator must first obtain a permit from the state. State permitting procedures vary, but usually involve the following: the submission of detailed engineering and geological analyses, and mining and reclamation plans; the acceptance by the operator of various restrictions the state imposed upon his mining activities; and the posting of a bond, which would be returned to the operator after the satisfactory completion of required reclamation procedures.

The establishment of regulations for surface-mining control required enabling legislation, and the establishment of administrative units to, first, promulgate detailed regulations and, then, enforce them. The enabling legislation was subject to judicial review on constitutional grounds, the regulations were subject to judicial review to ensure that they fulfilled but did not exceed the authority granted under the enabling legislation, and the actions of the administrative agency were subject to judicial review to ensure that the agency did not exceed its authority.

Citizens and interest groups exerted influence on this process, at every stage: in electoral politics, by which legislative and certain key administrative posts, including that of chief executive, are filled; at legislative hearings; as plaintiffs in judicial proceedings; and as participants in various administrative processes established specifically to permit and encourage citizen participation. These last arrangements may provide for public hearings or comment prior to the adoption of regulations; public hearings or comment, or the filing of individual written objections, prior to the granting of a surface mining permit; etc. Citizens may also use the press and other public forums in an attempt to influence the regulatory process at every stage.

State governments also have considerable powers of taxation. Severance taxes may be placed upon coal, in general. Alternatively, a differential severance tax may be placed upon surface-mined coal, to provide a fund with which the state could reclaim abandoned surface mines, to (in a sense) compensate the general public for environmental damage caused by surface mining, or simply to discourage surface mining. The differential severance taxation of surface-mined coal would, surely, be challenged in the courts on the grounds that it violates the equal-protection clauses, but it may quite possibly survive such challenge.

State governments may also directly undertake reclamation activity, financing it from general revenues, from severance-tax revenues, or, more commonly, from the bonds forfeited by surface-mine operators who fail to complete reclamation satisfactorily.

By the early 1970's, the various states in which surface mining for coal is a significant activity had used some or all of these powers to influence the pattern of surface mining and to control its external effects. State laws differed in their stringency, and state enforcement differed in its effectiveness.[2]

A rationale for federal legislation to control surface mining and reclamation was being developed. Since surface mining affected water quality, and watersheds often crossed state boundaries, it was argued that surface mining could not be considered purely the concern of the state in which it occurred. It was also argued that individual states suffered some disadvantages, which would not be suffered by the federal government, in the attempt to control the external effects of surface mining. Given that resources useful in the extraction of coal are mobile across state boundaries, each state would establish its policy with respect to the control of surface mining with one eye on the damage caused by uncontrolled surface mining and the other eye on the activities of other states in which surface mining takes place. In other words, it was argued that, in the absence of collusion among the states, each state would be reluctant to insist upon internalizing the Pareto-relevant external diseconomies from coal mining, for fear that the industry, and the income and employment it produces, would move to states with less stringent regulations. Therefore, so the argument goes, federal regulation of surface mining would eliminate the temptation of individual states to indulge the industry with weak regulations and enforcement.

THE FEDERAL GOVERNMENT

The federal government had long had some interest in matters pertaining to surface mining of coal. The U. S. Geological Survey and the Bureau of Mines had mapped and inventoried coal reserves. The various federal land-management agencies had been involved in the leasing of coal to surface-mine operators, on the lands over which they had jurisdiction. Agencies as diverse as the Environmental Protection Agency, the U. S. Forest Service, and the Bureau of Mines (under the cabinet-level departments of Health, Education and Welfare, Agriculture, and Interior, respectively) had established research programs pertaining to surface-mining and reclamation methods. The Environmental Protection Agency, under its water-quality program, was approaching the regulation of effluent from surface-mining sites.

Enabling legislation for the federal regulation of surface mining and reclamation was introduced into the U. S. Congress on several occasions during the 1970's, and was passed by Congress but vetoed by President Ford in 1975. Eventually, in 1977, the Surface Mining Control and Reclamation Act was passed by the Congress and signed into law by President Carter, following a change in administrations. The legislative process was lengthy, and involved many legislative hearings, at which conflicting scientific evidence about the damage from surface mining and the costs of reclamation was presented.

The federal enabling legislation of 1977 contained the following general provisions: the Office of Surface Mining was established, to write and adopt detailed regulations, and to oversee their enforcement; regulations for the permitting of surface mines, the prevention of off-site damages during and after mining, and the reclamation of surface-mine sites were, as is usually the case in enabling legislation, delineated in broad outline, but not in specific detail; a fee, in essence a severance tax, was to be collected for each ton of coal mined and was to be used for the reclamation of lands already surface mined and abandoned (the tax applied to all coal, but surface-mined coal was to be taxed at a higher rate); and funding was provided for research into mining and reclamation practices and the utilization of coal, at various state universities. The regulations pertaining to the permitting of surface mines, the prevention of off-site damages during and after mining, and the reclamation of land and its restoration to productive use were, in aggregate, more stringent than the regulations at that time in force in any state.

Since the federal government does not enjoy the police power, how could it undertake police-power regulation of surface mining and reclamation? The answer is: through the power of the purse. The federal legislation required that, in order to avoid the withholding of certain categories of federal funds, each state must enact surface-mining control and reclamation legislation consistent with the federal act. Initially, the federal Office of Surface Mining was to enforce the federal regulations as they pertained to each surface mine in the United States. However, as each state demonstrated that its legislation was adequate, that regulations consistent with federal regulations had been adopted, and that an effective enforcement apparatus had been established within the state administration, day-to-day enforcement was to be turned over to state government. The Office of Surface Mining, nevertheless, was to retain some broad supervisory powers, to ensure that state regulation and enforcement complied with federal standards.

The federal legislation requires and permits extensive citizen participation at many stages in the regulatory process. In addition, it opens the federal and state courts to citizen complaints. The federal legislation itself, and the regulations adopted thereunder, may be challenged in federal court, and the state companion legislation and regulations may be challenged in state courts.

Federal regulation of surface mining and reclamation involves a very complex pattern of interaction among state and federal legislative, administrative, and judicial units. Since its purpose is to regulate behavior of an activity (i.e., surface mining for coal) undertaken by private individuals and firms, in order to prevent and mitigate damage that may be imposed upon other private individuals and firms, the pattern of institutional interactions it involves includes not just interactions among these various governmental units but also interactions, at every level, between governmental and market units. At the most elemental level, each individual attempts to exert influence within, and is simultaneously constrained by, governmental and market institutions.

FEDERAL WATER PROJECTS

Whereas the governmental activity with respect to surface mining for coal was addressed to the establishment and enforcement of incentives to influence the pattern of private-sector activity in coal mining, governmental activity with respect to federal water projects involves direct government investment of resources and provision of services.

THE PROBLEM

River basins are large units, which typically encompass many individuals and firms, and frequently cross local and state jurisdictional boundaries. Ownership of water in river systems is vested in the public sector, as a public trust. State governments establish and enforce water rights, which assign to individuals the right to withdraw and use water for various purposes. Where major rivers cross state boundaries, states may subordinate a part of their authority, with respect to the granting of water rights to individuals, to an interstate rivers compact or commission. The federal government, operating through the U. S. Army Corps of Engineers, has jurisdiction over all navigable waters.

River systems are unpredictable, in that flooding or periods of drought may occur. In addition, the possibility exists that massive modifications to river systems (e.g., the building and maintenance of dams, flood-control structures, or navigation locks) may render river systems more effective in providing services to individuals and communities. Given the massive size of river systems, the massive capital requirements for large-scale river-system modifications, the tradition of homesteading and the family farm (which has resulted in the division of river-basin lands into many small, independently owned tracts), and the vesting of ownership rights to rivers in the public sector, large-scale river-modification projects must be carried out by the public sector, and usually the federal government, or not at all. .

THE GENESIS OF THE PROJECT PROPOSAL

For many years now, the federal government has financed, constructed, and operated major structural projects concerned with water resources. In the last four decades, quite massive programs to develop and manage "water and related land resources" have become institutionalized. One or more of the federal water-resources agencies is active in every major river basin in America, operating those water-resources projects that have already been constructed, perhaps currently constructing (or actively proposing) additional projects, and, almost certainly, maintaining a continuously active program of river-basin planning. In this institutional environment, citizens of the river basins, and especially those with a particular economic interest in water resources, have developed the expectation that the federal government will fund the construction and operation of proposed water projects that enjoy substantial support in their immediately affected localities.

Given these expectations, and past patterns of institutional behavior, citizen pressure, in a river basin that has already enjoyed substantial federal investment in water projects, gradually develops for an additional project. Perhaps population growth and increasing economic activity have led to increasing demands for irrigation water; water for residential, commercial, and industrial uses; additional flood protection; river-flow augmentation to reduce the concentration of pollutants in the river; or water-based outdoor recreation facilities. Perhaps vague and scattered sentiment for an additional water-resources project congeals as a result of a severe flood or drought.

The initial sentiment in favor of a new water-resources project is likely to come from those groups that have been traditional supporters of water-resources programs, and from similarly placed groups who have not yet enjoyed the benefits of federally funded water-resources development and who feel that their turn is about due. These groups, most likely, already enjoy close relationships with the local and regional staff of the federal water-resources agency most active in their river basin. So it is a relatively easy task for the private interests who would benefit most from a new water-resources project to make their desires known to the local and regional staff of the federal agency most likely to lend staff resources, political influence, and power within the administration to designing a new project, proposing it, and lobbying for its eventual authorization, funding, and construction.

Even before support for a new project begins to appear among private individuals and interest groups, it is likely that the cognizant federal water-resources agency (which, for brevity, we shall simply call the Agency) will already have done some initial planning of new projects, under the guise of its continual planning process. Thus, at the time of initial discussions concerning the proposed new project between the Agency and its potential clientele groups, neither party is entirely unprepared. The parties are familiar, in a general kind of way, with each other's goals, perceived needs, and operating procedures, and each party is likely to have done some advance planning.

The Agency, sensing a degree of local support for a new project, the construction and operation of which would be conducive to the Agency's internal goals of security, longevity, and increasing size, moves its planning effort into high gear, and focuses it upon the planning of one or a small number of specific projects designed to meet the felt needs of its clientele groups. At this stage, there is considerable interaction between the Agency and its traditional clientele groups but, usually, considerably less interaction between the Agency and the regional "general public" at large. The outcome of this process of planning and interaction with clientele groups is often the proposal by the Agency's local or regional office of a specific new project (hereafter called the Project).

THE FEDERAL ROLE

The Agency's local or regional office prepares detailed plans for the Project and detailed documentation of the need for it. This documentation finds its first use in the efforts of the local or regional office to persuade its national leadership to place the Project on the Agency's list of projects to be proposed to the U. S. Congress for its authorization.

Since passage of the Flood Control Act of 1936, Congress may authorize water-resources projects only if it is first demonstrated that the benefits to whomsoever they accrue will exceed the costs. That is, a benefit cost analysis of the Project must be performed, and it must demonstrate that the Project will have a benefit/cost ratio in excess of 1.0.

The benefit cost analysis is performed by the Agency, which procedure places the Agency in the anomalous position of evaluating a project it has proposed and would implement if approved. The benefit cost analysis is performed in accordance with guidelines set by the Water Resources Council,[3] a body appointed by the President and including the Secretaries of cognizant cabinet-level departments or their designated representatives. In performing the benefit cost analysis, the Agency is expected to seek input from all other federal and state agencies and other identifiable groups that may be expected to have information or expertise relevant to the Project. The Office of Management and Budget, a federal executive "watchdog" agency, may examine the benefit cost analysis. Another federal agency (e.g., the Natural Resource Economics Division of the Economics, Statistics, and Cooperatives Service) may also be assigned to examine the benefit cost analysis and its supporting documents. Eventually, the Agency submits to the Congress a request for authorization of the Project, along with appropriate supporting documentation (including the mandated benefit cost analysis).

In the event that the benefit cost analysis indicates that the expected benefits from the Project would fail to exceed its costs, it is pointless even to submit a request for congressional authorization. This requirement, coupled with the arrangement whereby the agency that proposes the project and would implement it, if authorized and funded, performs the benefit cost analysis, seems to provide a built-in incentive for optimistic benefit cost analysis.

The request for authorization of the Project is assigned, along with many other similar requests, to a congressional subcommittee, which then holds legislative hearings. Agency staff, representatives of other federal and state agencies that may have pertinent information, and interested members of the public may testify. At this point, significant local opposition may be heard, perhaps for the first time. Assume, so that our narrative may continue, that Congress authorizes the Project. At this point, project opponents have no recourse to the judiciary: project authorization is considered a congressional decision, and the benefit cost analysis is considered a congressional document. Thus, neither the authorization decision nor the documentation that is a prerequisite for that decision may be reviewed by the courts.

The National Environmental Policy Act of 1969 requires that an environmental-impact assessment (EIA) of the Project must be performed and an environmental-impact statement (EIS) must be prepared and submitted.[4] The EIA is to consider and evaluate all the potential impacts that construction and operation of the Project would have on the quality of life in the affected region; the EIS is to report the findings of this assessment. The Agency has detailed guidelines for the performance of the EIA and the preparation of the EIS. These guidelines call for (1) the collection of pertinent information concerning the potential impacts of the Project from within the Agency, from other cognizant federal and state agencies, and from individuals and interest groups who may have information to offer; (2) the assessment of the expected environmental impacts of the Project; (3) the active solicitation of written comments from all interested individuals and groups; (4) the completion of a draft EIA, its circulation among all identifiable interested parties, and the active solicitation of written comments; (5) the holding of public hearings concerning the draft EIS; (6) the preparation of a revised draft of the EIS, taking due consideration of Agency and public comment, and of information brought to light in the course of public hearings; (7) a further round of public and Agency comment, and public hearings; and (8) the submission of a final EIS to the President's Council on Environmental Quality. Until this final step in the EIS process has been completed, federal funds and resources may not be used in implementation of the Project.

The EIS process requires the Agency, which is necessarily a proponent of the Project, to prepare and to publicly present information concerning both the beneficial and the adverse effects the Project may be expected to have. In addition, the elaborate requirements for public comment and public hearings provide a forum for opponents of the Project. Thus, the EIS process may be important in catalyzing opposition to projects whose potential impacts include some that may be considered adverse by various segments of the public (often, groups that are not among the

Agency's traditional clientele groups, and that thus played little or no part in the interactions that led to the original proposal for the Project). The effects of opposition thus catalyzed may be felt at several points in the continuing institutional processes through which water-resources projects must pass, if they are to be implemented.

The National Environmental Policy Act explicitly permits litigation to challenge the EIS, on procedural or substantive grounds (i.e., on the grounds that the prescribed procedures were not followed, or that the substance of the EIS is incomplete or misleading). Successful litigation by project opponents results, usually, in a court order that an adequate EIS be prepared and submitted, and an injunction against further work on the project until the court has approved the resubmitted EIS. Ironically, it is perfectly legal, under the EIS process, to construct a project whose environmental impacts are overwhelmingly adverse; all that is required is that the EIS accurately depict those impacts. Thus, litigation under the EIS provisions of the Act cannot guarantee that only those projects that are environmentally benign are implemented. Nevertheless, litigation may be effective in delaying construction of those projects that meet with significant opposition, and publicizing the arguments raised by project opponents.

Congressional authorization of the Project does not end the involvement of the Congress. The Project must be funded. In fact, if no funds are allocated to the Project for several consecutive years, project authorization lapses. Water projects are funded under the public-works sections of the federal budget, following subcommittee hearings, subcommittee approval, approval of the Congress, and presidential assent of the budget. The subcommittee hearings concerning funding provide another forum in which project proponents and opponents make their respective cases, for and against project funding.

Assume that Congress allocates funds for implementation of the Project. These funds cannot be spent until the EIS requirements under the National Environmental Policy Act have been satisfied. In addition, several further administrative and judicial hurdles remain. The Agency may have to obtain a permit from the U. S. Army Corps of Engineers, which has jurisdiction over all navigable waters. Depending on the precise specifications of the Project, permits may need to be obtained from other agencies. In order to implement the Project, it may be necessary to condemn, under the power of eminent domain, land or other resources owned by private individuals. The condemnation process may lead to litigation. If it is found that the Project may destroy the significant habitat of an endangered species, litigation under the Endangered Species Act may result in a permanent injunction against implementation of the Project, or a court order that the Project be modified in such a way that the significant habitat is not destroyed.

THE ROLE OF STATE GOVERNMENT

In the case of federal water-resources projects, the role of state government is limited, but not insignificant. Under many water-resources programs, state governments are required to share certain categories of project costs. In the case of projects intended to provide certain services to state and/or local governments (e.g., residential, commercial, and industrial water for delivery through municipal water systems), it is required that state governments enter into firm contractual agreements concerning these services. In addition, many but not all federal water-resources agencies maintain a firm tradition that they will not implement projects that are opposed by the government of the state in which the proposed project is located. Thus, state governments have several tools through which they can bring their feelings, in support of a proposed federal water-resources project or in opposition to it, to bear on the decision process. Individuals and groups who feel strongly in favor of or in opposition to the Project will attempt to influence the role that state government plays in this process.

CITIZEN ROLES

The complex institutional procedures through which federal water-resources projects are designed, proposed, authorized, funded, and implemented provide citizen access to federal and state governments, and to the legislative, administrative, and judicial processes, at many different points. Legislation passed in the last decade, especially the National Environmental Policy Act and the 1973 amendments to the Endangered Species Act, has expanded the opportunities for citizen input into administrative processes and for citizen suits. The net impact of this legislation has been to broaden the avenues available to project opponents, relative to project proponents.

Throughout this case study of the institutional arrangements through which water-resource projects are implemented, reference to citizen roles has consistently been made in terms of "traditional clientele groups," "project proponents," and "project opponents." These groups, it was implicitly assumed, are, for the most part, centered in the project region, and therefore most likely to directly experience the beneficial and adverse impacts of the Project, if implemented.

There is a much larger group of citizens, the taxpayers of the United States, who have an interest in the Project: most of them can expect to contribute to the Project's costs but not to directly enjoy its benefits. However, this group is large and diffuse, and the contribution of each individual toward the Project's costs is likely to be very small. Thus, there is a sense in which sound decision making with respect to the Project is a nonexclusive good for the general taxpayer, who would gain little direct and exclusive benefit from active participation in the decision process. On the other hand, the beneficial and adverse impacts upon citizens in the project region may be strictly exclusive or, at least, shared among a group very much smaller than the group of nationwide taxpayers.

If this is a reasonable statement concerning individuals, it will be reflected in the behavior of their congressional representatives. The implementation of a water-resources project that enjoys local support in a congressman's district will be an exclusive good to that congressman; the costs of that project will be a nonexclusive good for the remaining 434 members of the U. S. House of Representatives. For these reasons, it is widely believed that the existing institutional arrangements for the implementation of water projects, whose impacts are localized but whose costs are shared throughout the nation, result in an inefficiently large aggregate investment, not only of capital but also of environmental resources, in such projects.

Growing awareness of this phenomenon may be responsible for the apparent increase in the vigor and effectiveness of groups opposing federal water-resource projects. In addition, it is quite possible that, as time passes and the more desirable water projects become implemented, the menu of remaining water projects awaiting authorization and implementation becomes less attractive. It has been suggested that after several decades of intensive federal dam-building activity, dam building must necessarily become a declining industry, as the marginal dam on the marginal tributary of the marginal river moves closer and closer to authorization.

Perhaps for these reasons, and perhaps for others, a shift in citizen opinion seems to be gradually occurring, as more and more individuals seem willing to question or actively oppose federal water-resources projects.

RECENT PROPOSALS FOR INSTITUTIONAL REORGANIZATION

The administration of President Carter, perceiving (correctly or incorrectly) that the institutional arrangements under which water projects are implemented are biased in favor of overinvestment in such projects and that public opinion is shifting in favor of more stringent project-authorization procedures, has proposed a rather sweeping institutional reorganization with respect to federal water projects.[5]

Increased state cost-sharing has been proposed, presumably in order to more nearly align the local incidence of costs and benefits. Local project proponents would be more likely to consider project costs if they were forced to bear a substantial proportion of those costs.

The Water Resources Council has been instructed to prepare a new manual setting forth procedures that must be followed in benefit cost analysis. The intent is clearly to establish more rigorous procedures for benefit cost analysis.

President Carter has proposed, as part of his plan for administrative reorganization, that an agency be established, within the proposed Department of Natural Resources, for the specific purpose of performing benefit cost analyses for all proposed federal water-resources projects. If Congress were to act upon this proposal, the economic justification for water-resources projects would no longer be evaluated by the very same agencies that proposed them and hope to implement them. Pending congressional action, the President has established, by executive order, a unit within the Water Resources Council to independently evaluate all benefit cost documents for proposed water-resources projects, and to report its findings directly to Congress.

These proposals are clearly intended to continue the process, initiated in the past decade with the enactment of the National Environmental Policy Act and the Endangered Species Act Amendments of 1973, whereby the institutional arrangements for the authorization and implementation of federal water-resources projects are being gradually modified in ways that discourage (relative to previously established procedures) this kind of investment of federal funds and natural and environmental resources.

QUESTIONS FOR DISCUSSION

1. Control of the environmental damage from surface mining has been pursued via the regulatory route. Could a system of incentives conceptually similar to effluent taxes be developed as an alternative? How could such a system be administered?
2. In many Appalachian states, mineral rights were severed from and dominant to surface rights. In some western states, surface rights are owned by ranchers, while mineral rights were retained by the federal government. What would be the economic effects if current legislative efforts to make private surface rights dominant to federal mineral rights were successful?
3. Do you support President Carter's proposal to create a separate agency to perform economic evaluations of proposed federal water projects? Why, or why not?
4. Would you expect that proposal to be warmly received in Congress? Why, or why not?

FURTHER READINGS

Anderson, Frederick. 1973. *NEPA and the Courts*. Baltimore: Johns Hopkins University Press.
Ingram, Helen M., and David J. Allee. 1972. *Authorization and Appropriation Processes for Water Resource Development*. A Report to the National Water Commission. Ithaca: Cornell University.

Landy, Marc K. 1976. *The Politics of Environmental Reform: Controlling Kentucky Strip Mining.* Washington: Resources for the Future Inc.

ENDNOTES

1. Schneider, David A. 1970-71. "Strip Mining in Kentucky," *Kentucky Law Journal.* 59: 653-672. Also Caudill, James K. 1974-75. "Kentucky's Experience with the Broad form Deed," *Kentucky Law Journal.* 63: 107-144.
2. See, for example, Center for Science in the Public Interest. 1975. *Enforcement of Strip Mining Laws.* Washington.
3. Water Resources Council. 1973. *Water and Related Land Resources: Establishment of Principles and Standards for Planning.* Washington: *Federal Register* 38 (No. 174), Part III, September 10.
4. "National Environmental Policy Act of 1969," *U.S. Statutes at Large.* 91st Congress. 1st Session 83: 852-856.
5. Office of the President. 1978. *Improvements in the Planning and Evaluation of Federal Water Resources Programs and Projects.* Washington. July 12.

V. TECHNIQUES FOR EMPIRICAL ANALYSES

Resource economists are often called upon to perform empirical analyses, to inform the policy-making process by quantifying the benefits and costs of alternative projects and programs, and by clarifying the tradeoffs that must be made in a world where few things are free and most gains are achieved only at a significant cost. In resource economics, as in all other branches of the economics discipline, empirical analysis involves the application of statistical and accounting techniques, within a framework defined by economic theory. The theoretical structure outlined in Sections II and III provides the logical framework within which the methods for empirical analysis outlined in this section are applied.

In Chapter 15, methods for project and program evaluation are outlined, with emphasis on the techniques for benefit cost analysis. While it is, unfortunately, common to find errors in the performance of benefit cost analysis, the economic theory underlying the technique is relatively straightforward. The basic benefit cost criterion is the potential Pareto-improvement, a maximum value of social product criterion that requires Pareto-efficiency as a necessary condition for an optimum. Correct application of benefit cost analysis requires that benefit and cost items be accurately quantified and valued according to the principles of efficient pricing. Where project costs are incurred and benefits are enjoyed over many years, and the time stream of costs and benefits are often noncontemporaneous, benefits and costs are reduced to present value, in accordance with the criteria for efficiency in public investment.

Since public projects and programs addressed to natural and environmental resource management often use as inputs, or provide as outputs, goods that are unpriced because of nonexclusiveness or are inefficiently priced because of externality or indivisibility in consumption, valuation problems often arise in benefit cost analysis. In Chapter 16, a general concept of value, relying on consumer's surplus theory, is developed. The applications of this theory to the valuation of resources and resource services that are unpriced, inefficiently priced, and/or provided or foregone in inframarginal or nonmarginal increments and decrements, are developed, using an analysis that handles marginal changes in the quantities of efficiently priced goods as a special case. Certain commonly used techniques for valuing non-market resources and resource services are introduced, in broad outline.

Since enactment of the National Environmental Policy Act, environmental impact analysis has taken its place alongside benefit cost analysis among the empirical procedures with which the resource economist is expected to be familiar. Environmental impact analysis is multi-faceted, and involves the application, insofar as is practicable, of empirical techniques from a wide variety of natural and social sciences. In Chapter 17, techniques for economic impact analysis (a subset of the analyses required for a complete environmental impact assessment) are introduced and briefly discussed.

15

Project and Program Evaluation

For federal water projects, in which public funds are invested to provide a stream of public and private benefits, formal economic evaluation has been required, in the U. S., for more than four decades. This evaluation is to take the form of benefit cost analysis, and is to be performed in accordance with a set of guidelines that have been refined over the years. The resulting analysis and its supporting plans, specifications, and data are Congressional documents. As a precondition for project authorization, benefit cost calculations must be performed and displayed, and they must demonstrate that the projected benefits from implementation of the proposed project exceed the projected costs.

In the most recent two decades, there has been growing public recognition that many quite different kinds of governmental projects and programs dealing with natural and environmental resources involve some public or private economic sacrifice in order to obtain some public or private benefits. In other words, the decisions concerning a broad array of resource and environmental management programs have been recognized as economic decisions. This public awareness has extended to the Congress and to the administrative agencies, which now require economic analyses along benefit cost lines as a routine part of the planning process for a quite vast array of natural resource and environmental policy decisions. In these applications, benefit cost analysis takes its place as one of a considerable number and variety of planning and evaluative tools. There are no strict requirements that the benefits of a project or program must be found to exceed the costs, as a precondition for its implementation.

This chapter focuses upon the use of benefit cost analysis and similar tools in the evaluation of projects and programs dealing with natural and environmental resources. At the outset, it must be recognized that benefit cost analysis and similar evaluative tools comprise only one segment of the total planning and evaluation process. For most natural and environmental resource policy decisions, benefit cost analysis carries no special weight that would make it pre-eminent among the various kinds of planning and evaluative tools. The exception, of course, is federal water projects, in which case a favorable benefit/cost ratio is a prerequisite for project authorization; however, there is no requirement that, of the set of projects with favorable benefit/cost ratios, those proposed projects with the highest benefit/cost ratios must be implemented first.

EVALUATION FORMATS

Here we consider the benefit cost analysis framework and two variants thereof, cost effectiveness analysis and risk benefit analysis.

COST EFFECTIVENESS ANALYSIS

Cost effectiveness analysis seeks to identify the least-cost way in which to achieve a given objective, without asking whether there is any economic justification for achieving that objective. Obviously, cost effectiveness analysis is most appropriately applied in cases where there is overwhelming support for project objectives, and thus the real question is not whether the objective should be fulfilled but how it may be fulfilled least expensively. Unfortunately, the cost effectiveness format is also used, by default as it were, in cases where no clear consensus exists about how best to measure program benefits. If benefits may be quantified, but not in economic terms, while costs are economically quantifiable, the cost effectiveness criterion provides guidance as to the least-cost method of obtaining the specified benefits.

If several candidate projects or programs would achieve exactly the same benefits in quantifiable (but not economically quantifiable) terms, cost effectiveness analysis requires merely that the costs of the alternative projects or programs be arrayed. Strict application of the cost effectiveness criterion would require that the alternative with the lowest total cost be selected. Unfortunately, it often occurs that alternatives that have different costs also promise different arrays of benefits. Where different alternatives provide homogeneous benefits, but in different quantities, a cost effectiveness ratio (i.e., cost per unit of output) may be calculated. Such a ratio provides information about the average costs per unit of output of the alternative projects or programs and, it will be instantly recognized, provides insufficient information to determine the economic efficiency of the various alternatives. Where, as is often the case, alternative projects and programs promise to provide qualitatively different outputs, even the cost effectiveness ratio (with all of its obvious inadequacies) is no longer meaningful.

RISK BENEFIT ANALYSIS

With the recent and growing awareness of the risks involved in the creation of near-indestructible toxic and hazardous wastes, the use of risk benefit analysis has been growing. The underlying concept is that economic progress often entails the acceptance of some degree of risk to environmental quality or to human health and safety. A tradeoff between risk and economic productivity is thus explicitly recognized. Risk benefit analysis arrays the economic benefits from various project and program alternatives alongside quantitative estimates of the risks involved. In its most complete form, risk benefit analysis would compare expected project benefits with the expected economic value of potential environmental or human hazards. However, the latter are often unmeasurable in economic terms, and reliable estimates of the probabilities of various catastrophes or hazards of specified magnitudes are unavailable. In these cases, risk benefit analysis remains incomplete. Further, it should be immediately obvious that even a complete risk benefit analysis is only a partial guide to economic decision making.

BENEFIT COST ANALYSIS

Benefit cost analysis seeks to apply the principles of public-investment decision making (as outlined in Chapter 9) to the selection of particular projects or programs for implementation. The term "benefit cost analysis" is used to denote analyses that apply either the maximum present value criterion or the benefit/cost ratio criterion. Benefit cost analysis seeks to determine whether, in the phrase made famous by the Flood Control Act of 1936, "the benefits to whomsoever they accrue exceed the costs." This language is remarkably similar to the language used in discussing compensation tests and the potential Pareto-improvement: "if the gainers could afford to compensate the losers . . ." Benefit cost analysis, strictly applied, is an attempt to implement the potential Pareto-improvement criterion which, it will be remembered (Chapter 6), is synonymous with the criterion of maximum value of social product.

Benefit and cost items are identified, estimated in quantitative terms, valued at their efficient prices (or the best available estimates thereof), reduced to present value by application of the social discount rate, and compared. Under the maximum present value criterion, a given alternative is acceptable if the present value of its benefits exceeds the present value of its costs, and the preferred package of project alternatives is that which provides the maximum net present value of benefits while exhausting the investment budget. Under the benefit/cost ratio criterion, a given alternative is acceptable if its benefit/cost ratio is equal to or greater than 1.0, and the preferred package of projects is that which, while exhausting the investment budget, has the greatest ratio of total package benefits to total package costs.

BENEFIT COST ANALYSIS
IN PROJECT EVALUATION

In project evaluation, benefit cost analysis provides an application of the principles of efficiency, through the potential Pareto-improvement criterion, in public investment.

SELECTION OF THE CRITERION

The benefit cost criterion may be maximum present value, or the benefit/cost ratio, given that both benefits and costs are expressed in present value terms. If a benefit/cost ratio is to be calculated, there are several alternative forms of the ratio.

Maximum Present Value

To calculate the present value of any project alternative, the present value of the stream of costs is subtracted from the present value of the stream of benefits.

Benefit/Cost Ratios

The simplest form of benefit/cost ratio is the present value of benefits divided by the present value of costs; i.e.:

$$\frac{B}{C}.$$

There are, however, other forms of benefit/cost ratio, which are useful in particular circumstances. For instance, it may be reasonable to assume that, once the project is in operation, the flow of benefits in each year will be more than sufficient to cover the project's operation and maintenance costs. In such cases, an appropriate benefit/cost ratio may take the form:

$$\frac{B - C_{operating\ and\ maintenance}}{C_{capital}};$$

i.e., total benefits minus operation and maintenance costs are divided by total capital costs.

Where a project is designed to provide at public expense inputs for use in private-sector production, an appropriate benefit/cost ratio may take the form:

$$\frac{B - C_{private}}{C_{public}} \; ;$$

i.e., the total stream of benefits minus costs borne by the private sector is divided by public-sector costs. This form of the benefit/cost ratio gives explicit recognition to the fact that public funds for capital investment are limited at the outset, while private-sector costs may reasonably be assumed to be covered by benefits accruing to the private sector. The selection of a particular form of the benefit/cost ratio is made according to a simple principle: the denominator of the ratio should be whatever is truly scarce, in the context of the decision problem at hand.

If one is concerned only with determining whether the benefits exceed the costs (i.e., the benefit/cost ratio is greater than 1.0), the exact form of benefit/cost ratio chosen is of no consequence. For a given set of project specifications, the various forms of benefit/cost ratio will be in unanimous agreement as to whether the benefit/cost ratio is greater than, equal to, or less than 1.0. However, it can be readily demonstrated that, in comparing several projects all of which have benefit/cost ratios greater than 1 and similar to each other, the form of benefit/cost ratio chosen may influence the ranking of projects.

IDENTIFICATION OF BENEFIT AND COST ITEMS

All project outputs, positive-valued and negative-valued, should be identified, quantified, valued in economic terms with appropriate signs attached, and treated as benefits. All project-related inputs should be similarly treated as costs. Costs should also include opportunity costs, the net value of alternatives that would be foregone if the project were implemented. For example, consider a typical water-resources project, in which a dam is built, a valley is inundated, and land previously used for nonirrigated agricultural or pastoral production is to be converted for use in irrigated agriculture. Project costs must include the net value of productivity from the valley if not inundated; from the "dry land" farmland, if not irrigated; and from the flowing stream, if not dammed: all projected over the planned lifetime of the project. All these benefits would be lost if the project were implemented, and thus represent opportunity costs of the project. This analytical requirement is known as the *"with and without" principle*. Net project benefits are the net benefits with the project, minus the net benefits without the project. If benefit cost analysis is undertaken to justify, rather than to impartially evaluate, a project, violation of the "with and without" principle may often occur: "without project" benefits may be ignored, or undervalued.

PRICING

Benefit cost analysis, being an application of the potential Pareto-improvement criterion, must value all benefit and cost items at their efficient unit prices, or their efficient values. Efficient unit prices are relevant when the project would use all inputs and would produce all outputs in very small quantities relative to the total markets in those inputs and outputs; thus, much as in the analysis of the single firm in competitive markets, the supply and demand curves facing the project may be assumed horizontal. Efficient economic values are relevant when the assumption of marginality is invalid for at least some cost or benefit items, and are discussed at some length in Chapter 16.

Where observed market prices do not seem to diverge significantly from efficient prices, they should be used in estimating economic value of benefit and cost items. However, cases are sometimes encountered where observed prices are known to diverge from efficient prices. In these cases, it is the task of the benefit cost analyst to estimate the efficient prices and use them in benefit cost analysis. This may involve correction for the impacts of inefficient subsidies, price supports, or price controls; of monopolistic influences in input or output markets; of Pareto-relevant external-ity; of indivisibility in consumption; and of nonexclusiveness, which results in positive-valued inputs and outputs going unpriced. The problems that arise in valuation of goods that are unpriced, or are institutionally priced (where institutional prices bear no obvious relationship to market clearing prices) are discussed in Chapter 16.

THE SOCIAL DISCOUNT RATE

Selection of an appropriate discount rate, to represent the social rate of discount, is a pricing problem: the problem of determining the appropriate price for the use of capital, usually a major cost item. The economic principles which guide selection of an appropriate discount rate are discussed in Chapter 9.

When benefit cost analysis is performed subject to guidelines specified by some cognizant agency, those guidelines frequently specify a discount rate, or a permissible range of discount rates. In some cases, economists have objected that the discount rates specified by particular agencies violate the principles for efficient pricing of capital, and thus bias the benefit cost analyses performed under the auspices of those agencies.

INCREASED ECONOMIC ACTIVITY IN THE PROJECT REGION

Implementation of a large project often increases economic activity in the region where the project is located. This is a major reason for the strong local support often accorded to proposed projects. Project construction may bring additional workers into the project region, increasing the demand for goods and services provided by local businesses. Where a part of the local labor force is unemployed or underemployed, project construction may generate an effective demand for that labor. Some project inputs, other than labor, may be purchased locally. Following construction, operation of the project may increase local economic activity. A labor force will be employed for project operation and maintenance. Irrigation water, flood protection, and outdoor recreation facilities provided by the project may expand the opportunities open to local businessmen, provide employment for the local labor force, and attract new businesses and workers into the project region.

The proper handling of increased regional economic activity in benefit cost analysis has long been a subject of controversy. While the outputs directly provided by a project may be unambiguously identified as benefits, there are considerable objections to treating increased regional economic activity as project benefits in the benefit cost framework. In an economy where resources are mobile and fully employed, increased activity in the project region represents merely an interregional transfer of economic activity. Where resources in the nation are underemployed, or resources in the project region are both underemployed and immobile, an argument can be made that some portion of the value of increased regional economic activity represents a net economic benefit resulting from the project.

The controversy surrounding the proper handling of regional economic activity in benefit cost analysis was resolved, in a manner that many (including this author) accept as making the best of a difficult situation, in the Principles and Standards adopted in 1973 for the benefit cost evaluation of U. S. federal water projects.[1] The Principles and Standards identify two separate economic accounts, the National Economic Development (NED) account and the Regional Economic Development (RED) account. The NED account treats benefit cost analysis as a strict search for potential Pareto-improvements. Thus, the value of increased regional economic activity is not included in that account. The NED account is subject to a strict benefit cost rule: NED benefits must exceed NED costs. The RED account provides estimates of the net change in regional economic activity that would result from project implementation. It is both regarded as, and treated as, separate from any NED benefit cost analysis. It provides useful information about the effectiveness of alternative projects in stimulating local and regional economies, but is considered separate from the benefit cost analysis. "RED benefit/cost ratios" (whose economic meaning, in any event, would be very unclear) are not calculated.

It should be noted that the Principles and Standards also require the preparation of an Environmental Quality (EQ) account, in which beneficial and adverse environmental impacts of proposed projects are inventoried and displayed. The EQ account does not require quantification of beneficial and adverse environmental impacts in economic terms, and no benefit cost analysis is performed on that account. An additional account, Social Wellbeing (SW) may be developed, but is not required. Again, the SW account is not presented in economic terms, and is not subject to benefit cost analysis.

When economists raise criticisms of the system of accounts developed in the 1973 Principles and Standards, the issue is most commonly the assignment of costs among the various accounts. While the NED account is subject to a strict benefit cost rule, it is not required that all project costs be assigned to the NED account. It is recognized, correctly, that some project costs may be expended for the purpose of fulfilling RED, EQ, or SW objectives. The problem arises because the assignment of costs to the different accounts necessarily involves an element of arbitrariness, and therefore may provide an opportunity to subvert the application of the strict benefit cost criterion to the NED account. If enough of the costs are assigned to other accounts, almost any project can pass the NED test. While there are some safeguards pertaining to cost assignments, the possibility of arbitrariness makes some economists uneasy.

BENEFIT COST ANALYSIS
IN PROGRAM EVALUATION

Benefit cost analysis is being increasingly used to evaluate the potential effects of proposed programs on economic efficiency. In this use, benefit cost information is simply one of several different informational inputs used by legislative and administrative bodies in evaluating proposed programs, and therefore a strict benefit cost rule (i.e., programs whose benefits do not exceed their costs are automatically rejected) is not applied. A wide variety of programs may be subjected to benefit cost analysis, under these general conditions. Such programs may include regulatory programs — e.g., those concerned with air and water quality, nuclear and other hazardous wastes, and programs concerned with human health and safety — in addition to programs whose objectives are more directly concerned with regulating economic activity. In these applications, benefit cost analysis encounters even more difficulties than are encountered in project evaluation. Many program outputs are neither easily quantified nor easily valued in economic terms. Examples include atmospheric visibility, the avoidance of catastrophic events that have very low probabilities of occurrence, and increments in the expectation of human life and health. In addition, the kinds of programs being evaluated may include those where time horizons are very long and outcomes may be irreversible.

In addition to the problems encountered in the economic valuation of program outputs, special problems are encountered in the application of investment criteria. It makes little sense in the evaluation of programs designed to deal with hazardous and nuclear wastes, which may if improperly handled cause catastrophic damage hundreds or even thousands of years hence, to use an analysis based on social discount rates that trivialize costs and benefits only two or three generations hence. In evaluating some kinds of programs, the rationale for discounting (an investment decision rule) is unclear. Where a proposed regulatory program may prohibit the marketing of certain consumption items (e.g., aerosol cans using fluorocarbon propellants), investment decision criteria may be inappropriate, since the program, if implemented, would reduce current consumption rather than current investment. It seems unreasonable, when dealing with programs designed to deal with very-long-term consequences, to apply discounting rules to foregone consumption on the rather tenuous supposition that MTP = MEI.

QUESTIONS FOR DISCUSSION

1. In an (imaginary) economy that has achieved a Pareto-efficient competitive equilibrium, what is the highest conceivable benefit/cost ratio for a proposed project? Explain.
2. In the U. S., approximately 22 million of the 25 million irrigated acres currently produce relatively low-valued commodities (i.e., small grains, hay, pasture, or cotton). It was recently recommended that, in benefit cost analysis of all proposed irrigation projects, agricultural benefits should be calculated *as though* low-valued crops would be produced, *regardless* of what crops would actually be produced at the proposed project site. Develop the economic logic underlying this recommendation.
3. Some have argued that, in evaluation of proposed projects that would provide food in underdeveloped countries where malnutrition is prevalent, food should be valued not at its actual price but at the price that would prevail if everyone could afford to avoid malnutrition. Can you accept this argument? Why, or why not?
4. Make a list of the benefit and cost items you would consider in a benefit cost analysis of a proposed program to regulate the disposal of nuclear wastes. How would you attempt to estimate the value of benefits and costs associated with these items?
5. Consider a proposed project that would increase the incomes of a low-income population. In NED benefit cost analysis, is it appropriate to count as benefits *both* the total value of project output *and* the savings in public assistance (i.e., "welfare") expenditures that would result from the increase in earnings of low-income persons?

FURTHER READINGS

Eckstein, Otto. 1958. *Water Sources Development: The Economics of Project Evaluation*. Cambridge: Harvard University Press.
Mishan, E. J. 1976. *Cost-Benefit Analysis*. New York: Praeger. 2nd edition.
Sassone, Peter G., and William A. Schaffer. 1978. *Cost-Benefit Analysis: A Handbook*. New York: Academic Press, Inc.

Water Resources Council. 1973. *Water and Related Land Resources. Establishment of Principles and Standards for Planning.* Washington: Federal Register 38 (No. 174), Part III, September 10.

ENDNOTE

1. Water Resources Council. 1973. *Water and Related Land Resources: Establishment of Principles and Standards for Planning.* Washington: *Federal Register* 38(No. 174), Part III, September 10.

16

Problems in Resource Valuation

For benefit cost analysis, it is generally agreed that, where a proposed undertaking will use only small quantities of inputs and provide only small quantities of outputs relative to the total quantities of inputs and outputs in their respective markets, the appropriate measure of value is the quantity change multiplied by the efficient unit price. Where quantity changes are only marginal, and observed prices may reasonably be assumed efficient, valuation provides few problems for the benefit cost analyst. However, the benefit cost analyst often encounters situations where quantity changes arc nonmarginal and efficient prices (or any prices at all) are unobservable. This chapter presents a general framework for the valuation of changes in the level of provision of goods, services, and amenities, which is applicable to marginal and nonmarginal quantity changes and to the valuation of priced and unpriced goods. Then, several empirical techniques for valuation of unpriced goods are introduced and briefly discussed.

A GENERAL FRAMEWORK FOR VALUATION

Consider, first, the value of the output of a single small firm in a competitive industry. The unit price of output is determined by the intersection of the demand and supply curves for the industry's output, D_I and S_I, respectively. The demand curve for the output of a single firm, D_i, is then a horizontal line intersecting the price axis at the equilibrium price, P, for the industry's output. The output of the individual firm, Q_i is determined by the intersection of $P = D_i$ and the firm's supply curve, S_i. The total value, V, of the firm's output is given by:

$$V \equiv \text{TR} = P \cdot Q_i;$$

i.e., the value of the firm's output is identically equal to the total revenue (TR) of the firm, which is equal to the quantity of output multiplied by the competitive unit price of that output (Figure 16.1).

Now consider a large-scale project that permits a nonmarginal increase in industry supply, from S_I to S'_I, by permitting new firms to enter the industry. The total revenue of these new firms, TR_P is equal to their output, $Q'_I - Q_I$, multiplied by P', the new, lower, equilibrium price of the industry's output; i.e.:

$$TR_P = P'(Q'_I - Q_I).$$

However, the consumers benefit from the project in two ways: they enjoy an increase in total output from Q_I to Q'_I, and a decrease in the unit price from P to P'. The value to consumers of the increment in output attributable for the project, V_P is given by the area ABQ'_IQ_I, which is greater than $TR_P = P'(Q'_I - Q_I)$, by the area ABC (Figure 16.2).

THE CONCEPT OF CONSUMER'S SURPLUS

The area ABC in Figure 16.2 is the increment in *consumer's surplus* (or, more precisely, Marshallian consumer's surplus) attributable to the increment in industry output that would result from implementation of the project. The total value V_P of the increment in output attributable to the project is equal to TR_P, the total revenue to producers of that increment in output, plus the consumer's surplus, ABC. If, perchance, the output were unpriced and therefore provided without reference to efficient markets, the

FIGURE 16.1

Industry Demand, Supply, Price and Quantity; and the Price and Quantity of Output for a Competitive Firm

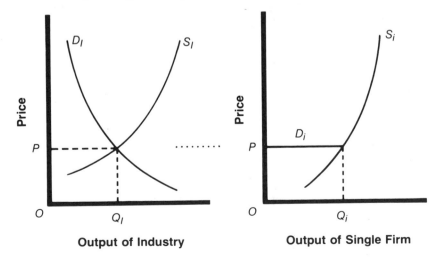

Output of Industry   **Output of Single Firm**

FIGURE 16.2

Price and Quantity Effects of a Nonmarginal Shift in Supply as a Result of Implementing a Proposed Project

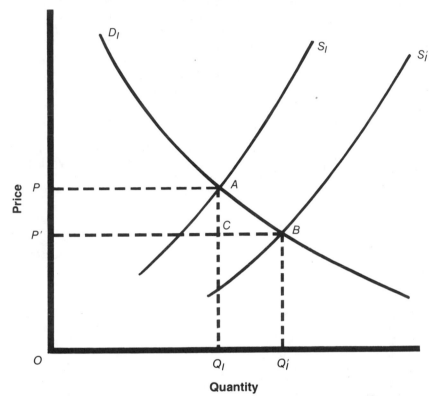

Quantity

supply curves S_I and S'_I would be no longer relevant; the project would increase the total output of the "nonmarket" good from Q_I to Q'_I; and the total value, V_P, of the increment in output attributable to the project would be equal to the consumer's surplus, which would be equal to the area, ABQ'_IQ_I (Figure 16.2).

Unfortunately, the above discussion of value and consumer's surplus requires a correction, which serves to complicate matters a little. The theoretically correct version of consumer's surplus is not the Marshallian version, but the Hicksian version. Hicksian consumer's surplus theory recognizes two concepts of consumer's surplus: a *compensating* version and an *equivalent* version. The compensating version defines the value of a change in output as the amount of compensation, paid or received, that would return the consumer to his *initial* welfare position *after* the change. The equivalent version defines the value of a change in output as the amount of compensation, paid or received, that would bring the consumer to his *subsequent* welfare position *if the change did not occur.*

To illustrate the application of Hicksian consumer's surplus concepts to valuation problems in benefit cost analysis, consider Figure 16.3, which modifies Figure 16.2 in the following ways: the supply curves, S_I and S'_I, are eliminated and replaced by broken vertical lines passing through Q_I and Q'_I (to indicate that without the project, output would be Q_I and with the project, output would be Q'_I); and, in addition to the Marshallian demand curve, D_I, two *Hicksian income-compensated demand curves*, D_I^H and $D_{I'}^H$ are presented. While the Marshallian consumer's surplus value of the increment in output attributable to the project is ABQ'_IQ_I, the Hicksian compensating value is $AB'Q'_IQ_I$ and the Hicksian equivalent value is $A'BQ'_IQ_I$.

It is important to note that if, instead of evaluating a project that would increase output from Q_I to Q'_I, one were evaluating a project that would decrease output from Q'_I to Q_I, the Hicksian compensating value of the decrement in output would be $A'BQ'_IQ_I$, while the Hicksian equivalent value would be $AB'Q'_IQ_I$.

FIGURE 16.3

Marshallian and Hicksian Concepts of Consumer's Surplus

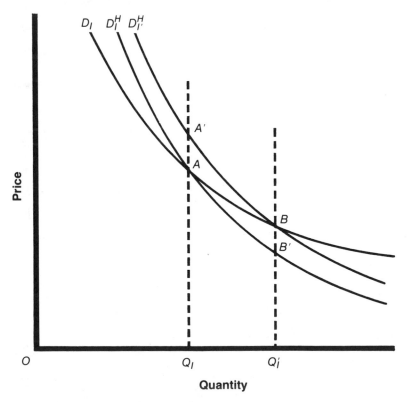

As Figure 16.3 indicates, the two Hicksian versions of consumer's surplus are different, in empirical magnitude, from each other and from the Marshallian version. Methods of empirically estimating the differences between the various versions of consumer's surplus have been developed but, unfortunately for our purposes, require a mathematics beyond the scope of this book. However, the results of this kind of analysis can be presented, in broad outline.[1] Where the value of the increment or decrement in goods, services and amenities that would result from implementation of a project is fairly small, relative to the consumer's total income, the differences between the three versions of consumer's surplus will be quite small, and a reliable estimate of any one of them will be serviceable in benefit cost analysis. However, where the value of the increment or decrement is large relative to the consumer's total budget, and where the responsiveness of total value to changes in income $(\Delta V_P/\Delta Y \cdot Y/V_P)$ is high and rises with income, the differences between the three versions of consumer's surplus may be quite large.

In this latter case, the correct application of benefit cost analysis, in accordance with the potential Pareto-improvement criterion, requires reliable estimates of the Hicksian compensating version of consumer's surplus.

A GENERAL MODEL FOR VALUATION OF INCREMENTS AND DECREMENTS IN OUTPUT[2]

Application of the potential Pareto-improvement criterion requires the use of the Hicksian compensating version of consumer's surplus. Thus, the value of an *increment* in output of goods, services, or amenities attributable to the project is equal to the maximum amount the consumer is willing to pay for that increment (which amount is denoted by WTP). The value of a decrement in output is equal to the minimum compensation that will induce the consumer to accept that *decrement* (which is denoted by WTA).

In Figure 16.4, the concept of a *total value curve* is introduced. In a four-quadrant diagram, the origin is placed at the consumer's initial position (which is consistent with the definition of the Hicksian compensating measure of value, which uses the consumer's initial welfare level as the reference). As one moves to the right of the origin, the quantity of output, Q, provided increases; as one moves to the left of the origin, the quantity provided decreases. As one moves up from the origin, the consumer's "income," Y, (or, more precisely, the value of all other goods and services he enjoys) decreases; as one moves down from the origin, his "income" increases. The total value curve is continuous on both sides of the origin. On the right side, it lies in the northeast quadrant, indicating that the consumer is willing to pay positive amounts of money (i.e., permit his "income" to decrease) in order to obtain increments in quantity. To the left of the origin, the total value curve lies in the southwest quadrant, indicating that the consumer is willing to accept positive amounts of

FIGURE 16.4
The Total Value Curve for an Individual Consumer

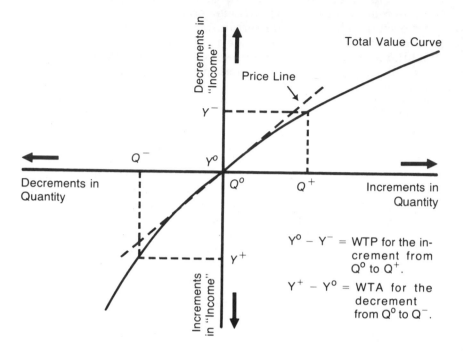

money (i.e., enjoy an increment in "income") concurrently with a decrease in quantity. The total value curve is, therefore, an indifference curve between "income" and quantities of a particular good, service, or amenity, passing through the origin of a diagram in which the horizontal axis represents quantity, in increasing amounts, and the vertical axis represents "income" in decreasing amounts.

Given an empirical estimate of the total value curve, the total value to an individual of increments or decrements (which may be nonmarginal) in the quantity provided of a good, service, or amenity (which may be unpriced) can be readily estimated, in a form entirely consistent with the potential Pareto-improvement criterion. For any proposed change in output, individual total values may be aggregated across the relevant population.

The total value curve provides a general framework for the valuation of increments and decrements in the quantities of goods, services, or amenities that would be provided, as a result of project implementation. There remains, however, a special case that is of interest. Consider a very small change in the quantity of a good provided in a very large competitive market. For such a good, the price line may be presented as a straight line (cf. Figures 5.2 and 5.3).

Since, for such a good, the consumer will be in equilibrium at the outset, the price line will be tangent to the total value curve (an indifference curve, remember) at the origin (Figure 16.4).

In a particular special case, valuation of increments and decrements in output, attributable to implementation of a proposed project, may be performed with reference to the price line, rather than to the total value curve. That special case occurs when the proposed project would result in small changes in quantity, relative to the total quantities exchanged in competitive markets with very low transactions costs. To provide a real-world example, the price line will provide a serviceable basis for the valuation of the increment in output of grain that would result from implementation of a project affecting a small local region. Grain markets are organized on a worldwide scale, and transactions costs in those markets are relatively small per unit of grain exchanged. Thus, $P(Q'_1 - Q_1)$ provides a serviceable indicator of the value of increments or decrements in grain resulting from implementation of such a project.

SOME TECHNIQUES OF "NONMARKET" VALUATION

In benefit cost analysis of projects and programs affecting natural and environmental resources, one frequently encounters the need to estimate the economic value of goods that are unpriced, or whose prices bear no obvious relationship to market-clearing prices. This phenomenon most commonly results from attenuation of property rights (leading to nonexclusiveness, or Pareto-relevant externality) or from indivisibility in consumption. Attenuation of property rights (Chapters 7 and 8) occurs in some cases because specification and enforcement of nonattenuated property rights would be prohibitively expensive, and in other cases because citizens acting through their governments choose to have certain goods, services, and amenities distributed through some mechanism that is not entirely budget-based (as opposed to distribution through the market, which is budget-based). These goods are commonly categorized as "nonmarket" goods — a term that is useful, if a little imprecise: it addresses not so much the strict absence of markets, but the substantial imperfection of any direct or indirect markets that may exist.

Researchers in natural resource and environmental economics have invested considerable ingenuity in the development and application of techniques for valuing nonmarket goods. The techniques that have been developed and applied take a number of rather different approaches, and some are clearly better-adapted than others for particular applications. Below, several of the more completely developed techniques of nonmarket valuation are introduced and briefly discussed.

INFERENTIAL TECHNIQUES

Inferential techniques use market-generated data pertaining to some marketed good in an attempt to infer the value of the nonmarket good under analysis. For valuation of a particular nonmarket good, the first step is the identification of some marketed good for which the demand may provide evidence of the value of the nonmarket good. Marketed goods may provide evidence of the value of nonmarket goods when both kinds of goods are complementary in consumption (as in the case of the travel-cost and land-value methods) or when the individual is confronted with a clearly defined trade-off between market goods and nonmarket goods (as in the case of methods that use labor-market observations for valuation of human health and safety).

Having identified an appropriate market good, the remaining tasks are to develop a rigorous theoretical model relating the value of the marketed good to the value of the nonmarket good, to acquire an appropriate data set, and to develop and perform a reliable statistical analysis of the data consistent with the theoretical valuation model.

The Travel-Cost Method

In order to enjoy the amenities provided by many outdoor recreation sites, it is necessary first to travel to the site, then to provide for one's subsistence at the site, and finally to return home. This observation led the late economist Harold Hotelling to suggest that the value of the amenities provided by outdoor recreation sites may be inferred from observation of the market for travel and subsistence purchased by users of the site. As implemented by Marion Clawson and Jack L. Knetch, and refined by these authors and a host of others,[3] the travel-cost method of inferring the demand of recreation sites proceeds as follows.

The total use of the recreation site is objectively measured, usually in visitor-days, using vehicle recorders, camper-registration records, etc. A random sample of users is then surveyed. A considerable variety of information may be collected, but emphasis is always placed on obtaining reliable information about the visitor's place of permanent residence, the distance he traveled to get to the site, and the expenses (e.g., for transportation, food, lodging, and any use or access fees) resulting from the visit. Information from the survey sample is then statistically analyzed and aggregated over the total population of users of the site. A relationship between distance traveled and expense of the trip is estimated statistically. By comparing survey data on the place of residence of the visitors and census data indicating the populations of the various localities surrounding the site, a statistical relationship between the cost of visiting the site and the proportion of those individuals facing that cost who choose to visit the site is estimated. This relationship is a kind of demand curve, since it relates travel costs (a surrogate for price) to usage of the site (an indicator of quantities demanded).

This estimated relationship is then transformed, using the assumption that potential visitors would respond to an increase in access fees for using the site in the same way they would respond to an increase in travel costs to get there, into a demand curve relating the price of using the site to the quantity of use demanded. This relationship is then used to estimate the value of services provided by the recreation site.

The travel-cost method of estimating the value of outdoor recreation services has been widely applied by researchers, and is accepted for use in official benefit cost analysis of federal water-resources projects. However, there are some unresolved difficulties in the use of the technique, and some limitations on its applicability. A major unresolved difficulty concerns the time cost of travel. Since the traveler invests both his time and his income in order to enjoy the services provided by a recreation site, his expenses alone will provide an underestimate of the total sacrifice made in order to use the site and, therefore (it is reasonably assumed), of his willingness to pay to use it. Unfortunately, since travel costs and travel time are highly correlated with each other, it has proven very difficult to obtain reliable statistical estimates that separate the influences of travel time and travel costs on use of the site. Solutions that simply add to the travel cost a "time cost" equal to travel time multiplied by a (usually small) fraction of the visitor's hourly wage are not entirely satisfactory.

The applicability of the travel-cost method is limited by the assumption that all expenditures during the trip may be regarded as paid specifically for the purpose of using the site. This assumption is violated when the trip itself is a source of utility, and when the trip involves visits to many different sites. The assumption that travel expenditures are an indicator of willingness to pay to use a site is violated when travel expenses themselves are small, and presumably an insignificant portion of the total sacrifices made by site users. This problem limits the use of the travel-cost method for valuing services provided by recreation sites in or near large urban areas.

The Land-Value Method[4]

It is reasonable to assume that some kinds of natural-resource and environmental amenities are enjoyed in a complementary manner with residential land. Thus, observations of markets in residential land have been used to attempt valuation of the amenities provided by beachfront, lakeside, and riverside environments. In large metropolitan areas, where the quality of ambient air varies within the metropolis, observations of the demand for residential land have been used to infer the value of increments in air quality. Below, the application of the land-value method for valuing increments in air quality is briefly discussed.

A large metropolitan area is divided into well-defined subregions, typically census tracts (so that many of the kinds of data to be used in the analysis are available from census information). Data on actual sales of residential land in each of the subregions are obtained, usually from local government authorities that record real-estate transactions. Observations of ambient-air quality (recorded by federal, state, and/or local environmental quality authorities) are arrayed by subregion. A detailed list of all other variables that may be expected to influence the sale price of residential land is made, and observations of these variables are obtained (from census and other information) by subregion. Relevant variables typically include indicators of the quality of residential structures on the land (e.g., number of rooms, total square feet of floor space, and the proportion of homes that provide amenities like central heating and air conditioning, and adequate plumbing); the distance from shopping centers, places of work, etc.; indicators of neighborhood quality (e.g., the density of housing, the proportion of land in the neighborhood devoted to parks, etc.); and the demographic characteristics of the neighborhood (e.g., per-capita income, the mix of ethnic groups, and the crime rate).

A statistical relationship in which the sale price of residential land is explained by ambient-air quality and an array of other variables such as those enumerated immediately above, is hypothesized and estimated. When the researcher is satisfied that he has estimated a reliable and statistically valid relationship, he then turns his attention to the regression coefficient for the air-quality variable. If that coefficient is statistically significant, he concludes that there does exist a relationship between ambient-air quality and the market value of residential land. If the (significant) coefficient has a positive sign, he concludes that residents are willing to pay more for land located in areas that enjoy relatively clean air.

Then, performing whatever mathematical manipulations are required by the particular form of the statistical equation estimated, he uses the significant positive coefficient of the air-quality variable to quantitatively estimate the increment in the sale price of residential land that may be attributed to a one-unit increment in the quality of the ambient air. This increment in sale price is the present value of the time stream of benefits from the increment in air quality. By a simple calculation, the annual benefits per household from a one-unit increment in air quality may be calculated, and the total annual benefits for an improvement in regional air quality may be calculated by aggregating over the number of households in the region.

The land-value method has been used in a considerable number of research studies. It encounters some statistical difficulties, since there is no foolproof way for the analyst to be sure that he has estimated the most reliable possible statistical relationship. The method encounters some conceptual difficulties:[5] (1) it is not clear that, because some residents are willing to pay a certain premium in order to enjoy a one-unit improvement in air quality *relative* to that obtained by other residents, all residents would be willing to pay the same premium for a one-unit improvement in air quality above their own homes; and (2) since residents typically spend a substantial portion of their time outside the home, one would expect that willingness to pay for improved ambient air in the vicinity of the home may underestimate willingness to pay for improved ambient air in the total metropolitan environment.

Using Labor-Market Observations to Estimate the Value of Human Health and Safety

Many policy decisions dealing with environmental quality, hazardous and toxic wastes, product safety, and workplace safety involve choices about the appropriate economic sacrifice in order to obtain improvements in human health and safety. Thus, the benefit cost analyst frequently encounters the need for estimates of the economic value of increments in human health and safety. Courts frequently confront a similar economic problem, when they are required to determine the appropriate compensation for death or injury.

Some courts and some policymakers have been willing to consider evidence of the present value of expected earnings foregone as a result of injury or premature death. However, this kind of evidence of the economic value of human health and safety is entirely unsatisfactory, because it places no value on the lives of the unemployed, retired persons, and homemakers, and values the lives of others in strict proportion to the market valuation of their labor. This method is based on the ethical supposition that human beings live to work, and have no worth beyond that of the labor they would provide in the course of a normal life span.

An approach that seems more acceptable, in its ethical implications, is based on the idea that life and health are the fundamental sources of utility for the individual. Thus, it asks not how much the labor market is willing to pay for an individual's services, but how much that individual himself is willing to accept in return for a decrement in his life expectancy.

The wage premium required to induce a worker to accept employment in a hazardous occupation may be interpreted as evidence of his willingness to accept compensation for decrements in his own expectancy of health, safety, and longevity. Richard Thaler and Sherwin Rosen obtained from insurance companies records that enabled them to estimate the probability of mortality on the job, for different kinds of occupations.[6] For workers in each of these occupations, they determined the wage rates, and the variables (e.g., education, occupational training, and demographic characteristics), that may influence the array of job opportunities available to each worker. Using statistical techniques similar to those used in application of the land-value method, they estimated the wage premium required to attract a worker into an occupation that would increase his probability of mortality in one year by .001. This technique provides a fairly reasonable method of estimating an individual's Hicksian compensating value for marginal changes in his expected health and safety, and is thus useful in many kinds of policy analyses. However, since the mortality expectancies associated with the various occupations ranged from roughly .003 to .007, the Thaler-Rosen analysis does not provide an acceptable basis for estimating the present value of an individual's life.[7]

Summary

This brief discussion of three kinds of inferential techniques developed and used for valuation of nonmarket goods should serve two purposes: (1) to suggest the quite considerable ingenuity that has been applied to the solution of nonmarket valuation problems, and (2) to indicate some of the conceptual and statistical difficulties that remain, in the application of inferential methods.

CONTINGENT VALUATION TECHNIQUES

Inferential techniques start with a data set that was generated by the actions of people facing real choices, and then use various theoretical assumptions and statistical methods to infer, from the real choices made, the value that individuals place on some nonmarket good. Contingent valuation techniques take a diametrically opposite approach: they address the individual's valuation of nonmarket goods directly but, in so doing, use data sets that are, in some respects, hypothetical or experimental.

The various techniques of contingent valuation all involve a process wherein the researcher creates a hypothetical market in a nonmarket good, invites a group of subjects (survey respondents or experimental subjects) to operate in that market, and records the results. The values generated through use of the hypothetical market are treated as estimates of the value of the nonmarket good, *contingent upon* the existence of the hypothetical market.

Contingent valuation techniques have two major advantages. (1) Careful design of the hypothetical markets results in collection of data in forms that are directly amenable to analysis using conceptual models such as that presented in Figure 16.4. The complex and sometimes unrealistic analytical assumptions used in some of the inferential methods are not necessary when using well-designed contingent valuation methods. (2) Hypothetical markets can be designed for use in a wide variety of valuation problems, some of which do not seem amenable to inferential methods. It is not necessary to identify some marketed good, the markets for which provide evidence for inferring the value of the nonmarket good. Therefore, contingent valuation techniques have a flexibility that permits the valuation of alternatives not currently available, and the estimation of option and existence values.

On the other hand, contingent valuation techniques have several disadvantages, all of which are related to the use of hypothetical rather than actual markets. (1) The flexibility and adaptability of contingent valuation techniques is constrained by the need to establish hypothetical markets that are comprehensible and credible to the subject; thus, contingent valuation techniques are less reliable when used to value alternatives that lie well beyond the experience of the subjects. (2) Given that the data set generated using contingent valuation techniques is generated in hypothetical markets, validation of that data is not easy. Replication, using different groups of subjects or a series of different contingent valuation techniques to value the same nonmarket good, is always possible but is never totally satisfying. Currently, there is considerable research under way, aimed at finding improved methods of validation, but no clear breakthrough has yet been reported. (3) It is sometimes argued that contingent valuation techniques provide opportunities and incentives for subjects to behave strategically. If a subject believes that the results of a contingent valuation exercise may influence the quantity of nonexclusive goods provided by the public sector and the total taxes collected, but that the actual increment or decrement in his personal tax payment will not be related to his stated contingent value, he may choose to distort his responses to the hypothetical market in order to exert undue influence on the public policy eventually adopted. In contingent valuation studies designed to test for this kind of strategic behavior, very little evidence that subjects actually behave that way has been found. Nevertheless, some economists remain skeptical of value data generated using contingent valuation techniques.

Below, three kinds of contingent valuation techniques are introduced and briefly discussed.

Direct Questions

While there is a wide variety of direct-question techniques, all of them involve some variation of the following kind of question: "How much would you be willing to pay in order to obtain some stated increment in a nonmarket good (or willing to accept in order to permit some stated decrement in the level of provision of the good)?"

In some formats, the hypothetical market is so poorly defined that the exercise scarcely qualifies as contingent valuation. For example, some public-opinion polls have used questions like, "Would you be willing to sacrifice, in order to obtain clean air?" This question provides the subject with no information on the extent of the sacrifice, the quantitative dimensions of the increment in clean air to be provided, or the structure of the market in which clean air is to be "bought."

More sophisticated direct-questioning techniques specify, in quantitive terms, the increment or decrement to be provided, and provide substantial detail about the institutional structure of the hypothetical market (which is designed in such a way as to minimize the temptations for strategic behavior on the part of subjects). The question format may be "open-ended," in which case the subject is asked "how much . . .?"[8]; or "closed-ended," in which case the subject is asked to answer "yes" or "no" to a question specifying both the precise amount of nonmarket good to be gained or lost and the precise amount of money to be paid or received.[9] This latter format is to be preferred, since it provides the subject with more information, and faces him with a hypothetical market more like those markets with which he is familiar.

For analysis, the responses to "how much . . .?" questions provides estimates of points on the total-value curve (Figure 16.4). Answers to the "yes or no?" questions do not provide estimates of total value of the nonmarket good to the individual subject: "Yes" answers do not indicate that the stated amount represents total value, but only that total value is at least as much as the stated amount. If the sample of subjects is subdivided into several groups, each responding to different stated amounts of money to be paid or received, analysis may proceed by estimating a schedule, much like a Marshallian demand curve, relating the stated amounts of money and the proportion of respondents who answered "yes."

Direct-question techniques, provided care is exercised in the specification of hypothetical markets, are serviceable devices for collecting value data with respect to nonmarket goods. They are widely used, because they are well-adapted to mail surveys, and thus permit inexpensive data collection. However, these techniques are regarded as less reliable than iterative bidding techniques.

Iterative Bidding Techniques

These techniques, which are best adapted to personal-interview surveys, but may also be used in telephone surveys and in group-administration experiments, are basically extensions of the "yes or no?" type of direct question. The interviewer or experimenter iteratively varies the stated amount of money to be paid or received, until the highest amount the subject is willing to pay, or the lowest amount the subject is willing to accept, is precisely identified. Thus, the identified amount is an estimate of a point on the total value curve (Figure 16.4).[10]

Experimental Techniques

Recently, several experimental techniques have been suggested, which include ingenious devices that penalize the experimental subject for attempts to engage in strategic behavior. These include the Clarke tax[11] and the experimental methods devised by Vernon Smith.[12] These techniques have been relatively little applied in research settings, and thus cannot be recommended for immediate widespread implementation. However, this author regards these techniques as promising. It is possible that the next decade will see a series of advances in these experimental techniques, comparable to the advances in direct-questioning and iterative bidding techniques that were made during the 1970's.

A TECHNIQUE OF LAST RESORT: COST OF THE LEAST-COST ALTERNATIVE

Some researchers and policymakers who have rejected contingent valuation techniques but are confronted with situations where no promising inferential technique has yet been developed, have used a valuation method based on the cost of the least-cost alternative. Using this method, the nonmarket good, service, or amenity to be valued is defined in quantitative terms. Then, marketed substitutes for that good, service, or amenity are identified. The total cost of providing the same quantity of good, service, or amenity using each marketed substitute is calculated, and the least-cost substitute is identified. The cost of this least-cost alternative is then used as an estimate of the value of the nonmarket good, service, or amenity.

The problem with this technique is that it pays no direct attention to demand. If one can be certain that the nonmarket good, service, or amenity would be demanded, in the quantity available, at a price equal to the price of the least-cost alternative, this technique is valid. However, if there is no assurance that the total quantity provided would be demanded at that price, the cost of the least-cost alternative provides only an upper bound on the value of the nonmarket good.

This author has seen studies that purport to estimate the value of waste-assimilation services provided by natural wetland environments by calculating the cost of installing and operating tertiary waste-treatment plants. These plants represent the least-cost alternative method of providing tertiary waste treatment. The problem with the "cost of the least-cost alternative" technique in this application is that there is no evidence that tertiary waste treatment is actually demanded at that price. On the contrary, relatively little demand for tertiary waste treatment at that price can be observed. It may be reasonably argued that this last observation is unfair, since markets in tertiary waste treatment are obviously imperfect. However, it remains reasonable to raise the question of demand, in the absence of hard evidence that such demand exists.

Without evidence that the quantity of the nonmarket good,

service, or amenity provided would be demanded at a price equal to the cost of the least-cost alternative, this technique can provide only an upper bound on its value.

SUMMARY

Accurate and comprehensive benefit cost analysis of alternative projects and programs for management of natural and environmental resources requires that the value of nonmarket goods, gained or lost, be included in the analysis. The above discussion is intended to suggest that (1) considerable effort and ingenuity have been invested in research to devise and refine techniques of nonmarket valuation, (2) definite progress has been made, and (3) considerable work remains to be done, in the development of new nonmarket-valuation techniques, and the refinement of those techniques which already exist in rudimentary form.

QUESTIONS FOR DISCUSSION

1. In some situations, the value of project inputs or outputs may be determined by multiplying quantity by price; in other situations, the appropriate measure of value is the aggregate change in consumer's surplus. For each of the items listed below, which is the appropriate approach to valuation?
   (a) A relatively small increase in the output of wheat.
   (b) Protection from a hazard, thereby improving the health and safety of a target human population.
   (c) Elimination of the last free-flowing trout stream in a geographic region of considerable size.
   (d) Cement for construction.
   (e) Hydroelectricity.
   (f) An exotic specialty crop.
2. Some have estimated the annual economic value of the services provided by homemakers, by itemizing all the useful things homemakers do, quantifying them, and calculating the total cost of buying the same bundle of services at market prices. For a mother of growing children, the amount often totals to between $30,000 and $45,000 annually. The average employed male head of a household with a homemaker spouse and growing children has an income of $19,000 before taxes.
   In light of the head's income, is this estimate of the value of the homemaker's services consistent with economic principles? Why, or why not?
3. Thaler and Rosen claim to have developed a serviceable method of estimating the willingness of workers to pay for reductions in work-related mortality and morbidity. Can you think of a suitable method of estimating the WTP of retired persons for an increment in life expectancy?
4. Why is the *cost of the least-cost alternative* method of valuation called "a technique of last resort"?

5. Can you think of one (or, better yet, several) technique(s) that could be used to determine the aggregate **value** to your class of the reference materials placed on reserve at the library for this course? Design a research project in which the technique(s) could be implemented.

FURTHER READINGS

All the publications listed in the Endnotes are worthwhile readings for the serious student. In addition, the following are recommended:

Freeman, A. Myrick III. 1979. *The Benefits of Environmental Improvement: Theory and Practice.* Baltimore: Johns Hopkins University Press.

Sinden, John A., and Albert C. Worrell. 1979. *Unpriced Values: Decisions Without Market Prices.* New York: Wiley-Interscience.

ENDNOTES

1. Willig, R. D. 1976. "Consumer's Surplus Without Apology," *American Economic Review.* 66: 587-597.
   And Alan Randall and John R. Stoll. 1980. "Consumer's Surplus in Commodity Space," *American Economic Review.* 70: 449-455.
2. This model is developed and applied in David S. Brookshire, Alan Randall, and John R. Stoll. 1980. "Valuing Increments and Decrements In Natural Resource Service Flows," *American Journal of Agricultural Economics.* 62: 478-488.
3. See Marion Clawson and Jack L. Knetch. 1965. *Economics of Outdoor Recreation.* Baltimore: The Johns Hopkins Press.
   And Jack L. Knetch. 1977. "Displaced Facilities and Benefit Calculations," *Land Economics.* 53: 123-129.
4. See A. Myrick Freeman III. 1974. "On Estimating Air Pollution Control Benefits from Land Value Studies." *Journal of Environmental Economics and Management.* 1: 74-83.
5. For a much more sophisticated discussion of the conceptual difficulties encountered in using the land-value method, see Karl-Goran Maler. 1974. *Environmental Economics.* Baltimore: The Johns Hopkins Press. 178-199.
6. Thaler, Richard H., and Sherwin Rosen. 1975. "The Value of Saving a Life: A Market Estimate," in *Household Production and Consumption.* Nestor Terleckyj, ed. *National Bureau of Economic Research Studies in Income and Wealth.* 40. New York.
7. Thaler and Rosen claim, however, that their method does provide an acceptable basis for estimating the combined willingness of 1,000 workers to pay to prevent one additional work-related death.
8. See, for example, Judd Hammack and Gardner Mallard Brown. 1974. *Waterfowl and Wetlands: Toward Bioeconomic Analysis.* Baltimore: Johns Hopkins University Press.
9. See, for example, Howard O. Ness. 1973. *Potential Markets for Selected Fee Hunting Enterprises in New Mexico.* Las Cruces: New Mexico State University, unpublished M.S. thesis.
10. See, for example, Alan Randall, Berry C. Ives and Clyde Eastman. 1974. "Bidding Games for Valuation of Aesthetic Environmental Improvements, *Journal of Environmental Economics and Management.* 1: 132-149.
11. See T. Nicholas Tideman and Gordon Tullock. 1976. "A New and Superior Process for Making Public Choices," *Journal of Political Economy.* 84: 1145-1159.
12. See Vernon L. Smith. 1977. "The Principle of Unanimity and Voluntary Consent in Social Choice," *Journal of Political Economy.* 85: 1125-1140.

17

Environmental-Impact Assessment: Economic Impacts

The environmental-impact assessment process under the National Environmental Policy Act (Chapter 14) requires that the economic, social, and environmental impacts of proposed projects and programs that will use federal resources be assessed. More than twenty states have similar legislation, which requires that projects and programs using state resources be subject to assessment of economic, social, and environmental impact. In addition, many jurisdictions have established licensing procedures (for electric generators, transmission lines, and other installations of a public-utility character) that include provisions for assessment of economic, social, and environmental impacts of the proposed facility. This is not a textbook on impact assessment. Nevertheless, in a textbook on resource economics, it seems essential to provide at least a brief introduction to the assessment of economic impacts.

ASSESSMENT PROCEDURES

The sequence of steps in impact assessment is as follows:

1. Assemble a profile of existing conditions in the planning area. This step involves the assembly and display of pertinent statistical and other information about existing conditions in the planning area. Judgment must be exercised, and decisions made, about the definition of the planning area (which may be delineated by a political jurisdiction, a hydrological unit, or by

the nature of the project or program impacts) and the kinds of economic conditions considered relevant for inclusion in the profile.

2. Make projections of "without project or program" conditions. The profile of existing conditions must be extended and projected, to portray future conditions without any project or program action. Projections should extend to cover the expected life of all project or program alternatives under consideration. The future is uncertain. Thus, for projection, a range of values, corresponding to a reasonable range of probable future conditions, should be used.

3. Make "with project or program" projections, identifying causative factors and tracing their effects. For each alternative under consideration, make projections of the "with project or program" conditions, including preconstruction, construction, and operation periods throughout its expected life. Causative factors and their likely economic effects should be identified. All significant interactive relationships should be considered. The interrelatedness of economic, social, and environmental aspects cannot be overlooked and must be considered.

4. Identify significant effects. A "significant" effect is one likely to have a material bearing on the decision-making process. An initial determination regarding significance should be made at the earliest stage possible in the assessment process. The determination should be reconsidered at each stage, particularly in the light of public input and reaction.

5. Describe and display all significant effects. Describe the effects of the various alternative plans in quantitative terms to the extent possible. The effects should be described objectively, and tentatively designated as beneficial or adverse.

6. Evaluate effects. Place values on the significant beneficial and adverse effects in monetary terms where applicable, quantitatively where possible, and qualitatively in any event. The assumptions or criteria on which a judgment is based should be made explicit, since segments of the public may perceive any single effect quite differently. The aggregate or systems interaction of combined economic, social, and environmental effects should be considered along with evaluation of individual effects.

7. Consider project modifications where adverse effects are significant. Since impact assessment is an integral part of the planning process, the identification of significant adverse effects should lead to a consideration of the possibility of (a) eliminating the effect or mitigating the effect by minimizing or reducing it to an acceptable level of intensity, or (b) compensating for it by including a counterbalancing positive effect. The possibility should always be recognized that an identified adverse effect may be of such magnitude or character that it cannot be accepted in the public interest, or be corrected

by project modification. In such a case, one or more new alternative plans must be formulated to avoid an unacceptable adverse consequence. "No action" is always one of the alternatives to be considered.

8. Seek assessment feedback from other sources. Adequate impact-assessment procedures require a variety of information sources, and continuous feedback. At an early stage, informal exchanges with federal, state, and local agencies, with private groups, and with interested individuals should be sought. As impact assessment proceeds, there must be formal consultation of cognizant federal, state, and local agencies, and identifiable interest groups and individuals; and the prescribed public-participation and public-hearing procedures must be fully utilized.

9. Use the impact assessment in making recommendations.

10. Prepare a statement of findings.

11. Use the impact assessment in drafting the Environmental Impact Statement.

As this brief summary of the steps in impact assessment suggests, the assessment process is comprehensive in nature, and integrated into the project- and program-planning process. The assessment process involves the utilization of many different kinds of expertise, and requires the mature judgment of senior agency personnel, supplemented by feedback from a wide variety of sources, obtained informally at first and, later, formally through public-participation and public-hearings processes.

ECONOMIC IMPACTS

For impact assessment, the variety of economic effects considered is substantially broader than that considered during benefit cost analysis. The focus is upon economic impacts in the project- or program-planning area and, more broadly, on the manner in which these economic impacts will influence quality of life in the planning area. Therefore, the specific focus of benefit cost analysis upon economic efficiency (or national economic development) is much narrower than the broad focus of economic-impact assessment. Below, an incomplete but illustrative list of economic effects is provided, and each kind of economic effect is briefly discussed.

NATIONAL ECONOMIC DEVELOPMENT

The national economic development impacts of proposed projects and programs should be assessed and estimated, following established procedures of benefit cost analysis.

This statement, which represents the author's opinion, is more controversial than one would expect. This controversy is largely attributable to the substantial differences between the Flood Control Act of 1936 (which requires benefit cost analysis of federal water projects) and the National Environmental Policy Act of 1969 (which requires environmental-impact assessment for all projects using federal resources). Under NEPA, the environmental-impact statement is subject to challenge in the courts. However, under the Flood Control Act, the benefit cost analysis is held to be a Congressional document and, therefore, not subject to judicial review. For this reason, judges have been reluctant to permit challenges to the benefit cost analysis, per se, under NEPA, thereby creating controversy as to whether the benefit cost (i.e., national economic development) analysis is in fact a part of the environmental-impact-assessment procedure. The author's statement that national economic-development impacts must be included in economic-impact assessment is based more upon his view of economic systems than upon legal precedent.

REGIONAL ECONOMIC DEVELOPMENT

"With project or program" regional economic growth should be projected. Projections of employment and labor-force participation, and business and industrial activity, by sector, must be made. "With project or program" projections should be compared to "without project or program" projections, in order to identify the effects attributable to the proposed project or program. The impact of the proposed impact program on real-income distribution should be estimated.

In addition to local and regional economic growth, employment, business and industrial activity, and real-income distribution, a number of other considerations must be addressed under the heading of regional economic development. These additional considerations include the following.

Population growth and migration patterns. Will the proposed alternative induce in-migration in the planning area, or will it reduce the rate of out-migration?

Land use. What will be the impacts of the proposed alternative on patterns of land use in the planning area?

Public services and public facilities. Are existing public services and facilities, given their expected growth and development, sufficient to serve the planning area if the proposed alternative is implemented? Or will the proposed alternative require a sudden increment in public services and facilities? If the latter, will the planning process ensure that additional public services and facilities will be provided in an orderly manner to accommodate the additional needs attributable to the project alternative?

Agricultural activity and prime land. Will the proposed project alternative displace farms and remove prime land, perhaps irreversibly, from agricultural production?

STATE AND LOCAL GOVERNMENT FINANCE

The impact of the proposed project alternative on state and local government finances must be projected. The impact of the project on tax revenues must be estimated, for each type of tax (income taxes, sales taxes, property taxes, and any other taxes). Estimates of regional economic-development impacts are essential for estimating project impacts on income and sales taxes. To estimate project impacts on property-tax revenues, it is necessary to identify any property that will be removed from tax rolls as a result of project implementation, and to estimate the impact of the project, if implemented, on the value of surrounding property. In order to estimate the impact of the proposed alternative on state and local government expenditures, it is necessary to make reliable estimates of the impact of the proposed alternative upon the demand for public services and facilities.

NATIONAL DEFENSE

If the proposed alternative is likely to influence the effectiveness of the national defense effort, or the costs of providing for the national defense, these effects should be estimated.

INTERACTIONS AMONG ECONOMIC, SOCIAL, AND ENVIRONMENTAL IMPACTS

Many of the economic impacts identified above are interactive with social and/or environmental impacts. For example, in-migration, out-migration, relocation of residents of the project "take area," and transformation of the pattern of industrial activity in the planning area, all regional economic impacts, have clear implications for the social structure of the planning area and the social cohesion in the impact region and its communities. Changes in the pattern of business, industrial, and agricultural activity, all regional economic impacts, have clear implications for environmental quality.

INPUT-OUTPUT ANALYSIS:
A TOOL FOR ESTIMATING REGIONAL
ECONOMIC-DEVELOPMENT IMPACTS

Local and regional economies are complex and interactive. An increase in economic activity in the agricultural sector, or in one or more business and industrial sectors, will typically increase activity in every sector of the local and regional economy. For example, an increase in agricultural activity due to irrigation, or an increase in industrial activity due to the provision of navigation services can be expected to induce increased economic activity in wholesale and retail trade, financial services, and the government sector. Input-output analysis provides a technique whereby the interactions within the regional economy can be modeled, and the effects of expansion in one or more sectors upon employment, output, and income in other sectors and the whole economy can be projected.

Input-output analysis is a substantially simplified method for analyzing economic interdependency. The industrial sector, rather than the firm, is taken to be the unit of production. The production function for each sector is assumed to be of the constant-coefficient type. Thus, the question of the optimal level of output is not addressed. The system contains no utility functions, and consumer demands are treated as exogenous. These are rather radical assumptions, but they have the virtue of permitting a simple interactive model that may be empirically estimated with relative ease.

Input-output analysis for a regional economy is based on a detailed accounting of the flow of goods and services, in dollar terms, at a particular time. Part of this flow is among industries within the regional economy, part may be between the region and "the rest of the world" through import and export sectors, and the remainder flows to an exogenously defined "final demand" sector. For an economy with n sectors, the inter-industry input-output coefficients are arranged as a matrix $A = [a_{ij}]$, where $i = 1,...,n$, and $j = 1,...,n$. The total output of industry i, x_i, must satisfy the following equation:

$$x_i = a_{i1}x_1 + a_{i2}x_2 + ... + a_{in}x_n + d_i$$

where d_i is the final demand for the output for industry i. Thus, the final demand vector, D, may be written:

$$(I - A)x = d,$$

where I is an $n \times n$ identity matrix. The solution to the set of n simultaneous equations represented by the above matrix equation is:

$$x = (I - A)^{-1}d.$$

Given this solution, it is a relatively simple matter to trace the income, output, and employment effects of a change in the level of activity in any industry i, or a change in final demand d. Input-output analysis has become accepted, despite its rigid and somewhat unrealistic assumptions, as the basic tool in the analysis of regional economic systems. The resource economist concerned with estimating regional economic-development impacts of proposed projects or programs will find input-output analysis an invaluable tool.

QUESTIONS FOR DISCUSSION

1. Some have insisted that it is an important and entirely worthwhile undertaking to invest research resources in order to develop improved methods of environmental-impact assessment. Others have claimed that the real significance of the environmental-impact-statement process under NEPA is that it provides a mechanism through which project opponents may obtain standing in court: therefore, there is little to be gained by developing more sophisticated impact-assessment methods. Which, if either, of these arguments do you support? Explain.
2. Should special provisions to expedite the environmental-impact assessment and EIS process be applied in the case of proposed energy-supply facilities?

FURTHER READINGS

Anderson, Frederick. 1973. *NEPA and the Courts*. Baltimore: Johns Hopkins University Press.

Krutilla, John V. (ed). 1972. *Natural Environments: Studies in Theoretical and Applied Analysis*. Baltimore: Johns Hopkins University Press.

McEvoy, James III. 1977. *Handbook for Environmental Planning: The Social Consequences of Environmental Change*. New York: Wiley-Interscience.

Miernyk, William. 1965. *The Elements of Input-Output Analysis*. New York: Random House.

Pearce, D. W. 1976. "The Limits of Cost Benefit Analysis as a Guide to Environmental Policy," *Kyklos*. 29: 97-112.

Warden, R. E., and W. T. Dagodag. 1976. *A Guide to the Preparation and Review of Environmental Impact Reports*. Los Angeles: Security World Publishing.

VI. APPLICATIONS

In this section, a series of specific applications is provided. The intent is to take a specific policy problem with respect to natural and environmental resources, and to apply to its solution the theoretical concepts of Sections II and III and, where appropriate, the empirical techniques of Section V, while cognizant of the institutional concepts discussed in Section IV. It is hoped that the student will gain an understanding of the dimensions of some important problems in resources policy, and a feel for what it is that resource economists actually do.

These applications chapters have a common dimension in that each one deals with a real-world policy problem. However, the various chapters take somewhat different approaches. Chapter 18 provides a narrative history of the Tellico Dam and Reservoir Project, in southeastern Tennessee. This narrative history is interesting reading, in and of itself. Beyond that, it is highly educational, since almost everything that can happen in the course of designing and implementing a federal water-resources project has happened, at one time or another, in the case of Tellico. The approach taken in the other applications chapters is quite different. In those chapters, the dimensions of the policy problem are delineated, and the application of resource economics principles and practices to their solution is discussed, without reference to specific localities. Where appropriate, one or more alternatives to present policies are suggested. The advantages of the alternatives are discussed, and any special problems or difficulties associated with them are identified.

Coming, as they do, toward the end of a rather lengthy book, these chapters are quite brief. The relevant theory, empirical techniques, and institutional concepts are provided in earlier sections. To take full advantage of these chapters, it is necessary for the student to refer to the pertinent materials in earlier sections each time an important concept or method is mentioned. These applications chapters do not provide a complete self-contained analysis of the policy problems they address. They do, however, provide the student a valuable opportunity to reinforce his knowledge of concepts and methods by applying them, with a considerable degree of independent initiative, to policy problems.

In these chapters, the relevant issues are highlighted, appropriate analyses are suggested, and conclusions are implicitly or explicitly stated. It is left to the reader to "flesh-out" the analysis. It may be that some of you will reach conclusions different from those implicitly or explicitly derived by the author. If you do, it is quite possible you may be right. But the burden of supporting your conclusions rests upon *you*.

18

Water Resources Projects: The Case of the Tellico Dam and Reservoir Project

The Little Tennessee River originates in the mountains of Georgia and converges with the Tennessee River near Knoxville, Tennessee. The upper sections of the Little Tennessee have been dammed, but for its lower 33 miles, the river is free-flowing. This free-flowing section is generally regarded as an outstanding trout stream in a region where trout streams are now very scarce. The lower 33 miles of the Little Tennessee flow through some of the finest farmland in East Tennessee.

The Tennessee Valley Authority (TVA) first proposed a dam on the lower Little Tennessee in 1936, as part of a comprehensive system of water-resources development projects for the Tennessee Valley.

When the Fort Loudoun dam was built, on the Tennessee River just upstream from its confluence with the Little Tennessee, the hydroelectric generators at Fort Loudoun were built at a size sufficiently large to handle the flow from the Little Tennessee in addition to that from the Tennessee. The idea was that the proposed project on the lower Little Tennessee, now called the "Fort Loudoun extension," could include a channel to divert the water from the Little Tennessee into the Fort Loudoun Reservoir and through the turbines at Fort Loudoun dam.

This "Fort Loudoun extension" was estimated to cost $10.7 million and, in 1942, Congress allocated funds to start its construction. The project was interrupted by World War II, and lay dormant for 20 years.

In 1963, the "Fort Loudoun extension" was reproposed as the Tellico Project. As formulated at that time, this project would involve the acquisition of 38,000 acres of land, and would provide for: the diversion of water into the Fort Loudoun Reservoir, to increase the load factor achieved by the Fort Loudoun generators; the extension of navigation into the lower section of the Little Tennessee River; flood control; slack-water recreation; and shoreline development. On the shoreline, a series of planned communities would be developed, providing for some 4,000 industrial jobs and 2,600 trades and service jobs. This shoreline development would be attracted by the availability of land, acquired under the Tennessee Valley Authority's exercise of eminent domain, and the navigation facilities to be provided by the project.

From the outset, the Tellico Project was controversial. While there was strong local support, there was also local opposition. The Eastern Band of the Cherokee Indian Nation opposed the project, which would result in inundation of the site of the ancient capital of the Cherokee Nation. While in 1963 the staff of the Tennessee State Planning Commission questioned the wisdom of the Tellico Project, in 1965 the state governor announced strong support for the project. In 1965 and 1966, proponents and opponents of the project pressed their respective cases vigorously before Congressional hearings. In 1966, the U. S. Congress approved the initial appropriation for the Tellico Project, and construction began in 1967. Congress has appropriated funds for the project each year thereafter.

In 1971, a suit was filed in federal court to halt the project on the grounds that an adequate environmental impact statement (EIS), as required under the National Environmental Policy Act, had not been filed. This suit was upheld, and TVA was enjoined from continuing construction of the Tellico Project for 21 months, until a final EIS was ruled acceptable to the court in 1973. The final EIS included a benefit cost statement,[1] which estimated the benefit/cost ratio for the Tellico Project to be 1.7.

Throughout the early 1970's, opposition to the project continued. Winfield Dunn, governor of Tennessee at the time, urged TVA to reappraise the project and consider discontinuing it. Dunn was impressed by the agricultural productivity and the recreational potential of the valley, with its Cherokee and pioneer archaeological relics and the free-flowing trout stream.

It is notable that the environmental-impact assessment, conducted under court order, included archaeological studies which permitted, perhaps for the first time, an appreciation of the immense archaeological resources of the valley. Following publication of the EIS, project opponents began pressing an alternative plan that included agricultural development of the valley's farmland, recreational development of the free-flowing stream, and development of major archaeological sites as a national treasure.

The Endangered Species Act of 1966, amended in 1973, precludes federal agencies from authorizing, funding, or implementing any action that would destroy the significant habitat of an endangered species. In 1971, the Tennessee Game and Fish Commission had informed TVA that three endangered fish species "probably" live in the impoundment area. In 1973, Dr. David Etnier, a biologist at the University of Tennessee, discovered an unfamiliar fish, a small darter (genus *Percina*), in the lower reaches of the Little Tennessee. Following intensive biological study, the fish was determined to be a distinct species. It was named the "snail darter" (*Percina tenasi*), since snails are a significant part of its diet. The snail darter survives, insofar as is known, only in free-flowing streams and, therefore, would predictably be eliminated from the Little Tennessee if the Tellico project were completed.

In 1975, the U. S. Fish and Wildlife Service, acting under the Endangered Species Act amendments of 1973, declared the snail darter an endangered species and the lower Little Tennessee River its critical habitat.

In 1976, a suit (Hill vs Tennessee Valley Authority) was filed in federal district court, asking that the Tellico Project be enjoined as being in violation of the Endangered Species Act. The suit was dismissed in district court, but plaintiffs appealed the case to the Sixth Circuit Court of Appeals, which reversed the District Court decision on January 31, 1977. At that time, the Court of Appeals prohibited TVA from performing any construction activity that would destroy or modify the critical habitat of the snail darter. By then, construction of the Tellico Project (which had continued apace during the period from when *Hill vs TVA* was filed until the Circuit Court ruling) was more than 90% complete, and more than $100 million had been spent. TVA appealed the Court of Appeals decision to the United States Supreme Court. However, the Supreme Court, in June 1978, affirmed the decision of the Court of Appeals.

Summary of the Project History, to June 1978

The Tellico Project, which had been controversial from the outset, but which had been authorized and funded by the U. S. Congress, was more than 90% complete, as of 1978. TVA's benefit cost calculations indicated a benefit/cost ratio of 1.7, but those calculations themselves were controversial. Throughout the 1960's and 1970's, water-resources projects, in general, were encountering more opposition than in previous decades. There was a growing awareness that, as more and more water-resources projects were completed, free-flowing streams were becoming more scarce while slack-water reservoirs were becoming more plentiful. A suit under the National Environmental Policy Act had halted the project for 21 months, but upon submission of an adequate EIS, construction recommenced. The Endangered Species Act had provided literally the last opportunity to halt the project permanently. However, the Supreme Court decision in favor of the snail darter was itself controversial.

The snail darter was a small fish of no apparent commercial value, and was burdened with a common name that was less than majestic. Some argued that, even if the snail darter were to become extinct, more than 100 similar species of darter would remain.

Newspaper articles featured the story of the "little fish that stopped a 100-million-dollar dam." During the winter of 1977-78, which featured unusually cold weather and a strike by coal miners, TVA lost no opportunity to remind the public that the snail darter was preventing or at least delaying construction of a project that would provide hydroelectricity.

THE ENDANGERED SPECIES COMMITTEE STAFF REPORT[2]

In response to the U. S. Supreme Court decision of June 1978, Congress again amended the Endangered Species Act. The amendments of 1978 established the Endangered Species Committee to consider applications for exemptions from the requirements of the Act, under certain specified criteria. The amendments provided for accelerated consideration of exemption applications for the Tellico Project and one other project.

The Committee was empowered to grant an exemption for any project that met the following independent criteria: (1) there are no reasonable and prudent alternatives to the proposed action, and (2) the benefits of the proposed action clearly outweigh the benefits of alternative courses of action consistent with preserving the endangered species or its critical habitat. If these criteria are met, the Committee is authorized to grant an exemption to the Endangered Species Act, provided it also requires actions (such as, but not limited to, transplanting the endangered species to a new habitat) that would minimize the adverse effects of the proposed action upon the species and its critical habitat.

The Endangered Species Committee is a high-level committee, consisting of several cabinet-level officers or their designated representatives. The Committee's staff was assigned the task of preparing a report that would examine the factual basis for determining whether the Tellico Project satisfies the criteria for an exemption from the provisions of the Act. The Staff Report was submitted on January 19, 1979, and the Committee took action in that same month.

At this point, it is appropriate to briefly review the findings of the Staff Report, upon which the Committee based its eventual decision.

REASONABLE AND PRUDENT ALTERNATIVES TO THE TELLICO PROJECT

After considering several alternatives to the project, the Staff focused its attention on River Development (the alternative) and Reservoir Development (essentially, the completion of the Tellico Project as originally planned, albeit with modifications to mitigate insofar as possible the adverse effects on the snail darter). The Staff found that River Development was a reasonable and prudent alternative to the project. Partial removal of the dam (which was substantially completed, but had not been closed) would be required under this alternative, thus permitting the survival of the snail darter.

River Development would permit maintenance of the free-flowing stream and its trout fishery, development of the archaeological sites, and the resumption of agriculture in the valley. Clearly, a number of sub-alternatives must be considered, under the River Development alternative. Recreational development could be more, or less, intensive. Development of the archaeological sites may involve the full-scale re-creation of a working replica of the ancient Cherokee Nation headquarters in the valley, or it may involve a less elaborate plan. Agricultural development may involve the leasing of farmland to large operators under arrangements whereby TVA would retain substantial control of farm management and the marketing of agricultural products, or it may involve liquidation of TVA's land holdings in order to restore the traditional pattern of family farm operation. While these various sub-alternatives existed, the Committee Staff identified a River Development alternative with sufficient specificity to permit comparison of its benefits and costs with those of Reservoir Development.

BENEFITS AND COSTS OF ALTERNATIVES

In a draft document issued jointly by the Tennessee Valley Authority and the United States Department of the Interior, on August 10, 1978, it was recognized that the total benefit/cost ratio for the Tellico Project, if calculated under guidelines operative in 1978, would be about 0.5 rather than 1.7 as was calculated in the EIS (Table 18.1). The major differences between the two calculations are: the 1978 calculation uses a more realistic discount rate; construction costs, by 1978, had increased considerably, even when adjusted for inflation; estimates of recreation benefits were sharply reduced in 1978, while the "shoreline development" and "redevelopment" categories of benefits were eliminated in 1978; and the electricity and flood-control benefit estimates had risen sharply by 1978.

However, since the Tellico Project was more than 90% complete and all costs that were already expended (i.e., an amount in excess of $100 million) must be considered fixed, the relevant efficiency criterion compares not total benefits and total costs but *incremental benefits* and *incremental costs* starting from the present situation.

Estimates of incremental NED benefits and costs, for the Reservoir Development and River Development alternatives, were provided by TVA and by the Committee Staff (Table 18.2). The benefit and cost estimates are briefly discussed below; and, where the TVA estimates differ substantially from those of the Committee Staff, these differences are discussed.

Agriculture (and Forestry). Under the Reservoir Development alternative, agricultural benefits will be quite small. On the other

TABLE 18.1
Total NED Benefits and Costs of Tellico Project
(Annualized)

Item	EIS Estimate* (1971)	TVA-DOI Estimate** (1978)
Economic Analysis		
Price level	1968	1978
Economic life (years)	100	50
Discount rate	3¼%	6⅝%
Annual Costs		
Total annual costs ($000)	2,250	9,710
Annual Benefits ($000)		
Flood Control	505	1,040
Navigation	400	540
Electricity	400	2,700
Recreation, fish and wildlife	1,660	450
Cultural	—	60
Water supply	70	60
Shoreline development	710	—
Redevelopment	15	—
Total annual benefits	3,760	4,950
B/C	1.7:1	0.5:1

*Environmental Statement, 1972.
**TVA-Department of Interior, Alternatives for Completing the Tellico Project, August 10, 1978.

hand, agricultural benefits under the River Development alternative were projected to fall into the range of 0.99 to 2.99 million dollars annually.

Electricity Generation. The Reservoir Development alternative would result in annual benefits from power generation of 2.7 million dollars, whereas there would be no such benefits from the River Development alternative.

Flood Control. TVA estimates that the Reservoir Development alternative would result in annual flood-control benefits of 1.04 million dollars, while the River Development alternative would provide no such benefits. After some comment, the Staff Report concludes that TVA's estimate of flood-control benefits from reservoir development is an upper-bound estimate.

Land Enhancement. TVA claims that land-enhancement benefits of roughly 0.4 million dollars would result from implementation of either the Reservoir Development or the River Development alternatives. The Committee Staff Report expressed some doubts about these benefits. Given these doubts, and the fact that, in quantitative terms, the claimed benefits are similar for each alternative, the Staff Report recommends that land-enhancement benefits be disregarded.

Recreation. TVA estimates the recreation benefits from Reservoir Development at 2.1 to 2.5 million dollars annually, and from River Development at 2.4 to 3.1 million dollars annually. The Committee Staff Report indicated a preference for the upper estimate, in each case.

Navigation, Employment, and Income. TVA assumes that the navigation facilities provided by Reservoir Development would generate direct benefits and, in addition, would result in the development of new industrial communities on the lakeshore, which would provide income and employment benefits. The Staff Report suggests that TVA's estimate of navigation benefits from River Development should be substantially reduced. The Staff expresses some uncertainty and confusion about the legitimacy of including employment and income benefits, and notes that the claimed benefits in these categories for Reservoir Development and River Development are of a similar order of magnitude.

Unmeasured Benefits and Costs. The Staff Report recognizes that some categories of benefits and costs cannot be effectively measured, in monetary terms, but are important and therefore should be considered. These include the effects on the cultural, archaeological, and historical resources of the valley; the losses in life-style amenities of the displaced farmers; and gains in life-style amenities of the individuals who would be attracted by Reservoir Development or River Development.

Regional Development. To this point, the discussion of benefits has focused upon national economic-development benefits. The Staff Report recognizes that regional economic-development benefits may exist, but concludes that such benefits are inappropriate for inclusion in benefit cost analysis.

Costs. The incremental capital costs of completing the Reservoir Development alternative were estimated at 3.19 million dollars, on an annual basis; the capital costs of completing River Development were estimated, on a similar basis, at 2.26 million dollars. In addition, the Committee Staff estimates that the opportunity cost of land amounts to 4.03 million dollars annually, regardless of whether Reservoir Development or River Development is selected.

Comparison of Benefits and Costs. Total incremental benefits and costs of both alternatives, reduced to an annual basis, are compared in Table 18.2. The Committee Staff finds that the (measured) incremental benefits of Reservoir Development are a little less than the incremental costs, while the (measured) incremental benefits of River Development are also a little less than the incremental costs. The ratio of incremental benefits to incremental costs is similar, for both development alternatives.

Since there are recognized but unmeasured benefits and costs, under both alternatives, the Committee Staff is reluctant to directly compare incremental benefits and costs, for either alternative. Such a comparison might seem to suggest that, since measured incremental benefits fail to exceed costs for either alternative, the appropriate solution would be to just walk away and leave the uncompleted project sitting there. However, that alternative is

TABLE 18.2
Benefit Cost Summary (NED): Additional Benefits and Costs,
in $ Millions (annualized)

	Reservoir Development		River Development	
	TVA*	CS**	TVA*	CS**
Additional Benefits				
Land enhancement	0.34	—	0.04	—
Flood control	1.04	1.04	—	—
Navigation	0.00-0.62	0.10	—	—
Electricity	2.70	2.70	—	—
Recreation	2.10-2.50	2.50	2.40-3.10	3.10
Water supply	0.045	0.045	—	—
Agriculture and forestry	0.11	0.11	0.99-2.99	2.00
Total Additional Benefits	6.34-7.36	6.52	3.43-6.13	5.10
Additional Costs:				
Capital costs	3.19	3.19	2.26	2.26
Opportunity cost of land	0.00	4.03	0.00	4.03
Total Additional Costs	3.19	7.22	2.26	6.29

Source: Endangered Species Committee Staff Report.
*Source: TVA: *Alternatives for Completing the Tellico Project,* December 1978.
**Denotes committee-staff estimate.

entirely unacceptable, since it would leave the snail darter unprotected (the unclosed dam wall has interfered with its migratory patterns) and would expose the watershed to continuing environmental damage.

The Committee Staff concludes that the benefits of Reservoir Development do not clearly outweigh the benefits of River Development. In the terms of the 1978 amendments to the Endangered Species Act, the benefits of the proposed action do not clearly outweigh the benefits of alternative courses of action consistent with preserving the endangered species and its critical habitat.

THE VALUE OF THE SNAIL DARTER

The Staff Report considers the ecological, aesthetic, educational, historical, recreational, and scientific value of the snail darter. These values are not quantified in monetary terms, but are generally assumed to be positive. The general principles enunciated in Chapter 11 suggest that, in the face of considerable uncertainty as to the value of the endangered species, the conscious exercise of caution and risk aversion is appropriate. In the Tellico case, this consideration leads to an obvious conclusion in favor of River Development. Since the economic costs and benefits of Reservoir Development and River Development are similar, the opportunity cost of exercising caution and risk aversion with respect to the snail darter species is trivial.

THE ENDANGERED SPECIES
COMMITTEE DECISION

On the motion of Charles L. Schultze, Chairman of the President's Council of Economic Advisors, and a member of the Endangered Species Committee, the Committee unanimously refused to grant the Tellico Project an exemption from the Endangered Species Act. In offering his motion, Schultze commented: "The interesting phenomenon is that here is a project that is 95% complete and, if one takes just the cost of finishing it against the benefits and does it properly, it doesn't pay, which says something about the original design."[3]

Under the Endangered Species Act amendments of 1978, the Tellico Project cannot be completed in a Reservoir Development form. The snail darter and its critical habitat must be protected. The specific River Development alternative evaluated by TVA and the Committee Staff may be implemented, or other nonreservoir alternatives may be considered for implementation. There can be no reservoir; the free-flowing trout fishery, the fertile bottomlands and the archaeological sites cannot be inundated; and many Tellico Project opponents (some of whom, ironically, place no very great value on the preservation of the snail darter species) are pleased with the outcome.

The economic reconsideration prompted by legal action under the Endangered Species Act was most enlightening. The difference between the total benefit/cost ratios estimated in 1971 and 1978 (Table 18.1) is astounding. If, as economists believe, the guidelines for benefit cost analysis operative in 1978 are more conducive to accurate evaluation of the efficiency of proposed projects, one can conclude that the Tellico Project was initially authorized on the basis of optimistic but unreliable benefit cost calculations.

A FINAL COMMENT

The narrative history of the Tellico Project is, perhaps, incomplete. As this is written, there is speculation that a further amendment to the Endangered Species Act, specifically exempting the Tellico Project from the provisions of the Act, will be introduced in Congress. As of now, it is not known whether such an amendment will be introduced and whether, if introduced, it will be passed.[4]

The history of the Tellico Project brings into sharp focus the interaction of economic and legal considerations in the processes by which federal water-resources projects are proposed, authorized, and implemented. It suggests some of the pitfalls that bedevil the application of benefit cost analysis, and provides the warning that benefit cost analyses prepared by agencies that are themselves proposing to implement the project under consideration should be carefully reviewed by independent authorities.

Finally, it should be pointed out that the Tellico Project was selected for this narrative history because of the rich detail it provides, not because the author believes it to be typical of federal water-resources projects.

QUESTIONS FOR DISCUSSION

1. Examine Table 18.1. How do you account, item by item, for the major differences in the total benefit cost calculations made for the Tellico Project in 1971 and 1978? Where there are important differences, which seems to be the more reliable estimate? Why?
2. If the Endangered Species Committee Staff Report is to be believed, the Tellico Project is economically unjustified. Yet, it was halted under the Endangered Species Act. What, if anything, can be done to halt economically unjustified water-resources projects that do not happen to threaten the critical habitat of an endangered species?

FURTHER READINGS

For further study of the Tellico Project, the Environmental Statement and the Staff Report (endnotes 1 and 2, respectively) provide a good beginning. For more general reading on the performance of water resources projects, see:

Haveman, Robert H. 1972. *The Economic Performance of Public Investments: An Expost Evaluation of Water Resource Investments.* Baltimore: Johns Hopkins University Press.

ENDNOTES

1. Tennessee Valley Authority. 1972. *Environmental Statement: Tellico Project.* Knoxville. 1-1-49.
2. *Tellico Dam and Reservoir,* Staff Report to the Endangered Species Committee, Washington. January 19, 1979.
3. Quoted from the record.
4. After three attempts to pass legislation permitting completion of the Reservoir Development version of the Tellico Project had failed in the U. S. Senate, a rider exempting the project from the Endangered Species Act — and any other law that could prevent its completion as a reservoir project — was successfully attached to the general appropriations bill for public-works projects, in the House of Representatives. The bill — with the "Tellico Rider" in place — passed the Senate and was signed by President Carter in late September, 1979. Construction of the reservoir was then resumed.

   Soon afterwards, a suit requesting that continued construction be enjoined was filed on behalf of a group of Cherokees. This suit was promptly dismissed. (This footnote was added at the time of copy editing.)

19

Land-Use Policy

In the classical capitalist economy, land was typically privately owned. Interests in land were protected and rights were established under private-law concepts of property (such as those briefly discussed in Chapter 13). Fee-simple title vested the owner with very substantial rights to decide for himself the uses he would make of his land. The laws of nuisance, trespass, etc., while restricting the choices a landowner could make insofar as those choices may affect the welfare of other landowners, provided the landowner with protection against annoyances others may thoughtlessly or deliberately impose upon him.

Since the Industrial Revolution, however, a number of developments have tended to reduce the effectiveness of private law in resolving conflicts about the use of land. Industrial and technological innovations have increased the capacity of landowners to impose annoyances upon one another and upon nonowners. In their determination to avoid erecting impediments to industrial progress, the courts have narrowed the interpretation of nuisance and trespass law, so that it is ineffective at controlling many of the externalities in a modern technological society. At the same time, the increasing affluence permitted by technological progress has resulted in increasing demands for land resources to provide satisfactions for consumers. Single-family dwellings, each on its little plot of land, have become the norm; and, with increasing individual wealth, the desired plot of land seems to be growing larger over time. In addition, there are growing demands for land to serve recreational and esthetic purposes. The modern concept of "the good life" includes parklands, open spaces, natural environments, and wild and scenic rivers.

For these reasons, the concepts of "land-use policy," "land-use planning," and "land-use control," all of which are at least a little at odds with the strictly private-property concept of land, have become quite prominent in public discussions, and in the activities of bureaucracies, legislatures, and the courts.

Four general categories of perceived land-use problems may be identified.

INCOMPATIBLE USES

These occur where the use decision of a landowner imposes an external diseconomy on the user of another parcel of land. Many kinds of land use impose external diseconomies on the residential land user: noisy, ugly, or polluting industry; certain agricultural uses, such as hog feedlots, which generate noise, odor, and polluted runoff; commercial establishments, such as taverns, drive-in movies, and gasoline stations, which create noise and congestion; and many kinds of locally obnoxious public facilities, such as airports, jails, and garbage dumps. Certain kinds of residential use may impose external diseconomies on other residential users: unattractive and inexpensive housing may lower the value of nearby more elaborate residences; multi-family dwellings may increase congestion and cause drainage problems, thus reducing the value of nearby, expensive, single-family residences; more generally, any resident who fails to control noise and to maintain the appearance of his dwelling is unlikely to please his neighbors.

There may also be conflicts between industrial and commercial land users, and among different kinds of industrial users, and different kinds of commercial users. Professional offices and high-class boutiques are unlikely to choose locations in noisy and congested environments. High-technology, "clean" industries, like the data-processing and communications industries, prefer to avoid locations near older-technology, "dirty" industries, like steel milling and oil refining.

PUBLIC-FINANCE PROBLEMS AT THE RURAL/URBAN FRINGE

There is a class of services that is typically supplied to the consumer at his place of residence. Included are electricity and gas for household use, domestic water and sewage, garbage collection, roads, public transportation (if any), and transportation of children to school. These kinds of services are often provided by the public sector, or by regulated public utilities. The total cost of supplying these services to a given population is lower when that population resides in a relatively compact area. Conversely, the total cost of providing these services is higher when the population is arrayed haphazardly across a larger land area. This latter pattern is called "urban sprawl."

Where, as was common practice, each customer is charged for these services on the basis of the average cost of serving all customers in the community, the individual land developer or home buyer has no incentive to contribute to the orderly development of compact communities. In fact, the incentives work in just the opposite direction. Land that does not immediately adjoin an urban region is usually less expensive. The developer building on such land and the subsequent home buyer enjoy the cost advantages of less expensive land and, at least temporarily, the esthetic advantages of living in a small subdivision surrounded by farming activities. This pattern of "leapfrog development" results in substantially higher costs for the kinds of services we have been discussing. However, these additional costs are borne only to an insignificant degree by the developer or the home buyer: through average-cost pricing, they are borne by every resident of the community.

These kinds of inefficiencies in the financing of public services and utilities result in an inequitable distribution of costs, so that residents of long-established neighborhoods nearer the city center in effect subsidize urban sprawl and leapfrog development at the urban/rural fringe. The pattern of development that results may create external diseconomies (e.g., by degrading the esthetic quality of the fringe area, or by generating excess runoff, which may lead to siltation, pollution, and flooding problems in formerly rural streams), and may render agriculture nonviable in the immediate urban/rural fringe, resulting in the premature withdrawal of land from agricultural use.

DESTRUCTION OF ESTHETICALLY DESIRABLE FEATURES OF THE ENVIRONMENT

Some kinds of land, in some particular kinds of uses, generate external economies in that they provide esthetic or recreational enjoyment for persons other than the owner. Thus, nonowners may assert a "public interest" that would be violated if such land was converted to a quite different kind of use. Thus, we see calls for public action to preserve certain kinds of lands in esthetically pleasing uses. There are calls to preserve historic buildings, historic districts, and districts that have uniformly fine examples of regional or period architecture. There are pressures to prevent the land bordering wild and scenic rivers from being converted to commercial, industrial, or even intensive agricultural uses. Many are in favor of the preservation of agricultural land uses that have particular cultural or esthetic appeal; examples include the Pennsylvania Dutch farming country in heavily populated Southeastern Pennsylvania, and the thoroughbred-horse-breeding establishments surrounding Lexington, Kentucky. In many urban areas, there is popular sentiment for the maintenance of a viable agriculture on the land immediately surrounding the city, for the simple reason that agricultural land and the farming way of life represent esthetic and cultural attractions to urban dwellers.

DEGRADATION OF THE BIOLOGICAL PRODUCTIVITY OF LAND

There are many, often including farmers, rural people and agricultural professionals, who are concerned that urban sprawl is a wasteful use of land. They argue that a time will eventually come, if it is not nearly upon us, when man will regret the conversion of prime lands to urban uses. With increasing demands for food and fiber, it is argued, the value of prime lands in agricultural and forestry uses will increase rapidly and substantially. Since conversion of agricultural and forest land to urban uses is, if not strictly irreversible, at least not readily reversible, it is argued that wisdom and foresight require compact urban and suburban settlements in order to maintain the biological productivity of as much of the best land as is possible.

Others have argued that this is not an especially pressing concern. They argue that residential uses of land are as legitimate, in the economic sense, as agricultural uses, since the market provides substantial evidence that land provides utility for residential users. Some have challenged the notion of future shortages of land for the production of food and fiber.

The facts, insofar as they are known, are not especially definitive. From 1940 through 1974, land-utilization trends were fairly stable, for the most part, but exhibited some interesting developments (Table 19.1). Cropland used for crops declined steadily through 1969, while land devoted to "special uses" (which include urban uses) increased. However, with the buoyant markets for agricultural products in the early 1970's, farmers were able to divert an additional 28 million acres of land to crops between 1969 and 1974. This suggests that land utilization remains quite responsive to relative prices.

For a closer look at the land-use picture, let us examine some statistics assembled and interpreted by Sterling Brubaker.[1] In 1973, all urban and transportation uses of land together accounted for only 2.3% of U. S. land. In the period from 1967 to 1975, three million acres was diverted annually to urban, transportation, and reservoir uses. Of this three million acres, one quarter was cropland. Cropland abandonment in total (about 2.7 million acres annually) is several times greater than cropland diversion to urban and other uses, but is partly offset by the development of 1.3 million acres of new cropland annually. Brubaker expects the rate of diversion of land to urban uses to diminish in the future as urbanization is completed, population growth slows, and rising energy prices encourage more compact population centers.

These statistics suggest that the U. S. faces no immediate crises that could be attributed to the conversion of cropland to urban and other uses. Nevertheless, there is an established pattern of diversion of cropland to such uses. It would be thoroughly undesirable if all or most of the prime agricultural and forest land were converted to urban uses. However, that is very far from happening, and it seems reasonable to the economist to expect that relative prices, responding to changes in relative scarcity, will provide powerful disincentives for that kind of outcome.

Beyond traditional agriculture and lumber oriented forestry, there are some more specialized concerns with the maintenance of the biological productivity of land. After centuries of agricultural and industrial development, terrestrial, aquatic, and marine habitats of high quality have become relatively scarce. To preserve ecological diversity, it is essential that scarce or unique habitats be maintained. Inland wetlands play a highly significant role in surface drainage and recharge of aquifers and, as a result of continued drainage and land-fill efforts, are becoming scarcer. Coastal marshes are essential to the production of seafood, of the types that we currently enjoy and the types that we may learn to enjoy if and when the oceans achieve their potential as sources of food for mankind; however, they are under increasing pressure for conversion to urban, resort, and recreational development. The preservation of these relatively scarce, and sometimes unique, lands is likely to become an increasingly important priority.

Some of these kinds of lands are already in the public domain. However, that alone is insufficient to protect them: public lands are subject to pressures for both development and preservation. Some of these lands remain in private ownership. In that case, their preservation (in their current natural habitat uses) would generate substantial external economies. It would be unfortunate if ways were not found to internalize those external economies, thus bringing the full opportunity costs of conversion to bear upon the landowners.

LAND-USE POLICY TOOLS

Institutional devices to influence and direct land use are provided by private law, the law of eminent domain, the police power, and the power to tax, used separately and in various combinations.

PRIVATE LAW

Private law provides for the establishment and security of property rights, and thus facilitates the resolution of land-use conflicts through the market. Private law provides devices whereby individuals operating independently, and groups operating collectively, may pursue their goals with respect to land use.

Deed Restrictions

Deed restrictions provide a private-law device for the control of external diseconomies through elimination of incompatible land

TABLE 19.1

Land Utilization, by Type: 1940 to 1974

Type	1940		1950		1959		1969		1974	
	Land	Percent	Land	Percent	Land	Percent	Land	Percent	Land	Percent
Total land area	1,904	100.0	1,904	100.0	2,271	100.0	2,264	100.0	2,264	100.0
Cropland used for crops[1]	368	19.3	377	19.8	359	15.8	333	14.7	361	16.0
Idle cropland	31	1.6	32	1.7	33	1.5	51	2.3	21	0.9
Cropland used only for pasture	68	3.6	69	3.6	55	2.9	88	3.9	83	3.7
Grassland pasture[2]	650	34.1	631	33.1	633	27.9	604	26.7	598	26.4
Forest land[3]	608	31.9	601	31.6	728	32.1	723	31.9	718	31.7
Special uses[4]	—	—	—	—	148	6.5	174	7.7	182	8.0
Other land	179	9.4	194	10.2	304	13.4	291	12.9	301	13.3

1. Cropland harvested, crop failure, and cultivated summer fallow. 2. Grassland and other nonforest pasture and range. 3. Excludes reserve forest land in parks and other specified uses of land. Includes forest grazing land. 4. Includes urban and transportation areas, federal and state areas used primarily for recreation and wildlife purposes, military areas, farmsteads, farm roads and lanes, and miscellaneous other uses.

Source: Bureau of the Census. U. S. Department of Commerce. 1978. *Statistical Abstract of the United States:* 1174.

uses. A developer acquires a relatively large tract of land, with the intention of subdividing it into suburban, or sometimes rural, residential units. In order to increase the attractiveness of these units to prospective purchasers, the developer establishes a series of deed restrictions. These restrictions limit the choices a purchaser may make with respect to the use of his land. However, the purchaser cheerfully accepts these limitations, because he is assured that neighboring tracts of land will not be used in ways incompatible with his own intended land use. Prospective purchasers shop around among various subdivisions, attempting to find a subdivision offering the preferred set of deed restrictions, subject to the purchaser's budget constraint. Developers carefully evaluate the market potential of their land prior to subdivision, and seek to establish that set of deed restrictions which will maximize their profits from development.

In residential subdivisions, deed restrictions typically limit or eliminate industrial, commercial, and agricultural land uses. Deed restrictions may establish minimum lot size, minimum setback from roads and streams, and minimum size of the houses eventually built and the construction materials used. Some deed restrictions are remarkably detailed — for example, requiring particular modes of landscaping, prohibiting outdoor clotheslines, banning mobile homes or temporary structures during the construction period, banning disabled automobiles and/or limiting the number of automobiles and recreational vehicles that may be parked on each lot outside of an enclosed garage. The author lives in a small "baby farm" subdivision, where he is subject to minimum lot size restrictions, minimum setback from the road, minimum house size, restrictions on construction materials, and restrictions that eliminate industrial and commercial land uses while limiting agricultural land uses to "no hogs, no chickens, and a maximum of one head of livestock per acre."

In times past, deed restrictions banning certain racial and ethnic groups from particular subdivisions were routine, but these kinds of deed restrictions are no longer permissible nor enforceable.

Deed restrictions provide an effective mechanism for the elimination of incompatible land uses within subdivisions. They have the advantage that they are noncoercive, in that the developer may, within broad limits, select the kind of deed restrictions he will impose, and the buyer may choose among alternative subdivisions with different sets of deed restrictions. However, deed restrictions are generally ineffective in controlling externalities that cross subdivision boundaries. Since individual subdivisions tend to be small relative to whole communities or metropolitan areas, deed restrictions may effectively control incompatible uses within subdivision boundaries, but are usually ineffective as tools for implementing broader land-use policy on a community, metropolitan, or regional basis.

Easements and Fee-Simple Title Purchase

Where a public or governmental institution has a strong desire to maintain a particular land use on a particular tract of land, it may seek to purchase an easement, or to purchase the land in fee-simple title. It may seek to purchase riparian lands, low lying and flood prone lands, and lands that provide high class natural environments or habitats, with the specific intention of foreclosing industrial, commercial, or residential development. Alternatively, a public institution or governmental unit may seek to purchase an easement from the landowner, which would permit him to continue current and similar land uses, while foreclosing his right to convert the land to more intensive industrial, commercial, or residential uses. On the outskirts of certain large metropolitan areas, governmental units have purchased scenic easements that foreclose the landowner's option for intensive development, while permitting and encouraging the continued use of the land in working farms or, perhaps, esthetically pleasing "green" uses such as golf courses.

The purchase of easements or of land in fee-simple title is an effective way in which the public may assert and secure a right to preserve land in esthetically pleasing uses, or to foreclose developments thought to be undesirable. The main factor discouraging more widespread use of this tool is its expense. Public institutions and governmental units, with their limited budgets, are likely to avoid the purchase of easements or land in fee-simple title if they can achieve their land-use objectives with equal or similar effectiveness by using the police power or the power to tax. In instances where the governmental unit is willing to pay the fair market price for easements or for title to land, the owner, sensing his strategic position, may hold out, demanding a price that exceeds the fair market value of the land. In this instance, the governmental unit (subject to restrictions discussed in Chapter 13) may invoke its power of *eminent domain,* and thus purchase the land at fair market value.

THE POLICE POWER

State governments may use the police power directly or, by delegation, may permit local governments to use the police power, in order to regulate the use of land for the protection of the public health, welfare, safety, and morals. The police power has permitted land-use zoning, subdivision controls, building codes, and a variety of specialized restrictions, such as those that eliminate taverns in the immediate vicinity of churches, and those that confine sexually oriented businesses to particular designated locations. In addition, the police power permits the regulation of public utilities, and thus provides a legal basis for the use of public-utility regulation to eliminate some of the public finance problems that encourage urban sprawl.

Land-Use Zoning

Land-use zoning has been used with varying degrees of effectiveness, in one governmental unit or another, to attack each of the perceived land-use problems discussed above: nuisance externalities and incompatible uses; urban sprawl; the perceived need to preserve historic districts and green space; and the perceived need to maintain the biological productivity of land. In the United States, zoning is most commonly implemented by local government units. However, the zoning powers enjoyed by local government units vary from state to state. The extremes are Oregon, which was the first state to require local government units to zone on the basis of an approved comprehensive land-use plan under the threat that the state would withdraw its delegation of zoning authority and proceed to carry out the zoning itself, and Texas, which has persistently refused to delegate zoning powers to local government. In many states, different local-government units have responded differently to the delegation of zoning authority: some use all of the authority delegated, while others steadfastly refuse to use all of the powers at their disposal.

Zoning may seek to eliminate incompatible uses, by designating particular zones for particular types of uses. A typical zoning scheme established agriculture as the highest and best land use, with single-family residences as the next highest use, and, in any particular zone, permits higher but not lower uses. Thus, residences are permitted in industrial zones, but not vice versa.

A comprehensive program of land-use zoning is most effective when based upon a comprehensive land-use plan. In this way, the pattern of land use can be made compatible with transportation facilities, utilities, drainage and flood protection, and the provision of schools and similar public-sector services.

Zoning is usually carried out by elected local government bodies, or by zoning boards or commissions whose members are appointed by elected government bodies. Zoning authorities are empowered to zone land at the outset, to grant specific variances and exceptions from an existing zoning arrangement, and to rezone land in order to permit more-intensive uses of land that had been previously reserved for less intensive uses.

Initial zoning, by permitting intensive uses on some land but not other land, confers the potential for large capital gains on some landowners but not others. Individual applicants may have much to gain financially from the granting of a variance or exception to an existing zoning provision. When land is rezoned to permit more intensive use, in order to accommodate future growth in the community, some favored individuals will enjoy "windfall gains," while others will not. These circumstances place immense burdens upon members of zoning boards and commissions. They are subjected to intense pressures from competing private interests and "public interest" groups. Because of the large profit potentials at stake, it is not unknown for zoning board members to be tempted with bribes or other inducements that are illegal or of dubious morality. This is only to be expected, since zoning boards are empowered to redefine the rights that pertain to property, and to create, maintain, and on occasion modify an artificial scarcity of land that is available for various purposes. Thus, zoning regulations raise the "windfalls and wipe-outs" and "takings" issues (which are discussed in Chapter 13).

Let us now consider the effectiveness of zoning in achieving its various goals. In general, of course, the effectiveness of zoning regulations depends on the quality of the planning efforts on which they are based, on the willingness of zoning boards to make difficult decisions for the long-term benefit of the community at large, and on the integrity of zoning board or commission members. Beyond that, there are some more specific things that can be said. Zoning can be relatively effective at controlling or eliminating incompatible uses. It can be effective in directing development away from flood plains, steep and unstable slopes, and natural or built environments deemed worthy of preservation. Over time, as cities grow, zoning may be less effective at protecting residential landowners from the negative externalities associated with more intensive development. It may be impossible to resist pressures to permit multi-family dwellings in areas previously reserved for single-family residences or to permit commercial developments along residential streets that have, over time, become major traffic arteries.

Zoning has been even less effective in preserving agricultural land and limiting urban sprawl. There is powerful pressure to rezone agricultural land for residential uses as a metropolitan area grows. Ironically, agricultural zoning, which often requires that five or perhaps 10 acres must be owned before construction of one single-family dwelling is permitted, seems to have accelerated the subdivision of larger and more productive farms into "baby farms" of much lower agricultural productivity. A fairly accurate general statement is that while zoning may be effective in directing urban growth, it is typically ineffective in limiting or restraining such growth.

Subdivision Controls

To control urban sprawl and to limit the inequities resulting from average cost pricing of services provided by local governments and public utilities, many jurisdictions have initiated subdivision controls. A proposed subdivision must be approved by the cognizant authority. Evidence must be presented that the subdivision is "needed" and therefore does not represent a wasteful use of land. However, these provisions are quite easily satisfied, since the mere fact that a developer seeks to undertake subdivision provides considerable evidence that a demand for the proposed housing exists.

A more significant influence of subdivision controls is derived from provisions requiring that the developer bear the initial capital costs of providing at least some services to the subdivision. Typically, the developer may be required to provide roads within the subdivision and (perhaps) roads linking the subdivision to major traffic arteries, drainage for the subdivision, a domestic water system, and a system for the collection and treatment of sewage. In principle, these kinds of provisions are conducive to both economic efficiency and equity in land use, since the price of homes in new subdivisions reflects, at least in part, the costs of providing services and utilities to fringe areas of the metropolitan area.

In application, subdivision controls have exhibited two weaknesses. (1) They seldom specify that the developer must bear the initial capital costs of *all* relevant services and utilities. While many jurisdictions require the developer to build internal roads, fewer require him to build roads from the subdivision to major traffic arteries, and none require him to bear the costs of widening and upgrading major traffic arteries, if that should prove necessary. While many subdivision controls require the provision of water and sewer services, very few require the provision of electric transmission lines, natural gas pipelines, or schools. Under average cost pricing, residents of established neighborhoods bear a substantial portion of the costs of extending these services to new subdivisions. Subdivision controls have perhaps been more successful in requiring that the developer set aside open space and parkland, but less successful in requiring that the parkland be adequately landscaped and developed for recreational purposes. (2) Quality control with respect to the facilities provided by developers has often been inadequate. After a specified period of time, or after a specified portion of the lots in the subdivision have been sold, the service and utility facilities provided by the developer typically are sold to a corporation (which may be a cooperative of subdivision residents) or revert to the local government jurisdiction. Under these conditions, it is rational for the developer to plan and construct these facilities with only a short-time horizon in mind. Thus, one observes subdivision roads that soon deteriorate and sewage treatment plants that soon become significant sources of pollution. Eventually, the public sector may often be obligated to correct the situation at considerable expense. In this way, the effectiveness of subdivision controls is often reduced and their purposes are subverted.

Building Codes

Building codes are, for the most part, regulations aimed at the protection of health and safety. As such, they provide protection to the consumer, who may often lack the expertise to provide such protection for himself. On the other hand, they may increase construction costs and retard innovations in construction techniques.

Building codes may exert some relatively minor influence on land use, by eliminating some structures that would be esthetically inferior or would deteriorate rapidly, and by requirements such as those that specify a minimum distance of buildings from property boundaries, utility lines, etc.

Public-Utility Regulation

Public utilities, which typically enjoy a monopoly within their service areas, are regulated with respect to the services they provide and the charges they make for those services. Utility-regulatory commissions could, if they chose, eliminate some of the public finance problems that encourage urban sprawl, by restructuring rate schedules to impose the costs of providing services to new developments upon residences and businesses in those developments. However, and perhaps unfortunately, the various state regulatory commissions have been mostly unwilling to take this route.

TAXATION

State and local jurisdictions typically tax property, in order to raise revenues. But, as we have already seen, the power to tax is the power to modify prices, and thus to modify economic incentives. Thus, it is frequently suggested that property-taxation strategy should provide a tool for implementation of land-use policy.

Property-taxation strategies are most commonly implemented at the urban/rural fringe, with the intention of restricting urban sprawl and delaying the premature conversion of land from agricultural uses. A common strategy is *use-value taxation,* wherein property is taxed on the basis of its value in its current use, rather than its market value which may reflect the value of the land in an alternative and more intensive use. It is clear that use-value taxation, by reducing the taxes paid on land in agricultural uses, represents a subsidy for farmers. However, our purpose here is to examine its effectiveness as a tool for land-use policy.

It is often argued that market-value taxation imposes an unbearable cost upon farmers near the urban/rural fringe, making farming unprofitable and thus accelerating the conversion of land from agricultural uses. While this may be true, it is only a part of the story. To believe that use-value taxation alone will be sufficient to prevent premature conversion of farmland, it is necessary to believe that farmers are entirely aware of the costs they actually bear but entirely oblivious of opportunity costs. If the market value of land substantially exceeds its use value in agriculture, those farmers who respond to economic incentives are likely to find the inducements to sell their land to a buyer with nonagricultural uses in mind irresistible, regardless of use-value property-taxation provisions. Further, experience has shown that use-value taxation often serves merely to provide an unnecessary subsidy to speculators and land developers, who purchase farmland near the urban/rural fringe and leave it unused or in low-intensity agricultural uses while awaiting the optimal time for its conversion to urban uses.

In the political arena, property-taxation policy has, for the reasons suggested above, become a battleground between those who are most concerned that use-value taxation remain a subsidy for farmers, speculators, and land developers, and those who would prefer that it become a more effective tool for land-use policy. The latter usually take the approach that use-value taxation should be available only to those landowners who are bona fide farmers and who intend that their land remain in agricultural use for a considerable time period. In various jurisdictions, several mechanisms have been implemented, in an attempt to satisfy these objectives.

Rollback provisions require that, in the event that agricultural land is converted to urban uses, the difference between market-value taxes and use-value taxes and interest on that difference be collected for the previous several years. Various jurisdictions specify different periods for the collection of "back taxes"; periods of three, five, and 10 years are among the more common. Rollback provisions serve to correct, at least in part, the apparent inequities that occur when landowners enjoy the benefits of use-value taxation while preparing for conversion of the land to urban uses. However, the total back taxes plus interest is likely to be an insignificant sum when compared to the capital gains to be enjoyed from land conversion. Accordingly, rollback provisions provide only a limited disincentive for premature land conversion.

Some jurisdictions have attempted to formalize the informal understanding between landowners and their state or local governments expressed in rollback provisions, by establishing procedures whereby use-value taxation may be enjoyed only by landowners who enter into formal agreements to forego land conversion for a period of, say, 10 years. Violation of this kind of agreement usually invokes rollback provisions and additional penalties. Such arrangements have had limited effectiveness. Where such agreements are voluntarily entered into by individual landowners and their governments, those landowners most likely to be tempted by the profits from premature land conversion are those least likely to enter into such agreements. In addition, should conversion prospects improve markedly during the 10 year period, the rollback provisions and penalties are seldom sufficiently great to discourage conversion.

These kinds of agreements are in some ways analogous to the purchase by local governments of easements that foreclose development. Local government, by voluntarily limiting the amount of taxes it collects on the land, in a sense is purchasing the right to foreclose development inexpensively and on "time payment." Although this represents a cheap way to buy such a right, the right so obtained is much less valuable than an easement foreclosing development. Under an easement, the beneficiary (i.e., local government) is and remains the dominant party. However, under this kind of agreement, developments (of the type intended to be foreclosed) may proceed without penalty at the end of the agreement period or with only a relatively insignificant penalty while the agreement is in effect.

In recent years, some heavily urbanized states, anxious to preserve the rural character of their remaining agricultural regions, have experimented with *agricultural districts*.[2] These offer property tax benefits, and sometimes other inducements, for landowners to keep their land in agricultural uses. They differ from the typical "use-value taxation with rollback provision" arrangement in that they are not agreements between the government and rural landowners one by one, but require a collective agreement among the landowners who wish to be included in an agricultural district. The primary advantage claimed for agricultural districts is that they provide each landowner with assurance that the district will retain its agricultural character into the distant future, and thus provide encouragement for continued investment to maintain and increase the agricultural productivity of the land (an encouragement entirely absent when a rural landowner expects that surrounding land, and perhaps also his land, is a candidate for imminent conversion to urban uses). Since agricultural districts are relatively recent innovations, it is too early to pass judgment on their effectiveness.

SUMMARY: THE EFFECTIVENESS OF TRADITIONAL POLICE-POWER AND TAXATION POLICIES IN FORESTALLING PREMATURE AND UNDESIRABLE LAND-USE CONVERSION

We have seen that subdivision controls and public-utility regulations are usually insufficient to offset the incentives for premature conversion of rural land that are inherent in the customary modes of financing local government services and public utilities. Further, use-value taxation, even with rollback provisions, seems insufficient to cancel out the incentives for premature development. Zoning may be helpful in directing urban development away from specific, unsuitable lands, but it has not been especially effective in discouraging urban sprawl. Further, because of the immense effects specific applications of zoning regulations may have on individual fortunes, there is continuing concern that zoning tends to treat landowners inequitably and to provide sometimes irresistible temptations for the corruption of zoning authorities.

SOME INNOVATIVE SUGGESTIONS FOR LAND-USE POLICY

There have been a number of suggestions for land-use policy that make innovative use of some of the principles of economics. Below we briefly discuss two of these.

The Auctioning of Zoning Changes

The economist Marion Clawson has argued along the following lines. [3] The community has made increasingly valuable the right to use land in intensive urban uses, since it is community growth that creates the demand for land in such uses and the community activity of zoning that creates the valuable right to so use land. Developers who wish to convert land to more intensive uses find the right to do so valuable and would be willing to pay for that right in a market if they no longer could obtain it through the political process.

Accordingly, he proposed that zoning authorities, after deciding which lands should be subject to zoning changes and variances, should auction the rights so created to the highest bidder. Implementation of such a proposal would have the following effects. Because of a lessening of restrictions on the operation of the price mechanism, markets in land would tend to become more efficient, spatially and intertemporally. Land would be more likely to gravitate to its highest valued use. The activity of land speculation would become less profitable, because the economic surplus that arises from changes in rights pertaining to land use would flow in large part to the local government that conducts the auction and collects the sums of money bid. In this way, some of the obvious inequities that result from zoning would be eliminated, along with most of the incentives for corruption on the part of zoning authorities.

This proposal is yet to be implemented in any jurisdiction, perhaps because it is contrary to some deeply embedded political traditions, and perhaps because land speculators and developers form an unusually effective lobby which prefers business-as-usual to the Clawson proposal.

Transfer of Development Rights[4]

The proposal for transferable development rights (TDRs) is aimed at accommodating the pressures for more intensive development that arise from population growth and economic progress, while providing for the preservation of natural or built environments deemed worthy of preservation, and at the same time eliminating inequitable treatment of owners of different tracts of land. Ordinary zoning to prevent development in flood plains, agricultural areas, and areas of historical or architectural significance is often resisted by landowners in those areas, because it would foreclose their prospects for profit from land-use conversion while enhancing the profit prospects of landowners in other areas. Independent observers may also see inequity in such an arrangement. The TDR proposal is aimed at eliminating this inequity, and thus increasing the political acceptability of proposals to preserve the character of areas deemed worthy of preservation.

The TDR proposal is best conceptualized as a version of zoning, but one that increases the scope for market behaviors. In the simplest case, the zoning authority divides its jurisdiction into two zones: a zone in which intensive land development is to be concentrated (called the development zone, DZ) and a zone in which the current land use is to be continued (called the transfer zone, TZ). Transferable development rights would be created and would be distributed among landowners in both zones. The basis for initial distribution of TDRs is a matter of some contention, but a possible solution is that each landowner would receive one TDR for each $10,000 assessed valuation of land he owns in either zone. A schedule, relating the required number of TDRs to the intensity of proposed individual developments in the DZ, would be established by the zoning authorities.

In order to receive approval of a development proposal, a developer would need to own both land in the DZ and the requisite number of TDRs. Thus, a market in TDRs would be established, and as development proceeds in the DZ, it would soon become necessary to purchase TDRs from landowners in the transfer zone. In this way, landowners in the TZ would be able to share in the profits from development, without endangering the benefits the public at large obtains from the preservation of TZ land in its current use. The expense of purchasing TDRs would discourage premature development in the DZ and would tend to limit the profits obtained by DZ landowners from conversion to more intensive land uses. Thus, the TDR proposal would enable a community to enjoy many of the benefits from zoning, while eliminating the "windfalls and wipe-outs" and "takings" problems commonly associated with zoning.

In the United States, the TDR proposal has been implemented in a number of localities. Its initial implementation was associated with the preservation of historic districts and of beachfront environments, but it appears to have the potential for more widespread implementation in communities that would like to control the pattern and direction of intensive development. In a hypothetical study of the simulated implementation of a TDR program in a more traditional land-use-problem setting (land use in the vicinity of a freeway interchange), a number of potential difficulties were identified.[5] However, the authors of that study are quick to suggest that their results should be interpreted as identifying areas that need further study and careful planning, rather than as providing reasons to abandon the TDR proposal.

QUESTIONS FOR DISCUSSION

1. Evaluate the contention that individuals using deed restrictions (voluntary agreements) can achieve the objectives that are often pursued through zoning (a use of the police power by governments), equally effectively and without coercion.
2. Why do governments often seek to accomplish through the use of the police power land-use objectives that could be accomplished under the power of eminent domain?
3. A cynic once said, "Zoning to control the spread of suburban development is a process by which a continuous flow of small economic gains to many is converted to a discontinuous flow of large economic gains to a well-connected few, without influencing suburban spread to any significant degree."

   What did he mean? Do you agree with him? Why, or why not?
4. Is "use-value taxation" of property an effective land-use control tool? Is it justifiable, solely on the grounds that it is "fair to farmers"?
5. Try to devise a TDR plan for the city in which your university or college is located. Where should the DZ be? How should TDRs be initially distributed among property owners? Devise a schedule relating the number of TDRs required to the intensity of proposed development in the DZ.

   Do you think your TDR plan would be preferable to the land-use controls (if any) currently in effect in that city?

FURTHER READINGS

Babcock, Richard F. 1966. *The Zoning Game.* Madison: The University of Wisconsin Press.

Barron, James C., and James W. Thomson. 1973. "Impacts of Open Space Taxation in Washington," Bulletin 772, Washington Agricultural Experiment Station, Washington State University (Mar.).

Barrows, Richard L., and Bruce A. Prengruber. 1975. "Transfer of Development Rights: An Analysis of a New Land Use Policy Tool," *American Journal of Agricultural Economics.* 57: 549-557.

Clawson, Marion. 1971. *Suburban Land Conversion in the United States: An Economic and Governmental Process.* Baltimore: Johns Hopkins University Press.

Conklin, Howard E., and William R. Bryant. 1974. "Agricultural Districts: A Compromise Approach to Agricultural Preservation," *American Journal of Agricultural Economics.* 56: 607-613.

Costonis, John J. 1973. "Development Rights Transfers: An Exploratory Essay," *Yale Law Journal.* 83: 75-128.

Ervin, David, James Fitch, Kenneth Godwin, Bruce Shepard, and Herbert Stoevener. 1977. *Land Use Control: Evaluating Economic and Political Effects.* Cambridge, Mass.: Ballinger.

Libby, Lawrence W. 1974. "Comprehensive Land Use Planning and Other Myths," *Journal of Soil and Water Conservation.* 29(3): 106-108.

McHarg, Ian L. 1969. *Design With Nature.* Garden City, New York: Natural History Press.

Netzer, Dick. 1968. *Impact of the Property Tax: Effect on Housing and Urban Land Use.* Washington, D. C.: National Commission on Urban Problems.

Siegan, Bernard H. 1972. *Land Use Without Zoning.* Lexington, Mass.: Lexington Books.

Whyte, William H. 1968. *The Last Landscape.* Garden City, New York: Doubleday Anchor.

ENDNOTES

1. Brubaker, Sterling. 1977. "Land — The Far Horizon," *American Journal of Agricultural Economics.* 59:1037-1044.
2. See Howard E. Conklin and Willian G. Lesher. 1977. "Farm-Value Assessment as a Means for Reducing Premature and Excessive Agricultural Disinvestment in Urban Fringes," *American Journal of Agricultural Economics.* 59:755-759.

    And Howard E. Conklin and William R. Bryant. 1974. "Agricultural Districts: A Compromise Approach to Agricultural Preservation," *American Journal of Agricultural Economics.* 56:607-613.
3. Clawson, Marion. 1967. "Why Not Sell Zoning and Rezoning? (legally, that is)," *Land Use Controls.* 1:(No. 2):29-30.
4. See John J. Costonis. 1973. "Development Rights Transfer: An Exploratory Essay," *Yale Law Journal.* 83:75-128.
5. Barrows, Richard L., and Bruce A. Prengruber. 1975. "Transfer of Development Rights: An Analysis of a New Land Use Policy Tool," *American Journal of Agricultural Economics.* 57:549-557.

20

The Preservation of Natural Environments

Consider the diminishing area of natural environments in the developed countries today. Terrestrial environments, inland wetlands, and coastal marshes with substantially nondegraded ecosystems are, unfortunately, becoming increasingly rare. Nevertheless, these environments provide a vast array of services for mankind.

For many kinds of fish and wildlife, they provide year-round habitat. For other species, they provide nursery or migratory habitat. For still other kinds of fish and wildlife, important links in the food chain are provided by species that themselves use these environments as nursery or migratory habitats. Thus, people may enjoy utility from fish and wildlife, via commercial harvest, sport hunting and fishing, or observation, in some cases by venturing into the natural environment and in other cases by encountering in other locales species that are dependent upon natural environments for their survival. Those who enter substantially nondegraded natural environments for recreation enjoy more than the pleasures of hunting, observing, or fishing for a particular species. They enjoy a total esthetic and recreational experience provided by the wondrous diversity of the nondegraded natural environment.

Among these environments one usually finds the few remaining significant habitats of endangered species, which is only to be expected, since species that are well-adapted to intensively managed agricultural environments or urban environments are unlikely to become endangered in the modern world. Thus, natural environments provide the best hope of preserving endangered species, which is thought desirable for several reasons: to preserve the natural heritage for the cultural and spiritual benefit of mankind; to maintain the diversity of nature's pool of genetic

349

materials, and thus to avoid limiting the evolutionary potential of nature; and because there is no assurance that species which seem of little use to mankind today will not be recognized as useful in the future. The progress of science frequently provides examples of the last-mentioned phenomenon, when it is discovered that species previously considered useless play significant roles in the survival and productivity of species valued by mankind, and when science discovers important uses, medicinal and other, for chemical compounds produced by biological organisms.

Natural environments provide research and educational services associated with individual species that exist therein and with the ecological diversity of such environments. Ecologically diverse habitats provide the only opportunities for man to learn about the interactions in natural systems.

Natural environments also provide a wide variety of services considered important by individuals who are not especially concerned with natural systems and ecological diversity, per se. Terrestrial natural environments provide air-quality enhancement, through "greenbelt effects." Inland aquatic and wetland environments provide drainage, recharge of aquifers, flood-water retention, and buffering from flood damage. In addition, they provide silt retention that in the short term reduces expenditures on dredging of streams, navigation locks, harbors, etc., and in the long term assists the process of soil formation. Coastal estuarine and marsh environments provide buffering effects, reducing damage from high winds, wave impact, and the accumulation of debris during violent weather. In addition, they perform a vital role in the maintenance of global chemical balance. As with inland wetlands, coastal environments perform services in drainage, flood-water retention, silt accumulation, and soil formation. Wetlands, whether inland or coastal, provide vital services in water-pollution control, through assimilation of wastes and recycling of chemicals.

The foregoing is directed at establishing that natural environments — terrestrial, inland wetland, and coastal — perform a wide variety of significant services that are currently or potentially of value to mankind. However, the area of such environments that remains in a substantially nondegraded state is relatively small and rapidly diminishing in the developed countries. The situation with respect to wetland wildlife-habitat loss in the U.S. (Figure 20.1) is perhaps typical.

The federal government has active programs designed to preserve some of the remaining natural environments.[1] The wetlands-protection program involves a relatively low-budget program under which the Fish and Wildlife Service purchases and maintains important breeding and wintering habitat for migratory waterfowl. In addition, an executive order has been issued requiring all federal executive agencies to refrain from supporting construction activities in wetlands wherever there is a practical alternative. Coastal-zone-management legislation encourages the coastal states

FIGURE 20.1
Wetland Wildlife Habitat Loss, 1955-75

  <u>|||||||</u> Greatest impact, potential drainage of 100,000 acres or more
  ▓▓▓ Waterfowl breeding habitat needing protection
  ▨▨▨ Waterfowl wintering habitat needing protection
  ● Urban or industrial encroachment
  ◆ Destroyed by highway construction and water facilities

Source: U.S. Water Resources Council, *Preliminary Water Resources Problem
Statements* (Washington, D.C., 1977), p. 33.

and territories to prepare management programs for their coastal
zones. While these programs are not designed to foreclose further
coastal-zone development, the preservation of critical coastal-zone
habitats is one of their many goals. The program for wild and scenic
rivers included stretches of 19 rivers totaling 1,655 miles as of 1977.
A further 51 rivers had been proposed for inclusion in the program,
or were under study. In 1976, 1.7 million acres were added to the
national wilderness-preservation system, bringing the total area
included to 14.4 million acres. Under currently proposed legislation,
many more millions of acres, mostly in Alaska, would be added to
the wilderness system.

The area of natural environments covered by such governmental
programs in the U. S. is increasing. Yet this cannot be taken as
evidence that substantially nondegraded natural environments are
becoming less scarce. It will take many years before the pre-existing
pattern of degradation in some recently added areas can be
reversed. Many environments now included in such programs may

continue to suffer some degradation as a result of man's activity in neighboring (and, in some cases, quite distant) areas. Finally, the process of degradation of natural ecosystems will continue in those areas not included in such programs; and (except in Alaska) those areas not included far exceed the areas included.

AN ECONOMIC DIAGNOSIS OF THE PROBLEM

Many (in fact, almost all) of the services provided by natural environments are nonexclusive. Thus, the prospects for earning income by establishing ownership over natural environments and marketing the services they provide are not good. On the other hand, many of the services that could be provided by the same land, if it were modified and converted to uses that are incompatible with the maintenance of a nondegraded ecosystem, are high-valued, exclusive, and readily marketed. A recent study of the economic value of coastal marshlands in Virginia concluded that it was nearly impossible to determine the value of such land as marshland, but that its value for landfilling and conversion to residential and resort development use could be estimated with reasonable accuracy; in one example, it was about $17,000 per acre.[2]

As a result of the very poorly developed markets for the goods and services natural environments provide, the owners of land in such environments often find potential profits in converting it to other quite different uses, even when the total social value of the services it would provide in the new uses is less than the value of the services it provides in its natural condition. Such being the pressures for conversion of privately owned lands in natural environments, it is not surprising that much of the remaining land with substantially nondegraded natural environments is in public ownership.

Public ownership, however, is insufficient to ensure the preservation of natural environments. Public agencies are charged with managing public lands in the national interest. And, during the Four Hundred Year Boom, the national interest was interpreted more often than not as being served by development rather than preservation. Public-land-management agencies are charged with multiple-objective planning in order to encourage multiple use of the lands they control. Whether these agencies are bound to make decisions on the basis of the results of benefit cost analyses or not, they are invariably at least influenced by benefit cost logic. Since many of the services provided by natural environments are nonexclusive, and therefore unpriced, empirical benefit cost analyses have tended to undervalue the services provided by preserved natural environments relative to the services provided by the "development option." As a result, public-resource-management agencies may have permitted too much development of the natural environments under their control. We observe logging, grazing, and mineral extraction in natural terrestrial environments, drainage of inland wetlands, landfilling of coastal marshes, and dredging of estuaries. These things, of course, are not necessarily undesirable. However, they become undesirable when, at the margin, the benefits from such development activities are less than the benefits from preservation — if only the benefits from preservation could be quantified.

ECONOMIC EVALUATION OF THE PRESERVATION OPTION

The framework for multiple-objective planning involves consideration of national economic development (NED), regional economic development (RED), environmental quality (EQ), and social well-being (SW), all of which have been discussed earlier (Chapter 15). For economic evaluation, the NED and RED accounts are most pertinent, bearing in mind that those items that appear in the EQ account should, to the extent that it is possible to value them in economic terms, also appear in the NED account. There is a simultaneity between the economic accounts and the management plan for the natural environment, since the parameters for economic evaluation depend on the management plan, while the management plan itself should be selected only after consideration of the economic performance of alternative management plans.

THE MANAGEMENT PLAN

The management plan for a natural environment almost always involves multiple use, so that the environment may provide a variety of services. Management plans must be internally consistent, which is a more difficult task than it appears at first glance. The provision of some kinds of services is incompatible with the provision of other kinds. The selection of the mix of services to be provided almost always involves trade-offs. Maximization of the provision of recreational services would most likely involve congestion, pollution, and degradation of the very ecosystem that is intended for preservation. While certain kinds of natural environments have the capacity to provide substantial and valuable waste-assimilation services, it is always possible that excessive quantities of wastes, or wastes of particular kinds, may degrade the environment, exhausting its waste-assimilation capacities and making it less productive in other uses. Thus, the establishment of management plans is a delicate task, requiring consideration of myriad trade-offs in a complex systems framework. Final selection of a management plan should be made only after consideration of the relative contributions of alternative plans to economic and other objectives.

NATIONAL ECONOMIC DEVELOPMENT

Given a coherent and internally consistent management plan, the estimation of the contribution of the preservation option to national economic development is an exercise in the evaluation of "without project" benefits, in the benefit cost framework. Below are presented the rudiments of an appropriate analytical framework for estimation of the net NED benefits of the preservation option. In accordance with the potential Pareto-improvement criterion, an existing natural environment is valued at the seller's reservation price for a capital good. The capital value of a given environmental resource (E) is the net present value (PV) to the seller of the stream of services in each time period, S_t, where $t = 0,1,2,...,\infty$, and the present time period is defined at $t = 0$. Thus,

$$PV(E) = \sum_{t=0}^{\infty} \frac{V(S_t)}{(1 + r)^t} \qquad \text{(Equation 1)}$$

where $V(S_t)$ = the net value, at time t, of the bundle of services produced by the environment in time t, and r = the discount rate.

The bundle of services, S_t, provided by the environment is a vector of n types of environmental services, s_{it}, where $i = 1,...,n$. Thus,

$$V(S_t) = \sum_{i=1}^{n} V_{it}(s_{it}) \qquad \text{(Equation 2)}$$

Now let us consider, first, the production of environmental services and, then, the value of those services. The supply of an environmental service, s_i ($i = 1,...,n$), in any time period is a function, uniquely determined by geological, hydrological, and ecological relationships of the attributes, a_k ($k = 1,...,m$), of the environment. Thus, for all environment services in $i = 1,...,n$, we have:

$$s_1 = g_1(a_1,...,a_m)$$
$$\vdots \qquad \qquad \text{(Equation 3)}$$
$$s_n = g_n(a_1,...,a_m)$$

Man enters the production system as a modifier of environment attributes. He may do this directly — e.g., by reassigning land to other uses, diverting water, removing vegetation, disturbing soil for mining, etc. He may also modify the environment as a side effect (expected or unexpected) of some other decision — e.g., disturbing land elsewhere for cultivation or mining, deposition of wastes in water upstream, etc. For each kind of environmental attribute in $k = 1,....,m$, we have:

$$a_1 = h_1(n^s, x^u)$$
$$\vdots$$
$$\text{(Equation 4)}$$
$$a_m = h_m(n^s, x^u)$$

where n^s = a vector of "natural-system inputs" (e.g., geological, hydrological, atmospheric, and ecological), and x^u = a vector in inputs controlled by man.

Both n^s and x^u are subject to scarcity; and the attribute-production functions are determined by the laws that govern natural systems and by man's technology. The production system is now complete. It is entirely possible that the level of production of some kinds of services, s_i, influences the level of some attributes, a_k, by a feedback mechanism wherein s_i alters the level of some man-controlled inputs in x^u. For example, the attempt to enjoy high levels of waste-assimilation services involves high levels of pollution inputs, which may directly or indirectly modify environment attributes.

Now consider the value of environmental services. Each individual, j, enjoys utility in each time period, t:

$$U_{jt} = f_j(s_t^g, z_t^y, y_t^z) \qquad \text{(Equation 5)}$$

where s^g = a vector of environmental services, which are directly enjoyed for their amenity value,

z^y = a vector of goods and services for which environmental services are inputs, and

y^z = a vector of goods and services produced in processes bearing no immediate relationship to environmental services.

Each individual makes decisions in the initial time period, and subject to his initial budget constraint, in order to maximize the present value of expected lifetime utility.

By minimizing his expenditures, subject to the constraint that his utility must always be equal to or greater than the utility he enjoys with the existing natural environment, his Hicksian income-compensated demand curves for environmental services may be derived. From this, the Hicksian compensating measure (see Chapter 16) of the value of the loss the individual would incur in time t, should the natural environment be destroyed or degraded, may be calculated. The NED benefits from preservation of the natural environment (or, conversely, the NED loss from destruction or degradation of that environment) may be calculated by summing the Hicksian compensating measures of value across individuals, and across time periods.

This framework for estimating the NED benefits of preservation of natural environments is conceptually valid. Nevertheless, it is clear that massive empirical tasks remain. The relationships governing the production of habitat services (Equations 3 and 4) are, in many instances, very poorly understood. Values of environmental services are seldom revealed in the market, and must often be estimated using one or another variant of the techniques discussed in Chapter 16.

REGIONAL ECONOMIC DEVELOPMENT BENEFITS OF PRESERVATION

RED benefits must be considered, in the context of multiple-objective planning. In addition, where local attitudes play an important role in the political process by which natural environments may be preserved, the relative sizes of the RED benefits of the development and preservation options provide one useful indicator of likely local support or opposition to preservation. RED benefits (discussed in Chapter 15) may be estimated using techniques such as those described in Chapter 17.

PRESERVATION OR NOT: THE DECISION PROCESS

Even where the natural environment that is a candidate for preservation exists entirely on public lands, competing private and "public interest" groups may be expected to have considerable interest in the outcome of the preservation decision. The outcome will not be determined entirely by economic evaluation, for at least two reasons: (1) many of those interested will argue that economic considerations (and, especially, NED considerations) are not the only ones that matter; and (2) the information underlying any economic evaluations performed will be partly, and sometimes substantially, incomplete and therefore not decisive.

With respect to the completeness and accuracy of the economic analysis of NED benefits, the following arguments are likely to have considerable validity. The relationships governing the production of goods, services, and amenities from natural habitats are not well understood, and thus not reliably quantified. Techniques for evaluation of nonmarket goods and services are imperfect. Economic evaluations derived from the utility functions of individuals may reflect the myopia and ignorance of people whose understanding of complex ecological relationships varies from abysmal to poor. Given the uncertainties that exist with respect to future technologies and future demands, who can accurately estimate the value of service flows in distant-future time periods? Finally, the decision to preserve a natural environment or not has very-long-term consequences and a considerable element of irreversibility. Therefore, the arguments against the use of discounting procedures in circumstances where intergenerational equity is a prime concern (Chapter 11) are pertinent.[3]

The decision process will be substantially political, operating within the established institutional framework, which includes NEPA, the Endangered Species Act, and a myriad of specialized laws, statutes, regulations, and guidelines directing the operation of the agencies entrusted with managing public lands and protecting natural and environmental resources. Economic interests will be brought to bear, and dispassionate economic analysis will play a restricted, but perhaps influential, role. For the foreseeable future, one could predict that improved economic analyses of the value of natural environments will tend to strengthen the hands of those who favor preservation — not because such analyses are likely to be complete and decisive, but because such analyses by their very existence will tend to undercut the widespread notion that "economic considerations always favor the development option."

The above discussion has been concerned, for the most part, with natural environments that exist on public property. What about cases where natural environments exist on privately owned property? As previously indicated, the opportunity seldom exists for a private owner to enjoy the economic benefits from the preservation option. If a public purpose can be demonstrated, the public sector may always acquire the relevant property, using the power of eminent domain. This is a reasonable, but expensive, approach. There have been instances where the public sector has preferred to achieve preservation via police-power regulation. Developments that would destroy or degrade the natural environment are simply prohibited by regulation. Since this procedure may cause considerable economic loss to the owner by foreclosing profitable development options, the "takings" issue will often arise where the public attempts to enforce preservation by police-power regulation.[4]

QUESTIONS FOR DISCUSSION

1. Can you suggest serviceable methods for estimating the economic value of the following categories of services that may be provided by natural environments:
   (a) recreation and nature study?
   (b) nursery habitat for species that produce commercial seafood?
   (c) mitigation of property damage from high winds?
   (d) tertiary waste treatment?
   (e) a sense of tranquility and harmony with nature?
2. How might the private sector be encouraged to preserve natural environments?
3. This chapter has argued that the nonexclusive and unpriced nature of many of the benefits from natural environments most likely results in the underprovision of natural environments by both private and public sectors.
   Others have argued that the complex and time-consuming EIS, licensing, and resource-planning processes, many of which permit citizen access to public hearings and the courts, provide "roadblocks to

development" and, conversely, result in excessive provision of natural environments.

Is either (or, perhaps, are both) of these arguments valid? If there is some truth to both arguments, which influence has the strongest impact?

FURTHER READINGS

Hammack, Judd, and Gardner Mallard Brown, 1974. *Water Fowl and Wetlands: Toward Bioeconomic Analysis.* Baltimore: The Johns Hopkins University Press.

Krutilla, John V. (ed). 1972. *National Environments: Studies in Theoretical and Applied Analysis.* Baltimore: The Johns Hopkins University Press.

Krutilla, John V., and Anthony C. Fisher (eds). 1975. *The Economics of Natural Environments: Studies in the Valuation of Commodity and Amenity Resources.* Baltimore: The Johns Hopkins University Press.

ENDNOTES

1. See Council on Environmental Quality. 1977. *Environmental Quality.* Washington. Pages 86-110.
2. Shabman, Leonard, and Michael K. Bertelson. 1979. "The Use of Development Value Estimates for Coastal Wetland Permit Decisions," *Land Economics.* 55: 213-222.
3. See Ferejohn, John, and Talbot Page. 1978. "On the Foundations of Intertemporal Choice," *American Journal of Agricultural Economics.* 60(May): 269-275.
4. See Bosselman, Fred, David Callies, and J. Banta. 1973. *The Takings Issue.* Washington: Council of Environmental Quality.

21

The Control of Polluting Emissions

Air pollution existed even in pre-industrial times, when it typically resulted from combustion of biological materials. Smoke from the burning of wood frequently polluted the air above urban centers, and grass and forest fires made air pollution a transitory phenomenon in even the most rural environments. Following the Industrial Revolution, the combustion of fossil fuels, and the by-products from the manufacture and use of chemicals, have added greatly to the quantity and multiplied the variety of pollutants in the air. Rural regions such as the Ohio River valley now have significant air-pollution problems, as they are invaded by airborne pollutants generated in the cities, and also generate significant air pollutants locally from automobiles, local industries, and large installations such as coal-burning electric generators that are with increasing frequency being located in rural regions.

Air pollution is ugly, causing discoloration and reducing atmospheric visibility. It is costly, for example, when airborne corrosive materials increase the maintenance costs and accelerate the deterioration of buildings, industrial plant, and equipment. Some kinds of pollutants diminish the productivity of biological resources as they, for example, retard plant growth on farms and in forests. There is substantial medical and statistical evidence that increasing levels of air pollution are positively related to human morbidity and mortality[1] (that means, people get sick and die). All of this suggests that air pollution is most definitely a discommodity.

Since, insofar as is known, nobody goes around polluting the air for the sheer joy of it, it is reasonable to surmise that air pollution occurs because it is an inexpensive way for the producer of waste materials to dispose of them. Since the ambient air is both indivisible and nonexclusive (see Chapter 8), it is most unlikely that anyone disposing of wastes into the air would personally suffer all the costs of the resulting air pollution damage. Thus, air pollution is an external diseconomy (Chapter 8) such that the utility of the receptor is influenced by those things under his control, but also by the polluting activity that is under the control of the polluter. Air pollution, therefore, involves the economic phenomena of external diseconomy, indivisibility in consumption, and nonexclusiveness.

THE CURRENT APPROACH TO THE CONTROL OF AIR POLLUTANTS

Given the indivisible and nonexclusive characteristics of ambient air, pure Coasian market solutions have in general been ineffective at internalizing the external diseconomies that result in inefficiently large amounts of air pollution. It is relatively easy to demonstrate (as in Chapter 8) that, conceptually, policies that work through the price system, such as emissions taxes, provide a given level of air-pollution abatement at a lower resource cost than regulatory approaches such as emission standards. Nevertheless, state and federal air pollution control policies in the U. S. have emphasized various regulatory approaches.[2] This is consistent with U. S. political traditions, in which regulatory approaches are customarily selected in preference to approaches that rely on modification of price incentives, and is also consistent with the observation (Chapter 13) that the U. S. Constitution simply makes it easier for legislators to pursue policy objectives via the police power rather than the power to tax.

Air pollution control policies are currently pursued in the U. S. through a very complex regulatory approach, in which the federal government has taken the lead, in spite of the constitutional provisions that vest the police power in the states (see Chapters 13 and 14). There is a complex web of federal and state enabling legislation, regulations, and enforcement. Different provisions apply to different pollutants, different locations, and different emissions sources. It would be inappropriate and impracticable to provide all the details here. Rather, some of the more significant aspects of the current regulatory approach will be discussed in general terms.

The 1970 amendments to the Clean Air Act directed the U. S. Environmental Protection Agency (EPA) to determine standards for ambient air quality that would protect human health. These were designated the primary standards, and were to be achieved rapidly. Secondary standards, more stringent than the primary standards, and designed to protect property and the public welfare, were established to be implemented on more flexible time schedules. In those areas that had historically suffered substantial pollution from industrial and mobile sources, the primary standards represented the immediate air quality target. In areas that had historically enjoyed high levels of air quality, the EPA was instructed to achieve "prevention of significant deterioration" (PSD) of air quality. After a spate of litigation, in which it was determined that PSD meant pretty much what it said, the 1977 Clean Air Act amendments required that, in certain pristine areas, atmospheric visibility must be protected.

Thus, the operative ambient air quality standard varied across regions, ranging from the primary standards in heavily populated and industrialized regions, through the secondary standards in many areas, to standards that would maintain atmospheric visibility above certain remote and pristine lands, mostly in the western states.

Federal legislation requires that the states establish and implement air quality standards at least as stringent as the federal standards. Ironically, the U. S. Supreme Court has ruled that states may not enforce standards more stringent than the applicable federal standard when a federal source of emissions is involved.

Ambient air quality standards are established by regulatory agencies, following enabling legislation (in a process similar to that described in Chapter 14, in the case of surface-mining control and reclamation standards). The process involves an attempt to balance the various interests, in legislative, regulatory, and perhaps judicial processes. While benefit cost analysis is not strictly required to serve as a basis for decisions as to the appropriate ambient air quality standards, some economic information in terms of both national economic development and regional economic development is usually available and may play a role in the decision process.

Of course, it is impossible to regulate ambient air quality directly: it is necessary, instead, to regulate what goes into the atmosphere. Thus, ambient air quality standards are achieved through regulation of emissions into the atmosphere. This is a complex technical problem, requiring knowledge of the relationship between emissions and ambient air quality. It is necessary to know not only what goes into the atmosphere, but also what happens to it once it is in the atmosphere. Atmospheric-diffusion models, which are quite complex but nevertheless primitive relative to the tasks required of them, assist in establishing the relationships between emissions and ambient air quality.

Once a satisfactory determination has been made of the maximum total emissions in each location that are compatible with the ambient air quality standards applying to that location, it is necessary to divide the total permissible emissions among the various emissions sources. Having rejected as impracticable a program of continuous monitoring of all sources of emissions, the federal government is unable to follow a simple program of emissions standards (such as that conceptualized in Chapter 8). Instead, a complex regulatory program, which treats different categories of sources quite differently, has been instituted.

Sources may be dichotomized as stationary or mobile, or as area or point. Point sources are large stationary sources, such as power plants, while area sources include small stationary sources, such as home fireplaces, along with mobile sources. For all sources and selected categories, Table 21.1 indicates annual emissions of major pollutants in the U. S. in 1975.

For point sources, the 1970 Clean Air Act amendments directed the Environmental Protection Agency to require that new point sources use the "best adequately demonstrated control technology" (BACT). Concern with benefits and costs is not explicit in this criterion, although it may enter implicitly via careful definition of "adequately demonstrated." In addition, established point sources may be required to retrofit emissions control devices. If ambient air quality standards would be violated, permits for new installations may be denied.

These amendments put EPA into the business of regulating the use of emissions control inputs, rather than emissions control performance. EPA is obliged to undertake detailed study of control technology and, in the case of very large point sources, become involved in the design of individual installations.

For mobile sources, the 1970 amendments actually specified the permissible emissions levels for automobiles. These standards apply to new cars; the control of emissions from old cars remained a matter for the states to do something, or nothing, about.

Automobile emissions standards were defined in terms of grams of various pollutants per mile driven. By 1975, new cars could emit only about 5 percent of the typical pre-1967 emissions of hydrocarbons and carbon monoxide, and by 1976, new cars would meet a similar standard for nitrogen oxides. Since 1970, it has become clear that to meet these standards would be very expensive in terms of control devices and fuel costs. A series of delays has been granted, and it is not certain that the standards originally set for 1976 will ever be achieved.

The 1970 amendments permitted a bewildering array of federal and state regulations, in the event that fitting of emissions control devices proved insufficient to satisfy the ambient air quality standards. These included land use controls, transportation controls, and shutdown of major polluters. Taken seriously, these provisions would amount to an unprecedented mandate for joint federal-state efforts to regulate public and private life.

Has the federal program of air pollution regulations been effective? From 1970 to 1975, substantial progress was made in reducing particulate emissions, and minor progress was made in reducing hydrocarbon and carbon monoxide emissions (Table 21.2). Barely perceptible progress was made with respect to sulfur oxides, while nitrogen oxide emissions increased. Presumably, more recent data would indicate some further progress in reducing total emissions.

TABLE 21.1
Air-Pollution Emissions, United States, 1975

Emissions	Pollutant (thousand tons/year)				
	Particulates	SO$_x$	NO$_x$	HC	CO
A. Grand total	13,767	32,824	22,390	27,157	93,404
Area	2,995	2,158	11,752	21,718	83,369
Point	10,771	30,666	10,638	5,439	10,035
B. Selected Categories					
Fuel combustion					
Area	1,173	1,417	1,187	165	476
Point	4,375	24,022	9,770	266	695
Residential					
Area	201	299	339	122	392
Electric generation					
Point	3,077	20,503	7,349	130	313
Industrial fuel					
Area	852	696	450	20	42
Point	1,198	3,304	1,925	98	338
Commercial					
Area	119	421	396	22	42
Point	93	201	100	7	13
Industrial process					
Point	6,225	6,578	814	5,036	8,432
Solid-waste disposal					
Area	327	28	100	621	1,776
Point	165	33	35	137	906
Transportation					
Area	1,166	714	10,405	13,158	79,126
Gasoline vehicles	745	216	6,707	10,572	74,787
Diesel vehicles	289	369	3,391	509	1,772
Forest fires					
Area	175	0	41	248	1,445

Source: *1975 National Emissions Report.* EPA, Research Triangle Park, N. C.

TABLE 21.2
Air-Pollution Emissions, United States, 1970-75 (Million Tons)

Pollutant	1970	1971	1972	1973	1974	1975
Particulates	27.5	25.2	23.2	21.0	19.5	13.8
Sulfur Oxides	34.3	33.5	32.6	33.2	31.4	32.8
Nitrogen Oxides	20.4	20.8	22.2	23.0	22.3	22.4
Hydrocarbons	32.1	31.4	31.3	31.3	30.4	27.2
Carbon Monoxide	107.3	104.9	104.9	100.9	94.5	93.4

Sources: 1970-74: Council on Environmental Quality. 1976. *Environmental Quality,*
Table 32.
1975: Table 21.1

AN ECONOMIC EVALUATION OF CURRENT PROGRAMS

Has the federal program been economically justified, in benefit cost terms? In 1977, the incremental expenditures on air pollution abatement that are attributable to federal regulation amounted to $12.5 billion (Table 21.3). Annual incremental expenditures are projected to amount to $32.4 billion, in 1977 dollars, by 1986. These expenditures are not trivial. The 1977 expenditure was about one-half of one percent of GNP. The estimation of benefits from the air pollution abatement program is a rather poorly developed science, at this time (Chapter 16). An admittedly crude benefit projection made for the Council on Environmental Quality suggests that total annual benefits from the air pollution abatement program were of the same approximate magnitude as annual expenditures, in 1977. A similar relationship is projected for 1986 (Table 21.3 and Figure 21.1).

The economist can identify a number of obvious sources of inefficiency in the current air pollution abatement program. The use of regulatory approaches, as opposed to emissions taxes, is likely to increase the total resource costs of abatement (Chapter 8).

The regulatory approach applied to point sources is especially prone to inefficiency, since it regulates emissions control inputs rather than emissions control performance. This approach encounters severe difficulties in accommodating growth, since a continuing increase in the number of installations, each achieving the same percentage reduction in emissions by using the same BACT, will eventually result in violation of ambient standards. Following the 1977 Clean Air Act amendments, EPA has adopted a policy of "offsets." New installations, such as coal-burning electric generators, that are major polluters may be introduced into regions

TABLE 21.3
Estimated Total and Incremental* Air-Pollution-Abatement
Expenditures 1977-86 (Billion 1977 Dollars)

Source	1977 Incremental	Total	1986 Incremental	Total	Cumulative 1977-1986 Incremental	Total
Public	0.3	0.5	3.1	4.4	21.2	30.3
Private:						
Mobile	5.5	5.5	9.1	9.1	79.6	79.6
Industrial	4.1	5.1	8.2	9.9	61.2	75.0
Utilities	2.3	3.0	8.9	10.3	51.6	63.0
Total	12.2	14.1	29.3	33.7	213.6	247.9

*Incremental expenditures are those made pursuant to federal regulations beyond those that would have been made in the absence of federal regulations.

Source: Council on Environmental Quality. 1978. *Environmental Quality*, Tables 10-3 and 10-4.

FIGURE 21.1
Estimated Annual Costs of Air-Pollution Damage, 1970-86

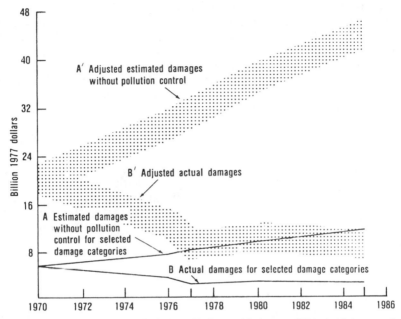

Source: Thomas E. Waddell, "Preliminary Update and Projections of Selected Categories of Damage Cost Estimates," prepared for the Council on Environmental Quality, May 1978.

where ambient air quality is already as low as the ambient standards permit only if assurances are provided that established polluters in the region will reduce emissions sufficiently to offset the emissions from the proposed new installation. In this way, a rudimentary market in the right to pollute has been established.

The BACT approach, which requires the use of particular inputs, discourages independent innovation in emissions control, and effectively prohibits the use of substitute control inputs. For example, electric utilities, if emissions were regulated on the basis of "tons per kilowatt hour of electricity produced," could satisfy the standards by burning low sulfur coal or by installing scrubbers and burning higher sulfur coal. The current BACT approach, combined with emissions control targets expressed not in "tons per unit of product" but in "percentage reduction of uncontrolled emissions," limits the possibility of substituting low sulfur coal for scrubbers. In effect, this kind of regulation penalizes the use of higher cost low sulfur coal. Not surprisingly, it gains most of its political support from those states that have predominantly high sulfur coal reserves.

Emissions control regulations, of course, must be backed up with effective enforcement. The most effective enforcement involves establishing penalties (*and* the probability that the penalty will actually be imposed) sufficiently high that the benefits a polluter may expect from violation are much lower than the costs. However, this approach has been considered politically unacceptable. Following detection of a violation, the usual enforcement approach involves negotiation and persuasion, although regulations often prescribe or at least permit monetary penalties for violation. The most significant powers of the enforcers derive from their persistence, from the threat of negative publicity and resulting damage to the corporate image of a major industrial polluter, and from the threat that monetary penalties may actually be imposed. A major industrial violator is not without bargaining power, since he may plausibly claim that strict enforcement would drive him out of business or force him to relocate, thus lowering regional employment and income. It is not uncommon for the work force, if organized, to join management in these kinds of arguments. A not uncommon outcome of this process of negotiation and persuasion is the issuance of a variance. If the enforcement agency accepts the argument that the polluter is making a good faith effort to comply but has been impeded by circumstances beyond his control, a variance may be granted permitting emissions beyond the standard for some period of time, at the end of which the variance will expire and the standard will be enforced.

The current approach to mobile source emissions, and especially to automobile emissions, may be subjected to many criticisms. It applies to new cars, but not to used cars. Testing of representative specimens of each make and model of new car is carried out by EPA. Periodic testing of the existing automobile stock is left to the states, if they so choose; and, most have not so chosen.

Manufacturers must provide 50,000-mile warranties for emissions control systems. However, there are some disincentives for owners to maintain these systems. Systems that do not use catalytic converters tend, for the most part, to reduce gasoline mileage and engine performance. The temptation to disconnect such systems remains strong, in spite of prescribed penalties which are seldom administered, where there is no provision for periodic emissions testing. Systems that do use catalytic converters require unleaded gasoline, which is more expensive and often less readily available than regular gasoline. It is very easy to fill one's gas tank with regular, and it is only necessary to do it a few times in order to render the catalytic converter ineffective.

The current approach to automobile emissions control requires expensive emissions control equipment on all new cars, but does almost nothing to require continuing and effective control of emissions.

An advantage of the regulatory approach to automobile emissions, compared with the BACT approach to point sources, is that automobile manufacturers are free to choose their preferred control technology provided that their test cars pass the emissions test.

On the other hand, the automobile emissions control program, unlike the point sources program, takes no account of regional differences in air quality. Permissible emissions per mile driven are the same for all regions (except California, and the California rules were instituted at state, not federal, initiative). It is easy to identify both inefficiency and inequity in a system that requires the same emissions control devices on cars used in crowded metropolitan areas and those used in remote rural regions.

The current approach to regulating air quality involves a complex array of legislative, administrative, and judicial procedures. The situation is considerably more complex than that described with respect to surface mining and reclamation controls (Chapter 14), since air pollution problems are more pervasive and more complex than surface mining problems. The decision process has all the advantages that accrue from giving the various interests their proverbial day in court, but also all of the transactions costs that entails.

Finally, any approach to air pollution control must have considerable flexibility. Since the relationship between emissions and ambient air quality varies with the weather, so that a level of emissions that is acceptable at most times leads to extreme deterioration of ambient air quality during temperature inversions, provisions are needed for extraordinary emissions controls during extraordinary weather conditions. The current regulatory structure has provisions for such extraordinary controls, including provisions that permit agencies to require that major polluting installations cease operations during periods of extreme weather conditions.

CAN ECONOMICS SUGGEST IMPROVED APPROACHES?

The economist's criticisms of the current approach to the control of polluting emissions should be fairly obvious to anyone who has read this far. The approach is inefficient, in that it does not encourage that most of the abating be done by the least cost abaters. It leads to interregional distortions, and is not well adapted to a dynamic economy. The use of negotiation and persuasion as primary enforcement tools weakens the effectiveness of regulations. To the extent that the current approach tends to require the use of particular pollution abatement inputs, it introduces inefficiencies by discouraging emissions reducing substitutions of inputs and innovations in pollution controls technology. Finally, emissions standards provide no encouragement for abatement beyond the standard, and make no provision for compensation of receptors for the pollution that remains.

Economists, for the most part, would recommend substantial

reliance upon incentives that operate through modification of prices, rather than upon regulatory requirements. Thus, their approach is aimed at taking maximum advantage from the efficiency of emissions taxes relative to emissions standards (Chapter 8).

Ambient air quality standards would be established, following benefit cost analysis based upon technical parameters established through careful research. Technical research would establish the relationships between emissions, ambient air quality, and the level of each of the various kinds of damage that results. Benefit cost analysis would compare, in total and at the margin, the benefits from abatement (i.e., the value of the damages that would be avoided by abatement) with the costs of achieving abatement. Ambient air quality standards would be established at the level where marginal benefits of additional abatement are equal to marginal costs. Of course, benefit cost analysis is not quite so simple as it sounds: major difficulties are introduced by the general ignorance about the long run consequences of various pollutants, and by the need to place economic values on reductions in human morbidity and mortality.

Following establishment of ambient air quality standards, a system of per unit emissions taxes would be established for each category of pollutants. In order to establish the appropriate emissions tax, it is first necessary to estimate the supply curve for abatement of each category of pollutants. Using this estimated relationship, the level of per unit tax that would result in the total amount of emissions consistent with the ambient air quality standard would be estimated. That per unit emissions tax would be levied on all emissions sources, a process that requires emissions monitoring and an agency to continuously collect the emission tax, just as the Internal Revenue Service continuously collects other kinds of taxes. Ambient air quality monitoring would continue. If, as most economists admit would be quite likely, errors in estimating the economic relationships discussed above result in imperfect consistency between the ambient air quality standard and the achieved ambient air quality, the level of per unit emissions taxes could be varied iteratively until the appropriate tax was determined by trial and error adjustment. To those who object that this process of iterative adjustment would generate uncertainty, some economists in cavalier manner respond that it is the proper role of the economic decision maker to respond to uncertainty; that, presumably, is what entrepreneurs are paid for.

Most economists would recommend that the ambient air quality standard and the level of emissions taxes should be permitted to vary across regions, in response to regional differences in the level of polluting activities, atmospheric conditions, and the demand for clean air.

Following a period in which much of the economic literature suggested that emissions taxes alone would constitute an entirely sufficient air pollution control policy, economists have more recently realized the importance of transient weather conditions to the relationship between emissions and ambient air quality.[3] A level of emissions that is tolerable under most weather conditions results in unacceptable ambient air quality during temperature inversions. Thus, recent and more sophisticated economic analyses have recommended that a generally applied system of emissions taxes be backed up with emissions standards (up to and including total prohibitions where necessary) to be invoked during periods of extreme weather conditions.

While many economists have been fairly satisfied with the above kinds of recommendations in the case of stationary sources, such as factories, they have recognized that mobile sources, such as automobiles, present special problems in the establishment and enforcement of emissions tax systems. While automobiles in aggregate are major polluters, each individual automobile is a relatively minor polluter and there are large numbers of them. Continuous monitoring of individual automobiles would be prohibitively expensive. In addition, automobiles, being designed for transportation, occasionally move across regional boundaries, even if they are most commonly used within the vicinity of the operator's residence. Thus, a policy involving regional differentials in emissions taxes poses particular problems in the case of mobile sources. Nevertheless, some economists have argued that a viable system of emissions charges for mobile sources is feasible.[4]

It has been suggested that automobiles should be tested for emissions at regular intervals, perhaps annually or semiannually. Following testing, each automobile would be issued a sticker that would indicate its "emissions class." The emissions classes would be based on emissions per gallon of gasoline used under "normal" driving conditions. The nation would be divided into regions, on the basis of the average cost of damages per unit of automobile emissions. Since, for an automobile in a given emissions class, total emissions are quite closely correlated with the quantity of fuel used, the emissions taxes could be collected at the fuel pump. The tax would be based on the quantity of fuel purchased, the emissions class of the automobile, and the air quality region in which the fuel pump is located.

Such a system would entail only a moderate increase in the bureaucratic hassles that confront the gasoline retailer. Gasoline pumps that automatically include the tax in the customer's bill could readily be designed. On the other hand, this system would have several significant advantages. Individual owners would choose their basic automobiles, the emissions controls devices to be fitted (as factory-fitted "options"), their maintenance programs, and their driving habits, in the same general way that they make other economic decisions. As a result, a given level of abatement would be achieved at the lowest opportunity cost. Incentives would exist for maintenance of emissions control devices, for continuous improvement in emissions control technology, and for retrofitting in the event that a highly effective and inexpensive emissions control device were developed. Finally, automobiles customarily operated in remote rural environments where air pollution does not present significant problems would no longer be required to have the same emissions control equipment as those customarily operated in regions that have serious air pollution problems. This would eliminate a major source of inefficiency and inequity in current policy with respect to pollution from automobiles.

QUESTIONS FOR DISCUSSION

1. How best can the economist counter the following arguments:
   (a) "Emissions taxes provide a license to pollute."
   (b) "Emissions taxes sell the environment to polluters."
   (c) "If emissions taxes were imposed, industrial polluters would not reduce their emissions but would merely pass the taxes on to the consumer."
2. Evaluate the contention that emissions charges are undesirable because they would make the country's products less competitive in international trade.
3. Do you think individual states should be free to determine air pollution control policies without supervision by the national government? Why, or why not?
4. If emissions taxes were imposed, what should be done with the revenues thus collected?
5. How do you explain the apparent reluctance of enforcement authorities to impose substantial penalties on large industrial firms found in violation of emissions standards?

FURTHER READINGS

Baumol, William J., and Wallace E. Oates. 1975. *The Theory of Environmental Policy.* Englewood Cliffs: Prentice-Hall.

Friedlander, Ann (ed.). 1978. *Air Pollution and Administrative Control.* Cambridge: M.I.T. Press.

Mills, Edwin S. 1978. *The Economics of Environmental Quality.* New York: Norton.

Portney, Paul R. (ed.). 1978. *Current Issues in U.S. Environmental Policy.* Baltimore: Johns Hopkins University Press. See Chapter 2 (A. Myrick Freeman III, "Air and Water Pollution Policy") and Chapter 3 (Eugene P. Seskin, "Automobile Air Pollution Policy").

ENDNOTES

1. Lave, Lester B., and Eugene P. Seskin. 1977. *Air Pollution and Human Health.* Baltimore: Johns Hopkins University Press.
2. See Edwin S. Mills. 1978. *The Economics of Environmental Quality.* New York: Norton. (Chapters 7 and 8.)

3. See William J. Baumol and Wallace Oates. 1975. *The Theory of Environmental Policy*. Englewood Cliffs: Prentice-Hall. (Chapter 11.)
4. See E. S. Mills and L. S. White. 1978. "Government Policies Toward Automotive Emissions Control," in *Air Pollution and Administrative Control*. Ann Friedlander, ed. Cambridge: M.I.T. Press. Note that the automobile emissions tax discussed below varies in some significant details from that discussed by Mills and White.

22

The Siting of Locally Obnoxious Facilities

There are some kinds of facilities that provide very useful services and therefore are considered, by consensus, "necessary." Most everybody agrees that these kinds of facilities ought to exist somewhere, but nobody wants to live next door to one. Historically, perhaps the most common example has been the garbage dump, but in recent decades the list has expanded considerably. Some are small in size and scope, affecting only a few city blocks: e.g., "half-way houses" to minimize the traumas as previously institution-alized alcoholics, mental patients, and prisoners return to society. Others may affect a significant section of a county: e.g., the sanitary landfill, the sewage-treatment works, and the city airport. Some are much larger in scope and may affect whole counties, or several county regions. Examples include large, maximum-security federal prisons; metropolitan and regional jetports; large-scale open-cut or strip mines; multi-megawatt coal burning electric power plants; coal-conversion facilities; and nuclear power plants.

These few examples suggest some of the factors these quite diverse facilities share in common.

First, they involve an external diseconomy in the immediate neighborhood, or sometimes a considerably larger region. They may threaten pollution, ugliness, or excessive noise. It may be feared that people considered "undesirables" may congregate in the immediate vicinity of the facility. There may be fears for the safety of residents of the surrounding areas, who may feel threatened by, e.g., nuclear hazards, or the possibility that violent prisoners may escape. Some of the various kinds of facilities listed above are likely to cause sudden and quite substantial increases in local employment. While some of the local citizenry can be expected to consider this a blessing, others can be expected to be more concerned about the possibilities of congestion, disruption of the local economy (facing local residents with higher prices, and local employers with more expensive labor and services), disruptions to local public-sector services (and tax increases to support the expansion of such services), and the social consequences of an influx of newcomers who may not share the regional and socioeconomic-class background of the local residents. The economic consequences discussed immediately above suggest that some of these facilities will not be locally obnoxious by universal consensus of the locals, but will be locally controversial.

Second, many of these facilities are operated by the public sector. Others may be owned by private investors but operated with substantial public-sector involvement. Coal-conversion facilities are likely to involve considerable public-sector financing or financial guarantees. Power plants, even when built by investor-owned utilities, involve the public sector in substantial ways: the land on which they are constructed may be acquired under the power of eminent domain; the public utility regulatory commission of the state involved must issue a certificate of necessity and convenience prior to construction, and will regulate the price at which the electricity is eventually sold. If the power plant is a nuclear installation, the federal Nuclear Regulatory Commission must authorize its construction and operation. In general, the public sector, whether it functions as owner, financial backer, or regulator, is substantially involved in the decisions as to whether the facility should be built and where it should be built.

Third, with the increasing adoption of large-scale, modern technologies, these kinds of facilities are becoming much larger, and more likely to be built in relatively remote rural regions where they threaten considerable shocks to the customary local way of life.

Fourth, as is discussed below, the various public-decision processes that are relevant to the planning and siting of locally obnoxious facilities (e.g., the licensing and environmental-impact-statement processes) provide considerable opportunity for local opposition to be organized and heard. Local opposition may succeed in having such a proposed facility sited elsewhere, or redesigned to mitigate its more offensive impacts. Plans for its construction may even be abandoned. However, there are few mechanisms by which a more satisfactory compromise — e.g., one in which installation of the facility proceeds as planned (or with modifications to provide an efficient degree of reduction of its harmful effects) but the local residents are compensated for the inconvenience they suffer — may be achieved. Thus, the decision process may be lengthy and expensive, while there is no assurance that its outcome will be a satisfactory accommodation between the regional "need" for the facility and the local opposition to it. While the locals are understandably reluctant to bear the brunt of the negative impacts of facilities that serve a larger clientele, the broader public is concerned that the public-decision processes for licensing and siting of such facilities, by causing delays and cost increases at some projects and the abandonment of others, may eventually result in serious shortages of some important services and commodities. Currently, this public concern is expressed in pressures to "cut the red tape" and get on with the construction of energy facilities.

EXISTING CONFLICT-RESOLUTION MECHANISMS

The existing mechanisms for conflict resolution with respect to the siting of locally obnoxious facilities rely substantially on police-power regulation, in its various forms.

LOCAL REGULATIONS

Subject to delegation by the states, most local governments enjoy the authority to impose police-power regulations in at least some of their various forms. Zoning regulations, for example, may be effective in keeping certain relatively small facilities of the locally obnoxious kind out of favored neighborhoods. Such regulations provide neither protection nor compensation to the residents of less favorably zoned neighborhoods, who may suffer various forms of economic injury when a locally obnoxious facility is located nearby. When confronted with decisions involving location of a large-scale facility, which may influence the quality of life in a multi-county region, local-government regulations are relatively ineffective. The possibility always exists that land may be rezoned, or variances granted to permit such a facility; thus, local authorities will come under intense political pressures. Further, it is quite likely that higher levels of government are involved as owners, backers, or regulators of the planned facility. Local governments are not well-situated to effectively use the police power to control annoyances in which state or federal governments have a considerable interest. States, after all, delegate the police power to local governments, and may withdraw that delegation. Courts have been inclined to rule that state and local governments may not impose upon a federal installation or operation any regulations that are more stringent than the pertinent federal regulations. For resolution of conflicts that involve large-scale locally obnoxious installations, local-government regulations are therefore relatively ineffective.

THE EIS PROVISIONS OF NEPA

The provision of the National Environmental Policy Act that requires the submission of Environmental Impact Statements prior to the implementation of any plan involving the commitment of federal resources is pertinent to a surprisingly large number of proposed major installations. Some will be constructed and

TABLE 22.1
Litigation under the Environmental Impact Statement Provisions of the National Environmental Policy Act, January 1970 through June 1976

Action	Projects Involved
EIS filed (not as a result of litigation)	7,265
Suits filed alleging EIS necessary	479
-EIS filed	69
-EIS ruled not required	71
-Case pending	339
EIS filed (total: 7,265 + 69)	7,334
Suits filed (total)	783
-Alleging EIS necessary	479
-Alleging EIS inadequate	288
-Other	16
Injunctions granted	177
Injunction-caused project delays:	
-Less than 3 months	32
-3 to 12 months	40
-More than 12 months	75
-Not indicated	30
Permanent injunctions	0
Projects cancelled after litigation filed (total)	42
-Federal agency decision to halt project	9
-State/Local agency decision to halt project	12
-Other reason(s)	21

Source: Council on Environmental Quality. 1977. *Environmental Quality.* Pages 122-129.

operated by federal agencies. Others will use land and water resources that are under federal control. Still others involve the use of the economic resources of the federal government, which may commit funds to the project, provide loan guarantees to aid in its financing, or provide purchase guarantees for the services or commodities that will eventually be produced. Thus, the EIS process provides opportunities through which local opposition to many kinds of proposed large-scale installations may be organized and heard.

The environmental impacts which, it is projected, would ensue from construction and operation of the facility must be documented. These impacts include effects on the local ecology, economy, social structure, and historical and archaeological resources. Adverse impacts must be documented, and local opponents of the project will have ample opportunity, in informal hearings, review and comment periods, formal hearings, and, perhaps, eventual litigation to ensure that their concerns are heard and widely publicized. The public discussion encouraged by the EIS process may be effective in mobilizing political opposition to the proposed project.

By shrewdly using the EIS process, local opponents of the proposed installation may be instrumental in delaying its construction, in forcing modifications that would mitigate some of its adverse impacts, or even in forcing the relocation or perhaps the abandonment of the proposed project.

As of June 30, 1976, environmental-impact statements had been filed for 7,334 proposed federal actions (Table 22.1). A total of 783 suits had been filed under NEPA. (Of these suits, 479 alleged that EIS were necessary prior to implementation of proposed actions; thus, the remaining 304 suits were directed at the 7,334 filed EISs.) A total of 177 temporary injunctions were granted, causing project delays. Following the filing of litigation, 42 projects were abandoned. These data provide some indication of the impacts of litigation under NEPA.

State "Companion Legislation"

Almost half the states have "companion legislation" to NEPA. This legislation usually sets up an EIS process that must be completed prior to the implementation of any project involving the use of resources under the control of state government. State "companion legislation," in those states that have enacted it, enlarges the EIS process for joint federal-state projects and extends it to projects in which state but not federal resources are involved.

LICENSES AND PERMITS

Many large-scale installations require the issuance of one or more licenses. Many projects require the withdrawal of significant quantities of water, for cooling or other purposes. Such commitments of water must be permitted by the U. S. Army Corps of Engineers, and perhaps by a state water-resources agency or an interstate rivers commission. State public-utilities regulatory commissions require that a certificate of necessity and convenience be granted prior to the initiation of construction of power plants, electric transmission lines, and gas pipelines. Nuclear power plants must be licensed by the Nuclear Regulatory Commission. Many other kinds of installations must meet licensing or permitting requirements established by various federal and state agencies.

The provisions pertaining to licensing and permitting usually involve considerable documentation, and provide the opportunity for public comment, formal public hearings, and, in certain circumstances, litigation. Thus, licensing and permitting procedures provide another opportunity for project opponents to present their arguments in such a way that the project may be delayed, relocated, or abandoned as an outcome of the licensing or permitting

TABLE 22.2

Average Reactor-Licensing and Total Lead Times, 1956-77

Calendar Year	Number of Construction Permits Issued	Average Megawatts	Average Construction-Permit Review Time[a] (in months)	Number of Reactors Completed as of 10/77	Average Total Lead Time[b] (in months)
1956	3	175	12	3	78
1957	1	175	16	1	49
1958	-	-	-	-	-
1959	1	22	9	1	44
1960	7	45	12	7	48
1961	-	-	-	-	-
1962	1	40	19	1	68
1963	1	50	5	1	57
1964	3	552	10	3	53
1965	1	610	14	1	54
1966	5	722	7	5	62
1967	14	764	10	14	70
1968	23	814	14	21	82
1969	7	910	18	5	55
1970	14	764	20	14	72
1971	4	963	21	3	93
1972	14	815	35	-	-
1973	14	1,076	34	-	-
1974	9	1,069	31	-	-
1975	9	1,166	26	-	-
1976	9	1,136	25	-	-
1977	11	1,120	39	-	-

[a] As measured from date of construction-permit application to date of construction-permit issuance, a period which constitutes the licensing phase of a reactor.
[b] As measured from date of construction-permit application to date of initial fuel loading.

Source: Department of Energy, *U. S. Central Station Nuclear Electric Generating Units: Significant Milestones,* March 1978.

process. At the least, these processes provide a forum in which public and political opposition to the project may be mobilized.

Licensing and permitting procedures are becoming more complex as more and more detailed studies are required and public-participation opportunities are expanded. Nuclear power provides an example. Total lead times, measured from construction-permit application to initial operation, have grown steadily over the last two decades. Construction-permit review (the licensing phase) has been responsible for much of the growth in total lead times. As of 1977, the most recently commissioned nuclear power plants had experienced an average total lead time of almost 8 years; they had been issued construction permits in 1971 after an average review period of 21 months. Since 1971, the construction-permit review time has increased, until those permits granted in 1977 had experienced an average 39-month review period (Table 22.2).

Construction-permit review obviously must be careful, consider-

TABLE 22.3
Source of Delays in the Licensing Phase of Reactor
Projects Issued Construction Permits, July 1, 1975, to
December 31, 1977

Source of Delay	Number of Cases
Public-Sector Delays:	
Substantive Issues:	
Safety	
Basic reactor-design changes	8
Radiological containment	6
External accidents	2
Environmental:	
Geology/seismology	7
Meteorology/hydrology	3
Site characteristics	2
Other:	
Corporate financial/managerial capability	3
Antitrust	1
Redundancy/Inefficiency:	
Bureaucratic delay/data transmission	5
Other government organizations	3
Public Participation	6
Private-Sector Delays:	
Reconsideration of need for power	1
Total number of reactor projects	24

Source: Derived from Nuclear Regulatory Commission, *Reactor Licensing Schedule Performance Critique* (1977).

ing the public perception of dangers associated with nuclear reactors. A Congressional Budget Office study of delays in nuclear-reactor licensing and construction reported that most delays in licensing were for substantive causes (Table 22.3). The same study reported that, after the construction permit had been issued, the typical plant experienced 5 months of delays in construction due to regulatory concerns (including Nuclear Regulatory Commission delays, forced retrofits, and judicial and referenda decisions).

The notion that care and patience should be invested in resolving concerns that arise in the licensing and construction of nuclear power plants is unassailable. The legitimate question is whether existing conflict-resolution mechanisms perform acceptably in terms of expense, delays, and the outcomes eventually achieved.

AN EVALUATION

The existing conflict-resolution mechanisms often involve considerable transactions costs and considerable delays in project implementation. Their eventual outcome may require no change in project plans, the mitigation of adverse project impacts, the relocation of the project, or its ultimate abandonment. Of course, project abandonment is not always an undesirable outcome: projects that are on balance undesirable have been proposed, from time to time, and the EIS, licensing, and permitting processes have performed a public service in revealing the inadequacies of these proposals. While some have complained that "red tape" has caused extended delays in the construction of nuclear power plants in the latter part of the 1970's, others have noted that demand for electricity did not grow as rapidly in that period as had been previously forecast. The delays in approving new nuclear installations may have actually saved some electric utilities and their customers from expensive premature investment.

Nevertheless, the existing conflict-resolution mechanisms seem unsatisfactory to people of almost every persuasion. Some are concerned that "essential" projects are delayed too long in a process whose transactions costs are too high. Others have claimed that while the decision process is expensive and lengthy, it does not seem to make very much difference to final outcomes. The proposed locally obnoxious facility is usually built eventually — and, more often than not, built at the proposed site. In such cases, neither project proponents nor opponents are satisfied with the outcome of the process.

AN ALTERNATIVE APPROACH: COMPENSATION OF COMMUNITIES RECEIVING LOCALLY OBNOXIOUS INSTALLATIONS[1]

There is no doubt that the siting of locally obnoxious facilities visits economic injury, in various forms, on local residents and communities. At best, these local residents are asked to accept injury for the benefit of a broader public. At worst, some proposed installations may, everything considered, do more harm than good. Can a mechanism be developed that would simultaneously provide a measure of the economic value of the local injury that would be caused by such a facility, ensure that the facility is located where it will do the least harm, and compensate those immediately affected for the harm that eventually occurs to them?

By using some of the notions presented in Chapter 6, it is possible to develop a system which, if implemented, would go a long way toward meeting these objectives. Given the initial endowments of each of its participants, a perfect market insures Pareto-safety for all. With adequate knowledge all around, voluntary exchange creates no losers: buyers and sellers are willing to entertain only those trades that leave them at least no worse off. The alternative approach discussed below is an attempt to introduce some of the advantages of voluntary exchange and Pareto-safety into the decision process that determines the siting of locally obnoxious facilities.

Voluntary exchange is seldom quite so desirable in practice as it is in theory: with imperfect knowledge, some participants may inadvertently trade to worse positions. Given the lack of knowledge about such issues as nuclear risk, and the long-run environmental impacts of massive coal-burning power plants and coal-conversion facilities, there is no assurance that voluntary exchange, if introduced into the decision process for siting of locally obnoxious facilities, would always work out for the best. In addition, large-scale installations may affect whole communities, whole counties, or multi-county regions. Thus, the appropriate decision units for the trading proposal offered below are not individuals, but local-government jurisdictions acting on behalf of their constituents. Since collective decision processes are always imperfect, individuals will not always be protected under a system that involves voluntary exchange at the community level. Nevertheless, in spite of these concerns, it seems appropriate to plow ahead.

It has been proposed that, after a new installation is planned and its projected impacts, beneficial and adverse, are documented (perhaps in a streamlined version of the EIS process), a "compensation auction" be conducted. Local-government jurisdictions would submit sealed bids indicating the minimum compensation they would be prepared to accept if the locally obnoxious facility were sited within their jurisdiction. The facility would be located in the jurisdiction making the lowest bid or, if all bids were deemed "too high," plans for it would be abandoned. Such a system would generate a fairly reliable measure of the economic injury the facility would visit upon citizens of the locality in which it would be sited, ensure that it was sited where it would do the least injury, and ensure that the offended local citizens were compensated in an amount at least equal to the damage they perceive. This proposal would sharply reduce the delays and the high transactions costs inherent in current procedures, since the receipt of compensation would tend to eliminate unquenched opposition to the installation.

Two issues remain to be settled, in order to complete the proposal: (1) the determination of the minimum and maximum size of jurisdictions, or coalitions of jurisdictions, bidding; and (2) the appropriate disposition of the compensation, after it is received by the local-government jurisdiction(s). The first of these issues should be settled, on a case-by-case basis, at the time when the compensation bids are invited, on the basis of documented projections of the environmental impacts of the installation. For installations that would affect only a part of the receiving jurisdiction, bids should be submitted by the jurisdiction acting as a trustee for the specific subjurisdictional region that is willing to accept the facility. Where the impacts are likely to spread across several local-government jurisdictions, bids should be submitted by formal coalitions of all the jurisdictions that would be simultaneously affected. By following these guidelines, compensation would be received only in the affected region, and the full extent of the affected region would be protected.

The second issue does not seem amenable to such simple and, at least at first glance, satisfactory solution. While the jurisdiction is the obvious unit to enter the "compensation auction" and to receive the compensation paid, individuals within the jurisdiction may suffer different degrees of injury. It seems most appropriate that the receiving jurisdiction should have considerable discretion as to how it uses compensation monies received, subject to the provision that those citizens who suffer most from the installation should receive most of the benefits from the compensation. Upon receipt of the compensation, the jurisdiction could reduce taxation rates or provide increased services, or both, thus making its citizens better-off than they would be in the absence of compensation. However, it seems there ought to be provisions that would direct the tax or public-works benefits toward those who suffer most of the adverse impacts from the installation. It may be appropriate to establish provisions that individuals who suffer disproportionate direct economic injury be permitted to seek monetary compensation.

Much as there have been complaints that pollution controls raise prices (Chapter 8), it may be objected that the need to pay compensation to communities accepting locally obnoxious facilities would increase the costs of the services they provide, thus raising charges or taxes. That would be correct, but only at the most superficial level of analysis. Under current procedures, users of the services provided pay only a part of the costs of those services, imposing the remainder on those citizens who are the reluctant hosts of the facility. In aggregate, the "compensation auction" would reduce the *total* costs of these services by ensuring that the facilities are sited where they would do the least perceived harm.

Some citizens, however, may rationally oppose the "compensation auction" if they believe that their locality will always have sufficient political power, under current procedures, to avert any plans to site such facilities nearby. If one believes that, one would expect, under current arrangements, to continue enjoying services at below cost by imposing a part of the costs upon others.

The "compensation auction" idea is not perfect. Its major imperfection lies in the necessity that bids be submitted and compensation be received at the level of the community, rather than the individual. Nevertheless, it seems that the "compensation auction" would be both more efficient and more equitable than the conflict-resolution mechanisms currently used. In that sense, it may be the kind of imperfect idea that has the substantial virtue that it would make the best of a very difficult situation.

Finally, some have objected that the "compensation auction" would result in a pattern whereby locally obnoxious facilities would be sited in economically disadvantaged jurisdictions. Such jurisdictions, it is argued, would be most attracted by the possibility of compensation, and therefore most likely to submit competitive compensation bids. Some have argued that this kind of outcome would be inequitable. Ironically, it can be plausibly argued that such an outcome would be considerably more equitable than that which typically emerges from the existing procedures. Under existing conflict-resolution mechanisms, economically disadvantaged jurisdictions are often finally selected as sites for locally obnoxious facilities. The citizens of such jurisdictions are often less able to bear the expense of mounting effective opposition and, to a middle-class power structure accustomed to regarding economically disadvantaged neighborhoods as (already) "ugly and unpleasant," such opposition may seem implausible. Also, where the locally obnoxious installation promises to introduce new employment opportunities and higher incomes, or to pay substantial taxes to local government, economically disadvantaged jurisdictions are less likely to oppose the installation, even where it threatens other impacts that would be considered locally obnoxious. It can be argued that a "compensation auction" procedure is little more likely than current procedures to result in the siting of locally obnoxious facilities in economically disadvantaged jurisdictions, but would at least ensure that the citizens of such jurisdictions were compensated to the extent of their perceived economic injury.

QUESTIONS FOR DISCUSSION

1. Is there any equitable way to decide on the location of facilities everybody considers necessary but nobody wants to live near?
2. If the "compensation auction" idea were to be implemented, how should the compensation received be distributed or spent?

FURTHER READINGS

O'Hare, Michael. 1977. "Not on My Block You Don't: Facility Siting and the Strategic Importance of Compensation," *Public Policy*. 25: 407-458.
Smith, Vernon L. 1977. "The Principle of Unanimity and Voluntary Consent in Social Choice," *Journal of Political Economy*. 85: 1125-1140.

ENDNOTE

1. The following discussion draws heavily upon O'Hare, Michael. 1977. "Not on My Block You Don't: Facility Siting and the Strategic Importance of Compensation," *Public Policy*. 25: 407-458.

23

Demand and Supply of Fossil Fuels

Fossil fuels represent deposits of stored solar energy that was photosynthetically collected in lush forests and compressed and stored in geological processes requiring eons of time. Within any concept of time relevant to human decisions, fossil fuels are exhaustible stock resources. Decisions about their use, then, are confined to decisions pertaining to their rate of discovery, extraction, and combustion.

Fossil fuels have contributed significantly to economic progress for little more than two hundred years (in the case of coal). Oil and natural gas have been used in significant quantities only in the last one hundred years. In this relatively brief period, however, fossil fuels have made a massive contribution to economic growth and material standards of living.

Extraction and combustion decisions have been made in an atmosphere of uncertainty with respect to the size of the total stocks (it is not known how large are the deposits awaiting discovery), but of absolute certainty that the total stocks are finite. To extract in any time period guarantees that there will be less available in later time periods. It is not necessarily true, however, that decisions made by each of the recent generations for higher rates of extraction and combustion were unreasonably selfish, or even foolhardy. Some have argued that the high rates of economic growth permitted by heavy use of fossil fuels have accelerated the formation of capital, and thus made it much more likely that high-cost fossil-fuel deposits will be exploited and adequate substitutes for fossil fuels will eventually be found. Nevertheless, it seems likely that fossil-fuel pricing and transportation policy decisions in the United States since the 1930's have encouraged high rates of current use, in activities that seem more nearly related to consumption than to capital-forming investment.

In North America in particular, economic growth, in the current and immediately preceding generations, has been highly fossil-fuel intensive. Some of the countries in western Europe have achieved standards of living similar to that in North America with roughly one-half the level of fossil-fuel consumption per capita. This seems to have been achieved almost entirely as the result of price incentives established by governments. In the United States, which had substantial oil and gas deposits and was, not so very long ago, a net exporter of oil, "cheap fuel" policies were followed, first by various subsidies to the oil and gas industries, and later by price controls that encouraged consumption. The countries of western Europe, however, had relatively small domestic deposits of oil and gas. In the years immediately following World War II, they also had severely limited reserves of foreign currencies. Petroleum needed to be imported, if it was to be used in large quantities, but imports had to be discouraged in order to protect the already weak positions of their economies in international trade. To discourage consumption and raise revenues, petroleum products were taxed heavily as luxuries. The result was the maintenance and improvement of public-transportation systems, the widespread use of motorcycles and small, fuel-efficient automobiles, and a conservative approach to the heating and air conditioning of buildings. Nevertheless, the western European postwar recovery was remarkable, and the material standard of living enjoyed in several western European countries is equal to or exceeds that in the United States.

The comparative performance of North America and western Europe, in terms of economic growth and the use of fossil fuel, is instructive. First, it refutes the notion, common in some circles in the United States, that there is a rigid relationship between economic productivity and fossil-fuel consumption (such that fossil-fuel consumption must grow if economic productivity is to grow). Second, it reminds us, once again, of the relationships between price and quantity demanded (Chapter 5).

While the economies of North America remain far and away the most fuel intensive, fossil-fuel consumption has been growing quite rapidly in all parts of the world: in the countries with modern economies; in developing countries such as Brazil, where industrialization is proceeding rapidly and a relatively affluent, automobile-oriented middle class is emerging; and in the poorest of the underdeveloped countries, where petroleum (to fuel industrial development, and as a feedstock for fertilizer production) is considered crucial to the hopes for economic development. Fossil fuels are used for transportation, electricity generation, heating and cooling, to fire industrial furnaces, and as feedstocks for the burgeoning petrochemical industry which produces synthetic fibers, plastics, synthetic chemicals, cosmetics, pharmaceutical products, and fertilizers and pesticides for agricultural applications (Table 23.1).

In discussing the demand for fossil fuels, it is appropriate to distinguish among the three major types of fossil fuels. There are

TABLE 23.1
Fossil-Fuel Consumption, by Type of Use, U. S., 1960-76

Fuel and Use		Consumption				Percent Use
		1960	1965	1970	1976	1976
Petroleum	mil. bbl	3,611	4,202	5,365	6,391	100
Fuel use	mil. bbl	3,301	3,802	4,787	5,676	89
Nonfuel use	mil. bbl	310	400	578	715	11
Residential and commercial	mil. bbl	853	978	1,129	1,095	17
Industrial	mil. bbl	644	740	961	1,175	18
Transportation	mil. bbl	1,934	2,272	2,903	3,503	55
Electrical generation	mil. bbl	90	119	334	553	9
Miscellaneous	mil. bbl	90	93	38	65	1
Natural gas	bil. cu. ft	12,269	15,598	21,367	19,947	100
Fuel use	bil. cu. ft	11,949	15,216	20,815	19,390	97
Nonfuel use	bil. cu. ft	320	382	552	557	3
Coal	mil. sh. tons	401	473	524	604	100
Fuel use	mil. sh. tons	395	468	518	604	100
Nonfuel use	mil. sh. tons	5	5	6	—	—
Residential and commercial	mil. sh. tons	37	26	16	10	2
Industrial	mil. sh. tons	175	201	187	139	22
Electrical generation	mil. sh. tons	177	245	321	476	76

Source: U. S. Department of Commerce. Bureau of the Census. 1978. *Statistical Abstracts:* 1321.

very few uses for which coal is the preferred fossil fuel, unless it is very much cheaper than oil or natural gas. Coal is expensive to extract. Deep mining requires considerable capital, and is damaging to the health and safety of workers. While both deep and surface mining have negative environmental consequences, the environmental impacts of surface mining are so devastating that stringent provisions have been enacted to control off-site damage during mining and to require reclamation thereafter. Coal is bulky, and is therefore not easy to handle and store. Coal is also dirty to burn, resulting in significant environmental damage, including damage to human health, and requiring expensive emissions controls. However, the energy content of the world's coal reserves far exceeds that of the oil and gas reserves. It is ironic that in the United States, where the energy content of known coal reserves is perhaps 50 times as great as that of the known oil and gas reserves, policies that have kept oil and gas prices low have resulted in increased use of oil and gas at the expense of coal.

Now consider the supply side of the equation. Oil and natural-gas production in the United States had peaked by 1970 (Table 23.2). Oil imports increased rapidly, so that imports amounted to more than

TABLE 23.2
Domestic Oil Production and Imports, U. S., 1940-77

Year	Producing Oil Wells		Completed Wells Drilled (1,000)				Domestic Oil Production			Imports, crude petroleum (mil. bbl.)	Refinery capacity (mil. bbl.)
	Total (1,000)	Daily output per well (bbl.)	Total	Oil	Gas	Dry	Total (mil. bbl.)	Value at wells (bil. dol.)	Avg. price per bbl. (dol.)		
1940	389	9.6	30	19	2	7	1,353	1.4	1.02	43	1,694
1945	416	11.3	27	14	3	7	1,714	2.1	1.22	74	1,935
1950	466	11.8	43	24	3	15	1,974	5.0	2.51	178	2,444
1955	524	13.2	57	32	4	21	2,484	6.9	2.77	285	3,074
1960	591	12.0	44	21	5	18	2,575	7.4	2.88	372	3,624
1965	589	13.3	40	19	5	16	2,849	8.2	2.86	452	3,933
1970	531	18.0	27	13	4	11	3,517	11.2	3.18	483	4,407
1971	517	18.1	25	11	4	10	3,454	11.7	3.39	613	4,752
1972	508	18.4	26	11	5	11	3,455	11.7	3.39	811	4,918
1973	497	18.3	26	10	6	10	3,361	13.1	3.89	1,184	5,038
1974	498	17.6	31	13	7	12	3,203	21.6	6.74	1,269	5,289
1975	500	16.8	37	16	8	13	3,057	23.4	7.67	1,498	5,537
1976	499	16.3	41	17	9	15	2,976	23.4	8.19	1,935	5,646
1977	507	16.3	45	19	11	15	2,985	25.6	8.57	2,397	6,063

Source: U. S. Department of Commerce, Bureau of the Census. 1978. *Statistical Abstracts:* 1320.

40% of all U. S. consumption by 1977. Early in the 1970's, there was serious discussion of massive imports of liquefied natural gas to the U. S. in supertankers. Elsewhere, the major petroleum exporters, many of which were Middle Eastern countries, and almost all of which had relatively backward economies heavily reliant upon the petroleum industry, were becoming increasingly aware that their reserves were finite and, in some cases, approaching exhaustion at current rates of extraction. In 1973, a number of Arab nations used an oil embargo against the United States and its allies in an attempt to influence U. S. policy with respect to Israel. The economic and political impacts of this move in the United States were immediate and pronounced. Soon afterward, the Middle Eastern members of the Organization of Petroleum Exporting Countries were successful in persuading that organization to exploit its strategic position as a cartel and dramatically increase the price of the oil they export. In 1979, following a political crisis in Iran (which reduced oil exports from that country and led to a situation in which the spot-market price for oil substantially exceeded the cartel price) and a continued decline in the value of the U. S. dollar relative to other currencies, the OPEC cartel significantly increased oil prices again.

Each of the importing countries reacted in its own way. Some, which imported almost all of the petroleum they use, made sure that the full price increase was reflected in the prices paid by users of refined petroleum products. The United States, a significant importer which, nevertheless, produces more than half of its crude oil domestically, seemed most concerned with keeping the prices of refined petroleum products as low as possible. Gradually and reluctantly, the price of "new" oil was allowed to rise to the world price. The price of "old" oil — i.e., oil from wells that were in production prior to the events of 1973 — remained strictly controlled. This policy was designed to provide price incentives for the discovery and production of new oil, while keeping the average price of petroleum products at the pump as low as possible.

There were some gestures in the direction of "conservation," which was interpreted to mean a reduction in the quantity of petroleum products demanded at any given price. Maximum speed on the highways was limited to 55 miles per hour, which was claimed to be a fuel-efficient speed for the peculiar breed of American automobiles, with their V-8 engines and their three-speed automatic transmissions. The fact that a four-cylinder car with a four-speed manual transmission could carry a similar number of passengers at 80 miles per hour while using less fuel than the typical American V-8 at 55 miles per hour, made no difference. The 55-miles-per-hour speed limit encouraged conservation of gasoline! Tax incentives were provided to encourage insulation and, to less effect in the short term, solar heating of homes; these measures were designed to reduce the quantity of oil demanded directly for heating, and for running electric power plants that provide fuel for electrically heated homes. Legislation was introduced requiring mandatory improvements in the fuel efficiency of American-built automobiles and establishing a time schedule for compliance. Power plants were, on the one hand, encouraged to switch from oil to coal fuel in order to conserve oil but, on the other hand, discouraged from burning coal by the high cost of controlling stack-gas emissions. There was considerable political discussion of gasoline rationing and the decontrol of retail prices of petroleum products along with decontrol of the wholesale price of "old" oil, but neither option was implemented. There was considerable discussion of large-scale plants to convert coal to synthetic oil or natural gas, and a few pilot-scale plants to achieve this purpose were constructed. However, it seemed clear that working-scale plants for these purposes would be very expensive, and the synthetic fuels produced would cost considerably more than OPEC oil.

There was considerable concern as to how the available refined products should be allocated, in the United States. Farmers and truckers demanded priority allocations, and representatives of various regions within the nation demanded that "a fair share" of the available petroleum products be expressly allocated to their regions. The U. S. Department of Energy got into the allocation business, devising a complex set of regulations to determine what products were refined from crude oil, to what regions the products were sent, what prices the retailers could charge, and which industrial sectors would receive first priority in having their demands met. Not surprisingly, quantity demanded, in aggregate, continued to increase; domestic production failed to grow at the desired rate; and, on occasion, there were short-term and localized shortages of gasoline, diesel fuel, and heating oil.

AN ECONOMIC DIAGNOSIS

As of 1979, it was clear that U. S. policy with respect to supply of and demand for fossil fuels was in disarray. The substantial deregulation of the price of "new" oil had failed to substantially increase production (Table 23.2). The reluctance to deregulate the price of "old" oil had dampened the effectiveness of price as a restraining influence on consumption (Tables 23.1 and 23.2; in the latter table, domestic production plus imports is an indicator of consumption). The allocation policy appeared to have exacerbated, rather than controlled, temporary disruptions in the domestic market for refined petroleum products. Significant quantities of synthetic oil and natural gas were no closer to reality than they had been five years earlier; and domestic coal production had increased, but at a disappointing rate (Table 23.3).

How could U. S. policy with respect to fossil fuels have been so totally ineffective? The United States, for two generations, had been committed to a "cheap fuel" policy, based on inexpensive heating and cooling, motor transportation, and automobile travel. This policy was deeply embedded in the fabric of American society. The

TABLE 23.3
U. S. Coal Production and Value, 1960-77

Item	1960	1965	1970	1975	1977
Bituminous (million tons)	416	512	603	648	672
Average value ($/ton)	4.69	4.44	6.26	19.23	21.00
Anthracite (million tons)	19	15	10	6	6
Average value ($/ton)	7.82	8.21	10.83	31.99	36.00

Source: U. S. Department of Commerce, Bureau of the Census. 1978. *Statistical Abstracts:* 1318.

huge private investment in motorized transport was paralleled by a massive public investment in superhighways. At the same time, the infrastructure for mass transportation was deliberately allowed to deteriorate and become obsolete. Instantaneous adjustment to the new fuel-price situation imposed by the increasing exhaustion of petroleum reserves and the actions of the OPEC cartel would have caused sudden economic injury to almost every individual. American society was ill-prepared to take the evasive action that would have been permitted by the availability of substitutes for petroleum in residential and transportation uses, or substitutes for household heating and cooling and automobile transportation themselves in the American consumption bundle. It is not surprising that governments were reluctant to administer this shock.

There was, and perhaps still is, a reluctance to believe that the current price of crude oil accurately reflects its scarcity. OPEC is perceived as a cartel that has, at least temporarily, raised the price of crude oil above its economic-equilibrium level. In addition, the giant multinational corporations that dominate the oil industry, from exploration through to the retailing of refined petroleum products, are not viewed sympathetically by the typical U. S. citizen. The industry is not viewed as competitive, and increasing industry profits at times when the "little man" faces higher prices and the inconvenience of temporary shortages, arouses the populist instincts that are often influential in American politics.

For these reasons, relatively little sentiment was expressed, in U. S. domestic politics in the 1970's, for immediate deregulation of the oil industry. Some economists, however, insisted that this simple policy would restrain consumption, encourage production, and encourage the development of substitute sources of energy. These results, if achieved, would restore an equilibrium condition in world oil markets, restrict the power of OPEC to increase the price of crude oil above equilibrium levels, and more efficiently ration the remaining stocks of oil and natural gas among the present and future generations. But, people worried, would such a policy be fair? Would it be fair to impose substantial price increases on a citizenry that has so few alternatives, and would it be fair to enrich an industry that, insofar as is known, has seldom gone out of its way to benefit its consumers?

In consideration of this dilemma, some academics and some policy advisers to the executive branch of government recommended the simultaneous policies of price decontrol and a "windfall profits tax." Price decontrol would restrain consumption, and provide powerful incentives for innovations that improve the thermodynamic efficiency of equipment and consumer durables that use fossil fuels. As yet, there is little evidence that those increases that have already occurred in the retail price of gasoline have reduced the rate of growth in consumption. On the other hand, evidence from the electricity market suggests that households are, in fact, responsive to increases in energy prices (Table 23.4). Preliminary data suggest that the post-1973 trend of sharply reduced growth in residential electricity demand is continuing. Thus, it is reasonable to expect retail-price increases in petroleum products to eventually influence household consumption. As yet, however, there is little evidence as to how much higher retail prices would need to rise before significant impacts would be observed.

Price decontrol, even with a "windfall profits" tax designed to ensure the public that oil companies would not unduly enrich themselves through windfall increases in the price of "old" oil, should provide incentives for discovery and exploitation of new oil reserves.

Some dissenters have argued that the "windfall profits" tax would deprive the oil industry of an important opportunity for capital formation. However, it was unclear whether capital formation was the real problem: some oil companies had conspicuously used accumulated capital to diversify their activities beyond the oil business.

TABLE 23.4
Trends in Consumption, Price, and Monthly Bill
for Residential Electricity (Investor-Owned
Utilities, U. S., 1960-76)

Year	Annual Growth in Residential Consumption (%)	Annual Change in: Price per Kilowatt-Hour (%)	Average Monthly Bill (%)
1960	6.2	−1.0	5.1
1965	5.2	−1.7	3.4
1970	7.5	0.5	7.9
1971	5.2	4.5	9.8
1972	4.9	4.3	9.5
1973	4.7	5.0	10.0
1974	−2.5	21.7	18.6
1975	3.8	13.6	17.8
1976	1.3	6.3	7.8

Source: Edison Electric Institute, *Statistical Yearbooks.*

In addition to providing the general public with some assurance that oil companies would not be unduly enriched by oil-price decontrol, the "windfall profits" tax would generate revenues. These receipts could be dedicated to research and development of substitute sources of fuel and fuel-saving innovations. It is clear that such innovations are needed on a massive scale if petroleum-consumption trends are to be reversed in a country whose infrastructure is so thoroughly attuned to increasing, rather than decreasing, dependence on fossil fuels.

By 1979, the proposal of simultaneous decontrol of oil prices and imposition of a "windfall profits" tax was gaining considerable political support.

WHAT IS THE SOLUTION?

The picture that has been painted of the fossil-fuel supply-and-demand situation is quite murky. Reasonable people — and, for that matter, reasonable people with considerable education in economics — may reasonably disagree. The theorems that provide the most comforting conclusions with respect to the efficiency of market economies (Chapters 5 and 6) are based on the notion of a multitude of small competitive firms operating in an environment where government limits its role largely to the establishment and enforcement of property rights. These theorems have never been reproduced for an economic sector dominated by a cartel of governments that supply most of a basic resource, and by a highly concentrated industry that extracts, refines, and markets that resource, subject to a complex web of intergovernmental agreements and domestic governmental policies in the consuming countries. Thus, to recommend a simple policy of price decontrol to permit market forces to solve the problem is substantially an act of faith, rather than a conclusion of economic science. That, however, is not an especially effective argument against a policy of simple price decontrol: there is no alternative policy that does not require, somewhere in the line of argument purporting to justify it, a similar act of faith.

Economics does suggest that price can effectively restrain current consumption and ration the remaining resource stocks among present and future generations. In spite of wishful thinking to the contrary, there is no economic evidence that the price established by the OPEC cartel in the last year of the 1970's is unduly high, relative to the efficient price for an exhaustible resource that appears to be within a generation of exhaustion. The arguments for price decontrol, therefore, are strong.

The more open questions, it seems, are those about a "windfall profits" tax, policies to encourage near-term substitution of other fuels for petroleum, and research policies for the longer-term future.

The public discussion of the "windfall profits" tax has been unusually unedifying because the nature of neither the "windfall profits" problem nor the proposed tax has been carefully defined. Those who perceive that price decontrol would permit the oil companies to enjoy massive "windfall profits" must have in mind the following. "Old" oil was discovered and brought into production in a market and institutional environment based on pre-embargo prices for imported oil and price controls on domestic oil and retail gasoline. Thus, it would be unfair to permit those who hold large inventories of "old" oil in the ground to enjoy a massive one-shot increase in the value of those inventories as a result of OPEC action and U. S. government policy.

The appropriate policy response to such a concern, if it is to be taken seriously, would be a one-shot "old" oil "inventory appreciation tax" designed to tax away all or part of the increment in the value of "old" oil in the ground without influencing the marginal incentives for its extraction. The tax would be calculated on the day of price decontrol and applied — only once — to all "old" oil deposits. Since the tax would amount to large sums, for many oil companies, and would cause serious disruptions in capital markets, it would be appropriate to permit oil companies to pay it in installments. The important thing is that the tax must be a one-shot affair, and each oil company's obligation must be calculated on the day of price decontrol and not influenced by events thereafter.

The arguments in favor of a one-shot "inventory appreciation tax" are as follows: (1) such a tax would be perceived by citizens as "fair," and may be essential to make price decontrol politically acceptable; (2) incentives for discovery and production of "new" oil, and extraction of "old" oil, would be undiminished by such a tax; and (3) there is a clear need to redirect energy research and development, and such a tax would provide government with the revenue to finance that endeavor. The arguments against such a tax are: (1) it would restrict the oil companies' opportunities for capital formation; and (2) there is no assurance that government-sponsored research is a better use of that capital than the investments oil companies would make.

What seems to be emerging from the political process under the guise of a "windfall profits" tax is not the "inventory appreciation tax" discussed above, but a complex system of severance taxes on "old" oil. This kind of tax would have the distinct disadvantage — in addition to the disadvantages associated with an "inventory appreciation tax" — of providing disincentives for the extraction of "old" oil. These disincentives would be of two kinds: (1) the disincentives for extraction which are usually associated with severance taxes (Chapter 10), and (2) additional disincentives provided by the possibility that reduced extraction in the near-term may encourage eventual repeal of the tax.

What, then, is the economist's advice with respect to a "windfall profits" tax to accompany decontrol of oil prices? I, for one, am convinced that any "windfall profits" tax should be a one-shot "inventory appreciation tax," not the complex system of severance taxes currently under consideration. But should there be a "windfall profits" tax at all? Economic reasoning is less persuasive on this question. I would personally support an "inventory appreciation tax," in large part because such a tax seems to be necessary to make price decontrol politically acceptable; but I make no claim that this position is unequivocally supported by economic science.

Near-term substitutes for petroleum products are largely confined to coal (to generate electricity and for conversion to synthetic oil and gas) and nuclear-generated electricity. These face serious problems of their own. Serious problems with nuclear waste disposal have long been recognized, and, since the incident at Three Mile Island in the spring of 1979, concerns about reactor safety have returned to prominence. Realistically, one must predict that the contribution of nuclear power will be relatively small in the near-term future.

Coal mining has serious environmental problems, as does the burning of coal in generators. Given the encouragement of coal utilization that would be provided by decontrol of oil prices, it seems that substitution of coal for petroleum will increase, even if current environmental policies are maintained. There seems no need to tolerate increased environmental externalities from coal mining and burning. However, it would be appropriate for coal-mine reclamation and coal-burning emissions-control policies to move in the direction of establishing price incentives rather than regulatory standards. This would encourage surface mining in those areas where environmental damage would be minimized, and the burning of cleaner coal (see Chapter 21).

Unfortunately, the arguments against a strong commitment to coal conversion to produce synthetic oil and gas seem stronger than those in favor. Coal conversion is heavily capital-intensive, and the products are expected to cost about twice as much, on a comparable basis, as the price of imported oil (and that does not consider the environmental cost). Even with a massive commitment of resources, the contribution of coal conversion to total fuel supplies by 1990 would be very small.

For the near term, and given the mixed prospects for substitute fuels, reduction in the demand for fuel energy seems to be an essential part of any effective solution to the "energy crisis."

In the longer term, one would hope that research-and-development policies would encourage the shift away from highly centralized energy facilities (e.g., giant power plants and coal-conversion facilities that distribute their products to the ultimate user via transmission grids and pipeline networks) toward more diffuse sources of energy. Especially, diffuse sources that use flow resources such as solar and wind energy have strong appeal, for the longer term. Similarly, one would hope for substantial increases in the efficiency with which energy is utilized. If these hopes are to be fulfilled, the economic power and political influence of the electric-utility and oil and gas pipeline industries must be diminished over time. These industries, understandably, are not much impressed with diffuse sources of energy, and their enthusiasm for conservation is diminished by their need to generate revenues.

The energy-importing countries in general, and the United States in particular, are confronted with new realities concerning the scarcity of fossil fuels, which are upsetting to the assumptions upon which economic progress in the twentieth century has been based. It is clear that major adjustments are essential, and that those adjustments will involve some pain and sacrifice.

It is also clear that economics is more effective at analyzing the competitive world upon which its favorite models are based than the complex world, noncompetitive in important ways, that exists. Economics, it seems, cannot provide a logically cohesive set of arguments leading to the perfect solution to the fossil fuel problem. Nevertheless, in this difficult situation, economics can provide certain suggestions that would surely result in improvements over the policies that have been pursued in the 1970's.

QUESTIONS FOR DISCUSSION

1. It seems to be commonly believed that in the late 1970's the actions of the U. S. Department of Energy made the energy situation worse rather than better. Do you share that opinion? Explain.
2. If, in a "food crisis," the price of "old wheat" (i.e., wheat produced on fields that had been initially cultivated prior to some specified date) were controlled while the price of "new wheat" was unregulated and higher, what would you predict, with respect to:
   (a) the total production of wheat?
   (b) the total consumption of wheat?
   (c) the prices, and quantities produced, of substitutes for wheat?
   (d) the longevity of the food crisis?
   (e) the prevalence of the unlawful practice of mislabeling "old wheat" as "new wheat" at the farm and wholesale levels?
3. Some have proposed that, in order to reduce total consumption while "equitably sharing the burden," gasoline should be rationed to consumers. If gasoline rationing were introduced, would it be desirable to make the ration coupons transferable? Explain.
4. Assume that the price of oil is to be decontrolled. Outline the arguments *for* and *against* simultaneous imposition of a "windfall profits" tax.
5. Assume the polluting emissions from burning of coal were controlled via emissions taxes (rather than standards). If the tax rate were unchanged, would you expect the total emissions from coal-burning installations to increase, decrease, or remain unchanged if the price of *oil* were to increase substantially? Explain.

FURTHER READINGS

Chapman, Duane (Chairman). 1974. "Energy Supply and Demand in the United States," *American Journal of Agricultural Economics.* 56: 397-435.

Darmstader, Joel, Joy Dunkerly, and Jack Alterman. 1977. *How Industrial Societies Use Energy*. Baltimore: Johns Hopkins University Press.

Mead, Walter J. 1979. "The Performance of Government in Energy Regulations," *American Economic Review Papers and Proceedings*. 69: 353-356.

Nordhaus, William D. 1973. "The Allocation of Energy Resources," in *Brookings Papers on Economic Activity* 3. A. M. Okun and G. L. Perry, eds. Washington: The Brookings Institution.

Schipper, Lee. 1979. "Another Look at Energy Conservation," *American Economic Review Papers and Proceedings*. 69: 362-371.

VII. EPILOG

24

Economic Science, Economic Policy, and Flying by the Seat of the Pants

I never said it was going to be easy. In Section I, the complexity of the natural and social systems that provide the context for resource-economics problems was emphasized. In Sections II and III, the failure of economic theory to provide perfect answers to some fundamental questions about efficiency and equity, in the static time frame and in the intertemporal context, was demonstrated. In Section IV, it was seen that complex and fundamentally imperfect institutional arrangements are the norm. In Section V, currently available techniques for empirical analyses were seen to be fundamentally inadequate for the analysis of complex systems, and subject to serious data limitations when applied in the partial analyses that substitute for systems analyses. Finally, the applications in Section VI demonstrated the inadequacy of existing practices, but also the limitations of resource economics in suggesting improved procedures: resource economics could often claim to recommend improvements, but never to find the perfect solution.

Nevertheless, resource economics can offer considerable insights in each of these areas. Section I presented a useful perspective on the problems of economic growth, resource scarcity, and environmental degradation; and a perspective on the role of economic systems within the broader context of natural and social systems, and the function of economic science in analyzing that system. Sections II and III presented the basic findings of economic science with respect to resource allocation, distribution, and economic well-being, in a static framework and in an intertemporal context. The theories presented are extremely useful and highly reliable in predicting the behavior of individual economic actors in response to changes in the pattern of relative scarcity and in the structure of incentives as influenced by institutions. These theories were less successful in defining the "perfect society" and elucidating the rules by which such a social and economic state of grace may be achieved. A little thought leads to the conclusion that this failure was only to be expected: who could expect economics to succeed in 200 years, where millennia of efforts in philosophy and theology have failed? Section IV elucidated the complex interrelationships between legal, political, and economic systems. If it succeeds, that section should increase the respect of lawyers and political scientists for economic relationships, while warning the economists that he who deals only with "economic" variables is condemned forever to working with abstract systems. The practicing resource economist works within the institutional framework, while always aware of the dynamism of that framework: thus, he evaluates changes in the institutional framework, in addition to predicting the response of individual economic actors to any existing or proposed institutional system. Section V demonstrated that the resource economist is not without useful tools for empirical analysis. In the last several decades, these tools have been substantially improved, and there is no reason to expect that this process will not continue. In Section VI, it was shown that, while the resource economist never knows all the answers, he is seldom unable to make useful suggestions.

ECONOMIC SCIENCE

There is a strong tradition within the discipline of economics that seeks to establish economics as a science, by emulating some of the features of the natural sciences. Economics, since it deals with complex systems, is often denied the possibility of controlled experimentation. But, so is meteorology — a natural science.

In response to the complexities of the systems with which it deals, economics has substituted for controlled experimentation the notion of *scientific objectivity*[1], which is usually taken to mean the following: the scientist has the freedom and the responsibility to (1) pose refutable and testable hypotheses, (2) test those hypotheses with relevant evidence, and (3) report the results in such a manner that they are accessible to any interested person. The idea of scientific objectivity thus includes the notions of positing relationships that *could* be proven invalid, testing the posited relationships with evidence, and exposing the posited relationship, the structure of the test, and the results of the test to criticism from within and without the economic discipline.

It is scientific objectivity that provides the basis for any claim that economic analysis is more than mere speculation.

ECONOMIC POLICY

Resource economics deals with policy. The resource economist, functioning as a scientist, tests refutable propositions about the response of individual actors, and thus economic aggregates, to existing and alternative policies. Beyond this, he is often called upon to make policy recommendations; and it is a fact that resource economists sometimes grow up to assume important roles in the decision-making process.

The processes of making recommendations and decisions goes beyond science. The notion of scientific objectivity provides a valuable element of quality control with respect to the information upon which recommendations and decisions may be based, but provides no instruction as to how to determine what should be recommended or decided. In making recommendations or decisions, the economist simply goes beyond the relatively secure confines of his science and into the thoroughly insecure world of normative policy.

It should be emphasized that the economist, merely because he *is* an economist, has no special and decisive qualifications for undertaking normative work. But, while the economist is no more qualified than others for this kind of activity, neither is he less qualified. It would be ironic if the economist, being overly conscious of the limitations of his science, withdrew from the policy arena, leaving it to others who have no more, and often less, scientific and philosophical basis upon which to make policy recommendations and decisions.

FLYING BY THE SEAT OF THE PANTS

In dealing with resource and environmental policy issues, which pertain to complex natural and social systems, the resource economist can draw upon the notion and processes of scientific objectivity as they apply to the generation of knowledge about those things that can be known, and the individualist ethic of modern welfare economics that provides him with a healthy skepticism about proposals claimed to be in the "public interest" or for the "public welfare." These things, however, seldom provide an entirely sufficient basis for recommendations or decisions. Almost always, the economist has inadequate information about the workings of the systems under study, in addition to an inadequate philosophical basis for determining the "best" solutions to policy problems.

The economist in the policy arena must eventually fall back upon his intuition, or "fly by the seat of his pants." It is good that his adherence to the notion of scientific objectivity and the individualist ethic of his discipline should make the economist modest, and even a little nervous, in this role. Such feelings are a good antidote for the self-importance that sometimes afflicts those active in the policy process. Nevertheless, these feelings should not lead the economist to withdraw from the public-policy process. He has too much to offer.

THE MARKET IN IDEAS

There is an unfortunate notion, which is all too prevalent in economics, systems-analysis, and operations-research circles, that the role of "the analyst" is to provide information for "the decision maker." I do not believe that "The Decision Maker" exists, beyond the household and the classical capitalist firm; and my belief that he does not exist in the policy arena gives me considerable comfort. Rather, I conceptualize a very complex policy-decision process, in which individual citizens, "experts" and subject-matter specialists, elected representatives, the personnel of bureaucratic agencies, the judiciary, and various organized interest groups all play significant roles.

Informational inputs, broadly defined to include statements on matters of fact and on normative propositions, play an important role in this decision process. However, informational inputs are not made directly (e.g., from "analyst" to "decision maker"), and they are not automatically taken as authoritative. Rather, informational inputs concerning both factual matters and normative propositions are evaluated by all parties in a "market in ideas," which is a subsystem of the complex system from which decisions eventually emerge. In such an environment, there is not much reason to fear that the value system of the economist and the normative propositions that arise therefrom will be imposed upon society on the mere basis of the economist's authority. Instead, as Kenneth Boulding has written, considerable protection from that kind of outcome is provided through the market in ideas by "the criticism within the scientific community and the acute perception that we all have of the impact of the norms of others on their own thought, however blind we may be to the impact of our own norms on our own thought."[2]

The most important role of the resource economist and of the other kinds of professionals who claim expertise on the basis of their education and intellectual development is to actively participate in the market in ideas, while always endeavoring to keep that market open and competitive. The market in ideas provides the best protection of society against the entrenched power of established economic interests and against the growing army of "professional experts" that is attempting to establish itself as the new decision-making class.

ENDNOTES

1. See Popper, Karl. 1957. "Philosophy of Science: A Personal Report," in *British Philosophy in Mid-Century*. C. H. Mace (ed.). London: George Allen and Unwin.
2. Boulding, Kenneth. 1977. "Prices and Other Institutions," *Journal of Economic Issues*. 11: 809-821.

INDEX